Better Homes and Gardens®

Biggest Book of Cookies

Better Homes and Gardens® Books
Des Moines, Iowa

Better Homes and Gardens® Books
An imprint of Meredith® Books

Biggest Book of Cookies
Project Manager: Shelli McConnell
Contributing Editors: Janet Figg, Linda J. Henry, Lisa Kingsley,
    Winifred Moranville, Mary Williams
Graphic Designers: Craig Hanken, Bethanie Aswegan—Studio P2
Copy Chief: Terri Fredrickson
Copy and Production Editor: Victoria Forlini
Editorial Operations Manager: Karen Schirm
Managers, Book Production: Pam Kvitne, Marjorie J. Schenkelberg,
    Rick von Holdt
Contributing Copy Editor: Kim Catanzarite
Contributing Proofreaders: Emmy Clausing, Gretchen Kauffman,
    Donna Segal
Indexer: Kathleen Poole
Electronic Production Coordinator: Paula Forest
Editorial and Design Assistants: Karen McFadden, Mary Lee Gavin
Test Kitchen Director: Lynn Blanchard
Test Kitchen Product Supervisor: Colleen Weeden

Meredith® Books
Editor in Chief: Linda Raglan Cunningham
Design Director: Matt Strelecki
Executive Editor, Food and Crafts: Jennifer Dorland Darling

Publisher: James D. Blume
Executive Director, Marketing: Jeffrey Myers
Executive Director, New Business Development: Todd M. Davis
Executive Director, Sales: Ken Zagor
Director, Operations: George A. Susral
Director, Production: Douglas M. Johnston
Business Director: Jim Leonard

Vice President and General Manager: Douglas J. Guendel

Better Homes and Gardens® Magazine
Editor in Chief: Karol DeWulf Nickell
Deputy Editor, Food and Entertaining: Nancy Hopkins

Meredith Publishing Group
President, Publishing Group: Stephen M. Lacy
Vice President-Publishing Director: Bob Mate

Meredith Corporation
Chairman and Chief Executive Officer: William T. Kerr

Chairman of the Executive Committee: E. T. Meredith III

All of us at Better Homes and Gardens® Books are dedicated to providing you with the information and ideas you need to create delicious foods. We welcome your comments and suggestions. Write to us at: Better Homes and Gardens Books, Cookbook Editorial Department, 1716 Locust St., Des Moines, IA 50309-3023.

If you would like to purchase any of our cooking, crafts, gardening, home improvement, or home decorating and design books, check wherever quality books are sold. Or visit us at: bhgbooks.com

Our seal assures you that every recipe in *Biggest Book of Cookies* has been tested in the Better Homes and Gardens® Test Kitchen. This means that each recipe is practical and reliable, and meets our high standards of taste appeal. We guarantee your satisfaction with this book for as long as you own it.

Table of Contents

We admit it! We're *crazy about cookies!*

Get ready to spread even more sweetness and joy. Inside these pages, you'll find more than 475 of our all-time favorite cookie recipes, ranging from the simple to the sumptuous, from the old-fashioned to the newfangled. Here you can rediscover beloved heirloom recipes of Old World cooks. You can salute the American cooks, too, with a full gamut of treats invented or perfected in our country: the classic chocolate chip, soft sugar cookies, brownies, and more, as well as tantalizing twists and variations on those themes. You'll find simple bars that taste best with a glass of milk, sophisticated sandwich cookies worthy of a champagne toast, and plenty of pleasures in between. Now the only thing left for you to do is to decide which wonderful cookie to bake first.

As always, you'll appreciate knowing that every recipe has been perfected by the experts in the Better Homes and Gardens® Test Kitchen. Think of our testers not only as seasoned kitchen pros but also passionate cookie lovers who can't wait to share their cookie recipes with you. They also offer dozens of tips, gleaned from over 75 years of cookie-baking expertise in our test kitchen.

In short, we've gathered the best cookie recipes ever and all the information you need to know to achieve cookie perfection.

Cookie Basics

The Better Homes and Gardens® Test Kitchen has been developing and perfecting cookie recipes for 75 years. That's a lot of time spent weeding out successes and failures—time well spent to bring you only the best of the best in recipes and advice. Tap into our know-how, and you can make your best cookies ever.

Your Cookie Questions Answered

When it comes to cookie queries, we've heard them all. Here are the answers to the most commonly asked questions we culled from cooks across the country.

How do I store baked cookies? Can I make cookie dough ahead of time to bake later?

For instructions on how to store baked cookies, check out the guidelines listed with each recipe. We think you'll find this feature one of our most helpful.

You can refrigerate or freeze most cookie doughs for baking later. The exceptions are thin batters, such as bar cookie batters, and meringue or macaroon mixtures.

Store cookie dough in a tightly covered container in the refrigerator up to three days or freeze up to three months. To freeze cookie dough, pack it into freezer containers or shape slice-and-bake dough into rolls and wrap in foil. If you wish, you can go a step further with drop cookie dough. Use a small ice cream scoop to form balls of dough and freeze them on a cookie sheet; after they freeze, transfer them to a plastic freezer container or bag.

Before baking, thaw frozen dough in the container in the refrigerator. If the thawed dough is too stiff to work with, let it stand at room temperature for a few minutes. Or place the small balls of frozen dough on the cookie sheet as directed in recipe. Bake as directed, adding a couple more minutes to the baking time.

My family doesn't like nuts. Can they be omitted from recipes?

We love the added texture and flavor that nuts give cookies, but we're aware that some people are allergic to them and still others simply don't care for them. In most cases, you can think of nuts as an optional ingredient and leave them out if you wish. Keep in mind a couple of exceptions, however: First, if a recipe calls for ground nuts, the nuts take the place of some of the flour and some of the fat, so they can't be omitted without a drastic change in the structure. Second, if the nuts play a starring role in the cookie's overall flavor, omitting them might leave behind what made the recipe a dazzler in the first place.

How should I adjust my cookie recipes for baking at high altitudes?

Cookie recipes need little adjustment for high-altitude environments. Increase the oven temperature by 25 degrees, and decrease the baking time by a minute or two. If further adjustment is necessary, reduce the sugar by just a couple of tablespoons. If a recipe calls for baking powder or baking soda, you may need to reduce the amount by ⅛ teaspoon. Make just one change to a recipe at a time, and see how each affects the results.

Can I mix cookie dough with a handheld portable mixer or do I need a stand mixer?

You can make all of the recipes in this book with a portable mixer, though you may need to work a little harder. Most portable mixers are less powerful than stand mixers, so when it comes to adding the last of the flour, you'll probably need to stir it in with a wooden spoon. Whether you're using a portable or a stand mixer, begin stirring in the flour once the mixer starts to strain.

Can I substitute margarine for butter in cookie recipes?

Butter is the gold standard for cookie baking, and some recipes garner scrumptious flavor and great texture only when butter is used. Many margarines contain more water than oil and therefore yield undesirable results. If you wish to use margarine instead of butter, use only stick margarine that contains at least 80 percent fat. If the fat percentage is not stated on the front of the box, check the nutrition label; the margarine should have 100 calories per tablespoon. You may have to read a lot of labels until you find one that works. Note, too, that stick margarines may produce a softer dough, so you may need to chill the dough longer than directed in the recipe, or even freeze it, before baking.

Low-fat, liquid, and soft vegetable oil spreads are for table use—not for baking. Their lower fat content often causes cookie dough to spread, become tough, and dry out faster.

What should I use to grease a cookie sheet, and how much of it should I use?

A light greasing with shortening or a quick spray with nonstick cooking spray is adequate for most recipes and will make it easier to remove the cookies and to wash the cookie sheet after baking. Using too much fat, or greasing when a recipe doesn't call for it, causes cookies to spread excessively, have very thin edges, and brown too quickly around the edges.

Cookie Sheet Smarts

All cookie sheets are not created equal. Before you start on your cookie-making spree, take a look at what's in your cupboard. If your cookie sheets are thin and warped or dark with baked-on grease—or you have nothing

but pans with 1-inch sides—it's time to buy some new equipment. When selecting cookie sheets, keep the following in mind:

- **Seek out shiny,** heavy-gauge sheets with very low or nonexistent sides. Avoid dark cookie sheets, which may cause cookie bottoms to overbrown.

- **Use jelly-roll pans** (15×10×1-inch baking pans) only for bar cookies. Other types of cookies won't bake evenly in a pan with such high sides. If you must use a jelly-roll pan, turn it over and bake on the bottom.

- **Dull or shiny finish?** For most cookies, select sheets with a dull finish so cookie bottoms brown more evenly. Use shiny sheets for cookies that should not brown on bottoms, such as shortbread.

- **Nonstick cookie sheets** let you skip the greasing step. However, the dough may not spread as much, resulting in thicker, more cakelike cookies.

- **Insulated cookie sheets** promote slow baking and tend to yield pale cookies with soft centers. When using insulated sheets, you may have trouble with cookies that contain a large proportion of butter, such as sugar cookie cutouts, because the butter may melt out before the dough is set. Don't bake cookies on insulated cookie sheets long enough to brown the bottoms; the other parts of

the cookies will be too dry. On the other hand, if your oven runs a bit hot or browns cookies rapidly, insulated cookie sheets may improve results.

Ask the Cookie Doctor

After years of trial and error in our Test Kitchen, we're pretty good at solving most cookie problems. Here are some common cookie quandaries you may have encountered and how to avoid them.

Why do my cookies always seem to require an extra minute or two of baking time?

Two different issues might be at work here: cookie size and oven temperature.

First, you might have used more dough per cookie than called for in the recipe; this results in larger cookies that take longer to bake. If this is the case, simply make smaller cookies next time.

Second, your oven may not be running at the right temperature. Buy an oven thermometer at a hardware store, and check your oven temperature occasionally. To do this, set the oven at 350°F and let it heat at least ten minutes. Place the thermometer in the oven. Close the door and let it heat at least five minutes. If the thermometer reads higher than 350°F, reduce the setting by the number of degrees' difference each time you bake. On the other hand, if the thermometer reads lower than 350°F, increase the setting by the number of degrees' difference. If your oven is more than 50 degrees off, have a service person adjust the thermostat.

What makes cookies too dry?

The cookies probably contain too much flour. Maybe the measuring didn't measure up! When you measure flour, stir it in the canister to lighten it (you don't need to sift). Gently spoon the flour into a dry measuring cup and level the top with the straight edge of a metal spatula or knife. Don't pack the flour into the cup and don't tap the cup with the spatula or on the counter to level it.

Measure flour and other dry ingredients, such as sugar, in nested metal or plastic measuring cups. Glass or plastic cups that have a spout are meant only for liquids. If you use a liquid-measuring cup for flour, you'll get an extra tablespoon or more of flour per cup—enough to make cookies dry and hard.

What makes cookies hard and tough?

Cookies become hard when they have too much flour (see preceding question); overbaking can also be the culprit. Check the oven temperature with an oven thermometer, and reduce the temperature, if needed. If the temperature is correct, reduce the baking time one to two minutes. Another cause of hard cookies is overmixed dough. After adding the flour, mix just until combined.

What makes cookies spread too much?

Sheets greased with too much fat cause cookies to overly spread, as does using a margarine that contains too much water (see related questions, page 6). Hot cookie sheets may also cause excessive spreading. Always let cookie sheets cool between batches.

More Cookie-Making Tips

- **For the freshest cookies**, start with the highest quality, freshest ingredients.

- **Chill dough** in the refrigerator or freezer when instructed to do so. This makes the dough easier to work with; in turn, you'll work it less, resulting in more tender cookies.

- **Preheat the oven** at least ten minutes before baking.

- **For even baking**, bake the cookies on the middle rack of the oven.

- **Check for doneness** at the minimum baking time specified in the recipe. Use a kitchen timer so you don't forget when you put the cookies in the oven.

- **Follow directions closely** for removing cookies from the cookie sheets. Some cookies require immediate removal; others need to remain on the sheet a specified amount of time.

- **Transfer hot cookies** to wire racks for even cooling.

Sweet Spoonfuls

Chocolate Chip Cookies

This cookie, an all-time favorite version of the classic, calls for both butter and shortening. The butter lends its undeniable flavor, while the shortening adds a soft, light texture. *(photo, page 35)*

Makes: about 60 cookies

Oven: 375°F

½ **cup butter, softened**

½ **cup shortening**

1 **cup packed brown sugar**

½ **cup granulated sugar**

½ **teaspoon baking soda**

2 **eggs**

1 **teaspoon vanilla**

2½ **cups all-purpose flour**

1 **12-ounce package (2 cups)**
    semisweet chocolate pieces
    or miniature candy-coated
    semisweet chocolate pieces

1½ **cups chopped walnuts, pecans,**
    or hazelnuts (filberts)
    (optional)

1. In a large mixing bowl beat butter and shortening with an electric mixer on medium to high speed for 30 seconds. Add brown sugar, granulated sugar, and baking soda. Beat until combined, scraping sides of bowl occasionally. Beat in eggs and vanilla until combined. Beat in as much of the flour as you can with the mixer. Stir in any remaining flour with a wooden spoon. Stir in chocolate pieces and, if desired, nuts.

2. Drop dough by rounded teaspoons 2 inches apart onto an ungreased cookie sheet. Bake in a 375° oven for 8 to 10 minutes or until edges are lightly browned. Transfer cookies to a wire rack and let cool.

Chocolate Chip Cookie Bars: Prepare as above, except press dough into an ungreased 15×10×1-inch baking pan. Bake in a 375° oven for 15 to 20 minutes or until golden. Cool on a wire rack. Cut into bars. Makes 48 bars.

Big Chocolate Chip Cookies: Prepare as above, except use a ¼-cup measure or scoop to drop mounds of dough about 4 inches apart onto an ungreased cookie sheet. Bake in a 375° oven for 11 to 13 minutes or until edges are lightly browned. Makes about 20 cookies.

Macadamia Nut and White Chocolate Chip Cookies: Prepare as above, except substitute white baking pieces for the semisweet chocolate pieces. Stir in one 3½-ounce jar macadamia nuts, chopped, with the baking pieces.

TO STORE: Place in layers separated by waxed paper in an airtight container; cover. Store at room temperature up to 3 days or freeze up to 3 months.

Chips and More *Cookies*

Chocolate chips are dandy, but why stop there? This recipe calls for an assortment of stir-ins sure to please and surprise everyone.

Makes: about 70 cookies

Oven: 350°F

1 cup butter, softened

1 cup packed brown sugar

1 cup granulated sugar

1 cup cooking oil

1 egg

1 teaspoon baking soda

1 teaspoon cream of tartar

1 teaspoon vanilla

$\frac{1}{2}$ teaspoon salt

$3\frac{1}{2}$ cups all-purpose flour

1 cup rolled oats

1 cup crisp rice cereal

1 cup semisweet chocolate

    pieces

1 cup coconut

$\frac{1}{2}$ cup chopped nuts

1. In a large mixing bowl beat butter with an electric mixer on medium to high speed for 30 seconds. Add brown sugar, granulated sugar, and cooking oil. Beat until combined, scraping sides of bowl occasionally. Beat in egg, baking soda, cream of tartar, vanilla, and salt until combined. Beat in flour. Stir in oats, rice cereal, chocolate pieces, coconut, and nuts with a wooden spoon.

2. Drop dough by rounded teaspoons 2 inches apart onto an ungreased cookie sheet. Bake in a 350° oven for 12 to 14 minutes or until edges are lightly browned. Transfer cookies to a wire rack and let cool.

TO STORE: Place in layers separated by waxed paper in an airtight container; cover. Store at room temperature up to 3 days or freeze up to 3 months.

Is it done yet? The doneness test for baked drop cookies couldn't be less tricky—they're done when the dough looks set and the edges and bottoms are lightly browned.

Brown Sugar *Christmas* Cookies

In keeping with the holidays, these brown sugar-flavored cookies are jazzed up with candies in festive colors. You can make them any time of year using any colors you like. *(photo, page 34)*

Makes: about 60 cookies

Oven: 375°F

¹⁄₂ **cup butter, softened**

¹⁄₂ **cup shortening**

1¹⁄₄ **cups packed brown sugar**

³⁄₄ **teaspoon baking soda**

¹⁄₄ **teaspoon salt**

3   **eggs**

2   **teaspoons vanilla**

3¹⁄₂ **cups all-purpose flour**

1   **cup red, green, and white candy-coated milk chocolate bits or red and green candy-coated chocolate pieces**

1   **cup chopped pecans**

1. In a large mixing bowl beat butter and shortening with an electric mixer on medium to high speed for 30 seconds. Add brown sugar, baking soda, and salt. Beat until combined, scraping sides of bowl occasionally. Beat in eggs and vanilla until combined. Beat in as much of the flour as you can with the mixer. Stir in any remaining flour, the chocolate bits, and pecans with a wooden spoon.

2. Drop dough by rounded teaspoons 2 inches apart onto an ungreased cookie sheet. If desired, flatten slightly with fingers. Bake in a 375° oven for 8 to 10 minutes or until edges are lightly browned. Transfer cookies to a wire rack and let cool.

TO STORE: **Place in layers separated by waxed paper in an airtight container; cover. Store at room temperature up to 3 days or freeze up to 3 months.**

The right mixer You can make all of the recipes in this book with a stand mixer or a handheld portable mixer. However, because most portable mixers are less powerful than stand mixers, when it comes to adding the last of the flour, you'll most likely need to stir it in with a wooden spoon. Whether you're using a portable or a stand mixer, if the mixer begins to strain while mixing dough, stir in the last bit of flour with a wooden spoon.

Double *Chocolate-Cherry* Cookies

With a sprinkling of nuts, dried cherries, and white baking pieces, this is one chocolate chip cookie worthy of the gourmet food lover.

Makes: about 60 cookies

Oven: 325°F

1 cup butter, softened

1⅓ cups granulated sugar

⅔ cup packed brown sugar

1 teaspoon baking soda

¼ teaspoon salt

2 eggs

1½ teaspoons vanilla

3 cups all-purpose flour

2 cups dried tart cherries

1½ cups chopped walnuts

1½ cups semisweet
    chocolate pieces

1 cup white baking pieces

1. In a large mixing bowl beat butter with an electric mixer on medium to high speed for 30 seconds. Add granulated sugar, brown sugar, baking soda, and salt. Beat until combined, scraping sides of bowl occasionally. Beat in eggs and vanilla until smooth. Beat in as much of the flour as you can with the mixer. Stir in any remaining flour with a wooden spoon. Stir in cherries, walnuts, chocolate pieces, and white baking pieces (dough will be stiff).

2. Drop dough by rounded tablespoons 2 inches apart onto an ungreased cookie sheet. Bake in a 325° oven for 14 to 16 minutes or until golden. Cool on cookie sheet for 1 minute. Transfer cookies to a wire rack and let cool.

TO STORE: Place in layers separated by waxed paper in an airtight container; cover. Store at room temperature up to 3 days or freeze up to 3 months.

Chocolate-Peanut *Blowouts*

In the world of special treats, peanuts and chocolate take the prize for most favored super duo. Make these candy- and peanut-studded delights for cookie monsters of all ages. *(photo, page 35)*

Makes: about 30 cookies

Oven: 350°F

½ cup butter, softened

½ cup peanut butter

½ cup packed brown sugar

¼ cup granulated sugar

1 teaspoon baking soda

¼ teaspoon salt

1 egg

¼ cup milk

1 teaspoon vanilla

2 cups all-purpose flour

¾ cup honey-roasted peanuts

¾ cup semisweet chocolate
      pieces

¾ cup coarsely chopped bite-size
      chocolate-covered peanut
      butter cups (about 15)*

1. In a large mixing bowl beat butter and peanut butter with an electric mixer on medium to high speed for 30 seconds. Add the brown sugar, granulated sugar, baking soda, and salt. Beat until combined, scraping sides of bowl occasionally. Beat in egg, milk, and vanilla until combined. Beat in as much of the flour as you can with the mixer. Stir in any remaining flour with a wooden spoon. Stir in peanuts, chocolate pieces, and chopped peanut butter cups.

2. Drop dough by generously rounded teaspoons 2 inches apart onto an ungreased cookie sheet. Bake in a 350° oven about 10 minutes or until lightly browned. Transfer cookies to a wire rack and let cool.

*NOTE: For easier chopping, freeze the bite-size chocolate-covered peanut butter cups in their wrappers for 1 hour. Remove wrappers before chopping the candies.

TO STORE: Place in layers separated by waxed paper in an airtight container; cover. Store at room temperature up to 3 days or freeze up to 3 months.

Peanut Butter and Oatmeal Rounds

Attention: health nuts! This cookie boasts the silky smoothness of peanut butter, wholesome goodness of oats, and healthy crunch of peanuts.

Makes: about 60 cookies

Oven: 375°F

¾ cup butter, softened

½ cup peanut butter

1 cup granulated sugar

½ cup packed brown sugar

1 teaspoon baking powder

½ teaspoon baking soda

2 eggs

1 teaspoon vanilla

1¼ cups all-purpose flour

2 cups rolled oats

1 cup chopped cocktail
    peanuts and/or semisweet
    chocolate pieces

1. In a medium mixing bowl beat butter and peanut butter with an electric mixer on medium to high speed for 30 seconds. Add granulated sugar, brown sugar, baking powder, and baking soda. Beat until combined, scraping sides of bowl occasionally. Beat in eggs and vanilla until combined. Beat in as much of the flour as you can with the mixer. Stir in any remaining flour with a wooden spoon. Stir in oats and peanuts.

2. Drop dough by rounded teaspoons 2 inches apart onto an ungreased cookie sheet. Bake in a 375° oven about 10 minutes or until edges are lightly browned. Transfer cookies to a wire rack and let cool.

TO STORE: Place in layers separated by waxed paper in an airtight container; cover. Store at room temperature up to 3 days or freeze up to 3 months.

A popular butter Today it's the taste of peanut butter that draws its many fans, but at the St. Louis World's Fair in 1904, it was touted as a health food. About half of the current United States peanut crop is made into peanut butter, and Americans top the world in peanut butter consumption.

By law, peanut butter must be 90 percent peanuts; no artificial flavor, colors, or preservatives are allowed. Peanut butter usually contains stabilizers to keep the oil from separating. Natural peanut butter, made with only peanuts and oil, must be stored in the refrigerator and stirred before use. Both kinds make delicious cookies.

Classic *Oatmeal* Cookies

This is it—a tried and true, perfected-through-the-ages version of the oh-so-homespun oatmeal cookie. If you're feeling a little splashy, throw in a few raisins or chocolate chips.

Makes: about 48 cookies

Oven: 375°F

¾ cup butter, softened

1 cup packed brown sugar

½ cup granulated sugar

1 teaspoon baking powder

¼ teaspoon baking soda

½ teaspoon ground cinnamon
      (optional)

¼ teaspoon ground cloves
      (optional)

2 eggs

1 teaspoon vanilla

1¾ cups all-purpose flour

2 cups rolled oats

1. In a large mixing bowl beat butter with an electric mixer on medium to high speed for 30 seconds. Add brown sugar, granulated sugar, baking powder, baking soda, and, if desired, cinnamon and cloves. Beat until combined, scraping sides of bowl occasionally. Beat in eggs and vanilla until combined. Beat in as much of the flour as you can with the mixer. Stir in any remaining flour with a wooden spoon. Stir in oats.

2. Drop dough by rounded teaspoons 2 inches apart onto an ungreased cookie sheet. Bake in a 375° oven for 8 to 10 minutes or until edges are golden. Cool on cookie sheet for 1 minute. Transfer cookies to a wire rack and let cool.

Oatmeal-Raisin Cookies: Prepare as above, except after stirring in oats, stir in 1 cup raisins or snipped dried tart cherries. Makes about 54 cookies.

Oatmeal-Chip Cookies: Prepare as above, except after stirring in oats, stir in 1 cup semisweet chocolate, butterscotch-flavored, or peanut butter-flavored pieces and ½ cup chopped walnuts or pecans. Makes about 54 cookies.

Giant Oatmeal Cookies: Prepare as above, except use a ¼-cup measure or scoop to drop mounds of dough 3 inches apart onto an ungreased cookie sheet. Press into a 3-inch circle. Bake in a 375° oven for 8 to 10 minutes or until edges are golden. Cool on cookie sheet for 1 minute. Transfer cookies to a wire rack and let cool. Makes about 10 cookies.

TO STORE: Place in layers separated by waxed paper in an airtight container; cover. Store at room temperature up to 3 days or freeze up to 3 months.

Favorite Oatmeal Cookies

Heart-healthful oatmeal flour and rolled oats enrich these drops. The chocolate-covered raisins sprinkle them with fun.

Makes: about 36 cookies

Oven: 350°F

- 1 **cup rolled oats**
- ⅓ **cup butter, softened**
- ⅓ **cup shortening**
- ¾ **cup granulated sugar**
- ¾ **cup packed brown sugar**
- 1 **teaspoon baking soda**
- 2 **eggs**
- 1 **teaspoon vanilla**
- 1 **cup all-purpose flour**
- 1 **cup rolled oats**
- 1 **cup coarsely chopped walnuts**
- 1 **cup chocolate-covered raisins**

1. For oat flour, place ½ cup of the rolled oats in a blender container or 1 cup in a food processor bowl. Cover and blend or process until oats turn into a powder. Transfer powder to a small bowl. If using a blender, repeat with the remaining ½ cup rolled oats. Set oat flour aside.
2. In a large mixing bowl beat butter and shortening with an electric mixer on medium to high speed for 30 seconds. Add granulated sugar, brown sugar, and baking soda. Beat until combined, scraping sides of bowl occasionally. Beat in eggs and vanilla until combined. Beat in oat flour and all-purpose flour. Stir in the remaining 1 cup rolled oats, walnuts, and raisins with a wooden spoon.
3. Drop dough by rounded teaspoons 2 inches apart onto an ungreased cookie sheet. Bake in a 350° oven for 8 to 10 minutes or until edges are lightly browned. Transfer cookies to a wire rack and let cool.

TO STORE: Place in layers separated by waxed paper in an airtight container; cover. Store at room temperature up to 3 days or freeze up to 3 months.

Finer fruit While raisins are the most often used dried fruit in baking, don't let it stop you from expanding your horizons. You can purchase apples, apricots, bananas, star fruits, cherries, cranberries, currants, dates, figs, peaches, pears, persimmons, pineapples, plums, mixed fruits, and fruit bits in dried form. They're all intensely sweet, chewy, and great for cookie baking.

Oatmeal *Jumbos*

Jumbo size is great when you're really hungry, but sometimes your craving is on the smaller side.

If so, drop by rounded teaspoons onto a cookie sheet and reduce baking time to 10 minutes.

You'll end up with about 60 cookies. *(photo, page 34)*

Makes: about 26 cookies

Oven: 350°F

1 cup peanut butter

½ cup butter, softened

1½ cups packed brown sugar

½ cup granulated sugar

1½ teaspoons baking powder

½ teaspoon baking soda

3 eggs

2 teaspoons vanilla

4 cups quick-cooking rolled oats

1½ cups candy-coated milk
   chocolate pieces

¾ cup chopped peanuts, walnuts,
   or pecans

1. In a large mixing bowl beat peanut butter and butter with an electric mixer on medium to high speed for 30 seconds. Add the brown sugar, granulated sugar, baking powder, and baking soda. Beat until combined, scraping sides of bowl occasionally. Beat in eggs and vanilla until combined. Stir in oats, chocolate pieces, and nuts with a wooden spoon.

2. Drop dough by a ¼-cup measure or scoop 4 inches apart onto an ungreased cookie sheet. Bake in a 350° oven about 15 minutes or until edges are lightly browned. Cool on cookie sheet for 2 minutes. Transfer cookies to a wire rack and let cool.

TO STORE: **Place in layers separated by waxed paper in an airtight container; cover. Store at room temperature up to 3 days or freeze up to 3 months.**

Everything Good Cookies

Simplify and sweeten your mornings. With whole wheat flour, your choice of nuts, wheat germ, and raisins, these cookies double as a quick breakfast.

Makes: about 66 cookies

Oven: 375°F

½ cup butter, softened

½ cup shortening

1 cup granulated sugar

1 cup packed brown sugar

1 teaspoon baking powder

1 teaspoon baking soda

2 eggs

2 tablespoons milk

2 teaspoons vanilla

2 cups whole wheat flour

2 cups rolled oats

1 cup chopped nuts

1 cup raisins or other
   snipped dried fruit

¼ cup toasted wheat germ

1. In a very large mixing bowl beat butter and shortening with an electric mixer on medium to high speed for 30 seconds. Add granulated sugar, brown sugar, baking powder, and baking soda. Beat until combined, scraping sides of bowl occasionally. Beat in eggs, milk, and vanilla until combined. Beat in as much of the flour as you can with the mixer. Stir in any remaining flour with a wooden spoon. Stir in oats, nuts, raisins, and wheat germ.

2. Drop dough by rounded teaspoons 2 inches apart onto an ungreased cookie sheet. Bake in a 375° oven about 8 minutes or until lightly browned. Transfer cookies to a wire rack and let cool.

TO STORE: Place in layers separated by waxed paper in an airtight container; cover. Store at room temperature up to 3 days or freeze up to 3 months.

Plumping fruit If you prefer moister fruit in cookies, plump the dried fruit before adding it to the dough. Cover the fruit with water in a small saucepan and bring to boiling. Remove from the heat, cover, and let stand five minutes. Drain fruit well, patting excess moisture with a paper towel.

Fruit and Nut *Oatmeal* Cookies

Expect the unexpected—this is no ordinary oatmeal cookie! While sprightly orange flavor infuses both the cookie and the frosting, cranberries and hazelnuts stand in for the more routine raisins and walnuts.

Makes: about 54 cookies

Oven: 375°F

½ cup butter, softened

½ cup shortening

1 cup granulated sugar

1 cup packed brown sugar

2 teaspoons finely shredded
   orange peel

1 teaspoon ground cinnamon

½ teaspoon baking soda

½ teaspoon salt

2 eggs

2 tablespoons orange juice

3 cups all-purpose flour

1¾ cups quick-cooking rolled oats

⅔ cup finely chopped dried
   cranberries, dried tart
   cherries, or dried currants

½ cup finely chopped hazelnuts
   (filberts) or walnuts

1 recipe Orange Icing

1. In a large mixing bowl beat butter and shortening with an electric mixer on medium to high speed for 30 seconds. Add the granulated sugar, brown sugar, orange peel, cinnamon, baking soda, and salt. Beat until combined, scraping sides of bowl occasionally. Beat in eggs and orange juice until combined. Beat in as much of the flour as you can with the mixer. Stir in any remaining flour, oats, dried fruit, and nuts with a wooden spoon.

2. Drop dough by rounded teaspoons 2 inches apart onto an ungreased cookie sheet. Bake in a 375° oven about 8 minutes or until edges are lightly browned. Cool on cookie sheet for 1 minute. Transfer cookies to a wire rack and let cool. Drizzle Orange Icing over cookies; let icing dry.

Orange Icing: In a medium bowl stir together 2 cups sifted powdered sugar and enough orange juice (2 to 3 tablespoons) to make drizzling consistency.

TO STORE: Place in layers separated by waxed paper in an airtight container; cover. Store at room temperature up to 3 days or freeze undrizzled cookies up to 3 months. Thaw cookies; drizzle.

Old-fashioned oats or quick oats? Unless a cookie recipe calls specifically for either regular or quick-cooking rolled oats, you can use whichever you happen to have on hand. Because they're thicker, old-fashioned oats impart a more rugged texture than quick-cooking oats. Do not, however, use instant or steel-cut rolled oats for baking: the instant is too powdery; the steel-cut, too coarse.

Ranger Cookies

Have you forgotten this classic childhood favorite? If so, it may be time for another taste. Whether you bake up regular size or jumbos, the next generation in your family will be glad to help usher in a revival!

Makes: about 48 cookies

Oven: 375°F

½ **cup butter, softened**

½ **cup granulated sugar**

½ **cup packed brown sugar**

½ **teaspoon baking powder**

¼ **teaspoon baking soda**

1 **egg**

1 **teaspoon vanilla**

1¼ **cups all-purpose flour**

1 **cup quick-cooking rolled oats**

1 **cup coconut**

1 **cup raisins, dried cherries,
dried cranberries, or
mixed dried fruit bits**

1. In a large mixing bowl beat butter with electric mixer on medium to high speed for 30 seconds. Add granulated sugar, brown sugar, baking powder, and baking soda. Beat until combined, scraping sides of bowl occasionally. Beat in egg and vanilla until combined. Beat in as much of the flour as you can with the mixer. Stir in any remaining flour with a wooden spoon. Stir in rolled oats, coconut, and raisins.

2. Drop dough by rounded teaspoons 2 inches apart onto an ungreased cookie sheet. Bake in a 375° oven about 8 minutes or until edges are golden. Cool on cookie sheet for 1 minute. Transfer cookies to a wire rack and let cool.

Jumbo Ranger Cookies: Prepare as above, except use a ⅓-cup measure or scoop to drop mounds of dough 3 inches apart onto an ungreased cookie sheet. Press into 4-inch circles. Bake in a 375° oven for 8 to 10 minutes or until edges are golden. Cool on cookie sheet for 1 minute. Transfer cookies to a wire rack and let cool. Makes about 10 cookies.

TO STORE: Place in layers separated by waxed paper in an airtight container; cover. Store at room temperature up to 3 days or freeze up to 3 months.

Peanut *Brittle* Cookies

Cookie lovers can't get enough variety when it comes to the good old peanut butter and chocolate variation. The peanut brittle crunch used here sets this one apart from the rest. Hint: Purchase the peanut brittle from a local candy shop. *(photo, page 35)*

Makes: about 24 cookies

Oven: 350°F

½ **cup butter, softened**

¼ **cup shortening**

1 **cup packed dark brown sugar**

½ **teaspoon baking powder**

¼ **teaspoon baking soda**

1 **egg**

1 **teaspoon vanilla**

1¼ **cups all-purpose flour**

1¼ **cups quick-cooking rolled oats**

4 **ounces bittersweet or semisweet chocolate, chopped**

1 **cup crushed peanut brittle**

1. Line a cookie sheet with foil and grease the foil; set aside.

2. In a medium mixing bowl beat butter and shortening with an electric mixer on medium to high speed for 30 seconds. Add brown sugar, baking powder, and baking soda. Beat until combined, scraping sides of bowl occasionally. Beat in egg and vanilla until combined. Beat in as much of the flour as you can with the mixer. Stir in any remaining flour with a wooden spoon. Stir in oats, chopped chocolate, and ½ cup of the crushed peanut brittle.

3. Drop dough by rounded teaspoons 2 inches apart onto prepared cookie sheet. Flatten each mound slightly. Bake in a 350° oven for 8 minutes. Remove cookie sheet from oven. Sprinkle each cookie with some of the remaining crushed peanut brittle, carefully pressing brittle slightly into cookies. Bake for 4 to 5 minutes more or until edges are lightly browned. Cool on cookie sheets for 2 minutes. Transfer cookies to a wire rack and let cool.

TO STORE: Place in layers separated by waxed paper in an airtight container; cover. Store at room temperature up to 3 days or freeze up to 3 months.

Tropical Jumbles

Go nuts—in a very civilized way—with these rich and luscious goodies packed with buttery macadamias, coconut, and dried tropical fruits. (photo, page 69)

Makes: about 60 cookies

Oven: 375°F

½ cup butter, softened

½ cup shortening

1¼ cups packed brown sugar

½ teaspoon baking soda

2 eggs

1 teaspoon vanilla

2½ cups all-purpose flour

1 3½-ounce jar macadamia nuts, chopped (about 1 cup)

1 cup coconut

½ cup chopped candied pineapple, raisins, or snipped dried apricots

½ cup chopped dried papaya or mango

½ cup dried banana chips, broken (optional)

1 recipe Citrus Icing

1. In a large mixing bowl beat butter and shortening with an electric mixer on medium to high speed for 30 seconds. Add brown sugar and baking soda. Beat until combined, scraping sides of bowl occasionally. Beat in eggs and vanilla until combined. Beat in as much of the flour as you can with the mixer. Stir in any remaining flour with a wooden spoon. Stir in nuts, coconut, pineapple, papaya, and, if desired, banana chips.

2. Drop dough by rounded teaspoons 2 inches apart onto an ungreased cookie sheet. Bake in a 375° oven for 8 to 10 minutes or until edges are lightly browned. Transfer cookies to a wire rack and let cool. Drizzle Citrus Icing over cookies; let icing dry.

Citrus Icing: In a medium bowl stir together 2 cups sifted powdered sugar and enough orange, lemon, or lime juice (2 to 3 tablespoons) to make drizzling consistency. Tint bright yellow, orange, or blue-green with food coloring for a tropical look. Or, if desired, divide the glaze into portions and tint each portion with a different color of food coloring.

TO STORE: Place in layers separated by waxed paper in an airtight container; cover. Store at room temperature up to 3 days or freeze undrizzled cookies up to 3 months. Thaw cookies; drizzle.

Chopping and snipping Both a sharp knife and kitchen shears make quick work of cutting large pieces of dried fruit into bite-size pieces. Dip the knife or shears into hot water frequently to keep the fruit from sticking.

Cranberry *Jumbles*

Perfected over the years, this basic brown sugar cookie dough has served as the foundation for many a great cookie. This variation surprises and delights with dried cranberries, almonds, and a zesty orange drizzle. (photo, page 34)

Makes: about 32 cookies

Oven: 350°F

1 cup all-purpose flour

$^{1}/_{3}$ cup whole wheat flour

$^{3}/_{4}$ cup packed brown sugar

$^{3}/_{4}$ teaspoon baking powder

$^{1}/_{8}$ teaspoon baking soda

$^{1}/_{2}$ teaspoon ground cinnamon

$^{1}/_{2}$ cup shortening

1 slightly beaten egg

2 tablespoons cranberry juice
    or orange juice

1 cup dried cranberries

$^{1}/_{2}$ cup slivered almonds

1 recipe Orange Frosting

1. In a large bowl stir together the all-purpose flour, whole wheat flour, brown sugar, baking powder, baking soda, and cinnamon. Using a pastry blender, cut in shortening until mixture resembles fine crumbs. Combine egg and juice; stir into flour mixture. Stir in cranberries and almonds.
2. Drop dough by rounded teaspoons 2 inches apart onto an ungreased cookie sheet. Bake in a 350° oven for 12 to 14 minutes or until bottoms are lightly browned. Transfer cookies to a wire rack and let cool. Drizzle Orange Frosting over cookies; let frosting dry.

Orange Frosting: In a small bowl stir together 1 cup sifted powdered sugar, $^{1}/_{2}$ teaspoon finely shredded orange peel, and enough orange juice (3 to 4 teaspoons) to make drizzling consistency.

TO STORE: Place in layers separated by waxed paper in an airtight container; cover. Store at room temperature up to 3 days or freeze undrizzled cookies up to 3 months. Thaw cookies; drizzle.

Storing dried fruit Once a package of dried fruit has been opened, wrap any remaining fruit in an airtight container and store it in the refrigerator or freeze it for up to six months.

Coffee and *Cream* Drops

Why do people love these coffee and cream drops so much? Because they're two great cookies that add up to one great mocha sensation.

Makes: about 48 cookies

Oven: 375°F

2 tablespoons instant
    coffee crystals

3 tablespoons light cream
    or half-and-half

1 cup butter, softened

²/₃ cup granulated sugar

²/₃ cup packed brown sugar

1 teaspoon baking soda

¼ teaspoon salt

1 egg

1 teaspoon vanilla

2¼ cups all-purpose flour

¼ cup unsweetened
    cocoa powder

½ cup chopped nuts

½ cup miniature semisweet
    chocolate pieces

1. In a small bowl stir together instant coffee crystals and 1 tablespoon of the light cream until crystals dissolve; set aside.
2. In a large mixing bowl beat butter with an electric mixer on medium to high speed for 30 seconds. Add granulated sugar, brown sugar, baking soda, and salt. Beat until combined, scraping sides of bowl occasionally. Beat in the coffee mixture, egg, and vanilla until combined. Beat in as much of the flour as you can with the mixer. Stir in any remaining flour with a wooden spoon.
3. Divide dough in half. Stir the remaining 2 tablespoons light cream and cocoa powder into one portion; stir in nuts. Stir chocolate pieces into the remaining plain dough portion. Spoon a scant teaspoon of each dough side by side onto an ungreased cookie sheet. Press doughs together.
4. Bake in a 375° oven for 8 to 9 minutes or just until set. Cool on cookie sheet for 1 minute. Transfer cookies to a wire rack and let cool.

TO STORE: Place in layers separated by waxed paper in an airtight container; cover. Store at room temperature up to 3 days or freeze up to 3 months.

Coffee *Crisps*

Calling all lovers of coffee! With coffee in the dough and a coffee and cream icing, these crisps were made with you in mind. Serve them with—what else?—a cup of your beloved steaming hot java. *(photo, page 34)*

Makes: about 20 cookies

Oven: 350°F

  4 teaspoons water

  2 teaspoons instant coffee
     crystals or 1 teaspoon
     instant espresso
     coffee powder

½ cup butter, softened

  1 cup granulated sugar

¼ teaspoon salt

  2 eggs

1½ cups all-purpose flour

  1 recipe Coffee Icing
     Instant coffee crystals,
     coarsely crushed (optional)

1. Line a large cookie sheet with parchment paper; set aside. In a small bowl stir together water and coffee crystals until crystals dissolve; set aside.

2. In a large mixing bowl beat butter with an electric mixer on medium to high speed for 30 seconds. Add sugar and salt. Beat until combined, scraping sides of bowl occasionally. Beat in eggs and coffee mixture until combined. Beat in as much of the flour as you can with the mixer. Stir in any remaining flour with a wooden spoon.

3. Drop dough by slightly rounded teaspoons 2 inches apart onto prepared cookie sheet; spread dough into 2-inch circles. Bake in a 350° oven for 9 to 11 minutes or until edges are lightly browned. Cool on cookie sheet for 2 minutes. Transfer cookies to a wire rack and let cool.

4. Fill a pastry bag fitted with a very small round tip with Coffee Icing. Pipe icing onto cookies in a zigzag pattern; let icing dry. (Or thin icing with additional whipping cream to make drizzling consistency. Use fork tines to drizzle icing over cookies; let icing dry.) If desired, sprinkle cookies with crushed coffee crystals.

Coffee Icing: Stir together 1 tablespoon whipping cream and ⅛ teaspoon instant coffee crystals or dash espresso coffee powder until crystals dissolve. In a small bowl stir together 1 cup sifted powdered sugar, the coffee mixture, and enough additional whipping cream (1 to 2 tablespoons) to make piping consistency.

TO STORE: Place in layers separated by waxed paper in an airtight container; cover. Store at room temperature up to 3 days or freeze unfrosted cookies up to 3 months. Thaw cookies; frost.

Hermits

Talk about a classic! These chewy cookies have been around since colonial days. They're full of nuts and raisins, and actually improve with age.

Makes: about 30 cookies

Oven: 375°F

¾ **cup butter, softened**

¾ **cup packed brown sugar**

1 **teaspoon ground cinnamon**

½ **teaspoon baking soda**

¼ **teaspoon ground cloves**

¼ **teaspoon ground nutmeg**

¼ **cup strong brewed**

   coffee, cooled

1 **egg**

1 **teaspoon vanilla**

1½ **cups all-purpose flour**

2 **cups raisins**

1 **cup chopped pecans**

   Pecan halves (optional)

   Sifted powdered sugar

   (optional)

1. In a large mixing bowl beat butter with an electric mixer on medium to high speed for 30 seconds. Add brown sugar, cinnamon, baking soda, cloves, and nutmeg. Beat until combined, scraping sides of bowl occasionally. Beat in coffee, egg, and vanilla until combined. Beat in as much of the flour as you can with the mixer. Stir in any remaining flour, raisins, and chopped pecans with a wooden spoon. Drop dough by rounded tablespoons 2 inches apart onto an ungreased cookie sheet. If desired, lightly press a pecan half on top of each dough mound.

2. Bake in a 375° oven for 8 to 10 minutes or until edges are lightly browned. Transfer cookies to a wire rack and let cool. If desired, sprinkle with powdered sugar.

TO STORE: Place in layers separated by waxed paper in an airtight container; cover. Store at room temperature up to 3 days or freeze unsugared cookies up to 3 months. Thaw cookies; if desired, sprinkle with powdered sugar.

One rack at a time It's tempting to bake quick, multiple batches of cookies using all oven racks at the same time; however, it's best to bake just one batch on one oven rack at a time for even browning. If you wish to save time, do so by having a second prepared cookie sheet ready to go in the oven as soon as the first finished sheet of cookies comes out.

Pecan *Crispies*

Here's a '50s favorite that never lost its flavor. For chewier cookies with delectably crisp edges, bake only 10 minutes.

Makes: about 60 cookies

Oven: 350°F

- ½ **cup butter, softened**
- ½ **cup shortening**
- 2½ **cups packed brown sugar**
- ½ **teaspoon baking soda**
- ¼ **teaspoon salt**
- 2 **eggs**
- 2½ **cups all-purpose flour**
- 1 **cup chopped pecans**

1. Grease a large cookie sheet; set aside. In a large mixing bowl beat butter and shortening with an electric mixer on medium to high speed for 30 seconds. Add brown sugar, baking soda, and salt. Beat until combined, scraping sides of bowl occasionally. Beat in eggs until combined. Beat in as much of the flour as you can with the mixer. Stir in any remaining flour with a wooden spoon. Stir in pecans.

2. Drop dough by teaspoons 2 inches apart onto prepared cookie sheet. Bake in a 350° oven about 12 minutes or until edges are set and lightly browned. Transfer cookies to a wire rack and let cool.

TO STORE: Place in layers separated by waxed paper in an airtight container; cover. Store at room temperature up to 3 days or freeze up to 3 months.

To grease or not to grease? If a recipe calls for a greased cookie sheet, use only a very light coating or your cookies may spread too much as they bake. Regreasing the cookie sheet between batches is not necessary unless the recipes specifies doing so. If a recipe specifies ungreased cookie sheets, use regular cookie or nonstick sheets, but don't grease them.

Also remember to let cookie sheets cool between batches, as warm sheets also cause dough to spread.

holiday treat

Florentines

For a twist on tradition, these chewy fruit and nut wafers have a swirl of white chocolate in addition to the dark chocolate that classically coats them.

Makes: about 20 cookies

Oven: 350°F

⅓ **cup butter, cut up**

⅓ **cup milk**

¼ **cup sugar**

2 **tablespoons honey**

¾ **cup sliced almonds**

½ **cup finely chopped candied**

mixed fruits and peels

¼ **cup all-purpose flour**

¾ **cup semisweet**

chocolate pieces

2 **tablespoons shortening**

2 **ounces white baking bars**

2 **teaspoons shortening**

1. Grease and lightly flour two cookie sheets; set aside. (Repeat greasing and flouring cookie sheets for each batch.)
2. In a medium heavy saucepan combine butter, milk, sugar, and honey. Bring to a full rolling boil, stirring occasionally. Remove from heat (mixture will appear curdled). Stir in almonds and candied fruits and peels. Stir in flour.
3. Drop batter by level tablespoons at least 3 inches apart onto prepared cookie sheets. Using the back of a spoon, spread the batter into 3-inch circles. Bake in a 350° oven for 7 to 9 minutes or until the edges are lightly browned. Cool on cookie sheet for 2 minutes. Carefully loosen edges and remove cookies with a wide metal spatula. Transfer cookies to waxed paper and let cool.
4. In a small heavy saucepan melt the semisweet chocolate pieces and the 2 tablespoons shortening over low heat, stirring constantly. Spread the bottom of each cookie with about 1 teaspoon of the chocolate mixture. Place chocolate sides up on a wire rack.
5. In another small heavy saucepan melt the white baking bars and the 2 teaspoons shortening over low heat, stirring constantly; drizzle over dark chocolate. To marble, draw the tines of a fork through the white drizzle; let stand until set.

TO STORE: Place in layers separated by waxed paper in an airtight container; cover. Store in the refrigerator up to 3 days or freeze cookies before spreading with chocolate up to 3 months. Thaw cookies; spread with dark chocolate and drizzle.

Crisp *Cranberry* Rounds

These dainty cookies make a terrific teatime treat. The secret is to spread each mound

of batter with the back of a spoon so the cookies will be thin and crisp.

Makes: about 30 cookies

Oven: 350°F

¹/₃ **cup butter, cut up**

¹/₃ **cup milk**

¹/₄ **cup sugar**

³/₄ **cup finely chopped**

almonds, toasted

²/₃ **cup dried cranberries,**

finely snipped

¹/₄ **cup all-purpose flour**

1 **teaspoon finely shredded**

orange peel

3 **ounces white chocolate**

baking squares or

white baking bars

2 **teaspoons shortening**

1. Grease and flour two cookie sheets; set aside. (Repeat greasing and flouring cookie sheets for each batch.)

2. In a medium heavy saucepan combine butter, milk, and sugar. Bring to boiling, stirring occasionally. Remove from heat. Stir in almonds, cranberries, flour, and orange peel.

3. Drop batter from slightly rounded teaspoons 3 inches apart onto prepared cookie sheets. Using the back of a spoon, spread the batter into 2½-inch circles.

4. Bake in a 350° oven for 8 to 10 minutes or until the edges are deep golden brown (do not underbake, or the cooled cookies may be limp rather than crisp). Cool on cookie sheet for 2 minutes. Carefully loosen edges and remove cookies with a wide metal spatula. Transfer cookies to waxed paper and let cool.

5. In a small heavy saucepan melt the white baking squares and shortening over low heat, stirring constantly. Drizzle over cookies; let stand until set.

TO STORE: Place in layers separated by waxed paper in an airtight container; cover. Store at room temperature up to 3 days or freeze undrizzled cookies up to 3 months. Thaw cookies; drizzle.

Crispy Sunflower Cookies

These sweet, buttery cookies get their crispy texture from delicate, nutty sunflower seeds and coconut.

Makes: about 60 cookies

Oven: 350°F

1½ cups all-purpose flour

1 teaspoon baking soda

½ teaspoon baking powder

1 cup butter, softened

1 cup granulated sugar

1 cup packed brown sugar

2 eggs

1 teaspoon vanilla

2 cups quick-cooking rolled oats

1 cup coconut

1 cup shelled sunflower seeds

1. Line a large cookie sheet with foil; set aside. In a small bowl stir together flour, baking soda, and baking powder; set flour mixture aside.

2. In a large mixing bowl beat butter with an electric mixer on medium to high speed for 30 seconds. Add granulated sugar and brown sugar. Beat until combined, scraping sides of bowl occasionally.

3. Beat in eggs and vanilla until combined. Beat in as much of the flour mixture as you can with the mixer. Stir in any remaining flour mixture with a wooden spoon. Stir in oats, coconut, and sunflower seeds.

4. Drop dough by slightly rounded tablespoons 3 inches apart onto prepared cookie sheet. Bake in a 350° oven about 10 minutes or until edges are golden brown. Cool on cookie sheet for 5 minutes. Transfer cookies to a wire rack and let cool.

TO STORE: Place in layers separated by waxed paper in an airtight container; cover. Store at room temperature up to 2 days or freeze up to 3 months.

Mix now, bake later You can mix and refrigerate or freeze most drop cookie doughs for baking later. Store your favorite dough in a tightly covered container in the refrigerator for up to three days or pack the dough into freezer containers and freeze for up to six months.

Before baking, thaw the frozen dough in the container in the refrigerator. If it's too stiff to work with, let the dough stand at room temperature a few minutes to soften.

holiday treat

Frosted *Butterscotch* Cookies

Whatever you do, don't skip the frosting—it's what makes these cakelike gems perennial pleasers.

(photo, page 33)

Makes: about 60 cookies

Oven: 375°F

2½ cups all-purpose flour

1 teaspoon baking soda

½ teaspoon baking powder

½ teaspoon salt

1½ cups packed brown sugar

½ cup shortening

2 eggs

1 teaspoon vanilla

1 8-ounce carton dairy
    sour cream

⅔ cup chopped walnuts

1 recipe Browned Butter Frosting

Walnut halves (optional)

1. Grease a large cookie sheet; set aside. In a bowl stir together flour, baking soda, baking powder, and salt; set flour mixture aside.

2. In a large mixing bowl beat brown sugar and shortening with an electric mixer on medium to high speed for 30 seconds. Add eggs and vanilla. Beat until combined, scraping sides of bowl occasionally. Alternately add flour mixture and sour cream to egg mixture, beating well after each addition. Stir in chopped walnuts with a wooden spoon.

3. Drop dough by rounded teaspoons 2 inches apart onto prepared cookie sheet. Bake in a 375° oven for 10 to 12 minutes or until edges are lightly browned. Transfer cookies to a wire rack and let cool. Frost with Browned Butter Frosting. If desired, top each cookie with a walnut half. Let dry.

Browned Butter Frosting: In a medium heavy saucepan heat and stir ½ cup butter over medium-low heat until golden brown (do not scorch). Remove from heat. Stir in 3½ cups sifted powdered sugar, 5 teaspoons boiling water, and 1½ teaspoons vanilla. Beat to make a smooth, spreadable frosting. Immediately frost cookies. (If frosting begins to get stiff, add a small amount of boiling water and stir until smooth.)

TO STORE: Place in layers separated by waxed paper in an airtight container; cover. Store at room temperature up to 3 days or freeze unfrosted cookies up to 3 months. Thaw cookies; frost.

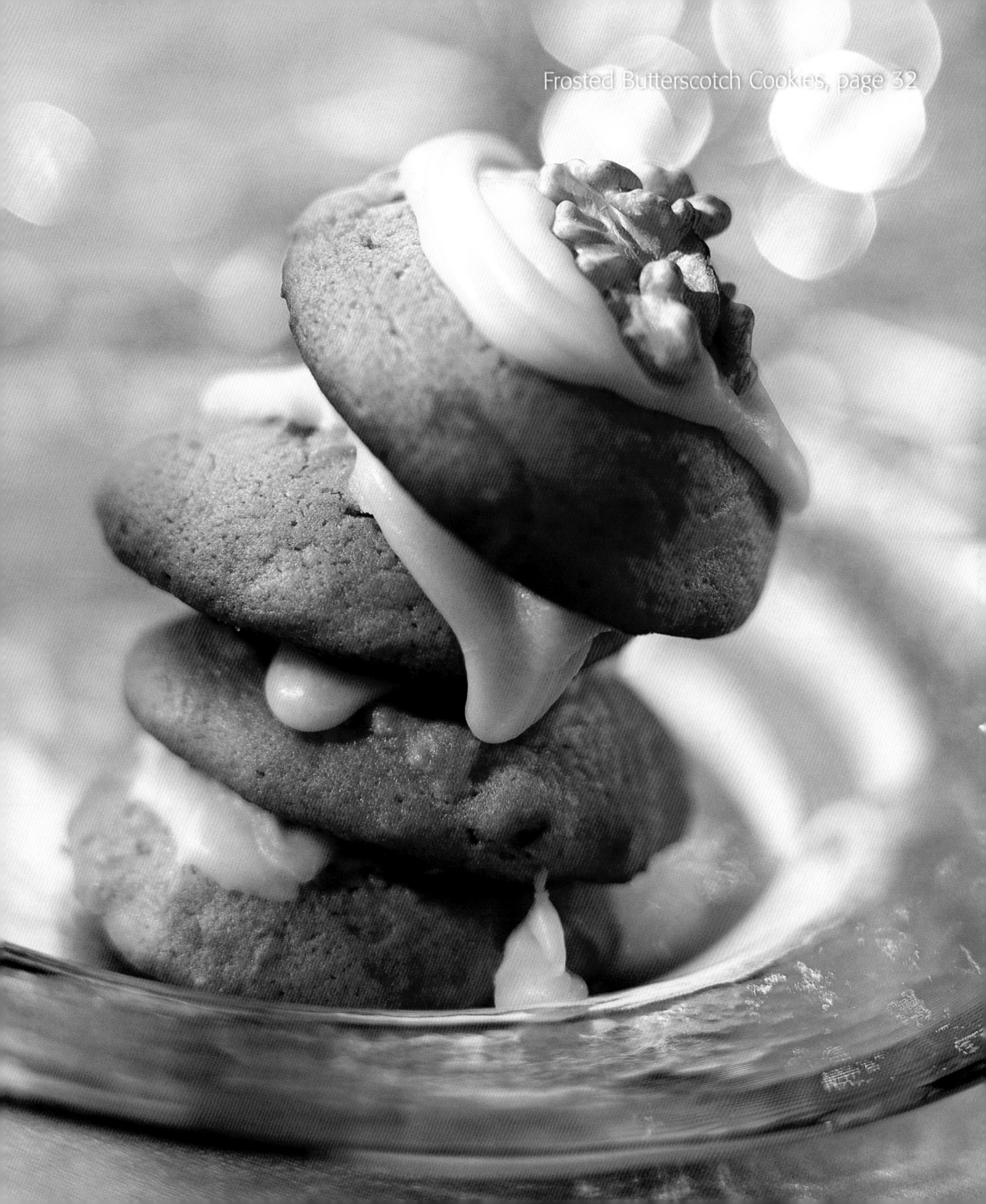

Frosted Butterscotch Cookies, page 32

ABOVE: Brown Sugar Christmas Cookies, page 12; Cranberry Jumbles, page 24
BELOW: Coffee Crisps, page 26; Oatmeal Jumbos, page 18

ABOVE: Chocolate-Peanut Blowouts, page 14 RIGHT: Chocolate Chip Cookies, page 10
BELOW: Peanut Brittle Cookies, page 22, and Malted Milk Cookies, page 44

Almond Sweets, page 37

holiday treat

Almond Sweets

Despite its sugary name, this Italian-style cookie is not overly sweet. Put it on your list of great additions to cookie trays. *(photo, page 36)*

Makes: about 48 cookies

Oven: 350°F

2½ cups all-purpose flour

2 teaspoons baking powder

½ teaspoon salt

3 eggs

½ cup granulated sugar

½ cup cooking oil

1 teaspoon vanilla

¼ teaspoon almond extract

1 recipe Almond Icing

Small multicolored decorative candies (optional)

1. Grease two large cookie sheets; set aside. In a bowl stir together flour, baking powder, and salt; set flour mixture aside.

2. In a large mixing bowl beat eggs, sugar, oil, vanilla, and almond extract with an electric mixer until combined. Beat in as much of the flour mixture as you can with the mixer. Stir in any remaining flour mixture with a wooden spoon.

3. Drop dough by teaspoons (about 1¼ inches in diameter) 1 inch apart onto the prepared cookie sheets. Bake in a 350° oven about 10 minutes or until golden. Transfer cookies to a wire rack and let cool. Frost with Almond Icing. If desired, sprinkle lightly with multicolored candies. Let icing dry.

Almond Icing: In a medium bowl stir together 1 cup sifted powdered sugar, ¼ teaspoon almond extract, and enough milk (2 to 4 teaspoons) to make a smooth, spreadable icing. If desired, tint with food coloring.

TO STORE: Place in layers separated by waxed paper in an airtight container; cover. Store at room temperature up to 3 days or freeze unfrosted cookies up to 3 months. Thaw cookies; frost and, if desired, sprinkle with multicolored candies.

Coconut *Jumbles*

When a cookie sports the surname jumble, you know it's a time-honored treat because jumble is an old-fashioned name for cookie.

Makes: about 24 cookies

Oven: 375°F

½ cup butter, softened

¾ cup sugar

1 egg

3 tablespoons milk

1 teaspoon vanilla

¼ teaspoon salt

1½ cups all-purpose flour

1 cup coconut

1 recipe Pink Frosting

¼ cup coconut, toasted

1. In a medium mixing bowl beat butter with an electric mixer on medium to high speed for 30 seconds. Add sugar; beat until combined, scraping sides of bowl occasionally. Beat in egg, milk, vanilla, and salt until combined. Beat in as much of the flour as you can with the mixer. Stir in any remaining flour and coconut with a wooden spoon.

2. Drop dough by rounded teaspoons 2 inches apart onto an ungreased cookie sheet. Bake in a 375° oven for 8 to 10 minutes or until edges are firm and bottoms are lightly browned. Transfer cookies to a wire rack and let cool. Frost with Pink Frosting; sprinkle with toasted coconut. Let dry.

Pink Frosting: In a medium bowl stir together 2 cups sifted powdered sugar, ½ teaspoon vanilla, and a drop of red food coloring. Stir in enough milk (2 to 3 tablespoons) to make a smooth, spreadable frosting.

TO STORE: Place in layers separated by waxed paper in an airtight container; cover. Store at room temperature up to 3 days or freeze unfrosted cookies up to 3 months. Thaw cookies; frost and sprinkle with coconut.

How big is a drop? When a cookie recipe calls for you to drop the dough from a teaspoon or a tablespoon, use the corresponding utensil from your flatware—not measuring spoons. Make sure the mounds are rounded and about the same size so they'll bake evenly.

Another option is to buy cookie scoops. Found in many sizes, the scoops help guarantee drop cookies of a uniform size and shape.

Orange Snowdrops

Heading to a potluck or cookie exchange? These unique citrus-inspired cookies will refreshingly stand out among platters of other sweet offerings. Hint: For special occasions, sprinkle with thin threads of orange peel.

Makes: about 36 cookies

Oven: 375°F

½ cup butter, softened

½ cup shortening

1 cup sifted powdered sugar

½ teaspoon baking soda

1 egg

½ of a 6-ounce can (⅓ cup) frozen orange juice concentrate, thawed

1 teaspoon vanilla

2 cups all-purpose flour

1 recipe Orange Frosting

Finely shredded orange peel (optional)

1. In a large mixing bowl beat butter and shortening with an electric mixer on medium to high speed for 30 seconds. Add powdered sugar and baking soda. Beat until combined, scraping sides of bowl occasionally. Beat in egg, orange juice concentrate, and vanilla until combined. Beat in as much of the flour as you can with the mixer. Stir in any remaining flour with a wooden spoon.

2. Drop dough by rounded teaspoons 2 inches apart onto an ungreased cookie sheet. Bake in a 375° oven about 8 minutes or until edges are lightly browned. Cool on cookie sheet for 1 minute. Transfer cookies to a wire rack and let cool. Frost with Orange Frosting. If desired, sprinkle with orange peel. Let dry.

Orange Frosting: In a medium bowl stir together 3 cups sifted powdered sugar; half of a 6-ounce can (⅓ cup) frozen orange juice concentrate, thawed; and ½ teaspoon finely shredded orange peel to make a smooth, spreadable frosting.

TO STORE: Place in layers separated by waxed paper in an airtight container; cover. Store at room temperature up to 3 days or freeze unfrosted cookies up to 3 months. Thaw cookies; frost and, if desired, sprinkle with orange peel.

Old-Fashioned Ginger Creams

Here you'll find all the homespun, grandmotherly goodness of gingerbread wrapped into a simple drop cookie. Serve with hot tea or cocoa to warm autumn and winter nights.

Makes: about 36 cookies

Oven: 375°F

¹⁄₃ **cup shortening**

¹⁄₂ **cup sugar**

1 **teaspoon ground ginger**

¹⁄₂ **teaspoon baking soda**

¹⁄₂ **teaspoon ground nutmeg**

¹⁄₂ **teaspoon ground cinnamon**

¹⁄₄ **teaspoon ground cloves**

¹⁄₄ **teaspoon salt**

1 **egg**

¹⁄₂ **cup mild-flavored molasses**

¹⁄₂ **cup water**

2 **cups all-purpose flour**

1 **recipe Butter Frosting**

1. In a large mixing bowl beat shortening with an electric mixer on medium to high speed for 30 seconds. Add sugar, ginger, baking soda, nutmeg, cinnamon, cloves, and salt. Beat until combined, scraping sides of bowl occasionally. Beat in egg, molasses, and water until combined. Beat in as much of the flour as you can with the mixer. Stir in any remaining flour with a wooden spoon. Cover and chill dough for 3 hours (dough will be soft).

2. Grease a large cookie sheet. Drop dough by rounded teaspoons 2 inches apart onto prepared cookie sheet. Bake in a 375° oven about 8 minutes or until edges are firm. Transfer cookies to a wire rack and let cool. Frost with Butter Frosting; let frosting dry.

Butter Frosting: In a medium bowl stir together 2 cups sifted powdered sugar; 2 tablespoons butter, melted; and 4 teaspoons milk. If necessary, stir in additional milk to make a smooth, spreadable frosting.

TO STORE: Place in layers separated by waxed paper in an airtight container; cover. Store at room temperature up to 3 days or freeze unfrosted cookies up to 3 months. Thaw cookies; frost.

Whole Wheat-*Fruit Drops*

This cookie rolls a host of classic baking ingredients—dates, raisins, nuts, and coconut—into one sweet, buttery gem.

Makes: about 40 cookies

Oven: 375°F

¾ cup whole wheat flour

¼ cup all-purpose flour

½ teaspoon baking powder

¼ teaspoon baking soda

¼ teaspoon salt

½ cup butter, softened

⅓ cup granulated sugar

⅓ cup packed brown sugar

1 egg

½ teaspoon vanilla

¾ cup quick-cooking rolled oats

½ cup snipped pitted
       whole dates

½ cup raisins

½ cup chopped walnuts

½ cup coconut

1½ teaspoons finely shredded
       orange peel

1. Grease a large cookie sheet; set aside. In a small bowl stir together whole wheat flour, all-purpose flour, baking powder, baking soda, and salt; set flour mixture aside.

2. In a large mixing bowl beat butter with an electric mixer on medium to high speed for 30 seconds. Add granulated sugar and brown sugar. Beat until combined, scraping sides of bowl occasionally. Beat in egg and vanilla until combined. Stir flour mixture into egg mixture with a wooden spoon. Stir in oats, dates, raisins, walnuts, coconut, and orange peel.

3. Drop dough by teaspoons 2 inches apart onto prepared cookie sheet. Bake in a 375° oven for 9 to 10 minutes or until edges are lightly browned. Cool on cookie sheet for 1 minute. Transfer cookies to a wire rack and let cool.

TO STORE: Place in layers separated by waxed paper in an airtight container; cover. Store at room temperature up to 3 days or freeze up to 3 months.

Flour power Most of the recipes in this cookbook use all-purpose flour, although a few may include some whole wheat flour. Store both types of flour in sealed plastic bags or transfer them to airtight storage containers; keep in a cool, dry place. All-purpose flour stays fresh for eight months; whole grain flour stays fresh for up to five months.

Pumpkin-Pecan Cookies

Pumpkin isn't just for Halloween. Whenever you find yourself with leftover pumpkin from another recipe, stir it into these spicy drop cookies!

Makes: about 40 cookies

Oven: 375°F

  2 **cups all-purpose flour**

1¹⁄₂ **teaspoons baking powder**

  1 **teaspoon ground cinnamon**

¹⁄₄ **teaspoon baking soda**

¹⁄₄ **teaspoon ground allspice**

  1 **cup butter, softened**

  1 **cup sugar**

  1 **egg**

  1 **cup canned pumpkin**

  1 **cup chopped pecans, toasted**

  1 **recipe Brown Sugar-**
      Butter Frosting

1. In a medium bowl combine flour, baking powder, cinnamon, baking soda, and allspice; set flour mixture aside.
2. In a large mixing bowl beat butter with an electric mixer on medium to high speed for 30 seconds. Add sugar. Beat until combined, scraping sides of bowl occasionally. Beat in egg until combined. Stir pumpkin and flour mixture into egg mixture with a wooden spoon. Stir in pecans.
3. Drop dough by rounded teaspoons 2 inches apart onto an ungreased cookie sheet. Bake in a 375° oven for 10 to 12 minutes or until bottoms are lightly browned. Transfer cookies to a wire rack and let cool. Frost with Brown Sugar-Butter Frosting; let frosting dry.

Brown Sugar-Butter Frosting: In a medium heavy saucepan heat and stir 6 tablespoons butter and ¹⁄₃ cup packed brown sugar over medium heat until butter melts; remove from heat. Stir in 2 cups sifted powdered sugar and 1 teaspoon vanilla. Stir in enough hot water (2 to 3 teaspoons) to make a smooth, spreadable frosting. Immediately frost cookies. (If frosting becomes grainy, add a few more drops of hot water and stir until smooth.)

TO STORE: Place in layers separated by waxed paper in an airtight container; cover. Store at room temperature up to 3 days or freeze unfrosted cookies up to 3 months. Thaw cookies; frost.

Spiced *Apple* Drops

Apples and spice and everything nice—that's what these cookies are made of. The buttery apple frosting gives them an extra dose of melt-in-your-mouth irresistibility.

Makes: about 40 cookies

Oven: 375°F

½ cup butter, softened

⅔ cup granulated sugar

⅔ cup packed brown sugar

1 teaspoon ground cinnamon

½ teaspoon baking soda

½ teaspoon ground nutmeg

⅛ teaspoon ground cloves

1 egg

¼ cup apple juice or apple cider

2 cups all-purpose flour

1 cup finely chopped
   peeled apple

1 cup chopped walnuts

1 recipe Apple Frosting

1. Grease a large cookie sheet; set aside. In a large mixing bowl beat butter with an electric mixer on medium to high speed for 30 seconds. Add granulated sugar, brown sugar, cinnamon, baking soda, nutmeg, and cloves. Beat until combined, scraping sides of bowl occasionally. Beat in egg and apple juice until combined. Beat in as much of the flour as you can with the mixer. Stir in any remaining flour, chopped apple, and walnuts with a wooden spoon.

2. Drop dough by rounded teaspoons 2 inches apart onto prepared cookie sheet. Bake in a 375° oven for 10 to 12 minutes or until edges are lightly browned. Cool on cookie sheet for 1 minute. Transfer cookies to a wire rack and let cool. Frost with Apple Frosting; let frosting dry.

Apple Frosting: In a large mixing bowl beat 4 cups sifted powdered sugar, ¼ cup softened butter, 1 teaspoon vanilla, and enough apple juice (3 to 4 tablespoons) with an electric mixer to make a smooth, spreadable frosting.

TO STORE: Place in layers separated by waxed paper in an airtight container; cover. Store in the refrigerator up to 3 days or freeze unfrosted cookies up to 3 months. Thaw cookies; frost.

Malted Milk Cookies

These cookies, flavored with malted milk balls and malted milk powder, seem to magically bring back favorite childhood memories. Hint: Coarsely chop the malted milk balls individually until you have a cupful. *(photo, page 35)*

Makes: about 36 cookies

Oven: 375°F

1 cup butter, softened

¾ cup granulated sugar

¾ cup packed brown sugar

1 teaspoon baking soda

2 eggs

1 teaspoon vanilla

2 ounces unsweetened
  chocolate, melted
  and cooled

2¾ cups all-purpose flour

½ cup instant malted
  milk powder

1 cup coarsely chopped
  malted milk balls

1. In a large mixing bowl beat butter with an electric mixer on medium to high speed for 30 seconds. Add granulated sugar, brown sugar, and baking soda. Beat until combined, scraping sides of bowl occasionally. Beat in eggs, vanilla, and melted chocolate until combined. Beat in as much of the flour as you can with the mixer. Stir in any remaining flour and the malted milk powder with a wooden spoon. Stir in chopped malted milk balls.

2. Drop dough by rounded teaspoons 2½ inches apart onto an ungreased cookie sheet. Bake in a 375° oven about 10 minutes or until edges are firm. Cool on cookie sheet for 1 minute. Transfer cookies to a wire rack and let cool.

TO STORE: Place in layers separated by waxed paper in an airtight container; cover. Store at room temperature up to 3 days or freeze up to 3 months.

holiday treat

Lemon Drops

A simple lemon glaze adds a sparkle to these dainty holiday treats. Make the glaze while the cookies are baking so it's ready to slather over the warm cookies.

Makes: about 36 cookies

Oven: 375°F

½ **cup butter, softened**

¾ **cup granulated sugar**

4 **teaspoons finely shredded lemon peel**

½ **teaspoon baking powder**

½ **teaspoon baking soda**

⅛ **teaspoon salt**

1 **egg**

½ **cup dairy sour cream**

⅓ **cup lemon juice**

2 **cups all-purpose flour**

1 **recipe Lemon Glaze**

Coarse sugar

Yellow gum drops, chopped

1. In a large mixing bowl beat butter with an electric mixer on medium to high speed for 30 seconds. Add the granulated sugar, lemon peel, baking powder, baking soda, and salt. Beat until combined, scraping sides of bowl occasionally. Beat in egg, sour cream, and lemon juice until combined. Beat in as much of the flour as you can with the mixer. Stir in any remaining flour with a wooden spoon.

2. Drop dough by slightly rounded tablespoons 3 inches apart onto an ungreased cookie sheet. Bake in a 375° oven about 8 minutes or until tops are firm. Transfer cookies to a wire rack. Brush the tops of the warm cookies with Lemon Glaze. Sprinkle with coarse sugar and decorate with chopped gumdrops. Let cookies cool.

Lemon Glaze: In a small bowl stir together ¼ cup granulated sugar and 2 tablespoons lemon juice.

TO STORE: Place in layers separated by waxed paper in an airtight container; cover. Store at room temperature up to 3 days or freeze up to 3 months.

holiday
treat

Pecan Drops

It's the powdered sugar that gives this cookie a light, cakelike texture. Hint: Select the nicest pecan halves to use for the cookie tops; coarsely chop the rest before stirring them into the dough.

Makes: about 36 cookies

Oven: 375°F

½ cup butter, softened

2 cups sifted powdered sugar

1¾ cups all-purpose flour

⅓ cup milk

1 egg

1 teaspoon baking powder

1 teaspoon vanilla

1 cup coarsely chopped pecans

Granulated sugar

Pecan halves (optional)

1. Grease a large cookie sheet; set aside. In a large mixing bowl beat butter with an electric mixer on medium to high speed for 30 seconds. Add powdered sugar, about half of the flour, half of the milk, the egg, baking powder, and vanilla. Beat until combined, scraping sides of bowl occasionally. Stir in remaining flour and milk with a wooden spoon. Stir in chopped pecans.

2. Drop dough by rounded teaspoons 2 inches apart onto prepared cookie sheet. Sprinkle with granulated sugar. If desired, lightly press a pecan half in the center of each cookie. Bake in a 375° oven for 8 to 10 minutes or until edges are lightly browned. Transfer cookies to a wire rack and let cool.

TO STORE: Place in layers separated by waxed paper in an airtight container; cover. Store at room temperature up to 3 days or freeze up to 3 months.

Converting recipes for convection ovens

You can convert most of the recipes in this book for use in a convection oven. Follow any specific instructions your oven manufacturer provides, and keep these general guidelines in mind.

When cooking in a convection oven, use the original recipe's temperature and time as a guideline, checking for doneness after three-quarters of the baking time has elapsed. Or reduce the original baking temperature by 25° and cook for the original amount of time. Open the oven door as little as possible during baking, and test food a few minutes before the minimum cooking time has elapsed, using the doneness test given in the recipe. Keep in mind that even when food appears golden brown, it may not be completely done.

Follow the user's manual for manufacturer's recommendations for preheating a convection oven. Be sure to position oven racks before you turn on the oven because they will heat up quickly.

Stuffed *Date* Drops

Valued in locales across America, community cookbooks are a plentiful source of terrific recipes that have been lovingly passed from one generation to another. The editors of a community cookbook share this uncommonly good date-studded recipe. *(photo, page 71)*

Makes: about 60 cookies

Oven: 375°F

1¼ cups all-purpose flour

½ teaspoon baking powder

½ teaspoon baking soda

¼ teaspoon salt

1 pound pitted whole dates

60 to 70 pecan halves

¼ cup butter, softened

¾ cup packed brown sugar

1 egg

½ cup dairy sour cream

1 recipe Browned Butter Icing

1. In a small bowl stir together flour, baking powder, baking soda, and salt; set flour mixture aside. Stuff each date with a pecan half; set aside.

2. In a medium mixing bowl beat butter with an electric mixer on medium speed for 30 seconds. Add brown sugar. Beat until combined, scraping sides of bowl occasionally. Beat in egg until combined. Alternately add flour mixture and sour cream to egg mixture, beating well after each addition. Gently stir in stuffed dates with a wooden spoon.

3. Drop dough by rounded teaspoons onto an ungreased cookie sheet, allowing one date per cookie. Bake in a 375° oven for 8 to 10 minutes or until edges are lightly browned. Transfer cookies to a wire rack and let cool. Drizzle Browned Butter Icing over cookies; let icing dry.

Browned Butter Icing: In a small heavy saucepan heat ½ cup butter over medium heat until golden brown, stirring occasionally. Remove from heat; stir in 3 cups sifted powdered sugar and 1 teaspoon vanilla. Stir in enough water (2 to 3 tablespoons) to make drizzling consistency.

TO STORE: Place in layers separated by waxed paper in an airtight container; cover. Store at room temperature up to 3 days or freeze undrizzled cookies up to 3 months. Thaw cookies; drizzle.

holiday treat

Cherry Winks

These cookie classics from the 1940s, with tiny dents that are filled with jellies and jams, have been called by many names over the years including thumbprints, thimble cookies, and Wee Tom Thumbs. A little cherry button is a winsome twist on the classic.

Makes: about 36 cookies

Oven: 400°F

- ½ **cup sugar**
- ⅓ **cup shortening**
- ½ **teaspoon baking powder**
- ¼ **teaspoon salt**
- 1 **egg**
- 1 **tablespoon milk**
- 1 **teaspoon vanilla**
- 1 **cup all-purpose flour**
- ½ **cup chopped raisins**
- ½ **cup chopped walnuts**
- 1 **teaspoon finely shredded lemon peel**
- 2 **cups wheat flakes cereal, crushed**
- 18 **candied cherries, halved**

1. In a large mixing bowl beat sugar, shortening, baking powder, and salt with an electric mixer on medium to high speed for 30 seconds. Add egg, milk, and vanilla. Beat until combined, scraping sides of bowl occasionally. Beat in as much of the flour as you can with the mixer. Stir in any remaining flour with a wooden spoon. Stir in the raisins, walnuts, and lemon peel.

2. Drop dough by rounded teaspoons into crushed cereal. Toss lightly to coat dough with cereal. Place cookies 2 inches apart onto an ungreased cookie sheet. Top each cookie with a candied cherry half. Bake in a 400° oven for 7 to 8 minutes or until bottoms are lightly browned. Transfer cookies to a wire rack and let cool.

TO STORE: Place in layers separated by waxed paper in an airtight container; cover. Store at room temperature up to 3 days or freeze up to 3 months.

Chewy *Coconut* Macaroons

Serve these sweet, airy gems with a dish of premium chocolate ice cream, and you'll have a dainty yet decadent dessert guests will rave about. *(photo, page 71)*

Makes: about 30 cookies

Oven: 325°F

2⅔ cups coconut

⅔ cup sugar

⅓ cup all-purpose flour

¼ teaspoon salt

4 egg whites

½ teaspoon almond extract

2 ounces semisweet chocolate (optional)

½ teaspoon shortening (optional)

1. Grease and flour a large cookie sheet; set aside. In a medium bowl stir together coconut, sugar, flour, and salt. Stir in egg whites and almond extract. Drop coconut mixture by rounded teaspoons 2 inches apart onto prepared cookie sheet.
2. Bake in a 325° oven for 20 to 25 minutes or until edges are golden brown. Transfer cookies to a wire rack and let cool.
3. If desired, in a small heavy saucepan melt chocolate and shortening over low heat, stirring constantly. Drizzle over cookies; let stand until set.

TO STORE: Place in layers separated by waxed paper in an airtight container; cover. Store at room temperature up to 3 days or freeze undrizzled cookies up to 3 months. Thaw cookies; drizzle.

Macaroons vs. meringues People often confuse macaroons with meringue cookies, but there is a difference. Although both are made with egg whites, the similarity ends there. Macaroons are chewy and may contain ground nuts, almond paste, or coconut. Meringue cookies contain egg whites and sugar. The meringue mixture is beaten until stiff and baked until crisp. For a meringue-style cookie, try Hickory Nut Meringues on page 50, Cashew Meringues on page 51, or Brownie Meringues on page 52.

Hickory Nut Meringues

This elegant meringue cookie dates back to the 1920s. The nuts determine the flavor here, so be sure to select your favorite among the options.

Makes: about 36 cookies

Oven: 325°F

4 egg whites

4 cups sifted powdered sugar

2 cups chopped hickory nuts,
    black walnuts, or
    toasted pecans

1. In a large mixing bowl allow egg whites to stand at room temperature for 30 minutes. Meanwhile, grease two cookie sheets; set aside.
2. Beat egg whites with an electric mixer on medium speed until soft peaks form (tips curl). Gradually add powdered sugar, about $\frac{1}{4}$ cup at a time, beating on medium speed just until combined. Beat on high speed about 2 minutes more or until stiff peaks form (tips stand straight). Fold in nuts.
3. Drop mixture by rounded teaspoons 2 inches apart onto prepared cookie sheets. Bake in a 325° oven about 15 minutes or until edges are very lightly browned. (Cookies puff and sides split during baking.) Transfer cookies to a wire rack and let cool.

TO STORE: **Place in layers separated by waxed paper in an airtight container; cover. Store at room temperature up to 2 days or freeze up to 3 months.**

Toasting nuts Toasting heightens the flavor of nuts, and it's simple to do: Spread the nuts in a single layer in a shallow baking pan. Bake in a 350°F oven for 5 to 10 minutes or until light golden brown, watching carefully and stirring once or twice so the nuts don't burn.

Almonds can also be "toasted" in a microwave (other nuts are trickier, as they burn more easily). Place $\frac{1}{2}$ to 1 cup slivered or sliced almonds in a 2-cup microwave-safe measure. Microwave, uncovered, on 100% power (high) for 1 minute; stir. Microwave $1\frac{1}{2}$ to 3 minutes more, stirring every 30 seconds. At the first sign of toasting, spread nuts on paper towels. (They will continue to toast as they stand.) Let stand for at least 15 minutes before using.

Cashew Meringues

As if ordinary meringue cookies aren't heavenly enough, this version is studded with buttery cashews and drizzled with silky caramel.

Makes: about 60 cookies

Oven: 325°F

2 egg whites

½ teaspoon vanilla

⅛ teaspoon cream of tartar

2 cups sifted powdered sugar

1 cup chopped cashews
   or mixed nuts

6 vanilla caramels, unwrapped

1 teaspoon milk

   Chopped cashews or mixed
      nuts (optional)

1. In a large mixing bowl allow egg whites to stand at room temperature for 30 minutes. Meanwhile, grease two cookie sheets; set aside.

2. Add vanilla and cream of tartar to egg whites. Beat with an electric mixer on medium speed until soft peaks form (tips curl). Gradually add the powdered sugar, about ¼ cup at a time, beating on medium speed just until combined. Beat on high speed for 1 to 2 minutes more. (Do not continue beating to stiff peaks.) Fold in the 2 cups nuts.

3. Drop mixture by teaspoons 2 inches apart onto prepared cookie sheets. Bake in a 325° oven about 15 minutes or until edges are very lightly browned. (Cookies puff and sides split during baking.) Transfer cookies to a wire rack and let cool.

4. In a small heavy saucepan heat and stir caramels and milk over low heat until caramels melt. Drizzle caramel mixture over cookies. If desired, sprinkle with additional chopped cashews. Let stand until set.

TO STORE: Place in layers separated by waxed paper in an airtight container; cover. Store at room temperature up to 3 days or freeze undrizzled cookies up to 3 months. Thaw cookies; drizzle and, if desired, sprinkle with nuts.

Brownie Meringues

Crisp and delicate on the outside with melt-in-your-mouth centers, these chocolate meringue cookies are a delightful melding of textures. A melted chocolate drizzle adds a luscious third dimension.

Makes: about 24 cookies

Oven: 350°F

   2 **egg whites**

½ **teaspoon vinegar**

½ **teaspoon vanilla**

   Dash salt

½ **cup sugar**

   1 **cup semisweet chocolate**
      pieces, melted and cooled

¾ **cup chopped walnuts**

½ **cup semisweet chocolate**
      pieces

   1 **teaspoon shortening**

1. In a large mixing bowl allow egg whites to stand at room temperature for 30 minutes. Meanwhile, grease two cookie sheets; set aside.

2. Add vinegar, vanilla, and salt to egg whites. Beat with an electric mixer on medium speed until soft peaks form (tips curl). Gradually add the sugar, 1 tablespoon at a time, beating on high speed about 4 minutes or until stiff peaks form (tips stand straight) and the sugar is almost dissolved. Fold in the melted chocolate and walnuts.

3. Drop mixture by teaspoons 2 inches apart onto prepared cookie sheets. Bake in a 350° oven for 10 to 12 minutes or until edges are firm. (Cookies puff and sides split during baking.) Transfer cookies to a wire rack and let cool.

4. In a small heavy saucepan melt the ½ cup semisweet chocolate pieces and shortening over low heat, stirring constantly. Drizzle chocolate mixture over cookies; let stand until set.

TO STORE: Place in layers separated by waxed paper in an airtight container; cover. Store at room temperature up to 3 days or freeze undrizzled cookies up to 3 months. Thaw cookies; drizzle.

Semisweet or bittersweet Semisweet chocolate and bittersweet chocolate, both sometimes referred to as "dark chocolate," contain at least 35 percent pure chocolate, with added cocoa butter and sugar. While no legal standards exist to differentiate the two, bittersweet chocolate is usually darker and less sweet than semisweet chocolate. You can use the two products interchangeably; experiment to discover which you prefer.

Fudge Ecstasies

Prepare to be wowed! You'll think you broke the chocolate bank when you bite into one of these chewy, double-chocolate, nut-filled wonders!

Makes: about 36 cookies

Oven: 350°F

1 **12-ounce package (2 cups) semisweet chocolate pieces**

2 **ounces unsweetened chocolate, chopped**

2 **tablespoons butter**

2 **eggs**

⅔ **cup sugar**

¼ **cup all-purpose flour**

1 **teaspoon vanilla**

¼ **teaspoon baking powder**

1 **cup chopped nuts**

1. Grease a large cookie sheet; set aside. In a medium heavy saucepan heat 1 cup of the chocolate pieces, the unsweetened chocolate, and butter until melted, stirring constantly. Remove from heat; add eggs, sugar, flour, vanilla, and baking powder. Beat with a wooden spoon until combined, scraping sides of pan occasionally. Stir in remaining 1 cup chocolate pieces and nuts.

2. Drop dough by rounded teaspoons 2 inches apart onto the prepared cookie sheet. Bake in a 350° oven for 8 to 10 minutes or until edges are firm and surfaces are dull and crackled. Transfer cookies to a wire rack and let cool.

TO STORE: Place in layers separated by waxed paper in an airtight container; cover. Store at room temperature up to 3 days or freeze up to 3 months.

Triple-Chocolate *Chunk* Cookies

For the true chocophile, there is no such thing as too much chocolate. If you belong to that camp, you'll be more than merely tempted by these chunky, oversize treats that boast a trio of chocolates!

Makes: about 22 cookies

Oven: 350°F

1 cup butter, softened

¾ cup granulated sugar

¾ cup packed brown sugar

1 teaspoon baking soda

2 eggs

1 teaspoon vanilla

3 ounces unsweetened chocolate, melted and cooled

2 cups all-purpose flour

1 8-ounce package semisweet chocolate, cut into ½-inch pieces, or 1⅓ cups large semisweet chocolate pieces

1 6-ounce package white baking bars, cut into ½-inch pieces, or 1 cup white baking pieces

1 cup chopped black walnuts or pecans (optional)

1. Grease a large cookie sheet; set aside. In a large mixing bowl beat butter with an electric mixer on medium to high speed for 30 seconds. Add granulated sugar, brown sugar, and baking soda. Beat until combined, scraping sides of bowl occasionally. Beat in eggs and vanilla until combined. Stir in melted chocolate. Beat in as much of the flour as you can with the mixer. Stir in any remaining flour with a wooden spoon. Stir in chocolate pieces, white baking pieces, and, if desired, nuts.

2. Use a ¼-cup measure or scoop to drop mounds of dough 4 inches apart onto prepared cookie sheet. Bake in a 350° oven for 12 to 14 minutes or until edges are firm. Cool on cookie sheet for 1 minute. Transfer cookies to a wire rack and let cool.

TO STORE: Place in layers separated by waxed paper in an airtight container; cover. Store at room temperature up to 3 days or freeze up to 3 months.

Chocolate-Cherry Drops

If you're making these treats at Christmastime, use dried tart red cherries and green-hued pistachios to reflect the colors of the season. When you're not looking for that holiday effect, substitute dried apricots or golden raisins for the cherries if you like. *(photo, page 69)*

Makes: about 40 cookies

Oven: 350°F

1 cup butter, softened

¾ cup granulated sugar

¾ cup packed brown sugar

1 teaspoon baking soda

3 ounces unsweetened chocolate, melted and cooled

2 eggs

1 teaspoon vanilla

2 cups all-purpose flour

1½ cups snipped dried tart cherries

1 cup pistachio nuts

3 ounces white baking bars

2 teaspoons shortening

¼ cup very finely chopped pistachio nuts

1. Grease a large cookie sheet; set aside. In a large mixing bowl beat butter with an electric mixer on medium to high speed for 30 seconds. Add granulated sugar, brown sugar, and baking soda. Beat until combined, scraping sides of bowl occasionally. Beat in the melted chocolate, eggs, and vanilla until combined. Beat in as much of the flour as you can with the mixer. Stir in any remaining flour, dried cherries, and the 1 cup pistachio nuts with a wooden spoon.

2. Drop dough by rounded teaspoons 2 inches apart onto the prepared cookie sheet. Bake in a 350° oven for 10 to 12 minutes or until edges are firm. Cool on cookie sheet for 1 minute. Transfer cookies to a wire rack and let cool.

3. In a small heavy saucepan melt white baking bars and shortening over low heat, stirring constantly. Drizzle over cookies; immediately sprinkle with the ¼ cup pistachio nuts. Let stand until set.

TO STORE: Place in layers separated by waxed paper in an airtight container; cover. Store at room temperature up to 2 days or freeze undrizzled cookies up to 3 months. Thaw cookies; drizzle and sprinkle with nuts.

White chocolate vs. white baking bar

White chocolate is a rich combination of cocoa butter, sugar, butterfat, milk solids, lecithin, and flavorings. The cocoa butter gives the white chocolate its richness. In products that are sometimes confused with white chocolate—white baking bars, white baking pieces, white candy coating, and white confectionery bars—vegetable fat substitutes for the cocoa butter. If your recipe calls for white chocolate exclusively, be sure to use an ingredient that's labeled as such. If an option is given for white chocolate or white baking bars or pieces, you can use them interchangeably.

Chocolate-Almond Sugar Cookies

The addition of your choice of liqueur gives these rich childhood favorites a grown-up slant.

If you plan to share them with children, use milk instead of liqueur.

Makes: about 72 cookies

Oven: 375°F

4 cups all-purpose flour

½ cup unsweetened
    cocoa powder

⅔ cup butter, softened

⅔ cup shortening

1½ cups sugar

2 teaspoons baking powder

2 eggs

3 tablespoons amaretto,
    coffee liqueur, crème
    de cacao, or milk

2 teaspoons vanilla

1 cup miniature semisweet
    chocolate pieces

¾ cup finely chopped
    almonds or pecans

Sugar

1. In a large bowl combine flour and cocoa powder; set flour mixture aside.

2. In a large mixing bowl beat butter and shortening with an electric mixer on medium to high speed for 30 seconds. Add the 1½ cups sugar and baking powder. Beat until combined, scraping sides of bowl occasionally. Beat in eggs, amaretto, and vanilla until combined. Beat in as much of the flour mixture as you can with the mixer. Stir in any remaining flour mixture with a wooden spoon. Stir in chocolate pieces and nuts.

3. Drop dough by rounded teaspoons 2 inches apart onto an ungreased cookie sheet. Flatten each piece of dough with a the bottom of a glass dipped in additional sugar.* Bake in a 375° oven for 7 to 9 minutes or until edges are firm. Transfer cookies to a wire rack and let cool.

*NOTE: So sugar will stick to the glass, first dip the bottom of the glass in the cookie dough. Next, dip it into sugar.

TO STORE: **Place in layers separated by waxed paper in an airtight container; cover. Store at room temperature up to 3 days or freeze up to 3 months.**

Dream Cookies

White chocolate and macadamia nuts add an air of sophistication to these dreamy chocolate chip cookies. *(photo, page 70)*

Makes: about 24 cookies

Oven: 350°F

½ cup butter, softened

½ cup shortening

¾ cup granulated sugar

¾ cup packed brown sugar

½ teaspoon baking powder

¼ teaspoon baking soda

¼ teaspoon salt

2 eggs

1 teaspoon vanilla

1⅓ cups all-purpose flour

⅓ cup unsweetened
   cocoa powder

2½ cups rolled oats

1 cup semisweet
   chocolate pieces

1 cup white baking pieces
   or peanut butter-
   flavored pieces

1 cup chopped macadamia nuts

1. Grease a large cookie sheet; set aside. In a large mixing bowl beat butter and shortening with an electric mixer on medium to high speed for 30 seconds. Add granulated sugar, brown sugar, baking powder, baking soda, and salt. Beat until combined, scraping sides of bowl occasionally. Add eggs and vanilla. Beat until combined. Beat in flour and cocoa powder on low speed just until combined. Stir in oats, chocolate pieces, white baking pieces, and macadamia nuts with a wooden spoon.

2. Drop dough by a ¼-cup measure or scoop 3 inches apart onto prepared cookie sheet. Press into 3-inch circles. Bake in a 350° oven for 12 to 14 minutes or just until set. Cool on cookie sheet for 1 minute. Transfer cookies to a wire rack and let cool.

TO STORE: Place in layers separated by waxed paper in an airtight container; cover. Store at room temperature up to 3 days or freeze up to 3 months.

Go Dutch Unsweetened cocoa powder is pure chocolate with most of the cocoa butter removed. Cocoas labeled "Dutch-process" or "European-style" have been treated to neutralize the natural acids, giving them a mellow flavor and reddish color. These products are generally more expensive than regular unsweetened cocoa powder that these recipes call for.

Frosted *Sour* Cream-Chocolate Drops

Here, the deep flavor of dark chocolate mingles with the extra richness sour cream imparts.

Topped off with Chocolate Butter Frosting, these cookies are decadent indeed! *(photo, page 71)*

Makes: about 42 cookies

Oven: 350°F

½ cup butter, softened

1 cup packed brown sugar

½ teaspoon baking soda

¼ teaspoon salt

1 egg

1 teaspoon vanilla

2 ounces unsweetened chocolate, melted and cooled

1 8-ounce carton dairy sour cream

2 cups all-purpose flour

1 recipe Chocolate Butter Frosting

1. In a large mixing bowl beat butter with an electric mixer on medium to high speed for 30 seconds. Add brown sugar, baking soda, and salt. Beat until combined, scraping sides of bowl occasionally. Beat in egg and vanilla. Add melted chocolate; beat until combined. Beat in sour cream. Beat in as much of the flour as you can with the mixer. Stir in any remaining flour with a wooden spoon.

2. Drop dough by slightly rounded teaspoons 2 inches apart onto an ungreased cookie sheet. Bake in a 350° oven for 8 to 10 minutes or until edges are firm. Transfer cookies to a wire rack and let cool. Frost with Chocolate Butter Frosting; let frosting dry.

Chocolate Butter Frosting: In a medium mixing bowl beat ¼ cup butter with an electric mixer on medium speed until fluffy. Gradually add 1 cup sifted powdered sugar and ⅓ cup unsweetened cocoa powder, beating well. Slowly beat in 3 tablespoons light cream or milk and 1 teaspoon vanilla. Gradually beat in 1½ cups sifted powdered sugar. If necessary, beat in additional light cream or milk to make a smooth, spreadable frosting.

TO STORE: Place in layers separated by waxed paper in an airtight container; cover. Store at room temperature up to 3 days or freeze unfrosted cookies up to 3 months. Thaw cookies; frost.

holiday treat

White Chocolate and *Raspberry* Cookies

The exact moment food lovers tapped into the magical melding of white chocolate and raspberries is lost to history. Since then, however, many great recipes in *Better Homes and Gardens*® books have combined this flavor duo. Here's one of the favorites! *(photo, page 71)*

Makes: about 48 cookies

Oven: 375°F

8 ounces white baking bars
    or white chocolate
    baking squares

½ cup butter, softened

1 cup sugar

1 teaspoon baking soda

¼ teaspoon salt

2 eggs

2¾ cups all-purpose flour

½ cup seedless raspberry jam

3 ounces white baking bars
    or white chocolate
    baking squares

½ teaspoon shortening

1. Grease a large cookie sheet; set aside. Chop 4 ounces of the white baking bars; set aside. In a small heavy saucepan melt 4 ounces baking bars over low heat, stirring constantly; cool.

2. In a large mixing bowl beat butter with an electric mixer on medium to high speed for 30 seconds. Add sugar, baking soda, and salt. Beat until combined, scraping sides of bowl occasionally. Beat in eggs and melted baking bars until combined. Beat in as much of the flour as you can with the mixer. Stir in any remaining flour with a wooden spoon. Stir in the 4 ounces chopped baking bars (dough will be stiff).

3. Drop dough from rounded teaspoons 2 inches apart onto the prepared cookie sheet. Bake in a 375° oven for 7 to 9 minutes or until edges are lightly browned. Cool on cookie sheet for 1 minute. Transfer cookies to a wire rack and let cool.

4. Just before serving, in a small heavy saucepan melt jam over low heat. Spoon about ½ teaspoon jam over each cookie. In another small heavy saucepan melt the remaining 3 ounces white baking bars and shortening over low heat, stirring constantly. Drizzle over cookies; let stand until set. (If necessary, chill cookies for 15 minutes or until drizzle is set.)

TO STORE: Place in layers separated by waxed paper in an airtight container; cover. Store in the refrigerator up to 3 days or freeze plain cookies up to 3 months. Thaw cookies; top with jam and drizzle with melted baking bars mixture.

Sachertorte Cookies

Over the years, *Better Homes and Gardens*® editors have become experts at parlaying the flavors of celebrated desserts into easy-to-make cookies. This one is modeled after the Sachertorte, a famous Viennese chocolate-and-apricot torte. *(photo, page 71)*

Makes: about 60 cookies

Oven: 375°F

2 cups all-purpose flour

⅓ cup unsweetened
      cocoa powder

1 teaspoon baking powder

¼ teaspoon baking soda

¼ teaspoon salt

¼ cup butter, softened

¼ cup cooking oil

1 cup packed brown sugar

⅓ cup granulated sugar

2 ounces unsweetened chocolate,
      melted and cooled

1 teaspoon vanilla

3 eggs

1 8-ounce carton dairy sour cream

½ cup apricot preserves

1 recipe Chocolate Frosting

1 cup milk chocolate pieces

1 teaspoon shortening

1. Grease a large cookie sheet; set aside. In a bowl combine flour, cocoa powder, baking powder, baking soda, and salt; set flour mixture aside.
2. In a large mixing bowl beat butter with an electric mixer on medium to high speed for 30 seconds. Add oil, brown sugar, granulated sugar, unsweetened chocolate, and vanilla. Beat until combined, scraping sides of bowl occasionally. Add eggs one at a time, beating well after each addition. Beat in sour cream until combined. Beat in as much of the flour mixture as you can with the mixer. Stir in any remaining flour mixture with a wooden spoon.
3. Drop dough by rounded teaspoons 2 inches apart onto prepared cookie sheet. Bake in a 375° oven for 8 to 10 minutes or until tops spring back when pressed lightly. Transfer cookies to a wire rack and let cool.
4. In a small heavy saucepan melt apricot preserves over low heat. Force preserves through a strainer with the back of a wooden spoon, discarding any large pieces. Brush tops of cooled cookies with strained preserves. Frost with Chocolate Frosting; let frosting dry.
5. In a small heavy saucepan melt milk chocolate pieces and shortening over low heat. Pipe or drizzle a letter S on each cookie; let stand until set.

Chocolate Frosting: In a small heavy saucepan melt 8 ounces semisweet chocolate and 2 tablespoons butter over low heat, stirring frequently. Remove from heat and stir in 2 tablespoons light-colored corn syrup and 2 tablespoons milk. Whisk until smooth.

TO STORE: Place in layers separated by waxed paper in an airtight container; cover. Store in the refrigerator up to 3 days or freeze cookies (before brushing with preserves) up to 3 months. Thaw cookies; brush with preserves, frost, and decorate.

Heavenly Hand-Shaped Cookies

Peanut Butter *Cookies*

Dress up the old-fashioned crisscrossed favorite with a drizzle of melted semisweet chocolate pieces, and a new classic is born!

Makes: about 36 cookies

Oven: 375°F

½ cup butter, softened

½ cup peanut butter

½ cup granulated sugar

½ cup packed brown sugar

    or ¼ cup honey

½ teaspoon baking soda

½ teaspoon baking powder

1 egg

½ teaspoon vanilla

1¼ cups all-purpose flour

    Granulated sugar

½ cup semisweet chocolate

    pieces (optional)

1 teaspoon shortening (optional)

1. In a large mixing bowl beat butter and peanut butter with an electric mixer on medium to high speed for 30 seconds. Add the ½ cup granulated sugar, brown sugar, baking soda, and baking powder. Beat until combined, scraping sides of bowl occasionally. Beat in egg and vanilla until combined. Beat in as much of the flour as you can with the mixer. Stir in any remaining flour with a wooden spoon. If necessary, cover and chill dough about 1 hour or until easy to handle.

2. Shape dough into 1-inch balls. Roll in granulated sugar to coat. Place balls 2 inches apart on an ungreased cookie sheet. Flatten by making crisscross marks with the tines of a fork.

3. Bake in a 375° oven for 7 to 9 minutes or until bottoms are lightly browned. Transfer cookies to a wire rack and let cool.

4. If desired, in a small heavy saucepan melt chocolate pieces and shortening over low heat, stirring constantly. Drizzle chocolate mixture over cookies; let stand until set.

TO STORE: Place in layers separated by waxed paper in an airtight container; cover. Store at room temperature up to 3 days or freeze up to 3 months.

The skinny on peanut butter Can you make your favorite peanut butter bars with reduced-fat peanut butter? You bet! Substitute the same amount of reduced-fat peanut butter for the regular product. The lower-fat cookies might be slightly chewier, but that shouldn't bother true peanut butter fans, who are used to peanut butter sticking to the roofs of their mouths.

Peanut Butter Blossoms

These days, they're known as Peanut Butter Blossoms, but your grandmother may have called them Black-Eyed Susans, thanks to their daisylike resemblance. No matter what you call them, the time-honored treats endure as a favorite.

Makes: about 54 cookies

Oven: 350°F

1/2 **cup shortening**

1/2 **cup peanut butter**

1/2 **cup granulated sugar**

1/2 **cup packed brown sugar**

1 **teaspoon baking powder**

1/8 **teaspoon baking soda**

1 **egg**

2 **tablespoons milk**

1 **teaspoon vanilla**

1 3/4 **cups all-purpose flour**

1/4 **cup granulated sugar**

Milk chocolate kisses,

   unwrapped, or stars

1. In a large mixing bowl beat shortening and peanut butter with an electric mixer on medium to high speed for 30 seconds. Add the 1/2 cup granulated sugar, brown sugar, baking powder, and baking soda. Beat until combined, scraping sides of bowl occasionally. Beat in egg, milk, and vanilla until combined. Beat in as much of the flour as you can with the mixer. Stir in any remaining flour with a wooden spoon.

2. Shape dough into 1-inch balls. Roll balls in the 1/4 cup granulated sugar. Place balls 2 inches apart on an ungreased cookie sheet.

3. Bake in a 350° oven for 10 to 12 minutes or until edges are firm and bottoms are lightly browned. Immediately press a chocolate kiss or star into center of each cookie. Transfer cookies to a wire rack and let cool.

TO STORE: Place in layers separated by waxed paper in an airtight container; cover. Store at room temperature up to 3 days or freeze up to 3 months.

Peanut Butter *Candy Bar* Cookies

Wrap peanutty cookie dough around bite-size candy bars to create two treats in one. If miniature candy bars aren't available, cut regular-size bars into 1-inch squares.

Makes: 24 cookies

Oven: 350°F

1³⁄₄ **cups all-purpose flour**

¹⁄₂ **cup sugar**

¹⁄₂ **teaspoon baking soda**

¹⁄₄ **teaspoon salt**

¹⁄₂ **cup butter**

¹⁄₂ **cup creamy peanut butter**

¹⁄₄ **cup honey**

1 **tablespoon milk**

24 **miniature chocolate-coated**

caramel-topped nougat

bars with peanuts

1. In a large bowl stir together flour, sugar, baking soda, and salt. Using a pastry blender, cut in butter and peanut butter until mixture resembles coarse crumbs. Beat in honey and milk with a wooden spoon until combined.

2. For each cookie, pat 1 tablespoon of the dough into a 2-inch circle. Place one candy bar in the center of the circle. Shape the dough around the candy bar to form a 1¹⁄₂-inch ball. Place balls 2 inches apart on an ungreased cookie sheet.

3. Bake in a 350° oven for 12 to 15 minutes or until edges are lightly browned. Transfer cookies to a wire rack and let cool.

TO STORE: Place in layers separated by waxed paper in an airtight container; cover. Store at room temperature up to 3 days or freeze up to 3 months.

Chocolate *Crinkles*

The sugary surfaces of these cookies crack as they bake, revealing irresistible fudgy centers. Kids love that zebra-stripe effect!

Makes: about 48 cookies

Oven: 375°F

3 eggs

1½ cups granulated sugar

4 ounces unsweetened
    chocolate, melted

½ cup cooking oil

2 teaspoons baking powder

2 teaspoons vanilla

2 cups all-purpose flour

Sifted powdered sugar

1. In a large mixing bowl beat eggs, granulated sugar, chocolate, oil, baking powder, and vanilla with an electric mixer on medium speed until combined. Beat in as much of the flour as you can with the mixer. Stir in any remaining flour with a wooden spoon. Cover and chill dough for 1 to 2 hours or until easy to handle.
2. Shape dough into 1-inch balls. Roll in powdered sugar to coat generously. Place balls 1 inch apart on an ungreased cookie sheet.
3. Bake in a 375° oven for 8 to 10 minutes or until edges are set and tops are crackled. Transfer cookies to a wire rack and let cool. If desired, sprinkle with additional powdered sugar.

Chocolate-Mint Cookies: Prepare as above, except add ¼ teaspoon mint flavoring with vanilla.

TO STORE: Place in layers separated by waxed paper in an airtight container; cover. Store at room temperature up to 3 days or freeze up to 3 months.

Unsweetened chocolate Sometimes called baking or bitter chocolate, this product is pure chocolate with no added sugar. It's generally used for baking and cooking rather than snacking.

Mocha *Latte* Crinkles

These crisp cookies and their cinnamon, coffee, and chocolate style take after the irresistible coffeehouse favorite they're named for.

Makes: about 40 cookies

Oven: 350°F

1/3 cup butter, softened

1 cup packed brown sugar

2/3 cup unsweetened
    cocoa powder

1 tablespoon instant
    coffee crystals

1 teaspoon baking soda

1 teaspoon ground cinnamon

2 egg whites

1/3 cup low-fat vanilla yogurt

1 1/2 cups all-purpose flour

1/4 cup granulated sugar

1. In a large mixing bowl beat butter with an electric mixer on medium to high speed for 30 seconds. Add brown sugar, cocoa powder, coffee crystals, baking soda, and cinnamon. Beat until combined, scraping sides of bowl occasionally. Beat in egg whites and yogurt until combined. Beat in as much of the flour as you can with the mixer. Stir in any remaining flour with a wooden spoon. Cover and chill dough for 2 to 3 hours or until easy to handle.

2. Place granulated sugar in a small bowl. Drop dough by teaspoonfuls into sugar; roll into balls. Place balls 2 inches apart on an ungreased cookie sheet.

3. Bake in a 350° oven for 8 to 10 minutes until edges are firm. Transfer cookies to a wire rack and let cool.

TO STORE: **Place in layers separated by waxed paper in an airtight container; cover. Store at room temperature up to 3 days or freeze up to 3 months.**

holiday
treat

Chocolate-Mint Creams

These treats with their pretty pastel candy centers have long delighted bakers. Look for the mints at candy stores, food gift shops, or department store candy counters. *(photo, page 72)*

Makes: about 48 cookies

Oven: 350°F

1¼ **cups all-purpose flour**

 ½ **teaspoon baking soda**

 ⅔ **cup packed brown sugar**

 6 **tablespoons butter**

 1 **tablespoon water**

 1 **cup semisweet**

   chocolate pieces

 1 **egg**

 ½ **to ¾ pound pastel-color**

   cream mint kisses

1. In a small bowl combine flour and baking soda; set aside. In a medium saucepan cook and stir brown sugar, butter, and water over low heat until butter melts. Add chocolate pieces; cook and stir until melted. Pour chocolate mixture into a large bowl; let stand for 10 to 15 minutes or until cool.

2. Beat egg into the chocolate mixture. Stir in flour mixture until combined (dough will be soft). Cover and chill dough for 1 to 2 hours or until easy to handle.

3. Shape dough into 1-inch balls. Place balls 2 inches apart on an ungreased cookie sheet.

4. Bake in a 350° oven for 8 minutes. Remove from oven and immediately top each cookie with a mint kiss. Return to oven and bake about 2 minutes more or until edges are set. Swirl the melted mints with a knife to frost cookies. Transfer cookies to a wire rack and let cool until mints are firm.

TO STORE: Place in layers separated by waxed paper in an airtight container; cover. Store at room temperature up to 3 days or freeze up to 3 months.

> ### *Softening brown sugar* You can soften brown sugar that has hardened or formed lumps in the microwave oven. Microwave ½ cup water, uncovered, in a 1-cup microwave-safe measuring cup or bowl on 100% power (high) for 1 to 2 minutes or until boiling. Place the brown sugar in a microwave-safe container near the water. Microwave, uncovered, on 100% power (high) until softened. Allow 1½ to 2½ minutes for ½ pound brown sugar or 2 to 3 minutes for 1 pound.

Peanut Butter-Filled *Chocolate* Cookies

Regally rich, each chocolate cookie has a heart of gold in the form of a satiny peanut butter filling.

(photo, page 69)

Makes: 32 cookies

Oven: 350°F

1½ cups all-purpose flour

½ cup unsweetened
    cocoa powder

½ teaspoon baking soda

½ cup butter, softened

½ cup granulated sugar

½ cup packed brown sugar

¼ cup peanut butter

1 egg

1 tablespoon milk

1 teaspoon vanilla

¾ cup sifted powdered sugar

½ cup peanut butter

Granulated sugar

1. In a medium bowl combine flour, cocoa powder, and baking soda; set aside. In a large mixing bowl beat butter, the ½ cup granulated sugar, brown sugar, and the ¼ cup peanut butter with an electric mixer until combined, scraping sides of bowl occasionally. Beat in egg, milk, and vanilla until combined. Beat in as much of the flour mixture as you can with the mixer. Stir in any remaining flour mixture with a wooden spoon. Shape dough into 1¼-inch balls (should have 32); set aside.

2. For peanut butter filling, in a medium bowl stir together powdered sugar and the ½ cup peanut butter until smooth. Shape mixture into ¾-inch balls (should have 32).

3. On a work surface, slightly flatten each chocolate dough ball and top with a peanut butter ball. Shape the chocolate dough over the peanut butter filling, completely covering the filling. Roll dough into balls.

4. Place balls 2 inches apart on an ungreased cookie sheet. Lightly flatten with the bottom of a glass dipped granulated sugar.*

5. Bake in a 350° oven about 8 minutes or until just set and surface is slightly cracked. Cool on cookie sheet for 1 minute. Transfer cookies to a wire rack and let cool.

*NOTE: So sugar will stick to the glass, first dip the bottom of the glass in the cookie dough. Next, dip it into the sugar.

TO STORE: Place in layers separated by waxed paper in an airtight container; cover. Store at room temperature up to 3 days or freeze up to 3 months.

LEFT: Peanut Butter-Filled Chocolate Cookies, page 68 ABOVE: Chocolate-Cherry Drops, page 55
BELOW: Tropical Jumbles, page 23

Dream Cookies, page 57

ABOVE: Frosted Sour Cream-Chocolate Drops, page 58, and Stuffed Date Drops, page 47; Sachertorte Cookies, page 60
BELOW: Chewy Coconut Macaroons, page 49; White Chocolate and Raspberry Cookies, page 59

ABOVE: Chocolate-Covered Cherry Cookies, page 77, and Chocolate-Pistachio Wreaths, page 82
BELOW: Chocolate-Mint Creams, page 67 RIGHT: Giant Ginger Cookies, page 83

White Chocolate *Snowcap* Cookies

These hidden-treasure treats are surefire crowd pleasers. What's the treasure? A kiss of chocolate tucked under a crisp cap of meringue.

Makes: 26 to 30 cookies

Oven: 350°F

$\frac{1}{3}$ **cup butter, softened**

$\frac{1}{3}$ **cup sugar**

 1 **egg yolk**

 1 **ounce white chocolate baking square, melted and cooled**

$\frac{1}{2}$ **teaspoon vanilla**

 1 **cup all-purpose flour**

26 **to 30 milk chocolate kisses with almonds, unwrapped**

 2 **egg whites**

$\frac{1}{2}$ **teaspoon vanilla**

$\frac{1}{4}$ **teaspoon cream of tartar**

 3 **tablespoons sugar**

1. Grease a cookie sheet; set aside. In a medium mixing bowl beat butter with an electric mixer on medium to high speed for 30 seconds. Add the $\frac{1}{3}$ cup sugar; beat until combined, scraping sides of bowl occasionally. Beat in egg yolk, white baking square, and $\frac{1}{2}$ teaspoon vanilla. Beat in as much of the flour as you can with the mixer. Stir in any remaining flour.

2. Shape dough into 1-inch balls. Place balls 2 inches apart on prepared cookie sheet. Flatten to $1\frac{1}{2}$-inch diameter with the bottom of a floured glass.*

3. Bake in a 350° oven about 8 minutes or until edges are set. Cool on cookie sheet 1 minute. Place a chocolate kiss in center of each cookie. Cool on cookie sheet until candy is firm. Reduce oven temperature to 300°.

4. For meringue, in a medium mixing bowl beat egg whites, $\frac{1}{2}$ teaspoon vanilla, and cream of tartar with an electric mixer on medium speed about 1 minute or until soft peaks form (tips curl). Gradually add the 3 tablespoons sugar, 1 tablespoon at a time, beating on high speed about 4 minutes more or until mixture forms stiff, glossy peaks (tips stand straight) and sugar dissolves. Pipe or spoon meringue over each chocolate kiss and onto the cookie base.

5. Bake in the 300° oven for 15 minutes or until meringue is lightly browned. Transfer cookies to a wire rack and let cool.

*NOTE: So flour will stick to the glass, first dip the bottom of the glass in the cookie dough. Next, dip it into the flour.

TO STORE: Place in a single layer in an airtight container; cover. Store at room temperature up to 3 days or freeze cookies without meringue up to 1 month. Thaw cookies; top with meringue and bake as above.

Fantasy *Chocolate-Caramel* Delights

With its dream team of chocolate, caramel, and nuts, this one's a triple delight. So delicious, these little morsels will probably get snatched up before the chocolate sets.

Makes: about 36 cookies

Oven: 350°F

1 **egg**

1 **cup all-purpose flour**

⅓ **cup unsweetened cocoa powder**

¼ **teaspoon salt**

½ **cup butter, softened**

⅔ **cup sugar**

2 **tablespoons milk**

1 **teaspoon vanilla**

16 **vanilla caramels**

3 **tablespoons whipping cream**

1¼ **cups finely chopped pecans**

½ **cup semisweet chocolate pieces**

1 **teaspoon shortening**

1. Separate egg, reserving yolk and white. Cover and chill egg white until needed. In a small bowl combine flour, cocoa powder, and salt; set flour mixture aside.

2. In a large mixing bowl beat butter with an electric mixer on medium to high speed for 30 seconds. Add sugar; beat until combined, scraping sides of bowl occasionally. Beat in egg yolk, milk, and vanilla until combined. Beat in as much of the flour mixture as you can with the mixer. Stir in any remaining flour mixture with a wooden spoon. Cover and chill dough about 2 hours or until easy to handle.

3. In a small saucepan heat and stir caramels and whipping cream over low heat until mixture is smooth. Set aside.

4. Lightly grease a cookie sheet; set aside. Slightly beat reserved egg white. Shape dough into 1-inch balls. Roll balls in egg white; roll in pecans to coat. Place balls 1 inch apart on prepared cookie sheet. Press your thumb into the center of each ball.

5. Bake in a 350° oven about 10 minutes or until edges are firm. Spoon some melted caramel mixture into indentation of each cookie. Transfer cookies to a wire rack and let cool. (If necessary, reheat caramel mixture to keep it spoonable.)

6. In another saucepan melt chocolate pieces and shortening over low heat, stirring constantly. Let cool slightly. Transfer the warm chocolate mixture to a self-sealing plastic bag. Close bag and cut a small hole in one corner of it. Drizzle cookies with chocolate mixture; let stand until set.

TO STORE: Place in layers separated by waxed paper in an airtight container; cover. Store at room temperature up to 3 days or freeze unfilled cookies up to 3 months. Thaw cookies; fill and drizzle.

Hidden *Surprise* Cookies

Surprise! Nestled inside this rich, buttery, almond-flavored cookie is a delightful contrast of cocoa-flavored filling. The chocolatey-nut combo can't be beat!

Makes: about 30 cookies

Oven: 375°F

½ **cup butter, softened**

¼ **cup butter-flavor shortening**

1 **cup granulated sugar**

½ **teaspoon baking powder**

½ **teaspoon salt**

1 **egg**

2 **egg yolks**

2 **teaspoons vanilla**

2½ **cups all-purpose flour**

⅓ **cup sifted powdered sugar**

2 **tablespoons unsweetened**
   cocoa powder

1 **tablespoon melted butter**

¼ **teaspoon almond extract**
   Coarse colored sugar
   or candy sprinkles

1. Grease a cookie sheet; set aside. In a large mixing bowl beat butter and shortening with an electric mixer on medium to high speed for 30 seconds. Add granulated sugar, baking powder, and salt. Beat until combined, scraping sides of bowl occasionally. Beat in egg, egg yolks, and vanilla until combined. Beat in as much of the flour as you can with the mixer. Stir in any remaining flour with a wooden spoon.

2. Transfer ¾ cup of the dough to a small bowl. Add powdered sugar, cocoa powder, and melted butter. Beat until combined. Shape chocolate dough into 1-inch balls.

3. Beat almond extract into remaining dough. Mold about 1 tablespoon of the almond-flavor dough around each chocolate ball. Roll gently to make a smooth, round ball. Roll each ball in colored sugar. Place balls 2 inches apart on prepared cookie sheet.

4. Bake in a 375° oven for 10 to 11 minutes or until bottoms are lightly browned. Cool on cookie sheet for 1 minute. Transfer cookies to a wire rack and let cool.

TO STORE: Place in layers separated by waxed paper in an airtight container; cover. Store at room temperature up to 3 days or freeze up to 3 months.

A bit about eggs We tested all of the recipes in this cookbook using large eggs. Store eggs in the egg carton for up to five weeks after the packing date printed on the carton. Or check for a "use by" date on the carton.

Mud *Pie* Cookies

As rich, dark, and gooey as their name, these double-chocolate mocha-filled cookies will satisfy any chocolate lover's craving.

Makes: about 60 cookies

Oven: 375°F

- ¾ **cup shortening**
- 1½ **cups sugar**
- ⅔ **cup unsweetened cocoa powder**
- 2 **teaspoons baking powder**
- 1 **teaspoon instant coffee crystals**
- 2 **teaspoons water**
- 3 **eggs**
- 1 **teaspoon vanilla**
- 2 **cups all-purpose flour**
- ¼ **cup finely chopped pecans**
- 1 **recipe Chocolate Frosting**

1. In a large mixing bowl beat shortening with an electric mixer on medium speed for 30 seconds. Add sugar, cocoa powder, and baking powder. Beat until combined, scraping sides of bowl occasionally. Dissolve coffee crystals in water. Add coffee mixture, eggs, and vanilla to sugar mixture; beat until combined. Beat in as much of the flour as you can with the mixer. Stir in any remaining flour and the pecans with a wooden spoon. Cover and chill dough for 1 to 2 hours or until easy to handle.

2. Shape dough into 1-inch balls. Place balls 2 inches apart on an ungreased cookie sheet. Press your thumb into the center of each cookie.

3. Bake in a 375° oven for 8 to 10 minutes or until edges are set. Transfer cookies to a wire rack and let cool. Fill centers with Chocolate Frosting; let frosting dry.

Chocolate Frosting: In a medium mixing bowl beat ⅓ cup softened butter and 1 teaspoon vanilla with an electric mixer on medium speed for 30 seconds. Slowly beat in ½ cup unsweetened cocoa powder and 1½ cups sifted powdered sugar. Beat in 2 tablespoons bourbon or milk. Gradually beat in 1½ cups sifted powdered sugar and enough milk (1 to 3 tablespoons) to make spreading consistency. Stir in ⅓ cup miniature semisweet chocolate pieces.

TO STORE: Place in layers separated by waxed paper in an airtight container; cover. Store at room temperature up to 3 days or freeze unfilled cookies up to 3 months. Thaw cookies; fill.

holiday treat

Chocolate-Covered Cherry Cookies

You'll find a lot to like about this cookie. Some bakers love the way the cookie is frosted before it cooks; others enjoy the buried cherry surprise. Nearly everyone finds the rich, fudgy flavor irresistible. *(photo, page 72)*

Makes: 48 cookies

Oven: 350°F

1½ **cups all-purpose flour**

½ **cup unsweetened cocoa powder**

½ **cup butter, softened**

1 **cup sugar**

¼ **teaspoon baking soda**

¼ **teaspoon baking powder**

¼ **teaspoon salt**

1 **egg**

1½ **teaspoons vanilla**

48 **maraschino cherries (about one 10-ounce jar), undrained**

1 **cup semisweet chocolate pieces**

½ **cup sweetened condensed milk**

1. In a small bowl combine flour and cocoa powder; set aside. In a large mixing bowl beat butter with an electric mixer on medium to high speed for 30 seconds. Add sugar, baking soda, baking powder, and salt. Beat until combined, scraping sides of bowl occasionally. Beat in egg and vanilla until combined. Beat in as much of the flour mixture as you can with the mixer. Stir in any remaining flour mixture with a wooden spoon.

2. Shape dough into 1-inch balls. Place balls about 2 inches apart on an ungreased cookie sheet. Press your thumb into the center of each ball. Drain maraschino cherries, reserving juice. Pat cherries dry with paper towels. Place a cherry in the indentation of each cookie.

3. For frosting, in a small saucepan combine chocolate pieces and sweetened condensed milk. Heat and stir over low heat until chocolate is melted. Stir in 4 teaspoons reserved cherry juice. Spoon about 1 teaspoon frosting over each cookie, spreading to cover cherry. (If necessary, thin frosting with additional cherry juice.)

4. Bake in a 350° oven about 10 minutes or until edges are firm. Cool on cookie sheet for 1 minute. Transfer cookies to a wire rack and let cool.

TO STORE: Place in layers separated by waxed paper in an airtight container; cover. Store at room temperature up to 3 days or freeze up to 3 months.

Chocolate *Thumbprints*

Can't get enough chocolate? This scrumptious recipe includes cocoa powder for flavor, a big chocolate candy kiss for extra chocolatey sweetness, and chocolate-flavored sprinkles for fun!

Makes: about 36 cookies

Oven: 375°F

²/₃ cup butter, softened

½ cup sugar

¼ cup unsweetened

　　cocoa powder

¼ teaspoon baking soda

⅛ teaspoon salt

1 egg

1 teaspoon vanilla

1¼ cups all-purpose flour

¾ cup chocolate-flavored or

　　multicolor sprinkles

　Milk chocolate kisses,

　　unwrapped

1. In a large mixing bowl beat butter with an electric mixer on medium to high speed for 30 seconds. Add sugar, cocoa powder, baking soda, and salt. Beat until combined, scraping sides of bowl occasionally. Beat in egg and vanilla until combined. Beat in as much of the flour as you can with the mixer. Stir in any remaining flour with a wooden spoon. Cover and chill dough about 1 hour or until easy to handle.

2. Grease a cookie sheet; set aside. Shape dough into 1-inch balls. Roll balls in sprinkles. Place balls 2 inches apart on prepared cookie sheet. Press your thumb into the center of each ball.

3. Bake in a 375° oven for 7 to 8 minutes or until edges are firm. Remove from oven; immediately press a chocolate kiss into the center of each cookie. Transfer cookies to a wire rack and let cool.

TO STORE: Place in layers separated by waxed paper in an airtight container; cover. Store at room temperature up to 3 days or freeze up to 3 months.

Being exact Looking for a surefire way to end up with the exact amount of cookies the recipe indicates? First, don't sample the cookie dough (especially since cookies generally contain raw eggs, which aren't considered safe to eat). Next, follow this tip:
　Pat the dough into a square. Cut the square of dough into the number of pieces the recipe should yield. If you want forty-eight cookies, for example, cut the dough into six equal strips in one direction and eight equal strips the other direction. Shape as directed into the forty-eight pieces.

Chocolate-Almond *Bonbons*

Half cookie, half confection, these almond-filled sweets are equally at home on a cookie tray or in a candy dish. *(photo, page 108)*

Makes: about 90 cookies

Oven: 350°F

1 **12-ounce package (2 cups) semisweet chocolate pieces**

¼ **cup butter**

1 **14-ounce can (1¼ cups) sweetened condensed milk**

1 **teaspoon vanilla**

2 **cups all-purpose flour**

1 **8-ounce can almond paste (made without syrup or glucose)**

1 **recipe Almond Glaze**

1 **recipe Chocolate Glaze (optional)**

   Assorted small candies (optional)

   Purchased decorator icing (optional)

1. In a medium saucepan combine chocolate pieces and butter. Cook and stir over low heat until melted and smooth. Stir in sweetened condensed milk and vanilla. Stir in flour until combined.

2. Shape a slightly rounded teaspoon of dough around ½ teaspoon of almond paste. Repeat with remaining dough and almond paste. Place balls on an ungreased cookie sheet.

3. Bake in a 350° oven for 6 to 8 minutes or until chocolate is soft and shiny (do not overbake). Transfer cookies to a wire rack and let cool.

4. Drizzle or spoon Almond Glaze over cookies, or, if desired, substitute Chocolate Glaze for the Almond Glaze. If desired, decorate with small candies and decorator icing; let icing dry.

Almond Glaze: In a small bowl stir together 1 cup sifted powdered sugar, ½ teaspoon almond extract, and enough milk (1 to 2 tablespoons) to make glaze of drizzling consistency. If desired, tint with a few drops of red food coloring.

Chocolate Glaze: In a small bowl stir together ½ cup sifted powdered sugar, 2 tablespoons unsweetened cocoa powder, and enough milk (2 to 3 teaspoons) to make of drizzling consistency.

TO STORE: Place in layers separated by waxed paper in an airtight container; cover. Store at room temperature up to 3 days or freeze unglazed cookies up to 3 months. Thaw cookies; glaze.

White Chocolate and Cherry Twists

Candied red cherries go into the pink dough, and chopped white baking squares go into the plain dough to produce a delightful two-color, two-taste combination.

Makes: about 56 cookies

Oven: 375°F

¾ cup butter, softened

1 cup sugar

1 teaspoon baking powder

1 egg

1 teaspoon vanilla

2½ cups all-purpose flour

⅓ cup finely chopped candied red cherries

Few drops red food coloring

2 ounces white baking squares, finely chopped

1. In a large mixing bowl beat butter with an electric mixer on medium to high speed for 30 seconds. Add sugar and baking powder. Beat until combined, scraping sides of bowl occasionally. Beat in egg and vanilla until combined. Beat in as much of the flour as you can with the mixer. Stir in any remaining flour with a wooden spoon. Divide dough in half.

2. Stir chopped candied cherries and food coloring into one half of the dough until combined; set aside. Stir chopped white baking squares into the remaining half of the dough. Wrap each dough in clear plastic wrap or waxed paper; chill about 30 minutes or until easy to handle.

3. For each cookie, on a lightly floured surface, shape a slightly rounded teaspoon of red dough into a 6-inch-long rope. Repeat with a teaspoon of white dough. Place ropes side by side and twist together. Place twists 2 inches apart on an ungreased cookie sheet.

4. Bake in a 375° oven for 8 to 10 minutes or until edges are firm and lightly browned. Cool on cookie sheet for 1 minute. Transfer cookies to a wire rack and let cool.

TO STORE: Place in layers separated by waxed paper in an airtight container; cover. Store at room temperature up to 3 days or freeze up to 3 months.

Black and White *Twists*

These sophisticated sweets are easy to make, but if you don't have time to do it all in one day,

do it in two instead. Mix and shape the twists, chill them overnight, and bake them the next day.

(photo, page 108)

Makes: about 48 cookies

Oven: 350°F

1½ **cups butter, softened**

2½ **cups sifted powdered sugar**

 ¼ **teaspoon salt**

 1 **egg**

 1 **teaspoon vanilla**

4¼ **cups all-purpose flour**

 2 **ounces unsweetened chocolate,**
    melted and cooled

 1 **tablespoon milk**

 1 **slightly beaten egg white**

 1 **cup finely chopped hazelnuts**
    (filberts) or pecans

1. In a large mixing bowl beat butter with an electric mixer on medium to high speed for 30 seconds. Add powdered sugar and salt. Beat until combined, scraping sides of bowl occasionally. Beat in egg and vanilla until combined. Beat in as much of the flour as you can with the mixer. Stir in any remaining flour with a wooden spoon.

2. Divide dough in half. Add melted chocolate and milk to one half of the dough. Using your hands, knead dough until well combined.

3. On a lightly floured surface, shape each dough half into a 12-inch-long log. Cut each log into 12 equal pieces. Roll each dough piece into a 12-inch-long rope. Place a chocolate rope and a vanilla rope side by side and gently twist together 8 to 10 times. Press lightly to seal ends and transfer to a cookie sheet. Repeat with remaining dough. Cover and chill for 2 to 24 hours or until firm.

4. Lightly grease a cookie sheet; set aside. Cut each twisted log into 2½-inch pieces. Dip one end of each piece into beaten egg white; dip into chopped nuts. Place about 2 inches apart on the prepared cookie sheet.

5. Bake in a 350° oven for 12 to 15 minutes or until vanilla dough is lightly golden. Transfer cookies to a wire rack and let cool.

TO STORE: Place in layers separated by waxed paper in an airtight container; cover. Store at room temperature up to 3 days or freeze up to 3 months.

holiday treat

Chocolate-Pistachio Wreaths

No cookie cutter needed! Simply roll and twist the nut-studded dough into very merry wreaths.

(photo, page 72)

Makes: 24 cookies

Oven: 375°F

¾ **cup butter, softened**

¾ **cup granulated sugar**

¼ **teaspoon baking powder**

1 **egg**

1 **teaspoon vanilla**

1¾ **cups all-purpose flour**

¼ **cup finely chopped**
    pistachio nuts

¼ **teaspoon almond extract**

3 **tablespoons unsweetened**
    cocoa powder

2 **tablespoons milk**

1 **recipe Berry Icing**

1. In a large mixing bowl beat butter with an electric mixer on medium to high speed for 30 seconds. Add granulated sugar and baking powder. Beat until combined, scraping sides of bowl occasionally. Beat in egg and vanilla until combined. Beat in as much of the flour as you can with the mixer. Stir in any remaining flour with a wooden spoon. Divide dough in half.

2. Stir pistachio nuts and almond extract into one half of the dough until combined; set aside. Stir cocoa powder and milk into remaining half of the dough until combined. Wrap each dough in clear plastic wrap or waxed paper; chill about 30 minutes or until easy to handle.

3. On a lightly floured surface, shape each dough portion into a 12-inch-long log. Cut each log into ½-inch pieces. Roll each piece into a 6-inch-long rope. Place a light and a dark rope side by side and twist together 5 or 6 times. Shape twisted rope into a circle, gently pinching ends together. Place wreath on an ungreased cookie sheet. Repeat with the remaining dough, placing wreaths 2 inches apart.

4. Bake in a 375° oven for 8 to 10 minutes or until edges are light brown. Cool on cookie sheet for 1 minute. Transfer cookies to a wire rack and let cool. Pipe clusters of berries on wreaths with Berry Icing; let icing dry.

Berry Icing: In a small bowl stir together ½ cup sifted powdered sugar and 1 to 2 teaspoons milk to make of piping consistency. Stir in red paste food coloring.

TO STORE: Place in layers separated by waxed paper in an airtight container; cover. Store at room temperature up to 3 days or freeze undecorated cookies up to 3 months. Thaw cookies; decorate.

Giant *Ginger* Cookies

Chewy and delicious, these cookies are giants in both size and snappy flavor. For a perfect gift, stack a few cookies, wrap in clear cellophane, and tie with a colorful ribbon. *(photo, page 72)*

Makes: about 24 cookies

Oven: 350°F

4½ **cups all-purpose flour**

4 **teaspoons ground ginger**

2 **teaspoons baking soda**

1½ **teaspoons ground cinnamon**

1 **teaspoon ground cloves**

¼ **teaspoon salt**

1½ **cups shortening**

2 **cups granulated sugar**

2 **eggs**

½ **cup molasses**

¾ **cup coarse sugar or granulated sugar**

1. Combine flour, ginger, baking soda, cinnamon, cloves, and salt; set aside. Beat shortening with an electric mixer on low to medium speed for 30 seconds. Add the 2 cups granulated sugar; beat until combined, scraping sides of bowl occasionally. Beat in eggs and molasses until combined. Beat in as much of the flour mixture as you can. Stir in any remaining flour mixture.

2. Shape dough into 2-inch balls using a ¼-cup measure or scoop. Roll balls in coarse sugar. Place balls 3 inches apart on an ungreased cookie sheet.

3. Bake in a 350° oven for 12 to 14 minutes or until bottoms are light brown and tops are puffed. (Do not overbake or cookies will not be chewy.) Cool on cookie sheet for 2 minutes. Transfer cookies to a wire rack and let cool.

Not-So-Giant Ginger Cookies: Prepare as above, except shape dough into 1-inch balls; roll in sugar. Place balls 1½ inches apart on an ungreased cookie sheet. Bake in a 350° oven for 8 to 9 minutes or until bottoms are lightly browned and tops are puffed (do not overbake). Cool on cookie sheet for 1 minute. Transfer cookies to a wire rack and let cool. Makes about 120 cookies.

TO STORE: Place in layers separated by waxed paper in an airtight container; cover. Store at room temperature up to 3 days or freeze up to 3 months.

Baking with molasses While mild-flavored and full-flavored molasses differ in taste, our cookie recipes rarely specify one or the other. Because both react the same in baking, the choice is a matter of personal preference. Choose full-flavor molasses if you prefer a more robust flavor and mild-flavor molasses if you're looking for more sweetness and a lighter molasses flavor.

Keep in mind that blackstrap molasses, which is slightly bitter and has almost no sweetness, is not used in baking.

Candied Ginger Cookies

The crystallized ginger–bits of fresh ginger cooked in sugar syrup and coated with sugar–adds a spicy-sweet touch to these cookies. You'll find it in the spice section at supermarkets.

Makes: about 48 cookies

Oven: 375°F

1 cup butter, softened

¾ cup granulated sugar

¾ cup packed brown sugar

1 teaspoon cream of tartar

1 teaspoon baking soda

½ teaspoon ground ginger

2 eggs

1 teaspoon vanilla

2¾ cups all-purpose flour

½ cup finely chopped
crystallized ginger

Granulated sugar

1. In a large mixing bowl beat butter with an electric mixer on medium to high speed for 30 seconds. Add the ¾ cup granulated sugar, brown sugar, cream of tartar, baking soda, and ground ginger. Beat until combined, scraping sides of bowl occasionally. Beat in eggs and vanilla until combined. Beat in as much of the flour as you can with the mixer. Stir in any remaining flour and the crystallized ginger with a wooden spoon. Cover and chill dough about 1 hour or until easy to handle.

2. Shape dough into 1¼-inch balls; roll in granulated sugar. Place balls 3 inches apart on an ungreased cookie sheet.

3. Bake in a 375° oven for 8 to 10 minutes or until edges are lightly browned. Transfer cookies to a wire rack and let cool.

TO STORE: Place in layers separated by waxed paper in an airtight container; cover. Store at room temperature up to 3 days or freeze up to 3 months.

Measuring brown sugar Our recipes call for packed brown sugar. This means the sugar is pressed firmly enough into a dry measuring cup that it holds the shape of the cup when it is turned out.

holiday treat

Frosties

These plump little fellows favor snowy forecasts, but they'll melt in your mouth whatever the weather.

Makes: about 24 cookies

Oven: 325°F

1 cup butter, softened

½ cup sugar

1 teaspoon vanilla

¼ teaspoon salt

2¼ cups all-purpose flour

    Miniature semisweet

        chocolate pieces

24 large gumdrops

1 recipe Decorating Icing

    Rolled fruit leather, cut into

        thin 3-inch-long strips

1. In a large mixing bowl beat butter with an electric mixer on medium to high speed for 30 seconds. Add sugar, vanilla, and salt. Beat until combined, scraping sides of bowl occasionally. Beat in as much of the flour as you can with the mixer. Stir in any remaining flour with a wooden spoon.

2. For each snowman, shape dough into three balls: one 1-inch ball, one ¾-inch ball, and one ½-inch ball. Place balls on an ungreased cookie sheet in decreasing sizes with edges touching. Press together slightly. Insert two chocolate pieces in the smallest ball for eyes, and one in the middle ball and two in the largest ball for buttons.

3. Bake in a 325° oven for 18 to 20 minutes or until set. Carefully transfer cookies to a wire rack and let cool.

4. For hat, roll a gumdrop into an oval shape (about 1½×1 inches) on a sugared surface. Roll oval into a cone shape; press to seal ends. Curl up bottom edge of cone to form hat brim. Attach to head with Decorating Icing. Wrap a fruit leather strip around each snowman's neck. Pipe on brooms and faces with Decorating Icing; let icing dry.

Decorating Icing: In a small bowl stir together 1 cup sifted powdered sugar and 1 tablespoon milk to make of piping consistency. Tint with paste food coloring.

TO STORE: Place in a single layer in an airtight container; cover. Store at room temperature up to 3 days or store undecorated cookies in freezer up to 3 months. Thaw cookies; decorate as desired.

holiday
treat

Berlinerkranzen

Immigrants from northern Europe introduced these buttery but not too sweet cookies to this country. A sprinkling with pearl sugar before baking is all the dressing up they need.

Makes: about 36 cookies

Oven: 325°F

 1 **cup butter, softened**

 ½ **cup sifted powdered sugar**

 1 **hard-cooked egg yolk, sieved**

 1 **raw egg yolk**

 1 **teaspoon vanilla**

2¼ **cups all-purpose flour**

 1 **slightly beaten egg white**

 2 **to 3 tablespoons pearl or**
     coarse sugar

1. In a large mixing bowl beat butter with an electric mixer on medium to high speed for 30 seconds. Add powdered sugar; beat until combined, scraping sides of bowl occasionally. Beat in hard-cooked and raw egg yolks and vanilla. Beat in as much of the flour as you can with the mixer. Stir in any remaining flour.

2. Cover and chill dough about 1 hour or until firm enough to handle. (Chilling it longer may make it too firm to roll.)

3. On a lightly floured surface, roll about 1 tablespoon dough into a 6-inch-long rope. Shape rope into a ring on an ungreased cookie sheet, crossing it over itself about 1 inch from ends. Repeat with remaining dough. Brush with egg white and sprinkle with pearl or coarse sugar.

4. Bake in a 325° oven for 18 to 20 minutes or until edges are lightly browned. Cool on cookie sheet for 1 minute. Transfer cookies to a wire rack and let cool.

TO STORE: Place in layers separated by waxed paper in an airtight container; cover. Store at room temperature up to 3 days or freeze up to 3 months.

Sandies

It's hard to resist one of these powdered sugar-coated cookie classics—and even harder to resist a second. Maybe that's why they're a classic!

Makes: about 48 cookies

Oven: 325°F

1 **cup butter, softened**

½ **cup sifted powdered sugar**

1 **tablespoon water**

1 **teaspoon vanilla**

2 **cups all-purpose flour**

1½ **cups finely chopped pecans**

1 **cup sifted powdered sugar**

1. In a large mixing bowl beat butter with an electric mixer on medium to high speed for 30 seconds. Add the ½ cup powdered sugar; beat until combined, scraping sides of bowl occasionally. Beat in water and vanilla until combined. Beat in as much of the flour as you can with the mixer. Stir in any remaining flour and the pecans.

2. Shape dough into 1-inch balls or 2½-inch logs. Place 1 inch apart on an ungreased cookie sheet.

3. Bake in a 325° oven about 15 minutes or until bottoms are lightly browned. Transfer cookies to a wire rack and let cool. Gently shake cooled cookies in a plastic bag with the 1 cup powdered sugar.

Cocoa Sandies: Prepare as above, except add ¼ cup unsweetened cocoa powder with the flour.

TO STORE: Place in layers separated by waxed paper in an airtight container; cover. Store at room temperature up to 3 days or freeze up to 3 months.

> *Cookie origination* One of the world's best-loved treats came about thanks to a bit of serendipity that took on a life of its own. The word "cookie" comes from the Dutch word for cake, *koekje*. The first cookies were actually tiny test cakes baked to make sure the oven temperature was right for baking a large cake. Someone obviously liked the test results.

Nutty Crescents

With their tender texture and buttery flavor, your friends will assume you bought these crescents at a Viennese coffee house.

Makes: about 48 cookies

Oven: 375°F

1 **cup butter, softened**

⅓ **cup packed brown sugar**

1 **tablespoon crème de**
 cacao or milk

1 **teaspoon vanilla**

2¼ **cups all-purpose flour**

1 **cup finely chopped pecans**

1 **recipe Chocolate Drizzle**

1. In a large mixing bowl beat butter with an electric mixer on medium to high speed for 30 seconds. Add brown sugar, crème de cacao, and vanilla. Beat until combined, scraping sides of bowl occasionally. Beat in as much of the flour as you can with the mixer. Stir in any remaining flour and pecans with a wooden spoon. (Knead with your hands, if necessary, until dough comes together.)

2. Shape rounded teaspoons of dough into 2-inch-long ropes; shape into crescents. Place 2 inches apart on an ungreased cookie sheet.

3. Bake in a 375° oven for 8 to 12 minutes or until edges are firm and bottoms are lightly browned. Cool on cookie sheet for 1 minute. Transfer cookies to a wire rack and let cool. Drizzle cooled cookies with Chocolate Drizzle; let stand until dry.

Chocolate Drizzle: In a small saucepan melt ¼ cup semisweet chocolate pieces and 2 teaspoons shortening over low heat, stirring constantly. Stir in ¾ cup sifted powdered sugar and 2 to 3 tablespoons milk to make of drizzling consistency.

TO STORE: Place in layers separated by waxed paper in an airtight container; cover. Store at room temperature up to 3 days or freeze undrizzled cookies up to 3 months. Thaw cookies; drizzle.

Pecan Balls

A Christmas cookie gift tray isn't complete without these little morsels. For even greater appeal, roll them in a mixture of the Colored Sugar and granulated sugar. *(photo, page 106)*

Makes: about 72 cookies

Oven: 350°F

1   cup butter, softened

½   cup granulated sugar

¼   teaspoon salt

2   teaspoons vanilla

2   cups all-purpose flour

1   cup finely chopped pecans

1   recipe Colored Sugar

    Granulated sugar (optional)

    Sifted powdered sugar

      (optional)

1. In a large mixing bowl beat butter with an electric mixer on medium to high speed for 30 seconds. Add granulated sugar and salt. Beat until combined, scraping sides of bowl occasionally. Beat in vanilla. Beat in as much of the flour as you can with the mixer. Stir in any remaining flour and the pecans with a wooden spoon.

2. Shape dough into ¾-inch balls. Place balls 1 inch apart on an ungreased cookie sheet.

3. Bake in a 350° oven about 12 minutes or until bottoms just begin to brown. Transfer cookies to a wire rack and let cool. Roll in Colored Sugar or, if desired, granulated sugar or powdered sugar.

Colored Sugar: Place ⅔ cup granulated sugar in a small bowl. Fill a ¼-teaspoon measure with water. Add 1 or 2 drops liquid food coloring to the water. Sprinkle colored water over sugar in bowl. Stir until combined and color is evenly distributed. Do not overmoisten or sugar will begin to dissolve.

TO STORE: Place in layers separated by waxed paper in an airtight container; cover. Store at room temperature up to 3 days or freeze unsugared cookies up to 3 months. Thaw cookies; roll in sugar.

Cashew-Butter Cookies

For this recipe, you process the cashews to make a luscious paste that becomes the starring ingredient in this nutty, buttery cookie.

Makes: about 24 cookies

Oven: 350°F

¾ **cup cashews**

⅓ **cup sugar**

3 **tablespoons butter, cut up**

1 **egg yolk**

1 **tablespoon milk**

¼ **teaspoon baking soda**

¼ **teaspoon vanilla**

½ **cup all-purpose flour**

1 **slightly beaten egg white**

¾ **cup finely chopped cashews**

1 **recipe Truffle Topping**

1. Place the ¾ cup cashews in a food processor bowl. Cover and process for 2 to 3 minutes or until a smooth paste is formed, stopping to scrape sides of bowl occasionally. Add sugar, butter, egg yolk, milk, baking soda, and vanilla. Cover and process about 30 seconds or until well combined. Add flour; cover and process just until combined. Remove dough. Wrap and chill dough about 30 minutes or until easy to handle.

2. Lightly grease a cookie sheet; set aside. Shape dough into 1-inch balls. Roll balls in egg white; roll in finely chopped cashews. Place balls 2 inches apart on prepared cookie sheet. Flatten slightly with your hand.

3. Bake in a 350° oven about 12 minutes or until edges are lightly browned. Transfer cookies to a wire rack and let cool. Pipe Truffle Topping on top of each cooled cookie.

Truffle Topping: In a small saucepan melt ½ cup semisweet chocolate pieces and 2 teaspoons butter over low heat, stirring constantly. Cool about 10 minutes. Gradually stir in 3 tablespoons whipping cream and 1 teaspoon coffee- or chocolate-flavored liqueur. Gradually stir in 1½ to 1¾ cups sifted powdered sugar until of piping consistency.

TO STORE: Place in layers separated by waxed paper in an airtight container; cover. Store at room temperature up to 3 days or freeze unpiped cookies up to 3 months. Thaw cookies; pipe on topping.

holiday treat

Pistachio *Balls*

When you shop for pistachio nuts, you'll find several varieties: those with pale tan shells, red-dyed shells, or no shells at all. Whichever way, the nuts themselves are the same.

Makes: about 48 cookies

Oven: 325°F

½ cup blanched almonds, toasted

¾ cup butter, softened

⅓ cup granulated sugar

1 tablespoon water

1 teaspoon vanilla

1½ cups all-purpose flour

½ cup finely chopped
    pistachio nuts

Halved pistachio nuts
    (optional)

Sifted powdered sugar

1. Place toasted almonds in a blender container or food processor bowl. Cover and blend or process until finely ground; set aside.

2. In a medium mixing bowl beat butter with an electric mixer on medium to high speed for 30 seconds. Add granulated sugar; beat until combined, scraping sides of bowl occasionally. Beat in water and vanilla until combined. Beat in as much of the flour as you can with the mixer. Stir in remaining flour, ground almonds, and chopped pistachio nuts with a wooden spoon.

3. Roll dough into 1-inch balls. Place balls 1 inch apart on an ungreased cookie sheet. If desired, place a pistachio nut half on top of each ball.

4. Bake in a 325° oven for 16 to 18 minutes or until bottoms are lightly browned. Transfer cookies to a wire rack and let cool. Sprinkle cooled cookies with powdered sugar.

TO STORE: **Place in layers separated by waxed paper in an airtight container; cover. Store at room temperature up to 3 days or freeze unsugared cookies up to 3 months. Thaw cookies; sprinkle with powdered sugar.**

Norwegian *Almond* Cookies

Some cookies hide the good stuff on the inside, but these inside-out treats wear a generous coating of almonds on the outside. What you see is what you get!

Makes: about 48 cookies

Oven: 375°F

⅔ cup butter, softened

½ cup sugar

¼ teaspoon baking powder

1 egg

1 teaspoon vanilla

1½ cups all-purpose flour

1 slightly beaten egg

1 cup coarsely chopped
   slivered almonds

1. In a large mixing bowl beat butter with an electric mixer on medium to high speed for 30 seconds. Add sugar and baking powder. Beat until combined, scraping sides of bowl occasionally. Beat in the 1 egg and vanilla until combined. Beat in as much of the flour as you can with the mixer. Stir in any remaining flour. Cover and chill dough for 2 to 3 hours or until easy to handle.

2. Grease a cookie sheet; set aside. Shape dough into ¾-inch balls. Roll balls in beaten egg; roll in almonds. Place balls 2 inches apart on the prepared cookie sheet. Flatten each ball slightly with a fork.

3. Bake in a 375° oven for 8 to 10 minutes or until edges are lightly browned. Transfer cookies to a wire rack and let cool.

TO STORE: Place in layers separated by waxed paper in an airtight container; cover. Store at room temperature up to 3 days or freeze up to 3 months.

Cherry *Chocolate* Kisses

With bits of maraschino cherries dotted throughout this shortbreadlike gem, this recipe is an upscale update on an old standby: the kiss-topped cookie.

Makes: about 48 cookies

Oven: 325°F

1 **cup butter, softened**

1 **cup sifted powdered sugar**

⅛ **teaspoon salt**

2 **teaspoons maraschino**
   cherry liquid

¼ **teaspoon almond extract**

2¼ **cups all-purpose flour**

½ **cup chopped maraschino**
   cherries

   Granulated sugar

   Milk chocolate kisses,
      unwrapped

1. In a large mixing bowl beat butter with an electric mixer on medium to high speed for 30 seconds. Add powdered sugar and salt. Beat until combined, scraping sides of bowl occasionally. Beat in cherry liquid and almond extract until combined. Beat in as much of the flour as you can with the mixer. Stir in any remaining flour and the cherries.

2. Shape dough into 1-inch balls. Place balls 2 inches apart on an ungreased cookie sheet. Flatten to ½-inch thickness with the bottom of a glass dipped in granulated sugar.*

3. Bake in a 325° oven about 14 minutes or until bottoms are lightly browned. Remove from oven; press a chocolate kiss into each cookie. Transfer cookies to a wire rack and let cool.

*NOTE: So sugar will stick to the glass, first dip the bottom of the glass in the cookie dough. Next, dip it into the sugar.

TO STORE: **Place in layers separated by waxed paper in an airtight container; cover. Store at room temperature up to 1 week or freeze up to 3 months.**

Cooking with kids Cookies are a great way to introduce children to the joys of baking, but a kitchen is not a playground. Here are some pointers to make your projects safe and successful:
- Supervise children in any step that involves dangerous equipment, such as a mixer, knives, the range top, and the oven.
- Keep plenty of towels handy for spills.
- Review each step before baking, and lay out the ingredients and equipment you'll be using.
- Clean as you go to set the best example for your budding bakers.

Orange and *Macadamia Nut* Cookies

One cup of cornstarch sounds like a lot, but it's the secret to the melt-in-your-mouth goodness of these buttery, nut-studded rounds.

Makes: about 72 cookies

Oven: 350°F

4   cups all-purpose flour

2   cups sifted powdered sugar

1   cup cornstarch

2   cups butter

1   cup chopped macadamia nuts
       or toasted walnuts

2   egg yolks

1   tablespoon finely shredded
       orange peel

4   to 6 tablespoons orange juice
       Granulated sugar

1   recipe Orange Frosting
       Finely chopped macadamia
          nuts or toasted walnuts
          (optional)

1. In a large bowl combine flour, powdered sugar, and cornstarch. Using a pastry blender, cut in butter until mixture resembles coarse crumbs. Stir in the 1 cup nuts. In a small bowl combine egg yolks, orange peel, and 4 tablespoons of the orange juice. Add egg yolk mixture to flour mixture, stirring until moistened. If necessary, add enough of the remaining orange juice to moisten.

2. On a lightly floured surface knead dough until it forms a ball. Shape dough into 1¼-inch balls. Place balls 2 inches apart on an ungreased cookie sheet. Flatten to ¼-inch thickness with the bottom of a fluted glass dipped in granulated sugar.*

3. Bake in a 350° oven for 12 to 15 minutes or until edges begin to brown. Transfer cookies to a wire rack and let cool. Frost with Orange Frosting. If desired, sprinkle with finely chopped nuts; let frosting dry.

*NOTE: So sugar will stick to the glass, first dip the bottom of the glass in the cookie dough. Next, dip it into the sugar.

Orange Frosting: In a medium bowl combine 2 cups sifted powdered sugar, 3 tablespoons softened butter, and 1 teaspoon finely shredded orange peel. Stir in 2 to 3 tablespoons orange juice to make of spreading consistency.

TO STORE: Place in layers separated by waxed paper in an airtight container; cover. Store at room temperature up to 3 days or freeze unfrosted cookies up to 3 months. Thaw cookies; frost, and, if desired, sprinkle with nuts.

Orange *Snowballs*

With a dusting of orange-infused sugar, these sparkling cookies are a lovely addition to a gift box of Christmas treats. *(photo, page 107)*

Makes: about 48 cookies

Oven: 325°F

1 **cup butter, softened**

¾ **cup sifted powdered sugar**

1 **tablespoon finely shredded orange peel (set aside)**

2 **teaspoons finely shredded orange peel (set aside)**

1 **tablespoon orange juice**

2⅔ **cups all-purpose flour**

Granulated sugar

¾ **cup granulated sugar**

1. In a large mixing bowl beat butter with an electric mixer on medium to high speed for 30 seconds. Add powdered sugar; beat until combined, scraping sides of bowl occasionally. Beat in orange juice until combined. Beat in as much of the flour as you can with the mixer. Stir in any remaining flour and the 1 tablespoon orange peel with a wooden spoon.

2. Shape dough into 1¼-inch balls; roll in granulated sugar. Place balls 2 inches apart on an ungreased cookie sheet.

3. Bake in a 325° oven about 15 minutes or until bottoms are lightly browned. Let cool on cookie sheet for 5 minutes.

4. Meanwhile, in a food processor or a blender container combine the ¾ cup granulated sugar and the 2 teaspoons orange peel. Cover and process or blend until mixture is combined. Roll warm baked cookies in the sugar mixture. Transfer cookies to a wire rack and let cool.

TO STORE: Place in layers separated by waxed paper in an airtight container; cover. Store at room temperature up to 3 days or freeze up to 3 months.

Peel now, juice later When a recipe calls for fresh citrus peel and juice, remember that it's easier to shred the peel and measure it before you cut open the fruit and squeeze it for the juice.

Roly-Poly Santas

These cute fellows are round and plump—just the way Santa should be! Hint: Press the balls of dough against each other as you flatten them so they won't separate after baking.

Makes: about 12 cookies

Oven: 325°F

 1 **cup butter, softened**

 ½ **cup sugar**

 1 **tablespoon milk**

 1 **teaspoon vanilla**

 2¼ **cups all-purpose flour**

   Red paste food coloring

   Miniature semisweet

      chocolate pieces

 1 **recipe Snow Frosting**

   Red cinnamon candies

1. In a large mixing bowl beat butter with an electric mixer on medium to high speed for 30 seconds. Add sugar; beat until combined, scraping sides of bowl occasionally. Beat in milk and vanilla until combined. Beat in as much of the flour as you can with the mixer. Stir in any remaining flour with a wooden spoon. Remove 1 cup of dough; set aside. Stir red paste food coloring into remaining dough to make desired color.

2. For each Santa, shape one ¾-inch ball and four ¼-inch balls from plain dough. From red dough, shape one 1-inch ball and five ½-inch balls. Flatten the 1-inch red ball on an ungreased cookie sheet until ½ inch thick. Attach the plain ¾-inch ball for head and flatten until ½ inch thick. Attach four ½-inch red balls for arms and legs. Shape remaining ½-inch red ball into a hat. Place plain ¼-inch balls at ends of arms and legs for hands and feet. Add chocolate pieces for eyes and buttons.

3. Bake in a 325° oven for 12 to 15 minutes or until edges are lightly browned. Cool on cookie sheet for 2 minutes. Carefully transfer cookies to a wire rack and let cool.

4. Using a decorating bag fitted with a medium star tip, pipe a Snow Frosting mustache, beard, and hatband on each cookie. For nose, attach a cinnamon candy with a small dab of frosting; let frosting dry.

Snow Frosting: In a small mixing bowl beat ½ cup shortening and ½ teaspoon vanilla with an electric mixer for 30 seconds. Beat in 1⅓ cups sifted powdered sugar until combined. Beat in 1 tablespoon milk. Beat in 1 cup sifted powdered sugar and enough milk (3 to 4 teaspoons) to make of piping consistency.

TO STORE: Place in a single layer in an airtight container; cover. Store at room temperature up to 3 days or freeze unfrosted cookies up to 3 months. Thaw cookies; frost.

Snickerdoodles

Popular for more than a century, these sweets have delighted many generations of children with their nonsensical name and their sugar-and-spice coating.

Makes: about 36 cookies

Oven: 375°F

½ **cup butter, softened**

1 **cup sugar**

¼ **teaspoon baking soda**

¼ **teaspoon cream of tartar**

1 **egg**

½ **teaspoon vanilla**

1½ **cups all-purpose flour**

2 **tablespoons sugar**

1 **teaspoon ground cinnamon**

1. In a medium mixing bowl beat butter with an electric mixer on medium to high speed for 30 seconds. Add the 1 cup sugar, baking soda, and cream of tartar. Beat until combined, scraping sides of bowl occasionally. Beat in egg and vanilla until combined. Beat in as much of the flour as you can with the mixer. Stir in any remaining flour with a wooden spoon. Cover and chill dough about 1 hour or until easy to handle.

2. In a small bowl combine the 2 tablespoons sugar and cinnamon. Shape dough into 1-inch balls; roll in sugar-cinnamon mixture to coat. Place balls 2 inches apart on an ungreased cookie sheet.

3. Bake in a 375° oven for 10 to 11 minutes or until edges are golden. Transfer to a wire rack and let cool.

TO STORE: **Place in layers separated by waxed paper in an airtight container; cover. Store at room temperature up to 3 days or freeze up to 3 months.**

Sugar smarts When a recipe calls for sugar, use white granulated sugar. Powdered sugar or confectioner's sugar refers to granulated sugar that has been pulverized (cornstarch is often added to it to prevent caking), and it's usually sifted before measuring. Brown sugar is a mix of granulated sugar and molasses; the amount of molasses determines whether the sugar is light or dark. Transfer boxes of sugars to sealed plastic bags or airtight containers. Stored in a cool, dry place, sugars keep indefinitely.

holiday
treat

Melt-in-Your-Mouth Sugar Cookies

Sturdier than traditional sugar cookie cutouts, but sporting the same yummy Mom's-kitchen flavor, these plump cookies beg to be mailed to much-missed out-of-town family and friends.

Makes: about 60 cookies

Oven: 300°F

½ cup butter, softened

½ cup shortening

2 cups sugar

1 teaspoon baking soda

1 teaspoon cream of tartar

⅛ teaspoon salt

3 egg yolks

½ teaspoon vanilla

1¾ cups all-purpose flour

1. In a large mixing bowl beat butter and shortening with an electric mixer on medium to high speed for 30 seconds. Add sugar, baking soda, cream of tartar, and salt. Beat until combined, scraping sides of bowl occasionally. Beat in egg yolks and vanilla until combined. Beat in as much of the flour as you can with the mixer. Stir in any remaining flour with a wooden spoon.

2. Shape dough into 1-inch balls. Place balls 2 inches apart on an ungreased cookie sheet.

3. Bake in a 300° oven about 15 minutes or until set (do not let edges brown). Cool on cookie sheet for 1 minute. Transfer cookies to a wire rack and let cool.

TO STORE: Place in layers separated by waxed paper in an airtight container; cover. Store at room temperature up to 3 days or freeze up to 3 months.

Small but significant Even when recipes call for only a small amount of baking soda or baking powder, these ingredients are essential for baking success. They are the reasons your cookies rise and become light. Store these ingredients in airtight containers in a cool, dry place. For best results, replace every six months or check the "use by" date.

Raisin Lovers' Sugar Cookies

This old-fashioned raisin-dotted cookie is true comfort food. Keep some in the freezer to pull out for rainy days, Mondays, and any other days that get you down.

Makes: about 36 cookies

Oven: 375°F

2 cups raisins

$\frac{1}{2}$ cup butter, softened

$\frac{3}{4}$ cup sugar

$\frac{1}{4}$ teaspoon baking powder

$\frac{1}{4}$ teaspoon salt

1 egg

1 tablespoon milk

2 teaspoons lemon extract

$1\frac{1}{2}$ cups all-purpose flour

   Sugar

1. In a small saucepan cover raisins with water; bring to boiling. Drain; let raisins cool.
2. In a medium mixing bowl beat the $\frac{1}{2}$ cup butter with an electric mixer on medium to high speed for 30 seconds. Add the $\frac{3}{4}$ cup sugar, baking powder, and salt. Beat until combined, scraping sides of bowl occasionally. Beat in egg, milk, and lemon extract until combined. Beat in as much of the flour as you can with the mixer. Stir in any remaining flour and the raisins. Cover and chill dough for 2 hours or until easy to handle.
3. Roll dough into $1\frac{1}{4}$-inch balls. Place balls 2 inches apart on an ungreased cookie sheet. Flatten balls with the bottom of a glass dipped in sugar.*
4. Bake in a 375° oven for 8 to 10 minutes or until bottoms are lightly browned. Transfer cookies to a wire rack and let cool.

*NOTE: So sugar will stick to the glass, first dip the bottom of the glass in the cookie dough. Next, dip it into the sugar.

TO STORE: **Place in layers separated by waxed paper in an airtight container; cover. Store at room temperature up to 3 days or freeze up to 3 months.**

holiday
treat

Spiral *Snowmen*

To achieve snowmen of uniform size, scoop out generous tablespoons of the dough using a measuring tablespoon. To shape each jolly snowman, roll the scoops of dough into ropes and curl them into coils.

Makes: about 24 cookies

Oven: 375°F

¾ cup butter, softened

¾ cup granulated sugar

¼ teaspoon baking powder

1 egg

1 teaspoon vanilla

2 cups all-purpose flour

   Fine sanding sugar* or
      granulated sugar*

   Red cinnamon candies

   Miniature semisweet
      chocolate pieces

   Black writing gel

1 recipe Gumdrop Hats
      (optional)

1. In a large mixing bowl beat butter with an electric mixer on medium to high speed for 30 seconds. Add the ¾ cup granulated sugar and baking powder. Beat until combined, scraping sides of bowl occasionally. Beat in egg and vanilla until combined. Beat in as much flour as you can with the mixer. Stir in any remaining flour with a wooden spoon. Cover and chill dough about 30 minutes or until easy to handle.

2. On a lightly floured surface, roll a generous tablespoon of the dough into a 10-inch-long rope. On an ungreased cookie sheet, loosely coil one end of the rope into a circle to make the head. Loosely coil the other end of the rope in the opposite direction to make the body. Repeat with remaining dough, placing cookies about 2 inches apart.

3. Sprinkle each cookie with sanding sugar. Add cinnamon candies for buttons and noses, and chocolate pieces for eyes.

4. Bake in a 375° oven for 10 to 12 minutes or until lightly browned. Cool on cookie sheet for 1 minute. Transfer cookies to a wire rack and let cool. Pipe on mouths with writing gel and, if desired, attach Gumdrop Hats.

*NOTE: Sanding sugar is a little coarser than granulated sugar. Look for it where cake decorating supplies are sold and in mail-order catalogs.

Gumdrop Hats: For each hat, roll a large gumdrop into an oval shape on a sugared surface. Roll oval into a cone shape; press to seal ends. Curl up bottom edge of cone to form a brim. If desired, attach each hat to the head of a snowman with frosting.

TO STORE: Place in a single layer in an airtight container; cover. Store at room temperature up to 3 days or freeze undecorated cookies up to 3 months. Thaw cookies; decorate.

Fairy Drops

This easy-to-handle dough takes on whatever fanciful shape you'd like, so check your cupboard for glasses, old-fashioned footed dishes, and sauce dishes with fanciful bases that can be used as molds.

Makes: 55 to 60 cookies

Oven: 350°F

4½ cups all-purpose flour

1 teaspoon baking soda

1 teaspoon cream of tartar

1 teaspoon salt

1 cup butter, softened

1 cup sifted powdered sugar

1 cup granulated sugar

1 cup cooking oil

2 eggs

2 teaspoons almond extract

Colored sugar (optional)

1 recipe Almond Frosting
    (optional)

Crushed candy canes (optional)

1. In a large bowl combine flour, baking soda, cream of tartar, and salt; set aside. In a large mixing bowl beat butter with an electric mixer on medium to high speed for 30 seconds. Add powdered sugar and granulated sugar. Beat until combined, scraping sides of bowl occasionally. Beat in oil, eggs, and almond extract until combined. Beat in as much of the flour mixture as you can with the mixer. Stir in any remaining flour mixture with a wooden spoon. Cover and chill dough about 30 minutes or until easy to handle.

2. Shape dough into 1-inch balls (the dough will be soft). Place balls 2 inches apart on an ungreased cookie sheet. Using the palm of your hand, the bottom of a glass, or a cookie stamp, gently flatten the balls to about ¼-inch thickness. If desired, sprinkle with colored sugar.

3. Bake in a 350° oven for 10 to 12 minutes or until edges are lightly browned. Transfer cookies to a wire rack and let cool. If desired, frost with Almond Frosting. If desired, sprinkle with crushed candy canes. Let dry.

Almond Frosting: In a small mixing bowl beat ½ cup butter with an electric mixer on medium speed for 30 seconds. Beat in ½ teaspoon almond extract and ½ teaspoon vanilla. Alternately add 2½ to 3½ cups sifted powdered sugar and 3 tablespoons light cream or milk, beating until smooth and of spreading consistency. If desired, stir in a few drops food coloring.

TO STORE: Place in layers separated by waxed paper in an airtight container; cover. Store at room temperature up to 3 days or freeze unfrosted cookies up to 3 months. Thaw cookies; frost.

Twisty Trees and Bows

For kids, the best part of cookie baking—beside sampling the results—is working with the pliable dough as they mold shapes such as these simple trees and bows.

Makes: about 24 cookies

Oven: 375°F

¾ cup butter, softened

¾ cup sugar

¼ teaspoon baking powder

1 egg

1 teaspoon vanilla

2 cups all-purpose flour

   Green paste food coloring

   Red paste food coloring

   Decorating candies

1. In a large mixing bowl beat butter with an electric mixer on medium to high speed for 30 seconds. Add sugar and baking powder. Beat until combined, scraping sides of bowl occasionally. Beat in egg and vanilla until combined. Beat in as much of the flour as you can with the mixer. Stir in any remaining flour with a wooden spoon.

2. For trees, knead green paste food coloring into dough to make desired color. Or, for bows, knead in red paste food coloring to make desired color. Cover and chill dough about 30 minutes or until easy to handle.

3. On a lightly floured surface, roll about 1½ tablespoons of dough into a 12-inch-long rope.

4. Shape trees about 2 inches apart on an ungreased cookie sheet: Leave about ¾ inch of the rope straight for top of tree and loop the remaining rope back and forth with each loop a little longer than the one before; leave about 1 inch below the longest loop for the trunk. Brush dough lightly with water; sprinkle with decorating candies.

5. Shape bows about 2 inches apart on an ungreased cookie sheet: Form a large U shape with the dough. Overlap the ends in the center of the U; twist ends once where they overlap. Brush dough lightly with water; sprinkle with decorating candies.

6. Bake in a 375° oven for 8 to 10 minutes or until lightly browned. Cool on cookie sheet for 1 minute. Transfer cookies to a wire rack and let cool.

TO STORE: Place in layers separated by waxed paper in an airtight container; cover. Store at room temperature up to 3 days or freeze up to 3 months.

Kringla

A Scandinavian tradition, these mildly sweet treats are almost breadlike. Savor them with a cup of hot coffee.

Makes: about 24 cookies

Oven: 425°F

3 cups all-purpose flour

2 teaspoons baking powder

   Dash salt

1⅓ cups sugar

2 tablespoons shortening

1 egg yolk

2 8-ounce cartons dairy
     sour cream

1 teaspoon baking soda

½ teaspoon vanilla

1. In a medium bowl combine flour, baking powder, and salt; set aside. In a large mixing bowl beat sugar and shortening with an electric mixer on medium to high speed for 30 seconds. Beat in egg yolk until combined.

2. In a small bowl combine sour cream, baking soda, and vanilla. Add sour cream mixture to sugar mixture. Beat until combined, scraping sides of bowl occasionally. Beat in as much of the flour mixture as you can with the mixer. Stir in any remaining flour mixture. Cover and chill dough overnight or freeze for 4 to 6 hours.

3. On a well-floured pastry cloth, roll 2 rounded tablespoons of dough into an 8-inch-long rope. Form the rope into a circle, placing one end looped under the other end. Place on an ungreased cookie sheet. Repeat with remaining dough.

4. Bake in a 425° oven about 7 minutes or until bottoms are lightly browned. Transfer cookies to a wire rack. If desired, serve warm.

TO STORE: Place in layers separated by waxed paper in an airtight container; cover. Store at room temperature up to 3 days or freeze up to 3 months.

> ### *Baking powder: It's not optional!* Because most cookie recipes call for baking powder and baking soda in such small amounts, it's easy to think the ingredients might be optional. They're not! Baking powder and baking soda are leavening agents; without them, baked products won't rise. Because the chemical properties of the two ingredients differ, one cannot be substituted for the other. If you're going to bake, it's best to keep both on hand.

Maple Log Cabins and Trees

Curl up with a cozy fire, a cup of coffee, and these tasty cabin- and tree-shape cookies.

(photo, page 105)

Makes: 24 cookies

Oven: 375°F

1½ **cups butter, softened**

1½ **cups packed brown sugar**

 2 **eggs**

¼ **cup maple-flavored syrup**

 4 **cups all-purpose flour**

 1 **cup finely chopped**

   toasted pecans

 1 **slightly beaten egg white**

 1 **tablespoon water**

 1 **recipe Maple Frosting**

   Nonpareils (optional)

1. Beat butter with an electric mixer for 30 seconds. Add brown sugar; beat until combined. Beat in eggs and syrup until combined. Beat in as much of the flour as you can. Stir in any remaining flour and the pecans.

2. Divide dough in half. Cover; chill 1 to 2 hours or until easy to handle. Divide each half of dough into 12 portions. Roll each portion into a 10-inch-long rope.

3. For a cabin, cut a rope into five 2-inch logs. To assemble, place the three logs horizontally on an ungreased cookie sheet; press together slightly to form cabin. Place remaining two logs in an inverted V shape above cabin; press ends against cabin corners to form roof.

4. For a tree, cut a rope into six pieces: one 3-inch piece, one 2½-inch, one 2-inch, two 1-inch, and one ½-inch. To assemble, place the 3-inch piece horizontally on the cookie sheet; add the 2½-inch piece, the 2-inch, a 1-inch, and the ½-inch piece; press together slightly to form tree. Place remaining 1-inch piece vertically below tree; press in place to form trunk.

5. Brush trees and/or cabins with a mixture of egg white and water. Bake in a 375° oven 8 to 10 minutes or until edges are lightly browned. Cool on cookie sheet 1 minute. Transfer to a wire rack; let cool. Decorate with Maple Frosting. If desired, while icing is still wet, sprinkle with nonpareils.

Maple Frosting: Beat 2 tablespoons butter for 30 seconds. Gradually beat in ¼ cup sifted powdered sugar. Beat in 3 tablespoons maple-flavored syrup. Gradually beat in enough sifted powdered sugar (½ to ¾ cup) to make of piping consistency. If desired, tint with food coloring.

TO STORE: Place in layers separated by waxed paper in an airtight container; cover. Store at room temperature up to 3 days or freeze undecorated cookies up to 3 months. Thaw cookies; decorate.

LEFT: Coffee Bean Cookies, page 110   ABOVE RIGHT: Eggnog Thumbprints, page 119
BELOW RIGHT: Pecan Balls, page 89

Orange Snowballs, page 95

ABOVE: Chocolate-Almond Bonbons, page 79; Yule Logs, page 109
BELOW: Black and White Twists, page 81; Kris Kringles, page 122

Yule Logs

Symbolic of a Yule log on a blazing fire, these little cookies add spicy sweetness to the warmth of the holiday season. *(photo, page 108)*

Makes: about 48 cookies

Oven: 350°F

1 **cup butter, softened**

¾ **cup granulated sugar**

¼ **cup packed brown sugar**

½ **teaspoon ground nutmeg**

½ **teaspoon ground ginger**

1 **egg**

1 **tablespoon dark rum**

1 **teaspoon vanilla**

3 **cups all-purpose flour**

1 **recipe Browned Butter Frosting**

Petal dust, powdered food coloring, or ground nutmeg

Purchased decorator icing (optional)

1. In a large mixing bowl beat butter with an electric mixer on medium to high speed for 30 seconds. Add granulated sugar, brown sugar, the ½ teaspoon ground nutmeg, and ginger. Beat until combined, scraping sides of bowl occasionally. Beat in egg, rum, and vanilla until combined. Beat in as much of the flour as you can. Stir in any remaining flour.

2. Divide dough into six portions. Wrap dough portions in plastic wrap and chill about 30 minutes or until easy to handle.

3. On a lightly floured surface, shape each dough portion into a ½-inch-thick rope. Cut ropes into 3-inch logs. Place logs 2 inches apart on an ungreased cookie sheet.

4. Bake in a 350° oven about 12 minutes or until lightly browned. Transfer cookies to a wire rack and let cool.

5. Spread Browned-Butter Frosting over each cookie. Run a fork lengthwise along log so frosting resembles bark. Sprinkle lightly with petal dust. If desired, add holly and berries of icing. Let frosting dry.

Browned Butter Frosting: In a small saucepan heat ½ cup butter over low heat until melted. Continue heating until butter turns a delicate brown. Remove from heat; pour butter into a medium mixing bowl. Add 5 cups sifted powdered sugar, ¼ cup milk, and 2 teaspoons vanilla. Beat with an electric mixer on low speed until combined. Beat on medium to high speed, adding additional milk (1 to 2 tablespoons), as necessary, to make of spreading consistency.

TO STORE: Place in layers separated by waxed paper in an airtight container; cover. Store at room temperature up to 3 days or freeze unfrosted cookies up to 3 months. Thaw cookies; frost and sprinkle with nutmeg.

Coffee Bean *Cookies*

If you're a coffee hound—or happen to be friends with one—bake up a batch of these fun, bean-shape cookies. Paired with a pound of real coffee beans from a gourmet java shop, they make a great gift for the coffee lover on your list. *(photo, page 106)*

Makes: about 48 cookies

Oven: 350°F

2 teaspoons instant
    coffee crystals

2 tablespoons milk

¾ cup butter, softened

1 3-ounce package cream
    cheese, softened

¾ cup packed brown sugar

1 teaspoon vanilla

2 cups all-purpose flour

1. In a small bowl stir together coffee crystals and milk until crystals dissolve; set aside.
2. Meanwhile, in a large mixing bowl beat butter and cream cheese with an electric mixer on medium to high speed for 30 seconds. Add brown sugar, vanilla, and the milk mixture. Beat until combined, scraping sides of bowl occasionally. Beat in as much of the flour as you can with the mixer. Stir in any remaining flour with a wooden spoon. Cover and chill dough about 1 hour or until easy to handle.
3. Shape dough into 1-inch balls. Shape balls into ovals. Press the thin edge of a wooden spoon (or a chopstick) lengthwise into the top of each oval, forming an indent that resembles those found on coffee beans. Place 1 inch apart on an ungreased cookie sheet.
4. Bake in a 350° oven for 9 to 11 minutes or until edges are firm and bottoms are lightly browned. Transfer cookies to a wire rack and let cool.

TO STORE: **Place in layers separated by waxed paper in an airtight container; cover. Store at room temperature up to 3 days or freeze up to 3 months.**

Espresso Delights

Make it a happy day at the office! Share these chocolate- and coffee-speckled crescents

with your co-workers and prevent that mid-afternoon slump.

Makes: about 32 cookies

Oven: 325°F

2   cups all-purpose flour

1   cup butter, softened

²⁄₃   cup sifted powdered sugar

1   ounce semisweet chocolate,
      finely chopped

1   tablespoon instant espresso
      coffee powder or regular
      instant coffee crystals

1   teaspoon vanilla

¹⁄₂   teaspoon ground cinnamon
      Sifted powdered sugar

1. In a large bowl combine flour, butter, the ²⁄₃ cup powdered sugar, chocolate, espresso powder, vanilla, and cinnamon. Stir until combined, kneading dough lightly with your hands to mix, if necessary.

2. Using 1 tablespoon dough for each, shape dough into 3-inch ropes. Place ropes on an ungreased cookie sheet, bending to form crescent shapes. Flatten slightly.

3. Bake cookies in a 325° oven about 15 minutes or until edges are set and bottoms are lightly browned. Transfer cookies to a wire rack and let cool. To serve, sprinkle with powdered sugar.

TO STORE: Place in layers separated by waxed paper in an airtight container; cover.
Store at room temperature up to 3 days or freeze up to 3 months.

Keeping spice nice **Follow these tips to preserve the flavor in your spices:**
- **Keep all spices in airtight containers, and store in a cool, dry place.**
- **The flavor in spices comes from volatile oils that lose their punch over time. Buy spices in small amounts, write the date of purchase on the container, and throw away any spices after 6 months.**
- **For the freshest flavor, buy whole spices and grind them just before using.**

holiday treat

Peppermint Candy Cookies

Though the mellow cream cheese dough contrasts with the snappy peppermint filling, a deliciously harmonious whole is the result. Hint: Be sure the cookies are still warm when you roll them in the candy mixture; otherwise the candy won't stick.

Makes: about 30 cookies

Oven: 325°F

1 cup butter, softened

1 cup sifted powdered sugar

1 tablespoon milk

1 teaspoon vanilla

2½ cups all-purpose flour

½ cup chopped pecans

½ cup finely crushed striped
round peppermint candies

1 3-ounce package cream
cheese, softened

1. In a large mixing bowl beat butter with an electric mixer on medium to high speed for 30 seconds. Add ½ cup of the powdered sugar, milk, and vanilla. Beat until combined, scraping sides of bowl occasionally. Beat in as much of the flour as you can with the mixer. Stir in remaining flour and the pecans with a wooden spoon.

2. For filling, combine the remaining ½ cup powdered sugar and the candy. In a bowl stir together cream cheese and 3 tablespoons of the candy mixture. Set remaining candy mixture aside.

3. Shape dough into 1½-inch balls. Press your thumb into the center of each ball. Spoon ¼ teaspoon peppermint filling into each thumbprint. Shape dough around filling and seal. Reroll into a ball. Place balls 1 inch apart on an ungreased cookie sheet.

4. Bake in a 325° oven about 15 minutes or until edges are firm but not brown. Transfer cookies to a wire rack and let cool 5 minutes.

5. Roll warm cookies in remaining crushed candy mixture. Cool completely on a wire rack. Roll cookies again in candy mixture before serving.

TO STORE: Place in layers separated by waxed paper in an airtight container; cover. Store in the refrigerator up to 1 week or freeze up to 3 months.

Buttery *Mint* Cookies

No colored sugar in your cupboard? These sparkling cookies provide a reason to discover the range of colors available from supermarkets, baking supply stores, and catalogs.

Makes: about 42 cookies

Oven: 350°F

³/₄ **cup butter, softened**

¹/₂ **cup granulated sugar**

1 **egg yolk**

2 **tablespoons milk**

¹/₄ **teaspoon mint extract**

2 **cups all-purpose flour**

Colored sugars (optional)

1. In a large mixing bowl beat butter with an electric mixer on medium to high speed for 30 seconds. Add granulated sugar; beat until combined, scraping sides of bowl occasionally. Beat in egg yolk, milk, and mint extract until combined. Beat in as much of the flour as you can with the mixer. Stir in any remaining flour with a wooden spoon. Cover and chill dough about 2 hours or until easy to handle.

2. Shape dough into 1-inch balls. Place on an ungreased cookie sheet. If desired, flatten cookies with the decorative bottom of a glass dipped in colored sugar.*

3. Bake in a 350° oven for 8 to 10 minutes or until edges begin to brown. Transfer cookies to a wire rack and let cool.

*NOTE: So sugar will stick to the glass, first dip the bottom of the glass in the cookie dough. Next, dip it into the sugar.

TO STORE: Place in layers separated by waxed paper in an airtight container; cover. Store at room temperature up to 3 days or freeze up to 3 months.

Make pastel-color sugars To make your own

pastel-color sugar, put ²/₃ cup granulated sugar in a self-sealing plastic bag. Place a few drops of a liquid food coloring in a ¹/₄ teaspoon measure. (Use two or three drops of red if you want light pink sugar, for example.) Add water to measuring spoon to fill. Sprinkle over sugar in bag. Seal bag and knead sugar with your hands until the color is well distributed. Empty tinted sugar into a pie plate. Let dry for several hours, stirring occasionally. When sugar is dry, store it in an airtight container.

To make an "original" pastel shade, mix together different colors of liquid food coloring in the ¹/₄ teaspoon measure. Try combining one drop of blue with one drop of green, for instance, or one drop of yellow with one drop of green.

Swirled *Mint* Cookies

Three colors of dough blend to form delightfully swirled slices. Make them dainty and petite, or big and beautiful, depending on how thick you slice the dough.

Makes: about 72 large or 144 small cookies

Oven: 375°F

2 cups all-purpose flour

½ teaspoon baking powder

1 cup butter, softened

1 cup sugar

1 egg

1 teaspoon vanilla

½ teaspoon peppermint extract

10 drops red food coloring

10 drops green food coloring

Sugar

1. In a medium bowl combine flour and baking powder; set aside. In a large mixing bowl beat butter with an electric mixer on medium to high speed for 30 seconds. Add the 1 cup sugar; beat until combined, scraping sides of bowl occasionally. Beat in egg, vanilla, and extract until combined. Beat in as much of the flour mixture as you can with the mixer. Stir in any remaining flour mixture with a wooden spoon.

2. Divide dough into three equal portions. Stir red food coloring into one portion, stir green food coloring into another, and leave remaining portion plain. Cover and chill dough about 1 hour or until easy to handle.

3. Divide each color of dough into four equal portions. On a lightly floured surface, roll each portion into a ½-inch-diameter rope. Place one red, one green, and one plain rope side by side. Twist together. Repeat with remaining ropes. Chill dough for 30 minutes. Cut ropes into ½-inch slices for larger cookies or ¼-inch slices for smaller ones. Carefully roll slices into balls, blending colors as little as possible. Place balls about 2 inches apart on an ungreased cookie sheet. Flatten to ¼-inch thickness with the bottom of a glass dipped in sugar.*

4. Bake in a 375° oven until edges are set (allow 8 to 10 minutes for larger cookies; 6 to 8 minutes for smaller ones). Transfer to a wire rack and let cool.

*NOTE: So sugar will stick to the glass, first dip the bottom of the glass in the cookie dough. Next, dip it into the sugar.

TO STORE: Place in layers separated by waxed paper in an airtight container; cover. Store at room temperature up to 3 days or freeze up to 3 months.

Farmyard *Friends*

Kids will want to help you shape this merry menagerie. Hint: If the dough sticks to your fingers, cover and chill it until it's firm.

Makes: about 25 cookies

Oven: 300°F

  4 **cups all-purpose flour**

  1 **tablespoon baking powder**

  ¼ **teaspoon salt**

  ¾ **cup butter, softened**

  ⅔ **cup shortening**

1½ **cups sugar**

  2 **eggs**

  1 **teaspoon peppermint extract**

     Paste or liquid food coloring

1. Combine flour, baking powder, and salt; set aside. Beat butter and shortening for 30 seconds. Add sugar; beat until combined. Beat in eggs and peppermint extract. Beat or stir in the flour mixture. Cover and chill dough at least 2 hours.

2. Divide dough into portions, one for each color you want to use. Knead desired food coloring into each portion. On an ungreased cookie sheet, form dough into animal shapes about ¼ inch thick. Decorate as suggested in shaping directions below. Place shapes about 1 inch apart.

3. Bake in a 300° oven for 18 to 20 minutes or until edges are firm and cookies look set but bottoms are not brown. Transfer to a rack; cool.

Polly Pig: For the body, flatten a ¾-inch colored ball of dough to about 2½ inches across. Roll a small colored ball for head. Use colored and untinted doughs to make legs, tail, ears, eyes, and snout. Attach pieces by pressing them gently onto body and head. If desired, add stripes or spots.

Roly-Poly Lamb: For the body, roll untinted dough into small balls of varying sizes and lay them on a cookie sheet so they touch each other. Use a small round ball of colored dough for the head and small ovals for the feet.

Holly Horse: For the body, flatten a 1-inch oval of untinted dough to about 2½ inches across. For the neck and head, place a heart-shaped piece of dough upside down next to the body. For the neck wreath, twist together two ⅛-inch ropes of colored dough. Use colored and untinted doughs to make legs, tail, mane, spots, and eye. Use the tines of a fork to draw mane and tail.

TO STORE: **Place in layers separated by waxed paper in an airtight container; cover. Store at room temperature up to 3 days or freeze up to 3 months.**

Peppermint Candy Canes

This easy shaping method differs from the way cookie candy canes usually are formed. The result is cookies of uniform thickness with clearly marked stripes.

Makes: about 36 cookies

Oven: 375°F

⅓ **cup butter, softened**

⅓ **cup shortening**

¾ **cup granulated sugar**

1 **teaspoon baking powder**

  Dash salt

1 **egg**

1 **tablespoon milk**

½ **teaspoon vanilla**

½ **teaspoon peppermint extract**

2 **cups all-purpose flour**

  Red paste food coloring

  Sanding sugar (optional)*

1. In a medium mixing bowl beat butter and shortening with an electric mixer on medium to high speed for 30 seconds. Add the ¾ cup granulated sugar, baking powder, and salt. Beat until combined, scraping sides of bowl occasionally. Beat in egg, milk, vanilla, and peppermint extract until combined. Beat in as much of the flour as you can with the mixer. Stir any remaining flour with a wooden spoon.

2. Divide dough in half. Stir red paste food coloring into one half of the dough. If necessary, cover and chill dough for 30 to 60 minutes or until easy to handle.

3. Divide each half of dough into six equal pieces. Roll each piece into a 12-inch-long rope. Lay ropes side by side on a lightly floured surface, alternating colors. With a rolling pin, roll assembled ropes into a 14×9-inch rectangle. Using a pizza wheel or long sharp knife, cut dough rectangle diagonally into ½-inch strips. Cut strips into pieces 5 to 7 inches long. (Press shorter strips together end to end to reach desired length.) Place strips on an ungreased cookie sheet. Curve one end of each piece to form a candy cane. If desired, sprinkle with sanding sugar.

4. Bake in a 375° oven for 7 to 8 minutes or until edges are firm and bottoms are very lightly browned. Transfer cookies to a wire rack and let cool.

*NOTE: Sanding sugar is a little coarser than granulated sugar. Look for it where cake decorating supplies are sold and in mail-order catalogs.

TO STORE: Place in layers separated by waxed paper in an airtight container; cover. Store at room temperature up to 3 days or freeze up to 3 months.

Birds' Nests

A quick dip in a beaten egg white bath ensures that the nuts cling to the dough. For variety, use cherry, strawberry, or apricot preserves in place of the raspberry suggested here.

Makes: about 36 cookies

Oven: 375°F

1 cup butter, softened

¹⁄₂ cup packed brown sugar

2 egg yolks

2 cups all-purpose flour

2 slightly beaten egg whites

2 cups finely chopped walnuts
   or pecans

¹⁄₂ cup seedless raspberry jam
   or preserves

1 recipe Powdered Sugar Icing
   (optional)

1. Lightly grease a cookie sheet; set aside. In a large mixing bowl beat butter with an electric mixer on medium to high speed for 30 seconds. Add brown sugar; beat until combined, scraping sides of bowl occasionally. Beat in egg yolks until combined. Beat in as much of the flour as you can with the mixer. Stir in any remaining flour with a wooden spoon.

2. Shape dough into 1¹⁄₄-inch balls. Roll balls in egg whites; roll in chopped nuts. Place balls 1 inch apart on prepared cookie sheet. Press your thumb into the center of each ball.

3. Bake in a 375° oven for 10 to 12 minutes or until edges are lightly brown. Transfer cookies to a wire rack and let cool. Before serving, fill centers with jam or preserves (about ¹⁄₂ teaspoon each). If desired, drizzle with Powdered Sugar Icing; let icing dry.

Powdered Sugar Icing: In a small bowl stir together 1 cup sifted powdered sugar and enough milk (1 to 2 tablespoons) to make of drizzling consistency.

TO STORE: Place in layers separated by waxed paper in an airtight container; cover. Store at room temperature up to 3 days or freeze unfilled cookies up to 3 months. Thaw cookies; fill and drizzle.

Jam *Thumbprints*

These tender rounds are a well-loved classic. Instead of jam, fill the centers with spoonfuls of your favorite frosting.

Makes: about 42 cookies

Oven: 375°F

⅔ **cup butter, softened**

½ **cup sugar**

2 **egg yolks**

1 **teaspoon vanilla**

1½ **cups all-purpose flour**

2 **slightly beaten egg whites**

1 **cup finely chopped walnuts**

⅓ **to ½ cup strawberry, cherry, or apricot jam or preserves**

1. In a large mixing bowl beat butter with an electric mixer on medium to high speed for 30 seconds. Add sugar; beat until combined, scraping sides of bowl occasionally. Beat in egg yolks and vanilla until combined. Beat in as much of the flour as you can with the mixer. Stir in any remaining flour with a wooden spoon. Cover and chill dough about 1 hour or until easy to handle.

2. Grease a cookie sheet; set aside. Shape dough into 1-inch balls. Roll balls in egg whites; roll in walnuts. Place balls 1 inch apart on the prepared cookie sheet. Press your thumb into the center of each ball.

3. Bake in a 375° oven for 10 to 12 minutes or until edges are lightly browned. Transfer cookies to a wire rack and let cool. Just before serving, fill centers with jam.

TO STORE: Place in layers separated by waxed paper in an airtight container; cover. Store unfilled cookies at room temperature up to 3 days (fill just before serving) or freeze unfilled cookies up to 3 months. Thaw cookies; fill just before serving.

Perfect cookie shapes When shaped cookie recipes call for chilling the dough, never shortcut this step—it's the key to perfectly shaped cookies! Chilled dough is easier to mold and helps the cookies better keep their shapes during baking.

If you're working in a warm kitchen, return the dough to the refrigerator between batches. Some doughs, even when chilled, tend to stick to your hands. When shaping these doughs, dust your hands lightly with flour as necessary.

holiday treat

Eggnog Thumbprints

This luscious holiday treat features walnut-covered butter cookies that serve as vessels for the rum-flavored filling. Pipe the filling in just before you serve them so it holds its shape.

(photo, page 106)

Makes: about 40 cookies

Oven: 375°F

3/4 **cup butter, softened**

1/2 **cup sugar**

1/8 **teaspoon ground nutmeg**

 2 **egg yolks**

 1 **teaspoon vanilla**

1 1/2 **cups all-purpose flour**

 2 **slightly beaten egg whites**

 1 **cup finely chopped walnuts**

 1 **recipe Rum Filling**

   Ground nutmeg

1. In a large mixing bowl beat butter with an electric mixer on medium to high speed for 30 seconds. Add sugar and the 1/8 teaspoon nutmeg. Beat until combined, scraping sides of bowl occasionally. Beat in egg yolks and vanilla until combined. Beat in as much of the flour as you can with the mixer. Stir in any remaining flour with a wooden spoon. Cover and chill dough about 1 hour or until easy to handle.

2. Lightly grease a cookie sheet; set aside. Shape dough into 1-inch balls. Roll balls in egg whites; roll in chopped walnuts to coat. Place balls about 1 inch apart on prepared cookie sheet. Press your thumb into the center of each ball.

3. Bake in a 375° oven for 10 to 12 minutes or until edges are lightly browned. Transfer cookies to a wire rack and let cool. Just before serving, pipe or spoon about 1/2 teaspoon Rum Filling into the center of each cookie. Sprinkle with additional nutmeg.

Rum Filling: In a small bowl beat 1/4 cup softened butter for 30 seconds. Beat in 1 cup sifted powdered sugar until fluffy. Beat in 1 teaspoon rum or 1/4 teaspoon rum extract and enough milk (1 to 2 teaspoons) to make of spreading consistency.

TO STORE: Place in layers separated by waxed paper in an airtight container; cover. Store unfilled cookies at room temperature up to 3 days (fill just before serving) or freeze unfilled cookies up to 3 months. Thaw cookies; fill just before serving.

Holiday Blossoms

Dressed in the appropriate colors, these candy-centered gems will never be out of season. For a subtle twist, add ¼ teaspoon of mint, peppermint, or almond extract along with the vanilla.

Makes: about 24 cookies

Oven: 350°F

½ **cup butter, softened**

1 **3-ounce package cream cheese, softened**

1½ **cups sifted powdered sugar**

½ **teaspoon baking powder**

¼ **teaspoon salt**

1 **egg**

½ **teaspoon vanilla**

2¼ **cups all-purpose flour**

Colored sugar

Pastel candy-coated mint chocolate balls

1. In a large mixing bowl beat butter and cream cheese with an electric mixer on medium to high speed for 30 seconds. Add powdered sugar, baking powder, and salt. Beat until combined, scraping sides of bowl occasionally. Beat in egg and vanilla until combined. Beat in as much of the flour as you can with the mixer. Stir in any remaining flour with a wooden spoon. Cover and chill dough about 1 hour or until easy to handle.

2. Shape dough into 1¼-inch balls; roll in colored sugar. Place balls 2 inches apart on an ungreased cookie sheet. With scissors, snip each ball in half from the top, cutting ¾ of the way through. Snip each half twice, making six wedges. Gently fold down wedges to make a flower shape. Sprinkle a little additional colored sugar in the center of each.

3. Bake in a 350° oven for 8 to 9 minutes or until edges are firm and bottoms are very lightly browned. Remove from oven; immediately place a chocolate ball in the center of each cookie. Transfer cookies to a wire rack and let cool.

TO STORE: Place in layers separated by waxed paper in an airtight container; cover. Store at room temperature up to 3 days or freeze up to 3 months.

Potato Chip *Crispies*

Sure, potato chips are great for snacks or with dips, but they make a surprisingly tasty cookie, too, especially if you're a fan of salty and sweet flavor combos.

Makes: about 20 cookies

Oven: 350°F

¾ **cup butter, softened**

½ **cup sugar**

1 **teaspoon vanilla**

1 **egg**

1¾ **cups all-purpose flour**

2 **cups crushed potato chips**

      (**about 6 cups uncrushed**)

1. In a large mixing bowl beat butter with an electric mixer on medium to high speed for 30 seconds. Add sugar and vanilla. Beat until combined, scraping sides of bowl occasionally. Beat in egg until combined. Beat in as much of the flour as you can with the mixer. Stir in any remaining flour and 1 cup of the potato chips.

2. Shape dough into 1½-inch balls. Roll balls in remaining crushed potato chips. Place balls 2 inches apart on an ungreased cookie sheet; flatten with hands until about ¼ inch thick.

3. Bake in a 350° oven about 12 minutes or until golden. Transfer cookies to a wire rack and let cool.

TO STORE: Place in layers separated by waxed paper in an airtight container; cover. Store at room temperature up to 3 days or freeze up to 3 months.

From the flour bin **When it comes to cookies, too much flour makes them hard as rocks; too little and they become flat as pancakes. Be sure to add just the right amount of flour by measuring correctly: Stir the flour prior to measuring. Flour settles as it sits; if you don't stir it, you may end up adding too much.**

   Spoon the flour into the measuring cup—dipping the whole cup results in too much flour.

Kris Kringles

Orange and lemon peel add a zesty edge to these rounds. Each jolly gem wears a bright cherry topknot, red or green, for the holidays. *(photo, page 108)*

Makes: about 26 cookies

Oven: 325°F

½ **cup butter**

¼ **cup sugar**

1 **egg yolk**

1 **teaspoon finely shredded lemon peel (set aside)**

1 **teaspoon lemon juice**

1 **cup all-purpose flour**

1 **tablespoon finely shredded orange peel**

   Dash salt

1 **slightly beaten egg white**

⅔ **cup finely chopped walnuts**

13 **whole candied red or green cherries, halved**

1. In a medium mixing bowl beat butter with an electric mixer on medium to high speed for 30 seconds. Add sugar; beat until combined, scraping sides of bowl occasionally. Beat in egg yolk and lemon juice until combined. Stir in flour, orange peel, salt, and lemon peel with a wooden spoon. Cover and chill dough about 1 hour or until easy to handle.

2. Grease a cookie sheet; set aside. Shape dough into 1-inch balls. Roll balls in egg white; roll in chopped walnuts. Place 1 inch apart on the prepared cookie sheet. Press a cherry half into each ball.

3. Bake in a 325° oven about 20 minutes or until lightly browned. Transfer cookies to a wire rack and let cool.

TO STORE: Place in layers separated by waxed paper in an airtight container; cover. Store at room temperature up to 3 days or freeze up to 3 months.

A shred of peel The little time it takes to shred fresh citrus peel is well worth the effort when you consider the lively burst of flavor it brings to recipes.

   If a recipe calls for shredded lime, orange, or lemon peel, use only the colored surface of the peel, not the bitter-tasting, spongy, white pith. Hand graters and zesters are convenient, but you can also use a vegetable peeler to remove thin layers of peel. Finely mince the peel with a sharp kitchen knife. Prepare extra peel to keep on hand, and freeze it in a resealable plastic freezer bag.

Molded and Pressed Shapes

Fudge *Brownie* Tassies

When tassie fans and chocolate lovers get together, sweet things happen. Try this new fudge brownie classic.

Makes: 24 tassies

Oven: 325°F

½ cup butter, softened

1 3-ounce package cream
  cheese, softened

1 cup all-purpose flour

½ cup semisweet
  chocolate pieces

2 tablespoons butter

⅓ cup sugar

1 beaten egg

1 teaspoon vanilla

Hazelnuts, almonds,
  macadamia nuts, or walnut
  pieces (optional)

1. For pastry, in a medium mixing bowl beat the ½ cup butter and cream cheese with an electric mixer on medium to high speed for 30 seconds. Stir in flour with a wooden spoon. Cover and chill dough about 1 hour or until easy to handle.

2. Shape dough into 24 balls. Press each ball evenly into bottom and up sides of an ungreased 1¾-inch muffin cup.

3. For filling, in a small heavy saucepan melt chocolate pieces and the 2 tablespoons butter over low heat, stirring constantly. Remove from heat. Stir in sugar, egg, and vanilla.

4. If desired, place a nut in each pastry-lined muffin cup. Spoon about 1 teaspoon of the chocolate mixture into each pastry-lined muffin cup. Bake in a 325° oven for 20 to 25 minutes or until pastry is golden and filling is puffed. Cool tassies slightly in pan on wire racks. Carefully remove tassies from pan by running a knife around the edges of each cup. Transfer tassies to a wire rack and let cool.

TO STORE: Place in layers separated by waxed paper in an airtight container; cover. Store at room temperature up to 3 days or freeze up to 3 months.

Pecan Tassies

These bite-size pecan pies have adorned holiday platters for years. For a subtle change of pace, use chopped mixed nuts in place of the pecans.

Makes: 24 tassies

Oven: 325°F

¹/₂ **cup butter, softened**

1 **3-ounce package cream cheese, softened**

1 **cup all-purpose flour**

1 **egg**

³/₄ **cup packed brown sugar**

1 **tablespoon butter, melted**

²/₃ **cup coarsely chopped pecans**

1. For pastry, in a medium mixing bowl beat the ½ cup butter and cream cheese with an electric mixer on medium to high speed for 30 seconds. Stir in flour with a wooden spoon. Cover and chill dough about 1 hour or until easy to handle.

2. Shape dough into 24 balls. Press each ball evenly into bottom and up sides of an ungreased 1¾-inch muffin cup.

3. For filling, in a small mixing bowl beat egg, brown sugar, and the 1 tablespoon melted butter with a rotary beater or a fork until combined. Stir in pecans.

4. Spoon about 1 heaping teaspoon of filling into each pastry-lined muffin cup. Bake in a 325° oven for 25 to 30 minutes or until pastry is golden and filling is puffed. Cool tassies slightly in pan on wire racks. Carefully remove tassies from pan by running a knife around the edges of each cup. Transfer tassies to a wire rack and let cool.

TO STORE: Place in layers separated by waxed paper in an airtight container; cover. Store at room temperature up to 3 days or freeze up to 3 months.

Any-occasion gifts Home-baked cookies make wonderful gifts for just about any occasion. To give the gift a special touch, pack the cookies in a decorative gift box or tin lined with colored tissue paper. Wrap the cookies individually or in pairs in clear plastic wrap before packing them in the box. Leave the box open to showcase the cookies or cover it with the lid to make it a surprise. Finish the package by tying sheer ribbon around the top or sides of the box.

Cranberry-Pecan *Tassies*

"Tassies," a word the Scottish use meaning "small cups," have incorporated many different flavors over the years. Here, the sweet and the tart—brown sugar filling and cranberries—come together for a delightful contrast.

Makes: 24 tassies

Oven: 325°F

½ cup butter, softened

1 3-ounce package cream cheese, softened

1 cup all-purpose flour

1 egg

¾ cup packed brown sugar

1 teaspoon vanilla

Dash salt

⅓ cup finely chopped cranberries

3 tablespoons chopped pecans

1. For pastry, in a medium mixing bowl beat butter and cream cheese with an electric mixer on medium to high speed for 30 seconds. Stir in flour with a wooden spoon. Cover and chill dough about 1 hour or until easy to handle.

2. Shape dough into 24 balls. Press each ball evenly into bottom and up sides of an ungreased 1¾-inch muffin cup.

3. For filling, in a small mixing bowl beat egg, brown sugar, vanilla, and salt with a rotary beater or a fork just until smooth. Stir in cranberries and pecans.

4. Spoon filling into pastry-lined muffin cups. Bake in 325° oven for 30 to 35 minutes or until pastry is golden brown and filling is puffed. Cool tassies slightly in pan on wire racks. Carefully remove tassies from pan by running a knife around the edges of each cup. Transfer tassies to a wire rack and let cool.

TO STORE: Place in layers separated by waxed paper in an airtight container; cover. Store at room temperature up to 3 days or freeze up to 3 months.

Apricot-Almond Tarts

Undeniably sophisticated, each tart boasts an apricot filling nestled beneath a puffy almond paste topping. That's one irresistible cookie!

Makes: 24 tarts

Oven: 325°F

½ **cup butter, softened**

1 **3-ounce package cream cheese, softened**

1 **cup all-purpose flour**

½ **cup water**

⅓ **cup snipped dried apricots**

2 **tablespoons sugar**

1 **egg**

½ **cup sugar**

½ **cup almond paste, crumbled**

1. For pastry, in a medium mixing bowl beat butter and cream cheese with an electric mixer on medium to high speed for 30 seconds. Stir in flour with a wooden spoon. Cover and chill dough about 1 hour or until easy to handle.

2. Meanwhile, for filling, in a small saucepan bring water, apricots, and the 2 tablespoons sugar to boiling. Reduce heat; simmer, covered, about 15 minutes or until apricots are tender. Remove from heat. Mash apricots with a fork until smooth. Cool completely.

3. Shape dough into 24 balls. Press each ball evenly into bottom and up sides of an ungreased 1¾-inch muffin cup.

4. In a small mixing bowl beat egg, the ½ cup sugar, and almond paste with an electric mixer on medium speed until combined. Spoon about ½ teaspoon of the apricot filling into each pastry-lined muffin cup. Top with a rounded teaspoon of the almond paste mixture.

5. Bake in a 325° oven for 25 to 30 minutes or until pastry is golden. Cool tarts slightly in pan on wire racks. Carefully remove tarts from pan by running a knife around the edges of each cup. Transfer tarts to a wire rack and let cool.

TO STORE: Place in a single layer in an airtight container; cover. Store at room temperature up to 3 days or freeze up to 3 months.

About almond paste Available in the baking aisle of larger supermarkets, almond paste is made from finely ground almonds and sugar. For best results, use an almond paste made without syrup or liquid glucose. Cookies made with almond paste that contains these ingredients may be softer.

Meringue-Topped *Fruit Tarts*

A date and apricot filling is tucked between a rich flaky pastry and a fluffy meringue topping.

Be sure to store these teatime treats in the refrigerator. *(photo, page 142)*

Makes: 24 tarts

Oven: 350°F

1¼ cups all-purpose flour

2 tablespoons brown sugar

⅓ cup butter

2 egg yolks

¼ cup dairy sour cream

½ teaspoon vanilla

½ cup snipped pitted dates

½ cup snipped dried apricots

⅓ cup dairy sour cream

⅓ cup apricot preserves or
orange marmalade

2 tablespoons candied
orange peel, chopped

1 egg white

¼ cup granulated sugar

¼ cup chopped walnuts

1. Grease twenty-four 1¾-inch muffin cups; set aside. For pastry, in a medium bowl stir together flour and brown sugar. Using a pastry blender, cut in butter until mixture resembles coarse crumbs. In a small bowl stir together egg yolks, the ¼ cup sour cream, and vanilla. Stir egg yolk mixture into flour mixture.

2. Shape dough into 24 balls. Press each ball evenly into bottom and up sides of a prepared muffin cup; set aside.

3. For fruit filling, in a small bowl stir together dates, apricots, the ⅓ cup sour cream, preserves, and orange peel. Spoon about 1 heaping teaspoon of filling into each pastry-lined muffin cup. Bake in a 350° oven for 10 minutes.

4. Meanwhile, for meringue topping, in a small mixing bowl beat egg white with an electric mixer on medium speed until soft peaks form (tips curl). Gradually add granulated sugar, beating on high speed until stiff peaks form (tips stand straight).

5. Carefully spoon or pipe a small dollop of meringue over fruit mixture in each muffin cup; sprinkle each with walnuts. Bake about 15 minutes more or until lightly browned. Cool tarts slightly in pans on wire racks. Carefully remove tarts from pan by running a knife around the edges of each cup. Transfer tarts to a wire rack and let cool.

TO STORE: **Place in a single layer in an airtight container; cover. Store in the refrigerator up to 3 days or freeze up to 1 month.**

Orange Curd Tarts

This easy recipe starts with a package of piecrust mix—a very up-to-date head start to an old-fashioned treat.

Makes: 32 tarts

Oven: 350°F

1 **package piecrust mix**

    (for 2 crusts)

¼ **cup finely chopped pecans**

⅓ **cup cold water**

1 **cup sugar**

2 **teaspoons cornstarch**

1 **tablespoon finely shredded**

    orange peel (set aside)

⅓ **cup orange juice**

1 **tablespoon butter, cut up**

3 **beaten eggs**

    Small orange peel curls

    (optional)

1. Lightly grease thirty-two 1¾-inch muffin cups; set aside. In a small bowl stir together piecrust mix and pecans. Add cold water and stir until moistened and dough holds together. Divide dough in half.

2. On a lightly floured surface, roll half of the dough at a time into a 10½-inch square; trim to a 10-inch square. Cut each square into sixteen 2½-inch squares. Fit squares into muffin cups, pleating sides and leaving corners standing up slightly.

3. For filling, in a medium saucepan combine sugar and cornstarch. Add orange juice and butter. Cook and stir over medium heat until thickened and bubbly. Cook and stir for 2 minutes more. Stir about half of the juice mixture into beaten eggs. Return egg mixture to saucepan. Remove from heat. Stir in finely shredded orange peel.

4. Spoon about 2 teaspoons orange filling into each pastry-lined muffin cup. Bake in a 350° oven for 18 to 20 minutes or until filling is set and crust is light brown. Cool tarts in pans on wire racks for 20 minutes. Carefully transfer tarts from pans to wire racks and cool completely. If desired, garnish each tart with a small orange peel curl just before serving.

TO STORE: Place in a single layer in an airtight container; cover. Store in the refrigerator up to 3 days.

Orange-Walnut *Madeleines*

To make madeleines, you need a special shell-shape cookie mold. Once you've invested in the molds, you might as well try as many versions of the cookie as possible, right? That was the thinking that led to this terrific take.

Makes: 24 cookies

Oven: 375°F

  2 **egg yolks**

  ½ **cup granulated sugar**

  ½ **cup butter, melted and cooled**

  1 **teaspoon finely shredded**

        orange peel

  1 **tablespoon orange juice**

  ½ **teaspoon vanilla**

  ½ **cup all-purpose flour**

  ½ **teaspoon baking powder**

  ¼ **teaspoon ground cardamom**

  ⅛ **teaspoon baking soda**

  ⅛ **teaspoon salt**

  ¼ **cup finely chopped**

        toasted walnuts

  2 **slightly beaten egg whites**

      Powdered sugar

1. Grease and flour twenty-four 3-inch madeleine molds; set aside. In a medium mixing bowl beat egg yolks and sugar with an electric mixer on medium to high speed about 30 seconds or until combined. Add melted butter, orange peel, orange juice, and vanilla. Beat on low speed until combined, scraping sides of bowl occasionally.

2. In a small bowl stir together flour, baking powder, cardamom, baking soda, and salt. Sift or sprinkle about one-fourth of the flour mixture over egg yolk mixture; gently fold in. Fold in remaining flour mixture one-fourth at a time. Fold in walnuts. Gently stir in egg whites.

3. Spoon batter into prepared molds, filling each mold about half full. Bake in a 375° oven for 10 to 12 minutes or until edges are golden and tops spring back when lightly touched. Cool in molds on wire racks for 1 minute. Using the point of a knife, loosen each cookie from mold; invert cookies onto wire racks. Remove molds and let cookies cool. Before serving, sift powdered sugar over tops of cookies.

TO STORE: Place in layers separated by waxed paper in an airtight container; cover. Store at room temperature up to 3 days or freeze up to 3 months. Thaw cookies; sift with powdered sugar.

Lemon-Almond Madeleines

The fact that madeleines are light, airy, buttery, and beautiful goes without saying. With a sprinkling of almonds and a hint of lemon, they become downright heavenly.

Makes: 24 cookies

Oven: 375°F

  2 **egg yolks**

  ½ **cup sugar**

  ½ **cup butter, melted and cooled**

  ½ **teaspoon finely shredded lemon peel**

  1 **tablespoon lemon juice**

  ½ **teaspoon vanilla**

  ½ **cup all-purpose flour**

  ½ **teaspoon baking powder**

  ⅛ **teaspoon baking soda**

  ⅛ **teaspoon salt**

  ¼ **cup finely chopped toasted almonds**

  2 **slightly beaten egg whites**

     Powdered sugar

1. Grease and flour twenty-four 3-inch madeleine molds; set aside. In a medium mixing bowl beat egg yolks and sugar with an electric mixer on medium to high speed for 30 seconds. Add melted butter, lemon peel, lemon juice, and vanilla. Beat on low speed until combined, scraping sides of bowl occasionally.

2. In a small bowl stir together flour, baking powder, baking soda, and salt. Sift or sprinkle about one-fourth of the flour mixture over egg yolk mixture; gently fold in. Fold in remaining flour mixture one-fourth at a time. Fold in almonds. Gently stir in egg whites.

3. Spoon batter into prepared molds, filling each mold about half full. Bake in a 375° oven for 10 to 12 minutes or until edges are golden and tops spring back when lightly touched. Cool in molds on wire racks for 1 minute. Using the point of a knife, loosen each cookie from mold; invert cookies onto wire racks. Remove molds and let cookies cool. Before serving, sift powdered sugar over tops of cookies.

TO STORE: Place in layers separated by waxed paper in an airtight container; cover. Store at room temperature up to 3 days or freeze up to 3 months. Thaw cookies; sift with powdered sugar.

Coffee Madeleines

If you prefer, add a sprinkle of powdered sugar to the tops of the cookies instead of the drizzle of icing.

Makes: 24 cookies

Oven: 375°F

　2　**egg yolks**

½　**cup granulated sugar**

⅓　**cup butter, melted and cooled**

　2　**teaspoons instant espresso**
　　　coffee powder

½　**teaspoon vanilla**

　2　**egg whites**

½　**cup all-purpose flour**

½　**teaspoon baking powder**

⅛　**teaspoon baking soda**

⅛　**teaspoon salt**

¼　**cup very finely**
　　　chopped almonds

　1　**recipe Espresso Icing**

1. Grease and flour twenty-four 3-inch madeleine molds; set aside. In a medium mixing bowl beat egg yolks and granulated sugar with an electric mixer on medium to high speed for 30 seconds. Add melted butter, espresso powder, and vanilla. Beat on low speed until combined, scraping sides of bowl occasionally. Beat in egg whites until combined.

2. In a small bowl stir together flour, baking powder, baking soda, and salt. Sift or sprinkle about one-fourth of the flour mixture over egg yolk mixture; gently fold in. Fold in remaining flour mixture one-fourth at a time. Fold in almonds.

3. Spoon batter into prepared molds, filling each mold about half full. Bake in a 375° oven for 10 to 12 minutes or until edges are golden and tops spring back when lightly touched. Cool in molds on wire racks for 1 minute. Using the point of a knife, loosen each cookie from mold; invert cookies onto wire racks. Remove molds and let cookies cool. Drizzle Espresso Icing over cooled cookies; let dry.

Espresso Icing: In a small bowl combine ½ teaspoon instant espresso coffee powder and 1 tablespoon water. Stir in 1 cup sifted powdered sugar. Stir in additional water, 1 teaspoon at a time, to make drizzling consistency.

TO STORE: Place in layers separated by waxed paper in an airtight container; cover. Store at room temperature up to 3 days or freeze undrizzled cookies up to 3 months. Thaw cookies; drizzle with icing.

Chocolate *Madeleines*

Thanks to a little cocoa in the mix, this classic tea cake shows up on the chocolate-lover's list of favorites too.

Makes: 24 cookies

Oven: 350°F

Butter

Unsweetened cocoa powder

²/₃ **cup butter**

 3 **ounces semisweet**

　　chocolate, chopped

¹/₂ **cup sugar**

¹/₃ **cup all-purpose flour**

¹/₈ **teaspoon salt**

 2 **eggs**

¹/₂ **teaspoon vanilla**

1. Generously butter twenty-four 3-inch madeleine molds. Sprinkle molds with cocoa powder; tap out excess. Set aside. In a small heavy saucepan melt the ²/₃ cup butter and semisweet chocolate over low heat, stirring occasionally. Remove from heat; cool to room temperature.

2. In a small bowl stir together sugar, flour, and salt; set aside. In a medium mixing bowl beat eggs with an electric mixer on medium speed about 2 minutes or until frothy. Reduce speed to low; beat in flour mixture just until combined. Beat in butter-chocolate mixture and vanilla. Let batter stand for 5 minutes until slightly thickened.

3. Using a slightly rounded tablespoon measure for each, spread batter into prepared molds. Bake in a 350° oven for 10 to 12 minutes or until tops spring back when lightly touched and a wooden toothpick inserted in center comes out clean. Using the point of a knife, loosen each cookie from mold; invert cookies onto wire racks. Remove molds; let cool.

TO STORE: Place in layers separated by waxed paper in an airtight container; cover. Store at room temperature up to 3 days or freeze up to 3 months.

Remembrance of great cookies past

Although madeleines were named after a French pastry chef (whose name was Madeleine), it was French writer Marcel Proust who made the little tea cake famous. As an adult, upon tasting one of these buttery shell-shape treats dipped into a cup of tea, a flood of childhood memories engulfed the writer. It was this moment, he claimed, that triggered his 3,500-page masterpiece, *Remembrance of Things Past.*

There is no guarantee that the cookie-size cake will have quite the same effect, but it's sure to be a memorable goodie indeed. It's easy to make too—just get yourself a shell-shape mold, available at specialty cookware stores and through mail-order sources.

Madeleine *Santas*

A lot of creative Santa cookies have come and gone over the years, but this has to be one of the best! Who would have thought that shell-shape madeleines make splendid beards? *(photo, page 142)*

Makes: 24 cookies

Oven: 375°F

2 eggs

½ teaspoon vanilla

½ teaspoon finely shredded
   lemon peel

1 cup sifted powdered sugar

⅔ cup all-purpose flour

¼ teaspoon baking powder

½ cup butter, melted and cooled

1 recipe Snow Frosting

1 recipe Powdered Sugar Icing
   Assorted decorative candies
   Powdered sugar

1. Grease and flour twenty-four 3-inch madeleine molds; set aside. Beat eggs, vanilla, and lemon peel on high speed for 5 minutes. Gradually beat in the 1 cup powdered sugar. Beat for 5 to 7 minutes or until thick and satiny.

2. Sift together flour and baking powder. Sift or sprinkle about one-fourth of flour mixture over egg mixture. Gently stir in flour mixture. Stir in remaining flour mixture one-fourth at a time. Stir in melted butter.

3. Spoon batter into prepared molds, filling each mold three-fourths full. Bake in a 375° oven for 10 to 12 minutes or until edges are golden and tops spring back when lightly touched. Cool in molds for 1 minute. Loosen cookies from molds; invert onto wire racks. Remove molds; let cool.

4. To decorate, pipe Snow Frosting from a decorating bag fitted with a medium star tip for a textured look. To add fine details, pipe Powdered Sugar Icing from a decorating bag fitted with a writing tip. Add decorative candies and a sprinkling of powdered sugar. Let frosting dry.

Snow Frosting: Beat ½ cup shortening and ½ teaspoon vanilla. Gradually beat in 1⅓ cups sifted powdered sugar. Add 1 tablespoon milk. Gradually beat in 1 cup sifted powdered sugar and enough milk (3 to 4 teaspoons) to make piping consistency. Color frosting with paste food coloring.

Powdered Sugar Icing: Combine 4 cups sifted powdered sugar, 1 teaspoon vanilla, and enough milk (3 to 4 tablespoons) to make drizzling consistency. Color icing as desired with paste food coloring.

TO STORE: Place in layers separated by waxed paper in an airtight container; cover. Store at room temperature up to 3 days or freeze undecorated cookies up to 3 months. Thaw cookies; decorate.

Peppermint Stars

If you want to dip the stars in chocolate, do so just before serving. Once the stars are dipped, the crispy meringue begins to soften.

Makes: 40 cookies

Oven: 300°F

  2 **egg whites**

½ **teaspoon vanilla**

¼ **teaspoon cream of tartar**

½ **cup sugar**

¼ **teaspoon peppermint extract**

    Red food coloring (optional)

  3 **ounces semisweet chocolate**

  1 **tablespoon shortening**

1. In a medium mixing bowl let egg whites stand, covered, at room temperature for 30 minutes. Line two large cookie sheets with parchment paper; set aside.

2. Preheat oven to 300°. Add vanilla and cream of tartar to egg whites. Beat with an electric mixer on medium speed until soft peaks form (tips curl). Gradually add sugar, 2 tablespoons at a time, beating on high speed until stiff, glossy peaks form (tips stand straight) and sugar dissolves. Quickly beat in peppermint extract, and, if desired, 2 to 3 drops red food coloring to tint mixture pink.

3. Using a decorating bag fitted with a ½-inch star tip, pipe meringue mixture 1½ inches in diameter onto prepared cookie sheets. Place cookie sheets on oven racks in the 300° oven. Turn off oven and let cookies dry in oven with door closed for 1 hour or until dry and crisp but still light in color. Let cool on parchment paper. Gently remove stars.

4. Just before serving, in a small heavy saucepan melt chocolate and shortening over low heat, stirring constantly. Dip bottom of each star into chocolate mixture, allowing excess to drip off. Place on waxed paper; let stand until set.

TO STORE: Place undipped cookies in layers separated by waxed paper in an airtight container; cover. Store at room temperature up to 3 days or freeze up to 3 months. If frozen, thaw cookies; just before serving, dip in melted chocolate.

Elf Hats

Heavenly meringues are made even more dreamy with chocolate and nuts. Hint: After baking, pipe on a bit of tinted icing. *(photo, page 142)*

Makes: about 48 cookies

Oven: 300°F

2 egg whites

½ teaspoon vanilla

⅛ teaspoon cream of tartar

Green or red food coloring

⅔ cup sugar

6 ounces bittersweet

chocolate or semisweet

chocolate, chopped

¾ cup finely chopped walnuts

Purchased decorator icing

(optional)

1. In a medium mixing bowl let egg whites stand, covered, at room temperature for 30 minutes. Grease two cookie sheets; set aside.

2. Preheat oven to 300°. Add vanilla, cream of tartar, and 2 or 3 drops food coloring to egg whites. Beat with an electric mixer on medium speed until soft peaks form (tips curl). Gradually add sugar, 1 tablespoon at a time, beating on high speed about 5 minutes or until stiff, glossy peaks form (tips stand straight).

3. Using a decorating bag fitted with a ½-inch round tip, pipe mixture into small 1-inch-high mounds that end in an angled tip about 1 inch apart on prepared cookie sheets. Place cookie sheets on oven racks in the 300° oven. Turn off oven and let cookies dry in oven with door closed for 1 hour or until dry and crisp but still light in color. Let cool on cookie sheets. Gently remove cookies.

4. In a small heavy saucepan melt chocolate over low heat, stirring frequently. When cookies are cool, dip bottoms into melted chocolate and into chopped walnuts. Place on waxed paper; let stand until set. If desired, add a dot of colored icing to each tip.

TO STORE: Place undipped cookies in layers separated by waxed paper in an airtight container; cover. Store at room temperature up to 3 days or freeze up to 3 months. Just before serving, dip in melted chocolate and in walnuts.

Spritz

Generations of kids have eagerly waited for their turn to squeeze the buttery spritz dough from the cookie press to the cookie sheet. For colorful variations, tint portions of the dough with paste food coloring.

Makes: about 84 cookies

Oven: 375°F

1½ **cups butter, softened**

  1 **cup granulated sugar**

  1 **teaspoon baking powder**

  1 **egg**

  1 **teaspoon vanilla**

¼ **teaspoon almond extract (optional)**

3½ **cups all-purpose flour**

  Colored sugar (optional)

  1 **recipe Decorative Frosting (optional)**

  Confetti and/or candies (optional)

1. In a medium mixing bowl beat butter with an electric mixer on medium to high speed for 30 seconds. Add granulated sugar and baking powder. Beat until combined, scraping sides of bowl occasionally. Beat in egg, vanilla, and, if desired, almond extract until combined. Beat in as much of the flour as you can with the mixer. Stir in remaining flour with a wooden spoon.

2. Pack dough into a cookie press. Force dough through press onto an ungreased cookie sheet. If desired, sprinkle cookies with colored sugar. Bake in a 375° oven for 8 to 10 minutes or until edges are firm but not brown. Transfer cookies to a wire rack and let cool. If desired, decorate unsugared cookies with Decorative Frosting and confetti and/or candies.

Chocolate Spritz: Prepare as above, except reduce all-purpose flour to 3¼ cups and add ¼ cup unsweetened cocoa powder with the granulated sugar.

Nutty Spritz: Prepare as above, except reduce granulated sugar to ⅔ cup and all-purpose flour to 3¼ cups. After adding flour, stir in 1 cup finely ground toasted almonds or hazelnuts (filberts).

Decorative Frosting: In a medium mixing bowl beat 4 cups sifted powdered sugar and 3 tablespoons milk with an electric mixer on medium to high speed until smooth. Beat in additional milk, 1 teaspoon at a time, until frosting is of piping consistency. Tint frosting as desired with paste food coloring.

TO STORE: Place in layers separated by waxed paper in an airtight container; cover. Store at room temperature up to 3 days or freeze undecorated cookies up to 3 months. Thaw cookies; decorate, if desired.

Almond Cream Spritz

Put a spin on the old reliable. This recipe imbues one of the world's favorite butter cookies with a delightful almondy essence.

Makes: about 48 cookies

Oven: 375°F

  1 **cup butter, softened**

  1 **3-ounce package cream
      cheese, softened**

 ½ **cup sugar**

 ½ **teaspoon almond extract**

 ¼ **teaspoon vanilla**

  2 **cups all-purpose flour**

      Finely chopped almonds

1. In a large mixing bowl beat butter and cream cheese with an electric mixer on medium to high speed for 30 seconds. Add sugar, almond extract, and vanilla. Beat until combined, scraping sides of bowl occasionally. Beat in as much of the flour as you can with the mixer. Stir in any remaining flour with a wooden spoon.

2. Pack dough into a cookie press. Force dough through press onto an ungreased cookie sheet. Sprinkle with almonds. Bake in a 375° oven for 8 to 10 minutes or until edges of cookies are firm but not brown. Transfer cookies to a wire rack and let cool.

TO STORE: Place in layers separated by waxed paper in an airtight container; cover. Store at room temperature up to 3 days or freeze up to 3 months.

Softening cream cheese in microwave

It happens—you're all ready to bake and your recipe calls for softened cream cheese. What to do? Use the microwave! Place the unwrapped cream cheese in a microwave-safe bowl. Microwave, uncovered, on 100% power (high). Allow 10 to 20 seconds for 3 ounces and 30 to 60 seconds for 8 ounces or until cream cheese begins to soften. Let stand for 5 minutes to completely soften.

Pumpkin *Spritz*

This version of the original is slightly softer than a classic spritz cookie, but the flavor—enhanced with pumpkin and spice—is every bit as delicious.

Makes: about 60 cookies

Oven: 400°F

- 1 **cup butter, softened**
- ½ **cup sugar**
- ¾ **teaspoon baking powder**
- ¾ **teaspoon ground cinnamon**
- ½ **teaspoon ground nutmeg**
- ¼ **teaspoon ground ginger**
- ⅓ **cup canned pumpkin**
- 1 **egg**
- 1 **teaspoon vanilla**
- 2¾ **cups all-purpose flour**
  Ground nutmeg (optional)

1. In a medium mixing bowl beat butter with an electric mixer on medium to high speed for 30 seconds. Add sugar, baking powder, cinnamon, ½ teaspoon nutmeg, and ginger. Beat until combined, scraping sides of bowl occasionally. Beat in pumpkin, egg, and vanilla until combined. Beat in as much of the flour as you can with the mixer. Stir in any remaining flour with a wooden spoon.
2. Pack dough into a cookie press. Force dough through cookie press onto an ungreased cookie sheet. If desired, sprinkle with additional nutmeg. Bake in a 400° oven for 6 to 8 minutes or until edges are firm but not brown. Transfer cookies to a wire rack and let cool.

TO STORE: Place in layers separated by waxed paper in an airtight container; cover. Store at room temperature up to 3 days or freeze up to 3 months.

Hazelnut Spritz

Contrary to popular belief, you don't need a cookie press to make these cookies. The narrow drizzles are simply piped from a pastry bag. A piping of melted semisweet chocolate dresses up the pretty sticks. *(photo, page 141)*

Makes: about 40 cookies

Oven: 325°F/350°F

¾ cup hazelnuts (filberts)

¾ cup butter, softened

½ cup sugar

1 egg

1½ teaspoons vanilla

1½ cups all-purpose flour

2 ounces semisweet
    chocolate, cut up

¼ teaspoon shortening

1. Spread hazelnuts in a shallow baking pan. Bake in a 325° oven about 15 minutes or until lightly toasted; cool. Place nuts between folds of a kitchen towel and rub with towel to remove skins. Place nuts in a food processor bowl or blender container. Cover and process or blend until finely ground; set aside. Increase oven temperature to 350°.

2. In a large mixing bowl beat butter with an electric mixer on medium to high speed for 30 seconds. Beat in sugar until combined, scraping sides of bowl occasionally. Beat in egg and vanilla until combined. Stir in flour and ground nuts with a wooden spoon.

3. Place dough in a pastry bag fitted with a large star tip (½-inch opening). Pipe dough in 2½-inch lengths onto an ungreased cookie sheet. Bake in a 350° oven about 10 minutes or until edges begin to brown. Transfer cookies to a wire rack placed over waxed paper and let cool.

4. In a small heavy saucepan melt chocolate and shortening over low heat, stirring frequently. Pour into a small, self-sealing plastic bag; seal. Cut a small hole in one corner of the bag and pipe chocolate onto cookies; let stand until set.

TO STORE: Place in layers separated by waxed paper in an airtight container; cover. Store at room temperature up to 3 days or freeze undrizzled cookies up to 3 months. Thaw cookies; drizzle with chocolate.

Hazelnut Spritz, page 140

ABOVE: Elf Hats, page 136; Chocolate Pizzelles, page 149
BELOW: Madeleine Santas, page 134; Meringue-Topped Fruit Tarts, page 128

ABOVE: Lemon Tuiles, page 156   RIGHT: Spicy Molasses Waffle Squares, page 154
BELOW: Speculaas, page 153

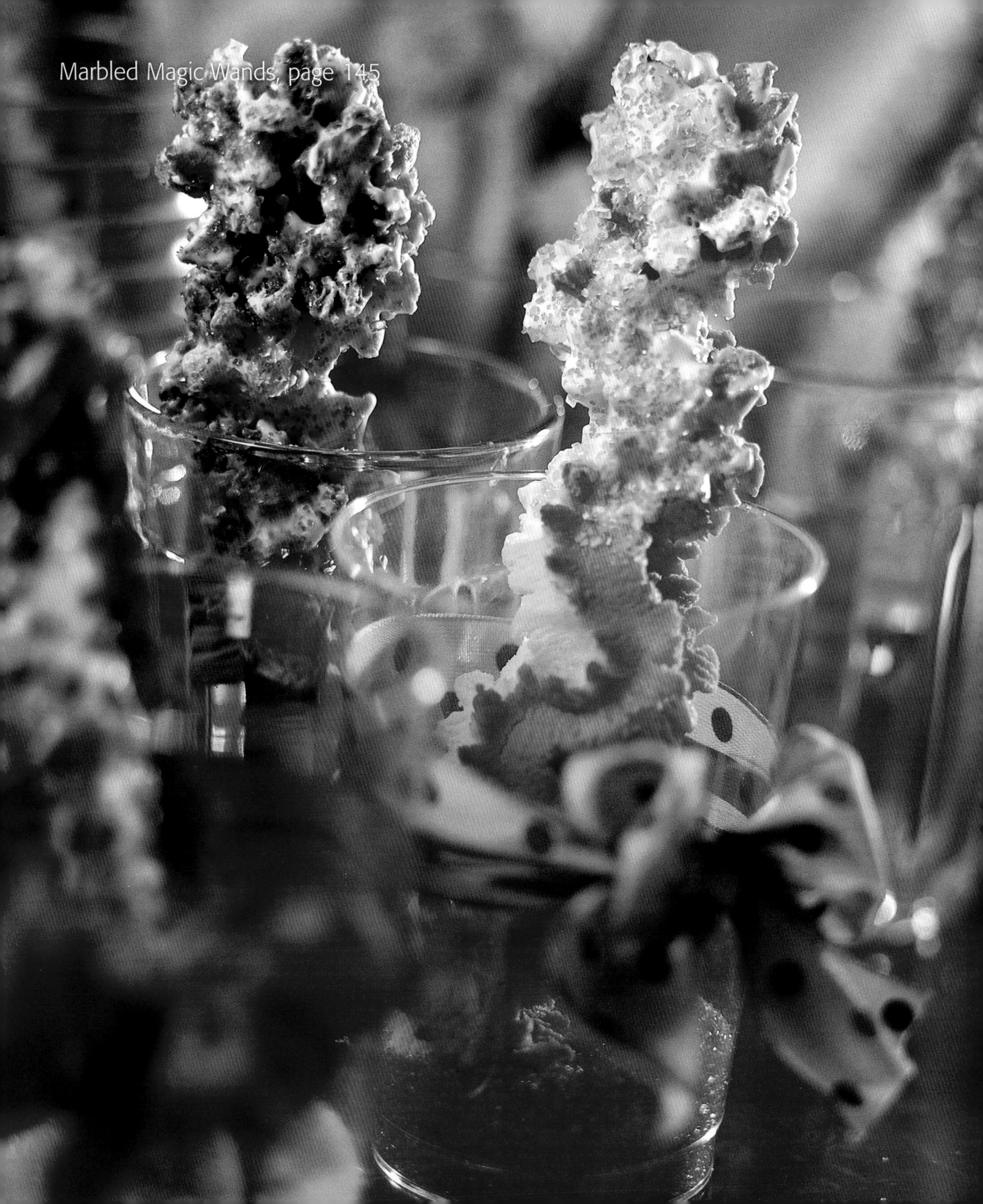

Marbled Magic Wands, page 145

Marbled Magic Wands

Dub yourself the royal baker and the kids your loyal students before making these treats. A little kitchen magic—food coloring, a cookie press, and colored sugars and candies—gives these wands the "wow!" factor kids love. (photo, page 144)

Makes: about 36 cookies

Oven: 375°F

1 cup butter, softened

1 cup granulated sugar

1 teaspoon baking powder

1 egg

2 teaspoons vanilla

3½ cups all-purpose flour

Assorted colors paste
   food coloring

1½ cups white baking pieces

1 tablespoon butter-flavored
   or regular shortening

Colored sugars or small
   multicolored decorative
   candies

1. In a large mixing bowl beat butter with an electric mixer on medium to high speed for 30 seconds. Add granulated sugar and baking powder. Beat until combined, scraping sides of bowl occasionally. Beat in egg and vanilla. Beat in as much of the flour as you can with the mixer. Stir in remaining flour with a wooden spoon.

2. Divide dough in half. Tint half of the dough as desired with paste food coloring. Leave remaining half of dough plain or tint with another color.

3. Pack both colors of dough into a cookie press, keeping doughs separate by placing them side by side in press. Using a large star plate in the press, force dough through press onto an ungreased cookie sheet to form wands about 5 inches long. Bake in a 375° oven about 10 minutes or until edges are firm but not brown. Cool on cookie sheet for 1 minute. Transfer cookies to wire racks and let cool.

4. In a small heavy saucepan melt white baking pieces and shortening over low heat, stirring constantly. Dip an end of each cookie into melted white baking pieces, allowing excess to drip off. Sprinkle with colored sugar or multicolored candies. Place cookies on waxed paper; let stand until set.

TO STORE: Place in layers separated by waxed paper in an airtight container; cover. Store at room temperature up to 3 days or freeze undipped cookies up to 3 months. Thaw cookies; dip in melted baking pieces and sprinkle with colored sugar.

holiday treat

Mocha *Logs*

The shape of these cookies may be playful, but their combination of coffee, chocolate, and pecans makes them very sophisticated. It's the perfect cookie for gourmets who don't take themselves too seriously!

Makes: about 72 cookies

Oven: 375°F

1	cup butter, softened
³/₄	cup sugar
4	teaspoons instant espresso coffee powder
¹/₂	teaspoon salt
¹/₄	teaspoon baking powder
1	egg
1	teaspoon vanilla
2¹/₃	cups all-purpose flour
8	ounces semisweet chocolate, chopped
1¹/₂	cups finely chopped pecans

1. In a large mixing bowl beat butter with an electric mixer on medium to high speed for 30 seconds. Add sugar, espresso powder, salt, and baking powder. Beat until combined, scraping sides of bowl occasionally. Beat in egg and vanilla until combined. Beat in as much of the flour as you can with the mixer. Stir in any remaining flour with a wooden spoon.

2. Pack dough into a cookie press. Using a star plate in the press, force dough through the press into 3-inch-long strips onto an ungreased cookie sheet. Bake in a 375° oven for 10 to 12 minutes or until edges are firm. Transfer cookies to a wire rack and let cool.

3. In a small heavy saucepan melt chocolate over low heat, stirring frequently. Remove from heat; cool slightly. Dip each end of cookies in melted chocolate, allowing excess to drip off. Sprinkle pecans over chocolate. Place cookies on waxed paper; let stand until set.

TO STORE: **Place in layers separated by waxed paper in an airtight container; cover. Store at room temperature up to 3 days or freeze undipped cookies up to 3 months. Thaw cookies; dip in chocolate and sprinkle with nuts.**

Out of pecans? Oh, nuts! What should you do if you don't have a specific nut a recipe calls for? In most recipes, nuts are selected for the particular flavor and appearance, so it may be worth a trip to the store. However, in general, walnuts may be substituted for pecans, and almonds for hazelnuts (filberts), and vice versa.

Citrus *Pinwheels*

Your medium of choice is an easy egg yolk "paint" that lets you get the decorating done before these citrus-twist cookies get to the oven.

Makes: about 48 cookies

Oven: 375°F

    1 cup butter, softened
    1 3-ounce package cream
       cheese, softened
 ½ cup sugar
    2 teaspoons finely shredded
       orange peel
    1 teaspoon finely shredded
       lemon peel
 ½ teaspoon finely shredded
       lime peel
 ½ teaspoon vanilla
2¼ cups all-purpose flour
    1 recipe Egg Yolk Paint

1. In a large mixing bowl beat butter and cream cheese with an electric mixer on medium to high speed for 30 seconds. Add sugar, orange peel, lemon peel, lime peel, and vanilla. Beat until combined, scraping sides of bowl occasionally. Beat in as much of the flour as you can with the mixer. Stir in any remaining flour with a wooden spoon.

2. Pack dough into a cookie press. Using a pinwheel plate in the press, force dough through press onto an ungreased cookie sheet. Brush a pattern on top of each cookie with all three Egg Yolk Paint colors. Bake in a 375° oven for 12 to 14 minutes or until edges are firm but not brown. Transfer cookies to a wire rack and let cool.

Egg Yolk Paint: To make green, yellow, and orange paints, in each of three small bowls combine 1 egg yolk and 1 teaspoon water. Add 1 or 2 drops of green food coloring to one bowl, 1 or 2 drops of yellow food coloring to the second bowl, and 1 drop of red food coloring plus 4 drops of yellow food coloring to the third bowl.

TO STORE: Place in layers separated by waxed paper in an airtight container; cover. Store at room temperature up to 3 days or freeze up to 3 months.

Pizzelles

Here's a classic version of Italy's crisp, wafflelike pizzelle (peets-TSEH-leh), one of the oldest cookie recipes known. You'll need a special, intricately designed iron—either an electric model or one that can be heated on the stove top—in order to make them.

Makes: 18 pizzelles

  2 **cups all-purpose flour**

  1 **tablespoon baking powder**

1½ **teaspoons ground nutmeg**

 ½ **teaspoon ground cardamom**

  3 **eggs**

 ¾ **cup sugar**

 ⅓ **cup butter, melted and cooled**

  2 **teaspoons vanilla**

1. In a medium bowl stir together flour, baking powder, nutmeg, and cardamom; set aside. In a large mixing bowl beat eggs with an electric mixer on high speed about 4 minutes or until thick and lemon-colored. Gradually beat in sugar on medium speed. Beat in cooled butter and vanilla, scraping sides of bowl occasionally. Add flour mixture, beating on low speed until combined.

2. Heat an electric pizzelle iron according to manufacturer's directions. (Or heat a pizzelle iron on the stove top over medium heat until a drop of water sizzles on the grid. Reduce heat to medium-low.)

3. For each pizzelle, place a slightly rounded tablespoon of batter on pizzelle iron, slightly off center toward back of grid. Close lid. Bake according to manufacturer's directions. (For a nonelectric iron, bake about 2 minutes or until golden brown, turning once.) Turn warm pizzelle out onto a paper towel to cool. Repeat with remaining batter.

TO STORE: Place in layers separated by waxed paper in an airtight container; cover. Store at room temperature up to 3 days or freeze up to 3 months.

Chocolate *Pizzelles*

You'll need a pizzelle mold to make these Italian treats, but that's a small inconvenience when you imagine how much the intricate wafers add to your cookie tray! Hint: Since these cookies get crispier as they cool, be sure to cut them in halves or quarters while they are hot. *(photo, page 142)*

Makes: about 36 pizzelle halves

1½ **cups toasted hazelnuts**
     (filberts)

2¼ **cups all-purpose flour**

3 **tablespoons unsweetened**
     cocoa powder

1 **tablespoon baking powder**

3 **eggs**

1 **cup granulated sugar**

⅓ **cup butter, melted and cooled**

2 **teaspoons vanilla**

1 **recipe Chocolate Glaze**

1. Finely chop 1 cup of the hazelnuts; set aside. Place remaining ½ cup hazelnuts in a blender container or food processor bowl. Cover and blend or process until very fine but dry and not oily.

2. Stir together ground hazelnuts, flour, cocoa powder, and baking powder; set aside. In a large mixing bowl beat eggs with an electric mixer on high speed about 4 minutes or until thick and lemon-colored. Gradually beat in sugar on medium speed. Beat in cooled butter and vanilla. Add flour mixture, beating on low speed until combined.

3. Heat an electric pizzelle iron according to manufacturer's directions. (Or heat a pizzelle iron on the stove top over medium heat until a drop of water sizzles on the grid. Reduce heat to medium-low.)

4. For each pizzelle, place a slightly rounded tablespoon of batter on pizzelle iron, slightly off center toward back of grid. Close lid. Bake according to manufacturer's directions. (For a nonelectric iron, bake about 2 minutes or until golden brown, turning once.) Turn warm pizzelle onto a cutting board; cut in half or into quarters. Transfer pizzelles to a paper towel to cool. Repeat with remaining batter.

5. Dip the rounded edge of each pizzelle piece into Chocolate Glaze; dip into reserved finely chopped hazelnuts. Place on a wire rack until glaze is set.

Chocolate Glaze: In a small bowl stir together 1½ cups sifted powdered sugar, 3 tablespoons unsweetened cocoa powder, and ½ teaspoon vanilla. Stir in enough milk (2 to 3 tablespoons) to make a glaze.

TO STORE: Place in layers separated by waxed paper in an airtight container; cover. Store at room temperature up to 3 days or freeze unglazed cookies up to 3 months. Thaw cookies; dip in glaze and in nuts.

Rosettes

Look for rosette irons at specialty kitchen shops or in mail-order catalogs. Savvy shoppers can find sets that offer more than one iron shape.

Makes: about 25 rosettes

1 **egg**

1 **tablespoon granulated sugar**

½ **cup all-purpose flour**

½ **cup milk**

1 **teaspoon vanilla**

Cooking oil for deep-fat frying

Colored sugar or powdered
  sugar

1. In a small mixing bowl stir together egg and granulated sugar. Add flour, milk, and vanilla. Beat with a rotary beater or wire whisk until mixture is smooth.
2. Heat a rosette iron in deep, hot oil (375°F) for 30 seconds. Remove iron from oil and briefly drain on paper towels. Dip hot iron into batter (batter should extend three-fourths of the way up sides of iron). Immediately dip iron into hot oil. Fry for 20 to 30 seconds or until rosette is golden. Lift out iron and tip slightly to drain. With a fork, push rosette off iron onto paper towels placed over wire racks.
3. Repeat with remaining batter, reheating rosette iron in oil about 10 seconds each time before dipping it into batter. Sprinkle with colored sugar while warm or sift powdered sugar over rosettes when cool.

TO STORE: Place in layers separated by waxed paper in an airtight container; cover. Store at room temperature up to 3 days or freeze up to 3 months. Thaw rosettes; sprinkle with additional powdered sugar, if using.

Nutmeg Rosettes

Swedish and Norwegian immigrants first brought these delicate fried cookies to Minnesota. From there, they became an American coffee-time tradition.

Makes: about 42 rosettes

2 **beaten eggs**

1 **cup all-purpose flour**

1 **cup milk**

1 **tablespoon granulated sugar**

1 **teaspoon ground nutmeg**

1 **teaspoon vanilla**

¼ **teaspoon salt**

Cooking oil for deep-fat frying

Powdered sugar or colored sugar

1. In a medium mixing bowl combine eggs, flour, milk, granulated sugar, nutmeg, vanilla, and salt. Beat with a rotary beater or wire whisk until mixture is smooth.

2. Heat a rosette iron in deep, hot oil (375°F) for 30 seconds. Remove iron from oil and briefly drain on paper towels. Dip hot iron into batter (batter should extend three-fourths of the way up sides of iron). Immediately dip iron into hot oil. Fry for 20 to 30 seconds or until rosette is golden. Lift out iron and tip slightly to drain. With a fork, push rosette off iron onto paper towels placed over wire racks.

3. Repeat with remaining batter, reheating rosette iron in oil about 10 seconds each time before dipping it into batter. Sift powdered sugar or sprinkle colored sugar over rosettes.

TO STORE: Place in layers separated by waxed paper in an airtight container; cover. Store at room temperature up to 3 days or freeze up to 3 months. Thaw rosettes; sprinkle with additional powdered sugar, if using.

Egg equivalents Recipes in this book were developed and tested using large eggs. If you purchase eggs in other sizes, adjust the number you use to ensure the best results for your cookies.

Large Eggs	Other Size Equivalents
1 large egg	1 jumbo, 1 extra-large, 1 medium, or 1 small egg
2 large eggs	2 jumbo, 2 extra-large, 2 medium, or 3 small eggs
3 large eggs	2 jumbo, 3 extra-large, 3 medium, or 4 small eggs
4 large eggs	3 jumbo, 4 extra-large, 5 medium, or 5 small eggs
5 large eggs	4 jumbo, 4 extra-large, 6 medium, or 7 small eggs
6 large eggs	5 jumbo, 5 extra-large, 7 medium, or 8 small eggs

Krumkake

You can enjoy these paper-thin cookies plain, or, for a special treat, fill the finished cones

with sweetened whipped cream and serve immediately.

Makes: 24 cookies

¹⁄₂ **cup butter**

3 **eggs**

¹⁄₂ **cup sugar**

¹⁄₂ **cup all-purpose flour**

1 **teaspoon vanilla or ¹⁄₂ teaspoon**
   almond extract

   Dash ground nutmeg

1. In a saucepan melt butter; cool slightly. In a medium mixing bowl beat eggs with an electric mixer on medium speed for 1 minute. Add sugar; beat about 3 minutes or until sugar is almost dissolved, scraping sides of bowl occasionally. Stir melted butter into egg mixture. Stir in flour, vanilla, and nutmeg just until smooth.

2. Heat a krumkake iron on the stove top over medium-low heat. For a 6-inch iron, spoon about 1 tablespoon of batter onto the hot, ungreased iron. Close gently but firmly. Cook over medium-low heat about 30 seconds. Open iron carefully. Loosen cookie with a narrow spatula; invert onto a wire rack. Immediately roll the cookie around a metal cone or cylinder. Let cookie cool around the cone or cylinder until it holds the shape. Place rolled cookies on a wire rack and let cool. Reheat the iron and repeat with remaining batter.

TO STORE: Place in a single layer in an airtight container; cover. Store at room temperature up to 3 days or freeze up to 3 months.

> **Why is butter best?** All of the recipes in this book call for butter because nothing beats the flavor and richness that butter brings. Many margarines contain more water than oil and yield undesirable results. If you decide to use margarine instead of butter, buy a stick margarine (not a tub) that contains at least 80% vegetable oil. If you can't determine the oil content from the front of the package, check the nutrition label; the best margarine for our purposes has at least 100 calories per tablespoon.

holiday treat

Speculaas

In North America, you may have seen these spice cookies in the shape of windmills; however, if you travel to Germany, the Netherlands, and Denmark, you'll find them in many shapes. Look for a variety of cookie molds in specialty kitchen shops and mail-order catalogs. *(photo, page 143)*

Makes: about 8 (6-inch) or 48 (2- to 2½-inch) cookies

Oven: 350°F

½ cup butter

¾ cup packed brown sugar

¾ teaspoon ground cinnamon

½ teaspoon baking powder

¼ teaspoon ground nutmeg

¼ teaspoon ground cloves

⅛ teaspoon salt

1 egg yolk

1 tablespoon milk

1⅓ cups all-purpose flour

3 tablespoons finely chopped blanched almonds (optional)

Powdered Sugar Glaze (optional)

1. In a large mixing bowl beat butter with an electric mixer on medium to high speed for 30 seconds. Add brown sugar, cinnamon, baking powder, nutmeg, cloves, and salt. Beat until combined, scraping sides of bowl occasionally. Beat in egg yolk and milk. Beat in as much of the flour as you can with the mixer. Stir in any remaining flour and, if desired, the almonds with a wooden spoon. Divide dough in half. Cover and chill about 1 hour or until dough is easy to handle.

2. Lightly grease a cookie sheet; set aside. Press a small amount of dough into a lightly oiled cookie mold.* Unmold dough onto the prepared cookie sheet. If cookie does not unmold easily, tap mold on counter to release dough. Place cookies 1 inch apart on prepared cookie sheet.

3. Bake in a 350° oven for 8 to 10 minutes or until edges are golden. Cool on cookie sheet for 1 minute. Transfer cookies to a wire rack and let cool. If desired, decorate cookies with Powdered Sugar Glaze.

*Note: If you do not own cookie molds, on a lightly floured surface, roll one portion of the dough at a time to a ⅛-inch thickness. Using cookie cutters, cut into desired shapes. Place cookies 1 inch apart on prepared cookie sheets. Bake as directed.

Powdered Sugar Glaze: In a small bowl combine 1½ cups sifted powdered sugar and 4 teaspoons milk. Stir in additional milk, 1 teaspoon at a time, to make a glaze of piping consistency.

TO STORE: Place in layers separated by waxed paper in an airtight container; cover. Store at room temperature up to 3 days or freeze undecorated cookies up to 3 months. Thaw cookies; decorate with glaze.

Spicy Molasses *Waffle* Squares

Sweet enough to eat for breakfast, these molasses-spice cookies are baked in a waffle baker.

(photo, page 143)

Makes: about 28 cookies

⅔ **cup all-purpose flour**

½ **cup whole wheat flour**

½ **cup packed brown sugar**

½ **teaspoon baking powder**

¼ **teaspoon salt**

¼ **teaspoon ground cinnamon**

⅛ **teaspoon ground ginger**

   Dash ground cloves

2 **slightly beaten eggs**

¼ **cup butter, melted**

2 **tablespoons molasses**

1 **recipe Orange Glaze**

1. Lightly grease a waffle baker; preheat. In a medium bowl stir together all-purpose flour, whole wheat flour, brown sugar, baking powder, salt, cinnamon, ginger, and cloves. Set flour mixture aside.

2. In small bowl combine eggs, melted butter, and molasses. Add egg mixture all at once to flour mixture. Stir just until mixture is moistened.

3. Drop batter by rounded teaspoons 3 inches apart onto grids of prepared waffle baker. Close lid. Bake about 1 minute or until cookies are golden brown. When done, use a fork to lift cookies off waffle baker. Transfer cookies to a wire rack and let cool. Repeat with remaining batter. Drizzle cooled cookies with Orange Glaze.

Orange Glaze: In a small bowl stir together 1 cup sifted powdered sugar and ½ teaspoon finely shredded orange peel. Stir in enough orange juice (3 to 4 teaspoons) to make glaze of drizzling consistency.

TO STORE: Place in layers separated by waxed paper in an airtight container; cover. Store in the refrigerator up to 3 days or freeze undrizzled cookies up to 3 months. Thaw cookies; drizzle with glaze.

Pecan Snaps with *Espresso* Cream

Add these elegant and scrumptious snaps to your list of special-occasion cookies. Prepare the coffee-spiked cream and fill the crispy cones just before serving. They're also delicious filled with plain whipped cream.

Makes: about 30 small or 11 large cookies

Oven: 350°F

¼ **cup packed brown sugar**

3 **tablespoons butter, melted**

2 **tablespoons dark-colored corn syrup**

1 **tablespoon coffee liqueur or brewed coffee**

½ **cup finely chopped pecans**

¼ **cup all-purpose flour**

1 **cup whipping cream**

¼ **cup sifted powdered sugar**

4 **teaspoons instant espresso coffee powder**

Grated chocolate (optional)

1. Lightly grease a cookie sheet or line with foil; set aside. In a small bowl stir together brown sugar, melted butter, corn syrup, and coffee liqueur. Stir in pecans and flour until combined.

2. For each cookie, drop batter by level teaspoons 3 inches apart, or level tablespoons 5 inches apart, onto the prepared cookie sheet. (Bake only 4 or 5 cookies at a time.) Bake in a 350° oven for 7 to 8 minutes for smaller cookies or 8 to 10 minutes for larger cookies or until cookies are bubbly and a deep golden brown. Cool cookies on cookie sheet for 1 to 2 minutes or until set. Using a wide spatula, quickly remove a cookie; roll cookie around a metal cone or the greased handle of a wooden spoon. When cookie is firm, slide cookie off cone or spoon and cool completely on a wire rack. Repeat with remaining cookies, one at a time. (If cookies harden before you shape them, reheat in oven about 1 minute or until softened.)

3. Up to 30 minutes before serving, in a large mixing bowl beat whipping cream, powdered sugar, and espresso coffee powder with an electric mixer on low speed until stiff peaks form. Pipe or spoon some of the whipped cream into each cookie. If desired, sprinkle with grated chocolate.

TO STORE: Place unfilled cookies in a single layer in an airtight container; cover. Store at room temperature up to 3 days or freeze up to 3 months. Thaw cookies; up to 30 minutes before serving, fill.

Lemon *Tuiles*

These light and lemony French cookies were named after the curved roof tiles they resemble.

To achieve the gentle curves, drape warm-from-the-oven cookies over a rolling pin.

(photo, page 143)

Makes: about 24 cookies

Oven: 375°F

  2 **egg whites**

¼ **cup butter, melted**

  2 **teaspoons finely shredded**

      lemon peel

¼ **teaspoon lemon extract**

½ **cup sugar**

½ **cup all-purpose flour**

1. In a medium mixing bowl let egg whites stand at room temperature for 30 minutes. Line a cookie sheet with foil or parchment paper. Lightly grease foil-lined cookie sheet; set aside. In a small bowl combine butter, lemon peel, and lemon extract; set aside.

2. Beat egg whites with an electric mixer on medium speed until soft peaks form (tips curl). Gradually add sugar, beating on high speed until stiff peaks form (tips stand straight). Fold in about half of the flour. Gently fold in butter mixture. Fold in remaining flour until combined.

3. For each cookie, drop a level tablespoon of batter onto the prepared cookie sheet (bake only 3 or 4 cookies at a time). Using the back of a spoon, spread batter into 3-inch circles. Bake in a 375° oven for 5 to 7 minutes or until cookies are golden brown around edges. Using a wide spatula, immediately remove cookies and drape in a single layer over a standard-size rolling pin (place cookies with the side that was against the cookie sheet against the rolling pin). Cool cookies on rolling pin until they hold their shape; carefully slide off rolling pin. Transfer cookies to a wire rack and let cool.

TO STORE: Place in layers separated by waxed paper in an airtight container; cover. Store at room temperature up to 3 days or freeze up to 3 months.

Slices of Delight

Oatmeal *Refrigerator* Cookies

These crisp slices are great for making ice-cream-filled cookie sandwiches. Hint: Because this particular dough is made with all shortening, you'll have to put it in the freezer to firm it up enough for slicing.

Makes: about 56 cookies

Oven: 350°F

1½ **cups all-purpose flour**

1 **teaspoon salt**

1 **teaspoon baking soda**

1 **teaspoon ground cinnamon**

1 **cup shortening**

1 **cup granulated sugar**

1 **cup packed brown sugar**

2 **eggs**

1 **teaspoon vanilla**

1½ **cups quick-cooking rolled oats**

½ **cup finely chopped walnuts**

1. In a bowl stir together flour, salt, baking soda, and cinnamon; set flour mixture aside. In a large mixing bowl beat shortening with an electric mixer on medium to high speed for 30 seconds. Add granulated sugar and brown sugar. Beat until combined, scraping sides of bowl occasionally. Add eggs, one at a time, beating well after each addition. Beat in vanilla until combined. Beat in as much of the flour mixture as you can with the mixer. Stir in any remaining flour mixture with a wooden spoon. Stir in oats and walnuts.

2. Divide dough in half. Shape each half into an 8-inch-long roll. Wrap in plastic wrap or waxed paper. Freeze for 8 to 24 hours or until firm enough to slice.

3. Grease a large cookie sheet; set aside. Cut rolls into ¼-inch slices. Place slices 2 inches apart on prepared cookie sheet. Bake in a 350° oven for 10 to 12 minutes or until edges are lightly browned. Cool on cookie sheet for 1 minute. Transfer cookies to a wire rack and let cool.

TO STORE: Place in layers separated by waxed paper in an airtight container; cover. Store at room temperature up to 3 days or freeze up to 3 months.

Brown Sugar *Icebox* Cookies

Refrigerators with freezers replaced iceboxes long ago, but the recipe's old-fashioned name is preserved. You have to admit it lends an air of grandmotherly goodness to these homemade gems.

Makes: about 72 cookies

Oven: 375°F

½ cup butter, softened

½ cup shortening

1¼ cups packed brown sugar

½ teaspoon baking soda

¼ teaspoon salt

1 egg

1 teaspoon vanilla

2½ cups all-purpose flour

¾ cup ground hazelnuts (filberts) or pecans, toasted

⅔ cup finely chopped hazelnuts (filberts) or pecans, toasted (optional)

1 recipe Browned Butter Icing

1. In a large mixing bowl beat butter and shortening with an electric mixer for 30 seconds. Add brown sugar, baking soda, and salt. Beat until combined, scraping sides of bowl occasionally. Beat in egg and vanilla until combined. Beat in as much of the flour as you can with the mixer. Stir in any remaining flour. Stir in the ¾ cup ground nuts.
2. Divide dough in half. Shape each half into a 10-inch-long roll. If desired, roll in the ⅔ cup chopped nuts. Wrap in plastic wrap or waxed paper. Chill for 4 to 24 hours or until firm enough to slice.
3. Cut rolls into ¼-inch slices. Place slices 1 inch apart on an ungreased cookie sheet. Bake in a 375° oven for 7 to 8 minutes or until edges are firm and lightly browned. Transfer cookies to a wire rack and let cool. Drizzle with Browned Butter Icing; let dry.

Browned Butter Icing: In a small heavy saucepan heat 2 tablespoons butter over medium heat until butter turns the color of light brown sugar, stirring frequently. Remove from heat. Using an electric mixer, slowly beat in 1½ cups sifted powdered sugar, 1 teaspoon vanilla, and enough milk (1 to 2 tablespoons) to make drizzling consistency.

TO STORE: Place in layers separated by waxed paper in an airtight container; cover. Store at room temperature up to 3 days or freeze undrizzled cookies up to 3 months. Thaw cookies; drizzle.

> ### *Skinning nuts* Some recipes call for the skin to be removed from nuts such as almonds and hazelnuts (filberts). To do this, toast the nuts lightly, place the nuts in between folds of a clean kitchen towel, and rub the nuts with the towel to remove the skins.

Praline Rounds

These crisp, tender cookies celebrate the famous Louisiana praline, a duo of brown sugar and pecans. Topping it off, a drizzle of brown sugar and cream frosting adds a welcome southern-style sweetness.

Makes: about 72 cookies

Oven: 375°F

½ cup butter, softened

½ cup shortening

1 cup packed brown sugar

½ teaspoon baking powder

¼ teaspoon baking soda

¼ teaspoon salt

1 egg

2 tablespoons milk

1 teaspoon vanilla

3 cups all-purpose flour

1 cup finely chopped pecans

1 recipe Brown Sugar Frosting

1. In a large mixing bowl beat butter and shortening with an electric mixer on medium to high speed for 30 seconds. Add brown sugar, baking powder, baking soda, and salt. Beat until combined, scraping sides of bowl occasionally. Beat in egg, milk, and vanilla until combined. Beat in as much of the flour as you can with the mixer. Stir in any remaining flour with a wooden spoon. Stir in ½ cup of the pecans.

2. Divide dough in half. Shape each half into a 10-inch-long roll. Wrap in plastic wrap or waxed paper. Chill for 4 to 24 hours or until firm enough to slice.

3. Cut rolls into ¼-inch slices. Place slices 2 inches apart on an ungreased cookie sheet. Bake in a 375° oven for 8 to 10 minutes or until edges are firm. Transfer cookies to a wire rack and let cool.

4. Drizzle Brown Sugar Frosting over cookies; immediately sprinkle with the remaining ½ cup pecans. Let dry.

Brown Sugar Frosting: In a small heavy saucepan combine 1 cup packed brown sugar, ¼ cup butter, and ¼ cup half-and-half or light cream. Heat and stir over medium heat until mixture comes to a full boil. Boil for 1 minute, stirring constantly. Remove from heat. Add 1⅓ cups sifted powdered sugar. Beat with a wire whisk to make drizzling consistency. (If frosting begins to get stiff, add a few drops hot water and stir until drizzling consistency.)

TO STORE: Place in layers separated by waxed paper in an airtight container; cover. Store at room temperature up to 3 days or freeze undrizzled cookies up to 3 months. Thaw cookies; drizzle and sprinkle with nuts.

Black Walnut *Pinwheels*

Black walnuts are tough nuts to crack, but true devotees find them well worth the effort.

The less devoted have the option of buying them shelled and ready to use at the supermarket.

Makes: about 44 cookies

Oven: 375°F

½ **cup shortening**

½ **cup packed brown sugar**

¾ **teaspoon baking soda**

¼ **teaspoon salt**

1 **egg**

1¾ **cups all-purpose flour**

⅓ **cup butter, melted**

⅔ **cup packed brown sugar**

½ **teaspoon black walnut**

flavoring (optional)

1 **cup finely ground**

black walnuts

1. In a large mixing bowl beat shortening with an electric mixer on medium to high speed for 30 seconds. Add the ½ cup brown sugar, baking soda, and salt. Beat until combined, scraping sides of bowl occasionally. Beat in egg until combined. Beat in as much of the flour as you can with the mixer. Stir in any remaining flour with a wooden spoon. Cover and chill dough for 1 to 2 hours or until easy to handle.

2. Meanwhile, in a small bowl combine melted butter, the ⅔ cup brown sugar, walnut flavoring (if desired), and walnuts.

3. On a lightly floured surface, roll dough into a 12-inch square. Spread walnut mixture evenly over the dough square to within ½ inch of edges. Carefully roll up dough. Moisten edges; pinch to seal. Wrap in plastic wrap or waxed paper. Chill for 3 to 24 hours or until firm enough to slice.

4. Cut rolls into ¼-inch slices. Place slices 2 inches apart on an ungreased cookie sheet. Bake in a 375° oven for 7 to 9 minutes or until edges are lightly browned. Cool on cookie sheet for 1 minute. Transfer cookies to a wire rack and let cool.

TO STORE: Place in layers separated by waxed paper in an airtight container; cover. Store at room temperature up to 3 days or freeze up to 3 months.

Brown Sugar-Brickle Rounds

Soft, with just the right amount of crunch, these cookies offer the best of both worlds. Brown sugar makes them moist and sweet; almond brickle adds the nutty crunch.

Makes: about 72 cookies

Oven: 350°F

½ cup butter, softened

½ cup shortening

1 cup packed brown sugar

½ teaspoon baking powder

½ teaspoon baking soda

¼ teaspoon salt

1 egg

2 tablespoons milk

½ teaspoon almond extract

3 cups all-purpose flour

1 7½-ounce package (1⅓ cups)
   almond brickle pieces

1. In a large mixing bowl beat butter and shortening with an electric mixer on medium to high speed for 30 seconds. Add brown sugar, baking powder, baking soda, and salt. Beat until combined, scraping sides of bowl occasionally. Beat in egg, milk, and almond extract until combined. Beat in as much of the flour as you can with the mixer. Stir in any remaining flour with a wooden spoon. Stir in almond brickle pieces.

2. Divide dough in half. Shape each half into a 10-inch-long roll. Wrap in plastic wrap or waxed paper. Chill for 4 to 24 hours or until firm enough to slice.

3. Cut rolls into ¼-inch slices. Place slices 2 inches apart on an ungreased cookie sheet. Bake in a 350° oven about 9 minutes or until edges are firm. Transfer cookies to a wire rack and let cool.

TO STORE: Place in layers separated by waxed paper in an airtight container; cover. Store at room temperature up to 3 days or freeze up to 3 months.

One at a time, please! Chilled dough is much easier to handle than warm dough; therefore, if a recipe makes more than one roll of dough, take only one roll at a time from the refrigerator to slice. Keep the other one chilled until you're ready for it.

Café Brûlot *Cookies*

At least one cup of café brûlot—a flaming drink of coffee, spices, citrus peels, and brandy—is a must for every visitor to New Orleans. This recipe brings the specialty home in a festive cookie.

Makes: about 40 cookies

Oven: 375°F

1 cup packed brown sugar

½ cup pecan pieces

1 teaspoon instant coffee
    crystals

½ teaspoon ground cinnamon

¼ teaspoon ground cloves

½ cup butter

1 tablespoon finely shredded
    lemon peel

1 tablespoon finely shredded
    orange peel

1 tablespoon brandy or milk

1 egg yolk

1¾ cups all-purpose flour

1 recipe Brandy Icing

1. In a food processor bowl combine brown sugar, pecans, coffee crystals, cinnamon, and cloves. Cover and process until nuts are finely chopped. Add butter, lemon peel, and orange peel; process until butter is evenly mixed. Add brandy and egg yolk; process until combined. Add flour gradually, processing until combined.

2. Divide dough in half. Shape each half into a 6-inch-long roll. Wrap in plastic wrap or waxed paper. Chill for 2 to 24 hours or until firm enough to slice.

3. Cut rolls into ¼-inch slices. Place slices 1½ inches apart on an ungreased cookie sheet. Bake in a 375° oven for 7 to 8 minutes or until lightly browned. Transfer cookies to a wire rack and let cool. Drizzle with Brandy Icing; let dry.

Brandy Icing: In a small bowl combine 1 cup sifted powdered sugar, 1 tablespoon brandy or strong coffee, and ½ teaspoon vanilla. Add milk, 1 teaspoon at a time, to make drizzling consistency.

TO STORE: Place in layers separated by waxed paper in an airtight container; cover. Store at room temperature up to 3 days or freeze undrizzled cookies up to 3 months. Thaw cookies; drizzle.

Pfeffernüesse

You'll come to know this one as the sweet and spicy cookie with the funny name. Pfeffernüesse has been a holiday favorite of German cooks for centuries. It's bite-size and, therefore, useful for punctuating a tray of larger cookies. *(photo, page 178)*

Makes: about 240 small cookies

Oven: 350°F

⅓ **cup mild-flavored molasses**

¼ **cup butter**

2 **cups all-purpose flour**

¼ **cup packed brown sugar**

¾ **teaspoon ground cinnamon**

½ **teaspoon baking soda**

¼ **teaspoon ground cardamom**

¼ **teaspoon ground allspice**

⅛ **teaspoon black pepper**

1 **beaten egg**

1. In a small saucepan combine molasses and butter. Cook and stir over low heat until butter melts; remove from heat. Pour into a large bowl and cool to room temperature.

2. In a medium bowl stir together flour, brown sugar, cinnamon, baking soda, cardamom, allspice, and pepper; set flour mixture aside.

3. Stir egg into cooled molasses mixture. Gradually stir in flour mixture until combined, kneading in the last of the flour mixture by hand, if necessary. Cover and chill dough about 1 hour or until easy to handle.

4. Divide dough into 12 portions. On a lightly floured surface, roll each portion into a rope about 10 inches long. Cut ropes into ½-inch pieces. Place pieces ½ inch apart in an ungreased shallow baking pan. Bake in a 350° oven about 10 minutes or until edges are firm and bottoms are lightly browned. Transfer cookies to paper towels and let cool.

TO STORE: Place in layers separated by waxed paper in an airtight container; cover. Store at room temperature up to 3 days or freeze up to 3 months.

Why chill out? Many cookie recipes call for chilling the dough in the refrigerator before shaping, slicing, or rolling because doing so helps to stiffen the butter or shortening and makes the dough more manageable. Chilling also results in a better finished product because you need to work chilled dough less than unchilled dough.

Chill all cookie doughs made with butter or shortening in the refrigerator for the time recommended in the recipe. If you're using margarine for sliced or shaped cookies, quick-chill the dough in the freezer for one-third of the refrigerator chilling time. Do not quick-chill cookie dough that's made with butter or shortening in the freezer; it will become too firm.

For rolled cookies made with margarine, refrigerate the dough at least five hours or freeze for two hours before rolling.

holiday
treat

Santa's *Whiskers*

The cloud of coconut that clings to each slice represents St. Nick's beard. Use these treats to remind your kids to be good for goodness' sake. *(photo, page 214)*

Makes: about 56 cookies

Oven: 375°F

³/₄ **cup butter, softened**

³/₄ **cup sugar**

1 **tablespoon milk**

1 **teaspoon vanilla**

2 **cups all-purpose flour**

³/₄ **cup finely chopped candied**

red and/or green cherries

¹/₃ **cup finely chopped pecans**

³/₄ **cup coconut**

1. In a large mixing bowl beat butter with an electric mixer on medium to high speed for 30 seconds. Add sugar. Beat until combined, scraping sides of bowl occasionally. Beat in milk and vanilla until combined. Beat in as much of the flour as you can with the mixer. Stir in any remaining flour with a wooden spoon. Stir in candied cherries and pecans.

2. Divide dough in half. Shape each half into an 8-inch-long roll; roll in coconut. Wrap in plastic wrap or waxed paper. Chill for 2 to 24 hours or until firm enough to slice.

3. Cut rolls into ¼-inch slices. Place slices 1 inch apart on an ungreased cookie sheet. Bake in a 375° oven for 10 to 12 minutes or until edges are golden brown. Transfer cookies to a wire rack and let cool.

TO STORE: Place in layers separated by waxed paper in an airtight container; cover. Store at room temperature up to 3 days or freeze up to 3 months.

Toasted *Coconut* Wafers

Each crispy bite celebrates the sweet taste of coconut inside and out. Shredded coconut is stirred into the dough, which is shaped into rolls that are enveloped with more coconut. *(photo, page 178)*

Makes: about 56 cookies

Oven: 375°F

1 **cup butter, softened**

1¼ **cups sifted powdered sugar**

½ **teaspoon almond**

  extract or vanilla

⅛ **teaspoon salt**

1 **egg yolk**

2¼ **cups all-purpose flour**

1 **cup coconut, toasted**

1 **beaten egg white**

1½ **cups coconut**

1. In a large mixing bowl beat butter with an electric mixer on medium to high speed for 30 seconds. Add powdered sugar, almond extract, and salt. Beat until combined, scraping sides of bowl occasionally. Beat in egg yolk until combined. Beat in as much of the flour as you can with the mixer. Stir in any remaining flour with a wooden spoon. Stir in the 1 cup toasted coconut.

2. Divide dough in half. Shape each half into an 8-inch-long roll. Brush rolls with egg white; roll in the 1½ cups coconut. Wrap in plastic wrap or waxed paper. Chill for 4 to 24 hours or until firm enough to slice.

3. Cut rolls into ¼-inch slices. Place slices 1 inch apart on an ungreased cookie sheet. Bake in a 375° oven for 10 to 12 minutes or until edges are lightly browned. Cool on cookie sheet for 1 minute. Transfer cookies to a wire rack and let cool.

TO STORE: Place in layers separated by waxed paper in an airtight container; cover. Store at room temperature up to 3 days or freeze up to 3 months.

Pretty up your cookies Slice-and-bake cookies are generally good-looking cookies that don't require embellishment. If you want to give them an extra touch of loveliness, roll the dough log in finely chopped nuts, colored sugar, or coconut. Press to make coating stick and chill as directed in the recipe.

Italian Fig Spirals

Fig cookies at Christmas are as Italian as opera, but don't be afraid to serve them any time of year, especially if you're in the market for an opulent treat. *(photo, page 214)*

Makes: about 56 cookies

Oven: 375°F

⅓ **cup butter, softened**

1 **cup sugar**

½ **teaspoon baking powder**

1 **egg**

3 **tablespoons milk**

½ **teaspoon vanilla**

2½ **cups all-purpose flour**

1 **cup finely snipped dried figs**

⅓ **cup orange marmalade**

¼ **cup orange juice**

1. In a large mixing bowl beat butter with an electric mixer on medium to high speed for 30 seconds. Add sugar and baking powder. Beat until combined, scraping sides of bowl occasionally. Beat in egg, milk, and vanilla until combined. Beat in as much of the flour as you can with the mixer. Stir in any remaining flour with a wooden spoon. Cover and chill dough about 1 hour or until easy to handle.

2. Meanwhile, for filling, in a small saucepan combine figs, marmalade, and orange juice. Cook and stir just until boiling; remove from heat. Set aside to cool.

3. Divide dough in half. Roll half of the dough between pieces of waxed paper into a 10×8-inch rectangle. Spread half of the filling over dough rectangle to within ½ inch of edges. Beginning with a short side, carefully roll up dough, using the waxed paper to lift and guide the roll. Moisten edges; pinch to seal. Wrap in plastic wrap or waxed paper. Repeat with remaining dough and filling. Chill for 4 to 24 hours or until firm enough to slice.

4. Line a large cookie sheet with foil. Grease foil; set aside. Cut rolls into ¼-inch slices. Place slices 2 inches apart on prepared cookie sheet. If desired, form each slice into a fig shape. Bake in a 375° oven for 9 to 11 minutes or until edges are firm and bottoms are lightly browned. Transfer cookies to a wire rack and let cool.

TO STORE: Place in layers separated by waxed paper in an airtight container; cover. Store at room temperature up to 3 days or freeze up to 3 months.

Cranberry-Orange Pinwheels

When it comes to pinwheel cookies, you can dress them up or down—these tangy cookies are definitely uptown.

Makes: about 72 cookies

Oven: 375°F

1   **cup cranberries**

1   **cup pecans**

¼   **cup packed brown sugar**

1   **cup butter, softened**

1½   **cups granulated sugar**

½   **teaspoon baking powder**

½   **teaspoon salt**

2   **eggs**

2   **teaspoons finely shredded orange peel**

3   **cups all-purpose flour**

1. For filling, in a blender container or food processor bowl combine cranberries, pecans, and brown sugar. Cover and blend or process until cranberries and nuts are finely chopped; set aside.

2. In a large mixing bowl beat butter with an electric mixer on medium to high speed for 30 seconds. Add granulated sugar, baking powder, and salt. Beat until combined, scraping sides of bowl occasionally. Beat in eggs and orange peel until combined. Beat in as much of the flour as you can with the mixer. Stir in any remaining flour with a wooden spoon. Cover and chill dough about 1 hour or until easy to handle.

3. Divide dough in half. Roll half of the dough between pieces of waxed paper into a 10-inch square. Spread half of the filling over the dough square to within ½ inch of the edges. Carefully roll up dough, using the waxed paper to lift and guide the roll. Moisten edges; pinch to seal. Wrap in plastic wrap or waxed paper. Repeat with remaining dough and filling. Chill for 2 to 24 hours or until firm enough to slice.

4. Cut rolls into ¼-inch slices. Place slices 2 inches apart on an ungreased cookie sheet. Bake in a 375° oven for 8 to 10 minutes or until edges are firm and bottoms are lightly browned. Cool on cookie sheet for 1 minute. Transfer cookies to a wire rack and let cool.

TO STORE: Place in layers separated by waxed paper in an airtight container; cover. Store at room temperature up to 3 days or freeze up to 3 months.

Bite-Size *Jam Swirls*

The coarse sugar, a crunchy topper, caps off the heavenly combination of fruit and nuts. Look

for coarse sugar at large supermarkets, specialty kitchen shops, or in mail-order catalogs.

Makes: about 52 cookies

Oven: 375°F

3   cups all-purpose flour

    Dash salt

1   8-ounce package cream cheese

1   cup butter

½   cup raspberry or

      strawberry jam

1   cup finely chopped walnuts

    Coarse sugar

1. In a large bowl combine flour and salt. Using a pastry blender, cut in cream cheese and butter until the mixture resembles fine crumbs and begins to cling together. Form mixture into a ball; knead until smooth. Divide dough in half. Wrap in plastic wrap or waxed paper. Chill about 1 hour or until easy to handle.

2. On a lightly floured surface, roll half of the dough at a time to ¼-inch thickness. Fold dough into thirds. Wrap in plastic wrap or waxed paper. Chill for 2 to 24 hours.

3. Line two cookie sheets with parchment paper; set aside. Remove one portion of dough from the refrigerator. On a lightly floured surface, roll dough into a 14×12-inch rectangle. Spread half of the jam evenly over the dough rectangle to within ½ inch of edges; sprinkle with half of the walnuts. Beginning with a long side, carefully roll up dough. Moisten edges; pinch to seal.

4. Cut rolls into ½-inch slices. Dip one cut side of each slice in coarse sugar. Place slices, sugar side up, 1 inch apart on prepared cookie sheets. Repeat with remaining dough, jam, and walnuts. Bake in a 375° oven about 15 minutes or until lightly browned. Transfer cookies to a wire rack and let cool.

TO STORE: Place in layers separated by waxed paper in an airtight container; cover. Store at room temperature up to 3 days or freeze up to 3 months.

> *Storing nuts* If you have nuts left over from a day of baking, be glad! Nuts have a long shelf life. Store unopened packages in a cool, dark place. Keep opened packages in an airtight container in the refrigerator for up to six months or in the freezer for up to one year.

Date *Pinwheels*

Some pinwheel enthusiasts can't get through the holidays without an appearance of these wonderfully old-fashioned homespun treats. Others eat them year-round.

Makes: about 88 cookies

Oven: 375°F

1   8-ounce package (1⅓ cups)
      pitted whole dates,
      finely snipped

½ cup water

⅓ cup granulated sugar

2   tablespoons lemon juice

½ teaspoon vanilla

½ cup butter, softened

½ cup shortening

½ cup granulated sugar

½ cup packed brown sugar

½ teaspoon baking soda

¼ teaspoon salt

1   egg

3   tablespoons milk

1   teaspoon vanilla

3   cups all-purpose flour

1. For filling, in a saucepan combine dates, water, and the ⅓ cup granulated sugar. Bring to boiling; reduce heat. Cook and stir about 2 minutes or until thick. Stir in lemon juice and the ½ teaspoon vanilla; set aside to cool.

2. In a large mixing bowl beat butter and shortening with an electric mixer on medium to high speed for 30 seconds. Add the ½ cup granulated sugar, the brown sugar, baking soda, and salt. Beat until combined, scraping sides of bowl occasionally. Beat in egg, milk, and the 1 teaspoon vanilla until combined. Beat in as much of the flour as you can with the mixer. Stir in any remaining flour with a wooden spoon. Cover and chill dough about 1 hour or until easy to handle.

3. Divide dough in half. Roll half of the dough between pieces of waxed paper into a 12×10-inch rectangle. Spread half of the filling over the dough rectangle to within ½ inch of the edges. Beginning with a long side, carefully roll up dough using the waxed paper to lift and guide the roll. Moisten edges; pinch to seal. Wrap in plastic wrap or waxed paper. Repeat with remaining dough and filling. Chill for 2 to 24 hours or until firm enough to slice.

4. Grease a large cookie sheet; set aside. Cut rolls into ¼-inch slices. Place slices 1 inch apart on the prepared cookie sheet. Bake in a 375° oven for 8 to 10 minutes or until edges are lightly browned. Transfer cookies to a wire rack and let cool.

TO STORE: Place in layers separated by waxed paper in an airtight container; cover. Store at room temperature up to 3 days or freeze up to 3 months.

Red *Raspberry* Twirls

This pretty, swirled cookie captures the magic of a classic Austrian linzertorte in a sweet that you can eat with your fingers.

Makes: about 56 cookies

Oven: 375°F

¹/₂ **cup butter, softened**

 1 **cup sugar**

¹/₂ **teaspoon baking powder**

 1 **egg**

 3 **tablespoons milk**

¹/₄ **teaspoon almond extract**

   (optional)

2³/₄ **cups all-purpose flour**

¹/₂ **cup seedless red raspberry jam**

1¹/₂ **teaspoons cornstarch**

¹/₂ **cup almonds, toasted**

   and ground

1. In a large mixing bowl beat butter with an electric mixer on medium to high speed for 30 seconds. Add sugar and baking powder. Beat until combined, scraping sides of bowl occasionally. Beat in egg, milk, and, if desired, almond extract. Beat in as much flour as you can with the mixer. Stir in any remaining flour with a wooden spoon. Cover and chill dough about 1 hour or until easy to handle.

2. Meanwhile, for filling, in a saucepan combine jam and cornstarch. Cook and stir until thickened and bubbly. Cook and stir for 1 minute more. Stir in almonds. Cover and set aside to cool.

3. Divide dough in half. Roll half of the dough between pieces of waxed paper into a 12×8-inch rectangle. Spread half of the filling over dough rectangle to within ¹/₂ inch of edges. Beginning with a short side, roll up dough, using the waxed paper to lift and guide the roll. Moisten edges; pinch to seal. Wrap in plastic wrap or waxed paper. Repeat with remaining dough and filling. Chill for 4 to 24 hours or until firm enough to slice.

4. Line a large cookie sheet with foil. Grease foil; set aside. Cut rolls into ¹/₄-inch slices. Place slices 2 inches apart on the prepared cookie sheet. Bake in a 375° oven for 9 to 11 minutes or until edges are firm and bottoms are lightly browned. Transfer cookies to a wire rack and let cool.

TO STORE: Place in layers separated by waxed paper in an airtight container; cover. Store at room temperature up to 3 days or freeze up to 3 months.

Citrus *Cheesecake* Slices

Love cheesecake? These lemony cream cheese cookies take after the real thing, suited up with a crust of graham crackers and nuts.

Makes: about 56 cookies

Oven: 375°F

¾ cup butter, softened

1 3-ounce package cream
    cheese, softened

¾ cup sugar

2 teaspoons finely shredded
    lemon peel

2 tablespoons lemon juice

2 teaspoons finely shredded
    orange peel

1 teaspoon vanilla

2 cups all-purpose flour

¼ cup finely chopped pecans

¼ cup finely crushed
    graham crackers

1. In a large bowl beat butter and cream cheese with an electric mixer on medium to high speed for 30 seconds. Add sugar, lemon peel, lemon juice, orange peel, and vanilla. Beat until combined, scraping sides of bowl occasionally. Beat in as much of the flour as you can with the mixer. Stir in any remaining flour with a wooden spoon. If necessary, cover and chill dough about 30 minutes or until easy to handle.

2. Stir together pecans and crushed crackers; set aside. Divide dough in half. Shape each half into an 8-inch-long roll; roll in nut mixture. Wrap in plastic wrap or waxed paper. Chill for 2 to 24 hours or until dough is firm enough to slice.

3. Cut rolls into ¼-inch slices. Place slices 2 inches apart on an ungreased cookie sheet. Bake in a 375° oven for 8 to 10 minutes or until bottoms are lightly browned. Cool on cookie sheet for 1 minute. Transfer cookies to a wire rack and let cool.

TO STORE: Place in layers separated by waxed paper in an airtight container; cover. Store at room temperature up to 3 days or freeze up to 3 months.

Sugar and Spice *Coffee* Slices

When life gets hectic, you can make this cookie in two easy-to-handle steps. Prepare the dough,

wrap the loaves in plastic, and put in the freezer for up to 1 week before slicing and baking.

(photo, page 178)

Makes: about 48 cookies

Oven: 375°F

2 **tablespoons instant espresso**
  coffee powder

1 **tablespoon hot water**

½ **cup butter, softened**

¼ **cup shortening**

1 **cup granulated sugar**

½ **cup packed brown sugar**

1 **teaspoon baking powder**

1 **teaspoon ground cinnamon**

¼ **teaspoon salt**

1 **egg**

2 **cups all-purpose flour**

1 **recipe Coffee Topping**

  Coffee beans (optional)

1. In a small bowl stir together the espresso powder and water until powder dissolves; set aside. In a large mixing bowl beat butter and shortening with an electric mixer on medium to high speed for 30 seconds. Add granulated sugar, brown sugar, baking powder, ground cinnamon, and salt. Beat until combined, scraping sides of bowl occasionally. Beat in egg and espresso mixture until combined. Beat in as much of the flour as you can with the mixer. Stir in any remaining flour with a wooden spoon.

2. Divide dough into three equal portions. Shape each portion into a 7-inch-long roll. Wrap in plastic wrap or waxed paper. Chill for 2 to 24 hours or until firm enough to slice.

3. Cut rolls into ⅜-inch slices. Place slices 2 inches apart on an ungreased cookie sheet. Sprinkle with Coffee Topping. If desired, gently press a few coffee beans into each slice. Bake in a 375° oven for 9 to 10 minutes or until edges are lightly browned. Cool on cookie sheet for 1 minute. Transfer cookies to a wire rack and let cool.

Coffee Topping: Stir together ¼ cup granulated sugar and 1 teaspoon instant espresso coffee powder.

TO STORE: Place in layers separated by waxed paper in an airtight container; cover. Store at room temperature up to 3 days or freeze up to 3 months.

Snickerdoodle Pinwheels

The popular cookie with the unusual name reinvents itself with a new shape and even more cinnamon.

(photo, page 214)

Makes: about 56 cookies

Oven: 375°F

⅓ cup sugar

1 tablespoon ground cinnamon

½ cup butter, softened

1 3-ounce package cream
    cheese, softened

1 cup sugar

½ teaspoon baking powder

1 egg

1 teaspoon vanilla

2⅔ cups all-purpose flour

1 tablespoon butter, melted

1. In a small bowl combine the ⅓ cup sugar and the cinnamon; set cinnamon-sugar mixture aside.

2. In a large mixing bowl beat the ½ cup butter and cream cheese with an electric mixer on medium to high speed for 30 seconds. Add the 1 cup sugar and baking powder. Beat until combined, scraping sides of bowl occasionally. Beat in egg and vanilla until combined. Beat in as much of the flour as you can with the mixer. Stir in any remaining flour with a wooden spoon. If necessary, cover and chill dough about 1 hour or until easy to handle.

3. Divide dough in half. Roll half of the dough between pieces of waxed paper into a 12×8-inch rectangle. Brush dough with half of the melted butter. Sprinkle with 2 tablespoons of the cinnamon-sugar mixture. Beginning with one of the short sides, carefully roll up dough, using the waxed paper to lift and guide the roll. Moisten edges; pinch to seal. Repeat with remaining dough, butter, and 2 tablespoons of the cinnamon-sugar mixture.

4. Roll each roll in the remaining cinnamon-sugar mixture. Wrap in plastic wrap or waxed paper. Chill for 4 to 24 hours or until firm enough to slice.

5. Cut rolls into ¼-inch slices. Place slices 1 inch apart on an ungreased cookie sheet. Bake in a 375° oven for 8 to 10 minutes or until edges are firm. Cool on cookie sheet for 1 minute. Transfer cookies to a wire rack and let cool.

TO STORE: Place in layers separated by waxed paper in an airtight container; cover. Store at room temperature up to 3 days or freeze up to 3 months.

Garden *Critter* Cookies

You'll keep the junior chefs busy with this one. Kids love molding this cookie dough into lively caterpillar and ladybug shapes. Simply roll up their sleeves and let the fun begin!

Makes: about 64 caterpillars or about 44 ladybugs

Oven: 375°F

1 cup butter, softened
1½ cups granulated sugar
1½ teaspoons baking powder
½ teaspoon salt
1 egg
1 teaspoon vanilla
2½ cups all-purpose flour
Paste food coloring
Purchased vanilla frosting (optional)
Semisweet chocolate, melted (optional)
Miniature candy-coated milk chocolate pieces

1. Beat butter with an electric mixer for 30 seconds. Add sugar, baking powder, and salt; beat until combined. Beat in egg and vanilla. Beat in as much of the flour as you can. Stir in any remaining flour.

Caterpillars: Divide dough in half. Using food coloring, tint half of the dough green and the other half blue. Divide each half of dough into four portions. Roll each portion into an 8-inch-long rope. Twist together one green rope and one blue rope; shape into a 1-inch-diameter roll. Repeat with remaining dough to make four rolls. Wrap rolls in plastic wrap. Chill 1 to 24 hours or until firm enough to slice. Cut rolls into ⅛-inch slices. For each caterpillar, overlap five to seven slices in a zigzag pattern on an ungreased cookie sheet. Bake in a 375° oven 5 to 6 minutes or until edges are lightly browned. Transfer to a wire rack; cool. Pipe colored frosting for eyes and mouths; let dry.

Ladybugs: Shape dough into a 12-inch-long roll. Wrap roll in plastic wrap. Chill for 1 to 24 hours or until firm enough to slice. Cut roll into ¼-inch slices. Place slices 1 inch apart on an ungreased cookie sheet. Bake in a 375° oven for 6 to 8 minutes or until edges are lightly browned. Transfer cookies to a wire rack and let cool. To decorate, use red paste food coloring to tint purchased vanilla frosting. Spread red frosting on top of cooled cookies. Pipe melted chocolate onto frosting to outline head and wings. Press miniature candy-coated milk chocolate pieces into frosting for spots; let dry.

TO STORE: Place in layers separated by waxed paper in an airtight container; cover. Store at room temperature up to 3 days or freeze undecorated cookies up to 3 months. Thaw cookies; decorate as desired.

Sugar Cookie Carolers

Turn ordinary sugar cookies into singing sensations. You can make every face in this chorus of carolers a one-of-a-kind treat. The possibilities are as limitless as your imagination.

(photo, page 177)

Makes: about 40 cookies

Oven: 375°F

¾ **cup butter, softened**

1 **cup granulated sugar**

½ **teaspoon baking powder**

½ **teaspoon salt**

1 **egg**

1 **teaspoon vanilla**

2½ **cups all-purpose flour**

   **Assorted colors of paste
     or liquid food coloring**

   **Small candies for decorating
    (optional)**

   Red petal dust (optional)

1 **recipe Powdered Sugar Icing
    (optional)**

1. Beat butter with an electric mixer on medium to high speed for 30 seconds. Add sugar, baking powder, and salt; beat until combined. Beat in egg and vanilla. Beat in as much of the flour as you can. Stir in any remaining flour.

2. Divide dough in half. Shape each half into a 6-inch-long roll. Wrap in plastic wrap or waxed paper. Chill for 2 to 24 hours or until firm enough to slice.

3. Cut rolls into ¼-inch slices. (Reserve several dough slices for decorating. Tint some of the dough with food coloring to form hats, hair, and earmuffs. To make hair, force dough through a garlic press.) For each caroler's face, place a dough slice on an ungreased cookie sheet. If desired, use a straw to make an oval-shape hole in the dough for the mouth. (It may be necessary to reform the mouth with the straw while baked cookie is still warm.) If desired, arrange small decorative candies for the eyes and nose and add other colored dough decorations before baking.*

4. Bake in a 375° oven for 6 to 8 minutes or until edges are lightly browned. Transfer to a rack; let cool. If desired, brush on petal dust to make cheeks.

*NOTE: If desired, instead of adding candy decorations before baking, tint Powdered Sugar Icing with food coloring and use a decorating bag and tips to pipe on icing, giving each caroler eyes and a nose after cookies have been baked and cooled.

Powdered Sugar Icing: Combine 1 cup sifted powdered sugar, ¼ teaspoon vanilla, and enough milk (2 to 4 teaspoons) to make piping consistency.

TO STORE: Place in layers separated by waxed paper in an airtight container; cover. Store at room temperature up to 3 days or freeze uniced cookies up to 3 months. Thaw cookies; decorate with icing.

LEFT: Sugar and Spice Coffee Slices, page 173   ABOVE RIGHT: Pfeffernüesse, page 164
BELOW: Toasted Coconut Wafers, page 166

ABOVE: Chocolate Ribbon Cookies, page 189; Chocolate Dotted-Orange Biscotti, page 194
BELOW: Lemon-Pistachio Biscotti, page 198; Scandinavian Almond Bars, page 191

Lemon and Poppy Seed Melts, page 181

holiday treat

Lemon and *Poppy Seed* Melts

To give these cookies a shimmering glow, add a tablespoon or two of edible glitter to the powdered sugar sprinkled on top. If necessary, freshen the sugar coating just before serving.

(photo, page 180)

Makes: about 32 cookies

Oven: 375°F

½ cup butter, softened

½ cup granulated sugar

1 tablespoon poppy seeds

⅛ teaspoon baking soda

1 egg yolk

1 tablespoon milk

2 teaspoons finely shredded
    lemon peel

½ teaspoon vanilla

1½ cups all-purpose flour

1 cup sifted powdered sugar

Yellow edible glitter (optional)

1. In a medium mixing bowl beat butter with an electric mixer on medium to high speed for 30 seconds. Add granulated sugar, poppy seeds, and baking soda. Beat until combined, scraping sides of bowl occasionally. Beat in egg yolk, milk, lemon peel, and vanilla until combined. Beat in as much of the flour as you can with the mixer. Stir in any remaining flour with a wooden spoon.

2. Divide dough in half. Shape each half into a 9-inch-long roll. Wrap in plastic wrap or waxed paper. Chill for 4 to 24 hours or until firm enough to slice.

3. Cut rolls into ½-inch slices. Place slices 1 inch apart on an ungreased cookie sheet. Bake in a 375° oven for 7 to 9 minutes or until edges are firm and bottoms are lightly browned.

4. Place powdered sugar in a plastic bag. If desired, add edible glitter to powdered sugar. While still warm, transfer several cookies at a time to the bag. Gently shake until coated. Transfer cookies to a wire rack and let cool. Gently shake cookies again in powdered sugar.

TO STORE: Place in layers separated by waxed paper in an airtight container; cover. Store at room temperature up to 3 days or freeze unsugared cookies up to 3 months. Thaw cookies; shake in powdered sugar.

Lemon and Poppy Seed Slices

When elegance is the effect you're after, choose these exquisite, buttery gems. They're a natural fit on a silver tea tray or as a gift for the sophisticate on your list.

Makes: about 56 cookies

Oven: 375°F

¾ cup butter, softened

1 cup sugar

1 egg

1 tablespoon milk

2 teaspoons finely shredded
   lemon peel

½ teaspoon vanilla

½ teaspoon lemon extract
   (optional)

2¼ cups all-purpose flour

2 tablespoons poppy seeds

Sanding sugar

1. In a medium mixing bowl beat butter with an electric mixer on medium to high speed for 30 seconds. Add sugar. Beat until combined, scraping sides of bowl occasionally. Beat in egg, milk, lemon peel, vanilla, and, if desired, lemon extract until combined. Beat in as much of the flour as you can with the mixer. Stir in any remaining flour with a wooden spoon. Stir in poppy seeds.

2. Divide dough in half. Shape each half into an 8-inch-long roll. Wrap in plastic wrap or waxed paper. Chill for 3 to 24 hours or until firm enough to slice.

3. Cut rolls into ¼-inch slices. Sprinkle with sanding sugar. Place slices 1 inch apart on an ungreased cookie sheet. Bake in a 375° oven for 11 to 12 minutes or until edges are golden. Transfer cookies to a wire rack and let cool.

TO STORE: Place in layers separated by waxed paper in an airtight container; cover. Store at room temperature up to 3 days or freeze up to 3 months.

No flats allowed Much of the appeal of slice-and-bake cookies is their pretty round shapes. To assure a clean shape, keep your dough in a perfect cylinder while it's chilling; slide the roll into a tall straight-sided drinking glass. While you're slicing, rotate the roll frequently to avoid flattening one side.

Mint *Swirls*

Crushed chocolate sandwich cookies—an easy filling—swirl through these mint-spiked cookies. Tinted a delicate shade of leprechaun green, they're just the thing to spread a bit of St. Patrick's Day cheer.

Makes: about 48 cookies

Oven: 375°F

¾ **cup butter, softened**

1 **cup sugar**

1 **teaspoon baking powder**

1 **egg**

¼ **teaspoon mint extract**

   Few drops green food coloring

2¼ **cups all-purpose flour**

½ **cup finely crushed chocolate sandwich cookies with white filling (about 6 cookies)**

½ **cup semisweet chocolate pieces (optional)**

1 **teaspoon shortening (optional)**

1. In a large mixing bowl beat butter with an electric mixer on medium to high speed for 30 seconds. Add sugar and baking powder. Beat until combined, scraping sides of bowl occasionally. Beat in egg, mint extract, and enough food coloring to tint dough light to medium green until combined. Beat in as much of the flour as you can with the mixer. Stir in any remaining flour with a wooden spoon. Cover and chill dough about 1 hour or until easy to handle.

2. Divide dough in half. Roll half of the dough between pieces of waxed paper into an 8×7-inch rectangle. Sprinkle half of the crushed cookies evenly over dough rectangle to within ¼ inch of the edges. Beginning with a short side, carefully roll up dough, using the waxed paper to lift and guide the roll. Moisten edges; pinch to seal. Wrap in plastic wrap or waxed paper. Repeat with remaining dough and crushed cookies. Chill for 4 to 24 hours or until firm enough to slice.

3. Cut rolls into ¼-inch slices. Place slices 2 inches apart on an ungreased cookie sheet. Bake in a 375° oven for 8 to 9 minutes or until edges are firm. Cool on cookie sheet for 1 minute. Transfer cookies to a wire rack and let cool.

4. If desired, in a small heavy saucepan melt chocolate pieces and shortening over low heat, stirring constantly. Drizzle over cookies; let stand until set.

TO STORE: Place in layers separated by waxed paper in an airtight container; cover. Store at room temperature up to 3 days or freeze undrizzled cookies up to 3 months. Thaw cookies; if desired, drizzle with melted chocolate.

Brownie Nut Slices

Are you subject to chocolate emergencies? Keep this dough in the freezer for whenever that chocolate urge strikes. Simply remember to thaw the dough in the refrigerator several hours for easier slicing.

Makes: about 60 cookies

Oven: 375°F

1 cup butter, softened

1½ cups sugar

1 teaspoon baking powder

¼ teaspoon baking soda

⅛ teaspoon salt

1 egg

4 ounces semisweet chocolate, melted and cooled

1 teaspoon vanilla

2½ cups all-purpose flour

Milk

¾ cup finely chopped walnuts

1. In a large mixing bowl beat butter with an electric mixer on medium to high speed for 30 seconds. Add sugar, baking powder, baking soda, and salt. Beat until combined, scraping sides of bowl occasionally. Beat in egg, chocolate, and vanilla until combined. Beat in as much of the flour as you can with the mixer. Stir in any remaining flour with a wooden spoon. If necessary, cover and chill dough for 1 to 2 hours until easy to handle.

2. Divide dough into three equal portions. Shape each portion into an 8½-inch-long roll. Brush rolls with milk; roll in walnuts. Wrap in plastic wrap or waxed paper. Chill for 4 to 24 hours or until firm enough to slice.

3. Cut rolls into ⅜-inch slices. Place slices 1 inch apart on an ungreased cookie sheet. Bake in a 375° oven about 10 minutes or until edges are set. Cool on cookie sheet for 1 minute. Transfer cookies to a wire rack and let cool.

TO STORE: Place in layers separated by waxed paper in an airtight container; cover. Store at room temperature up to 3 days or freeze up to 3 months.

Chocolate-Coconut Spirals

To the cookie that already has everything—cream cheese, nuts, and chocolate—coconut is added. Sometimes nothing impresses like excess.

Makes: about 72 cookies

Oven: 375°F

  1   **3-ounce package cream cheese, softened**
⅓   **cup sugar**
  1   **teaspoon vanilla**
  1   **cup coconut**
½   **cup finely chopped nuts**
⅓   **cup butter, softened**
  1   **cup sugar**
½   **teaspoon baking soda**
  1   **egg**
  1   **tablespoon milk**
¼   **cup unsweetened cocoa powder**
1½   **cups all-purpose flour**

1. For filling, in a small mixing bowl beat cream cheese, the ⅓ cup sugar, and the vanilla with an electric mixer on medium speed until smooth. Stir in coconut and nuts; set filling aside.

2. In a large mixing bowl beat butter with an electric mixer on medium to high speed for 30 seconds. Add the 1 cup sugar and the baking soda. Beat until combined, scraping sides of bowl occasionally. Beat in egg and milk until combined. Beat in cocoa powder and as much of the flour as you can with the mixer. Stir in any remaining flour with a wooden spoon. If necessary, cover and chill dough about 1 hour or until easy to handle.

3. Divide dough in half. Roll half of the dough between pieces of waxed paper into a 10×8-inch rectangle. Spread half of the filling over the dough rectangle to within ½ inch of the edges. Beginning with a long side, carefully roll up dough, using the waxed paper to lift and guide the roll. Moisten edges; pinch to seal. Wrap in plastic wrap or waxed paper. Repeat with remaining dough and filling. Chill for 4 to 24 hours or until dough is firm enough to slice.

4. Grease a large cookie sheet; set aside. Cut rolls into ¼-inch slices. Place slices 1 inch apart on prepared cookie sheet. Bake in a 375° oven about 8 minutes or until edges are firm. Transfer cookies to a wire rack and let cool.

TO STORE: Place in layers separated by waxed paper in an airtight container; cover. Store at room temperature up to 3 days or freeze up to 3 months.

Orange-Chocolate *Rounds*

Despite their intricate look, these fetching checkerboards are easy to make and shape. Add them to gift tins and party platters, and expect the compliments to come pouring in.

Makes: about 72 cookies

Oven: 375°F

1 cup butter, softened

1½ cups sugar

1½ teaspoons baking powder

¼ teaspoon salt

1 egg

1 teaspoon vanilla

2½ cups all-purpose flour

2 teaspoons finely shredded
   orange peel

2 ounces unsweetened chocolate,
   melted and cooled

1. In a large mixing bowl beat butter with an electric mixer on medium to high speed for 30 seconds. Add sugar, baking powder, and salt. Beat until combined, scraping sides of bowl occasionally. Beat in egg and vanilla until combined. Beat in as much of the flour as you can with the mixer. Stir in any remaining flour with a wooden spoon.

2. Divide dough in half. Stir orange peel into half of the dough. Stir melted chocolate into the other half of the dough. If necessary, cover and chill dough about 1 hour or until easy to handle.

3. Shape each half into a 10-inch-long roll. Wrap in plastic wrap or waxed paper. Chill for 2 to 24 hours or until firm enough to slice.

4. Cut rolls lengthwise into quarters. Reassemble rolls, alternating chocolate and orange quarters. Wrap and chill about 30 minutes more or until firm enough to slice.

5. Cut rolls into ¼-inch slices. Place slices 1 inch apart on an ungreased cookie sheet. Bake in a 375° oven for 7 to 9 minutes or until edges are firm and bottoms are lightly browned. Transfer cookies to a wire rack and let cool.

TO STORE: Place in layers separated by waxed paper in an airtight container; cover. Store at room temperature up to 3 days or freeze up to 3 months.

holiday
treat

Coffeehouse Flats

This stylish cookie is as rich as shortbread with the added delectability of cinnamon, coffee, and a half-moon coating of chocolate.

Makes: about 48 cookies

Oven: 350°F

2 **cups all-purpose flour**

1 **teaspoon ground cinnamon**
   (optional)

¼ **teaspoon salt**

1 **tablespoon instant**
   coffee crystals

1 **teaspoon water**

½ **cup butter, softened**

½ **cup shortening**

½ **cup granulated sugar**

½ **cup packed brown sugar**

2 **ounces unsweetened chocolate,**
   melted and cooled

1 **egg**

1½ **cups semisweet chocolate**
   pieces

2 **tablespoons shortening**

1. In a medium bowl stir together flour, cinnamon (if desired), and salt; set flour mixture aside. Stir coffee crystals and water until crystals dissolve; set aside.

2. In a large mixing bowl beat butter and the ½ cup shortening with an electric mixer on medium to high speed for 30 seconds. Add granulated sugar and brown sugar. Beat until combined, scraping sides of bowl occasionally. Beat in coffee mixture, melted chocolate, and egg until combined. Beat in as much of the flour mixture as you can with the mixer. Stir in any remaining flour mixture with a wooden spoon. Cover and chill dough about 1 hour or until easy to handle.

3. Divide dough in half. Shape each half into a 7-inch-long roll. Wrap in plastic wrap or waxed paper. Chill for 6 to 24 hours or until firm enough to slice.

4. Cut rolls into ¼-inch slices. Place slices 1 inch apart on an ungreased cookie sheet. Bake in a 350° oven about 8 minutes or until edges are firm and lightly browned. Transfer cookies to a wire rack and let cool.

5. In a small heavy saucepan melt chocolate pieces and the 2 tablespoons shortening over low heat, stirring constantly. Dip one half of each cookie into chocolate mixture; let stand until set.

TO STORE: Place in layers separated by waxed paper in an airtight container; cover. Store at room temperature up to 3 days or freeze undipped cookies up to 3 months. Thaw cookies; dip in melted chocolate.

Walnut-Chocolate Squares

You and your kids can have some fun decorating these toothsome, tile-shape treats. Pipe the vanilla or chocolate icing into pretty patterns or geometric mosaics. *(photo, page 214)*

Makes: about 42 cookies

Oven: 350°F

1 cup butter, softened

1 cup granulated sugar

⅓ cup unsweetened
    cocoa powder

1 teaspoon vanilla

⅛ teaspoon salt

1 cup walnuts, pecans, or
    hazelnuts (filberts),
    toasted and finely ground

2¼ cups all-purpose flour

1 recipe Vanilla Icing and/or
    Chocolate Icing

1. In a large mixing bowl beat butter with an electric mixer on medium to high speed for 30 seconds. Add sugar, cocoa powder, vanilla, and salt. Beat until combined, scraping sides of bowl occasionally. Beat in the ground nuts and as much of the flour as you can with the mixer. Stir in any remaining flour with a wooden spoon.

2. Shape dough into a 10×2-inch square log. Wrap in plastic wrap or waxed paper. Chill for 4 to 24 hours or until firm enough to slice.

3. Grease a large cookie sheet or line with parchment paper; set aside. Cut log into slightly less than ¼-inch slices. Place slices 1 inch apart on the prepared cookie sheet. Bake in a 350° oven for 8 to 10 minutes or until cookies look dry. Transfer cookies to a wire rack and let cool. Decorate as desired with Vanilla Icing and/or Chocolate Icing; let dry.

Vanilla Icing: In a small bowl stir together 1 cup sifted powdered sugar, ¼ teaspoon vanilla, and enough milk (1 to 2 tablespoons) to make drizzling consistency.

Chocolate Icing: In a small bowl stir together 1 cup sifted powdered sugar, 3 tablespoons unsweetened cocoa powder, ¼ teaspoon vanilla, and enough milk (1 to 2 tablespoons) to make drizzling consistency.

TO STORE: Place in layers separated by waxed paper in an airtight container; cover. Store at room temperature up to 3 days or freeze undecorated cookies up to 3 months. Thaw cookies; decorate as desired.

Chocolate *Ribbon* Cookies

These fancy striped cookies go as well with a frosty glass of milk as they do with a demitasse of espresso. *(photo, page 179)*

Makes: about 48 cookies

Oven: 375°F

½ **cup butter, softened**

½ **cup shortening**

1 **cup sugar**

½ **teaspoon baking soda**

⅛ **teaspoon salt**

1 **egg**

2 **tablespoons milk**

1 **teaspoon vanilla**

3 **cups all-purpose flour**

⅓ **cup miniature semisweet chocolate pieces, melted and cooled**

½ **cup finely chopped nuts**

½ **cup miniature semisweet chocolate pieces**

¼ **teaspoon rum flavoring**

1. In a large mixing bowl beat butter and shortening with an electric mixer on medium to high speed for 30 seconds. Add sugar, baking soda, and salt. Beat until combined, scraping sides of bowl occasionally. Beat in egg, milk, and vanilla until combined. Beat in as much of the flour as you can with the mixer. Stir in any remaining flour with a wooden spoon.

2. Divide dough in half. Stir the melted chocolate and nuts into half of the dough. Stir the ½ cup miniature chocolate pieces and rum flavoring into the other half of dough. Divide each portion of dough in half.

3. To shape dough, line the bottom and sides of a 9×5×3-inch loaf pan or baking dish with plastic wrap or waxed paper. Press half of the chocolate dough evenly into the pan; top with half of the vanilla dough. Repeat layers, pressing each layer firmly and evenly over the last layer. Cover and chill for 1 to 24 hours or until firm enough to slice.

4. Invert pan to remove dough. Peel off plastic wrap or waxed paper. Cut dough crosswise into thirds. Slice each third crosswise into ¼-inch slices. Place slices 2 inches apart on an ungreased cookie sheet. Bake in a 375° oven about 10 minutes or until edges are firm and bottoms are lightly browned. Transfer cookies to a wire rack and let cool.

TO STORE: Place in layers separated by waxed paper in an airtight container; cover. Store at room temperature up to 3 days or freeze up to 3 months.

holiday treat

Spumoni Slices

The festive Italian dessert rarely fails to bring smiles, and these tricolored takeoffs produce exactly the same effect.

Makes: about 72 cookies

Oven: 350°F

2½ cups all-purpose flour

1½ teaspoons baking powder

½ teaspoon salt

1 cup butter, softened

1½ cups sugar

1 egg

1 teaspoon vanilla

¼ teaspoon peppermint extract

5 drops red food coloring

¼ cup ground pistachio
    nuts or almonds

5 drops green food coloring

1 ounce unsweetened chocolate,
    melted and cooled

1. In a medium bowl stir together flour, baking powder, and salt; set flour mixture aside. In a large mixing bowl beat butter with an electric mixer on medium to high speed for 30 seconds. Add sugar; beat until combined, scraping sides of bowl occasionally. Beat in egg and vanilla until combined. Beat in as much of the flour mixture as you can with the mixer. Stir in any remaining flour with a wooden spoon.

2. Divide dough into three equal portions. Stir peppermint extract and red food coloring into one dough portion. Stir pistachio nuts and green food coloring into another dough portion. Stir melted chocolate into remaining dough portion.

3. Divide each portion of dough in half (you should have six portions total). Shape each portion into a 10-inch-long roll. Gently press one roll of pistachio dough and one roll of chocolate dough together, lengthwise, keeping the round shapes intact. Gently press one roll of peppermint dough on top, lengthwise, making a shape similar to a triangle. Repeat with remaining three rolls. Wrap each tricolored roll in plastic wrap or waxed paper. Chill for 2 to 24 hours or until firm enough to slice.

4. Cut rolls into ¼-inch slices. (Rotate the roll as you slice to avoid flattening the roll.) Place slices 1 inch apart on an ungreased cookie sheet. Bake in a 350° oven for 10 to 12 minutes or until edges are firm and lightly browned. Cool on cookie sheet for 1 minute. Transfer cookies to a wire rack and let cool.

TO STORE: Place in layers separated by waxed paper in an airtight container; cover. Store at room temperature up to 3 days or freeze up to 3 months.

Scandinavian Almond Bars

Like most Scandinavian cookies, this dainty bar is not overly sweet. Hint: Cut the rolls into strips while they're warm because if you wait, they'll become brittle and break. *(photo, page 179)*

Makes: about 44 bars

Oven: 325°F

1¾ cups all-purpose flour

2 teaspoons baking powder

¼ teaspoon salt

½ cup butter, softened

1 cup sugar

1 egg

½ teaspoon almond extract

Milk

½ cup sliced almonds,
   coarsely chopped

1 recipe Almond Icing

1. In a small bowl stir together flour, baking powder, and salt; set flour mixture aside. In a large mixing bowl beat butter with an electric mixer on medium to high speed for 30 seconds. Add sugar; beat until combined, scraping sides of bowl occasionally. Beat in egg and almond extract until combined. Beat in flour mixture.

2. Divide dough into four equal portions. Shape each portion into a 12-inch-long roll. Place two rolls 4 to 5 inches apart on an ungreased cookie sheet. Using your hands, flatten each roll until it is 3 inches wide. Repeat with remaining rolls. Brush flattened rolls with milk; sprinkle with almonds.

3. Bake in a 325° oven for 12 to 15 minutes or until edges are lightly browned. While still warm and soft on the cookie sheet, cut each roll diagonally into 1-inch-wide strips. Transfer cookies to a wire rack and let cool. Drizzle with Almond Icing; let dry.

Almond Icing: In a small bowl stir together 1 cup sifted powdered sugar, ¼ teaspoon almond extract, and enough milk (3 to 4 teaspoons) to make drizzling consistency.

TO STORE: Place in layers separated by waxed paper in an airtight container; cover. Store at room temperature up to 3 days or freeze undrizzled cookies up to 3 months. Thaw cookies; drizzle.

Chocolate Chip *Cookie* Sticks

What do you get when you cross America's favorite cookie—the chocolate chip—with Italy's favorite cookie, the biscotti? A yummy treat that's perfect for dunking in milk or coffee!

Makes: about 22 cookie sticks

Oven: 375°F/325°F

½ **cup butter, softened**

½ **cup shortening**

1 **cup packed brown sugar**

½ **cup granulated sugar**

½ **teaspoon baking soda**

2 **eggs**

2 **teaspoons vanilla**

2½ **cups all-purpose flour**

8 **ounces coarsely chopped**
   semisweet chocolate
   (2 cups)

1 **cup chopped walnuts, pecans,**
   or hazelnuts (filberts)
   (optional)

1. Line a 13×9×2-inch baking pan with foil; set aside. In a large mixing bowl beat butter and shortening with an electric mixer on medium to high speed for 30 seconds. Add brown sugar, granulated sugar, and baking soda. Beat until combined, scraping sides of bowl occasionally. Beat in eggs and vanilla until combined. Beat in as much of the flour as you can with the mixer. Stir in any remaining flour with a wooden spoon. Stir in chocolate and, if desired, nuts. Press dough evenly into the prepared pan.

2. Bake in a 375° oven for 22 to 25 minutes or until golden brown and center is set. Cool in pan for 1 hour.

3. Reduce oven temperature to 325°. Holding securely to foil lining, gently remove cookies from pan and place on a cutting board, leaving cookies on foil lining. Use a serrated knife to cut crosswise into 9×½-inch slices. Place slices, cut side down, 1 inch apart on an ungreased cookie sheet. Bake in a 325° oven for 6 to 8 minutes or until cut edges are crispy. Transfer cookies to a wire rack and let cool.

TO STORE: **Place in layers separated by waxed paper in an airtight container; cover. Store at room temperature up to 3 days or freeze up to 3 months.**

Cherry-Almond Slices

With its biscuitlike texture and jam-filled indentations, this delightful cookie makes a perfect teatime treat. Or try it as an unexpected addition to a breakfast or brunch spread.

Makes: about 32 cookies

Oven: 375°F

½ **cup butter, softened**

⅓ **cup packed brown sugar**

½ **teaspoon baking powder**

   Dash salt

2 **eggs**

1 **tablespoon kirsch**

   or orange juice

2¼ **cups all-purpose flour**

⅓ **cup finely chopped**

   almonds, toasted

1 **egg yolk**

1 **tablespoon milk**

½ **cup cherry preserves**

1 **ounce bittersweet chocolate,**

   chopped (optional)

¼ **teaspoon shortening (optional)**

1. Line a large cookie sheet with foil; set aside. In a large mixing bowl beat butter with an electric mixer on medium to high speed for 30 seconds. Add brown sugar, baking powder, and salt. Beat until combined, scraping sides of bowl occasionally. Beat in eggs and kirsch until combined. Beat in as much of the flour as you can with the mixer. Stir in any remaining flour with a wooden spoon. Stir in ¼ cup of the finely chopped almonds.

2. Divide dough in half. Shape each half into a 9-inch-long roll. Place rolls on prepared cookie sheet; flatten to 1 inch thick. Make an indentation that's 1 inch wide and ¼ inch deep down the middle of each log from end to end. Combine egg yolk and milk; brush over logs. Spoon cherry preserves in the indentations. Sprinkle with remaining almonds.

3. Bake in a 375° oven for 25 to 30 minutes or until a wooden toothpick inserted near center comes out clean. Cool on cookie sheet for 1 hour. Transfer to a cutting board. Use a serrated knife to cut each log crosswise into ½-inch slices.

4. If desired, in a small heavy saucepan melt chocolate and shortening over low heat, stirring constantly. Drizzle over slices before serving.

TO STORE: Place in layers separated by waxed paper in an airtight container; cover. Store at room temperature up to 24 hours or freeze undrizzled slices up to 3 months. Thaw cookies; drizzle.

Chocolate Dotted-Orange *Biscotti*

Orange and chocolate are a time-honored combination. Incorporate them in this traditional Italian cookie, and you've created an instant classic. Hint: A serrated knife works best for slicing the loaves of biscotti. *(photo, page 179)*

Makes: about 32 cookies

Oven: 375°F/325°F

⅓ cup butter, softened

⅔ cup sugar

2 teaspoons baking powder

2 eggs

2 teaspoons finely shredded
    orange peel (set aside)

2 tablespoons orange liqueur
    or orange juice

2 cups all-purpose flour

½ cup miniature semisweet
    chocolate pieces

⅓ cup semisweet
    chocolate pieces

½ teaspoon shortening

1. Grease a large cookie sheet; set aside. In a large mixing bowl beat butter with an electric mixer on medium to high speed for 30 seconds. Add sugar and baking powder. Beat until combined, scraping sides of bowl occasionally. Beat in eggs and orange liqueur until combined. Beat in as much of the flour as you can with the mixer. Stir in any remaining flour with a wooden spoon. Stir in orange peel and the ½ cup chocolate pieces.

2. Divide dough in half. Shape each half into a 9-inch-long roll. Place rolls about 4 inches apart on prepared cookie sheet; flatten to about 3 inches wide. Bake in a 375° oven for 20 to 25 minutes or until a wooden toothpick inserted near center comes out clean. Cool on cookie sheet for 1 hour.

3. Reduce oven temperature to 325°. Transfer rolls to a cutting board. Use a serrated knife to cut each roll diagonally into ½-inch slices. Place slices, cut side down, on an ungreased cookie sheet. Bake in a 325° oven for 8 minutes. Turn slices over and bake for 7 to 9 minutes more or until dry and crisp (do not overbake). Transfer to a wire rack and let cool.

4. In a small heavy saucepan melt the ⅓ cup chocolate pieces and shortening over low heat, stirring constantly. Dip ends of cookies into melted chocolate; let stand until set.

TO STORE: Place in layers separated by waxed paper in an airtight container; cover. Store at room temperature up to 3 days or freeze undipped cookies up to 3 months. Thaw cookies; dip ends into melted chocolate.

Double Chocolate Biscotti

Make room in the freezer for a batch of these super-chocolately biscotti. That way, you'll always have a terrific gift on hand for birthdays and other celebrations. For a special touch, present the cookies in a pretty mug.

Makes: about 32 cookies
Oven: 375°F/325°F

½ cup butter, softened
⅔ cup sugar
¼ cup unsweetened
      cocoa powder
2 teaspoons baking powder
2 eggs
1¾ cups all-purpose flour
¾ cup white baking pieces
½ cup large semisweet
      chocolate pieces or
      regular chocolate pieces

1. Grease a large cookie sheet; set aside. In a large mixing bowl beat butter with an electric mixer on medium to high speed for 30 seconds. Add sugar, cocoa powder, and baking powder. Beat until combined, scraping sides of bowl occasionally. Beat in eggs until combined. Beat in as much of the flour as you can with the mixer. Stir in any remaining flour with a wooden spoon. Stir in white baking pieces and chocolate pieces.

2. Divide dough in half. Shape each half into a 9-inch-long roll. Place rolls on prepared cookie sheet; flatten to about 2 inches wide. Bake in a 375° oven for 20 to 25 minutes or until a wooden toothpick inserted near center comes out clean. Cool on cookie sheet for 1 hour.

3. Reduce oven temperature to 325°. Transfer rolls to a cutting board. Use a serrated knife to cut each roll diagonally into ½-inch slices. Place slices, cut side down, on an ungreased cookie sheet. Bake in a 325° oven for 8 minutes. Turn slices over and bake for 7 to 9 minutes more or until dry and crisp (do not overbake). Transfer cookies to a wire rack and let cool.

TO STORE: Place in layers separated by waxed paper in an airtight container; cover. Store at room temperature up to 3 days or freeze up to 3 months.

Biscotti *D'Anici*

These days, you can find biscotti with all sorts of inventive stir-ins at ordinary supermarkets. If it's a classic you're after, however, make this simple version with anise, the traditional flavor of this beloved Italian cookie.

Makes: about 40 cookies
Oven: 375°F/325°F

½ cup butter, softened

1 cup sugar

1 tablespoon anise seeds,
    crushed, or 1 teaspoon
    anise extract

2½ teaspoons baking powder

3 eggs

3¼ cups all-purpose flour

1 tablespoon finely shredded
    lemon peel or orange peel

1. Lightly grease a cookie sheet; set aside. In a large mixing bowl beat butter with an electric mixer on medium to high speed for 30 seconds. Add sugar, anise seeds, and baking powder. Beat until combined, scraping sides of bowl occasionally. Beat in eggs until combined. Beat in as much of the flour as you can with the mixer. Stir in any remaining flour and lemon peel with a wooden spoon.

2. Divide dough in half. Shape each half into an 11-inch-long roll. Place rolls 5 inches apart on prepared cookie sheet; flatten to 2 inches wide. Bake in a 375° oven for 20 to 25 minutes or until lightly browned. Cool on cookie sheet for 1 hour.

3. Reduce oven temperature to 325°. Transfer rolls to a cutting board. Use a serrated knife to cut each roll diagonally into ½-inch slices. Place slices, cut side down, on an ungreased cookie sheet. Bake in a 325° oven for 10 minutes. Turn slices over and bake for 10 to 15 minutes more or until dry and crisp (do not overbake). Transfer cookies to a wire rack and let cool.

Sesame Seed Biscotti: Prepare as above, except omit anise seeds or anise extract. Shape dough into rolls as above; roll each roll in ⅓ cup (2 ounces) toasted sesame seeds. Place on cookie sheet; bake and cool as above.

TO STORE: Place in layers separated by waxed paper in an airtight container; cover. Store at room temperature up to 3 days or freeze up to 3 months.

Maple-Pecan Biscotti

Two indigenous ingredients—maple syrup and pecans—give this classic Italian cookie an American accent.

Makes: about 32 cookies

Oven: 375°F/325°F

⅓ cup butter, softened

½ cup sugar

2 teaspoons baking powder

2 eggs

¼ cup maple syrup

½ teaspoon vanilla

2¾ cups all-purpose flour

1 cup chopped pecans, toasted

⅓ cup finely chopped pecans

1 recipe Maple Drizzle

1. In a large mixing bowl beat butter with an electric mixer on medium to high speed for 30 seconds. Add sugar and baking powder. Beat until combined, scraping sides of bowl occasionally. Beat in eggs, maple syrup, and vanilla until combined. Beat in as much of the flour as you can with the mixer. Stir in any remaining flour with a wooden spoon. Stir in the 1 cup pecans. Divide dough in half. If necessary, cover and chill dough about 1 hour or until easy to handle.

2. Grease a large cookie sheet; set aside. Divide dough in half. Shape each half into a 9-inch-long roll. Place rolls 4 inches apart on prepared cookie sheet; flatten slightly. Sprinkle with the ⅓ cup pecans; press into tops of logs. Flatten to about 3 inches wide. Bake in a 375° oven for 25 to 30 minutes or until a wooden toothpick inserted near center comes out clean. Cool on cookie sheet for 1 hour.

3. Reduce oven temperature to 325°. Transfer rolls to a cutting board. Use a serrated knife to cut each roll diagonally into ½-inch slices. Place slices, cut side down, on an ungreased cookie sheet. Bake in a 325° oven for 8 minutes. Turn slices over and bake for 8 to 10 minutes more or until dry and crisp (do not overbake). Transfer cookies to a wire rack and let cool. Drizzle with Maple Drizzle; let dry.

Maple Drizzle: In a small bowl stir together 1¼ cups sifted powdered sugar and 1 tablespoon maple syrup. Stir in additional maple syrup (4 to 5 tablespoons) to make drizzling consistency.

TO STORE: Place in layers separated by waxed paper in an airtight container; cover. Store at room temperature up to 3 days or freeze undrizzled cookies up to 3 months. Thaw cookies; drizzle.

holiday treat

Lemon-Pistachio Biscotti

If you're passionate about pistachios, those deliciously sublime nuts, this is the cookie for you.

Hint: Don't skimp on the hour-long cooling time; it's necessary for good slicing without crumbling.

(photo, page 179)

Makes: about 42 cookies

Oven: 375°F/325°F

⅓ cup butter, softened

⅔ cup sugar

2 teaspoons baking powder

½ teaspoon salt

2 eggs

1 teaspoon vanilla

2 cups all-purpose flour

4 teaspoons finely shredded
  lemon peel

1¼ cups pistachio nuts

1 recipe Lemon Icing

1. Grease a very large cookie sheet; set aside. In a large mixing bowl beat butter with an electric mixer on medium to high speed for 30 seconds. Add sugar, baking powder, and salt. Beat until combined, scraping sides of bowl occasionally. Beat in eggs and vanilla until combined. Beat in as much of the flour as you can with the mixer. Stir in any remaining flour and lemon peel with a wooden spoon. Stir in pistachio nuts.

2. Divide dough into three equal portions. Shape each portion into an 8-inch-long roll. Place rolls at least 3 inches apart on prepared cookie sheet; flatten to about 2½ inches wide. Bake in a 375° oven for 20 to 25 minutes or until golden brown and tops are cracked (loaves will spread slightly). Cool on cookie sheet for 1 hour.

3. Reduce oven temperature to 325°. Transfer rolls to a cutting board. Use a serrated knife to cut each roll diagonally into ½-inch slices. Place slices, cut side down, on an ungreased cookie sheet. Bake in a 325° oven for 8 minutes. Turn slices over and bake for 8 to 10 minutes more or until dry and crisp (do not overbake). Transfer cookies to a wire rack and let cool. Drizzle with Lemon Icing; let dry.

Lemon Icing: In a small bowl stir together 1 cup sifted powdered sugar and 1 teaspoon finely shredded lemon peel. Stir in enough milk or lemon juice (1 to 2 tablespoons) to make drizzling consistency.

TO STORE: Place in layers separated by waxed paper in an airtight container; cover. Store at room temperature up to 3 days or freeze undrizzled cookies up to 3 months. Thaw cookies; drizzle

Rolling Pin Favorites

Sugar *Cookie* Cutouts

Although this is a classic holiday sugar cookie cutout, it's not only for Christmas. Use the dough—and your imagination—to make beautiful cookies for Easter, May Day, Mother's Day, or any special occasion. *(photo, page 217)*

Makes: about 36 cookies

Oven: 375°F

²/₃ **cup butter, softened**

³/₄ **cup sugar**

1 **teaspoon baking powder**

¹/₄ **teaspoon salt**

1 **egg**

1 **tablespoon milk**

1 **teaspoon vanilla**

2 **cups all-purpose flour**

1 **recipe Powdered Sugar Icing**

   (optional)

1. In a large mixing bowl beat butter with an electric mixer on medium to high speed for 30 seconds. Add sugar, baking powder, and salt. Beat until combined, scraping sides of bowl occasionally. Beat in egg, milk, and vanilla until combined. Beat in as much of the flour as you can with the mixer. Stir in any remaining flour with a wooden spoon. Divide dough in half. If necessary, cover and chill dough about 30 minutes or until easy to handle.

2. On a lightly floured surface, roll half of the dough at a time until ¹/₈ inch thick. Using a floured 2¹/₂-inch cookie cutter, cut into desired shapes. Place 1 inch apart on an ungreased cookie sheet.

3. Bake in a 375° oven for 7 to 8 minutes or until edges are firm and bottoms are very lightly browned. Transfer cookies to a wire rack and let cool. If desired, frost with Powdered Sugar Icing; let icing dry.

Candy Windowpane Cutouts: Prepare as above, except place cutout dough on a foil-lined cookie sheet. Cut small shapes out of cookie centers. Finely crush 3 ounces hard candy (about ¹/₂ cup). Fill each center cutout with some of the crushed candy. After baking, cool cookies on foil.

Powdered Sugar Icing: In a bowl combine 3 cups sifted powdered sugar, 3 tablespoons milk or orange juice, and 1 teaspoon vanilla. Stir in additional milk or orange juice, 1 teaspoon at a time, to make drizzling consistency.

TO STORE: Place in layers separated by waxed paper in an airtight container; cover. Store at room temperature up to 3 days or freeze unfrosted cookies up to 3 months. Thaw cookies; if desired, frost.

Old-Fashioned Sugar Cookies

Hankering for a taste of the good old days? These plump sugar cookies ought to do the trick. They might even be the kind your grandmother used to make. *(photo, page 215)*

Makes: about 32 cookies

Oven: 375°F

1¼ **cups shortening**

 2 **cups granulated sugar**

 2 **teaspoons baking powder**

 1 **teaspoon baking soda**

 ½ **teaspoon ground nutmeg**

 ¼ **teaspoon salt**

 2 **eggs**

 1 **teaspoon vanilla**

 ½ **teaspoon lemon extract**

4½ **cups all-purpose flour**

 1 **cup buttermilk or sour milk***

   Colored decorating sugar

1. In a large mixing bowl beat shortening with an electric mixer on medium to high speed for 30 seconds. Add granulated sugar, baking powder, baking soda, nutmeg, and salt. Beat until combined, scraping sides of bowl occasionally. Beat in eggs, vanilla, and lemon extract until combined. Alternately add flour and buttermilk to shortening mixture, beating until combined. Divide dough in half. Cover and chill dough about 3 hours or until easy to handle.

2. On a lightly floured surface, roll half of the dough at a time until ½ inch thick. Using a floured 2½-inch round cookie cutter, cut out dough. Place 2½ inches apart on an ungreased cookie sheet. Sprinkle with decorating sugar.

3. Bake in a 375° oven about 10 minutes or until set and edges just begin to brown. Transfer cookies to a wire rack and let cool.

***NOTE:** To make sour milk, place 1 tablespoon lemon juice or vinegar in a glass measuring cup. Add enough milk to make 1 cup total; stir. Let mixture stand for 5 minutes before using.

TO STORE: Place in layers separated by waxed paper in an airtight container; cover. Store at room temperature up to 3 days or freeze up to 3 months.

Sour Cream Sugar *Cookies*

Transform ordinary frosted cutouts into edible works of art. Your canvas is made of frosting; your tools, a paintbrush and food coloring. *(photo, page 219)*

Makes: about 48 cookies

Oven: 375°F

½ cup butter, softened

1 cup sugar

1 teaspoon baking powder

¼ teaspoon baking soda

Dash salt

½ cup dairy sour cream

1 egg

1 teaspoon vanilla

1 teaspoon finely shredded
   lemon peel

2½ cups all-purpose flour

1 recipe Meringue Powder Icing

Food coloring (optional)

1. In a large mixing bowl beat butter with an electric mixer on medium to high speed for 30 seconds. Add sugar, baking powder, baking soda, and salt. Beat until combined, scraping sides of bowl occasionally. Beat in sour cream, egg, vanilla, and lemon peel until combined. Beat in as much of the flour as you can with the mixer. Stir in any remaining flour with a wooden spoon. Divide dough in half. Cover and chill dough for 1 to 2 hours or until easy to handle.

2. On a well floured surface, roll half of the dough at a time until ⅛ to ¼ inch thick. Using floured cookie cutters, cut into desired shapes. Place 1 inch apart on an ungreased cookie sheet.

3. Bake in a 375° oven for 7 to 8 minutes or until edges are firm and bottoms are very lightly browned. Transfer cookies to a wire rack and let cool. Frost with Meringue Powder Icing; let icing dry. If desired, use a clean small paintbrush to paint designs on each cookie with food coloring.

Meringue Powder Icing: In a medium mixing bowl beat together ¼ cup warm water and 2 tablespoons meringue powder with an electric mixer until combined. Beat in 2¾ cups sifted powdered sugar to make a smooth, spreadable icing. If desired, tint icing with paste food coloring.

TO STORE: Place in layers separated by waxed paper in an airtight container; cover. Store at room temperature up to 3 days or freeze unfrosted cookies up to 3 months. Thaw cookies; frost.

holiday treat

Marbled **Holiday Greetings**

Pipe a sweet, seasonal sentiment on these cookie greeting cards. The recipients will not only love your kind wishes but also your great taste—each colorful swirl of dough has its own special flavor. *(photo, page 215)*

Makes: 144 cookies

Oven: 375°F

1   **cup butter, softened**

⅔   **cup shortening**

2   **cups sugar**

⅔   **cup dairy sour cream**

2   **eggs**

1   **teaspoon vanilla**

1½ **teaspoons baking powder**

½   **teaspoon baking soda**

⅛   **teaspoon salt**

5   **cups all-purpose flour**

     Rose petal pink, violet, leaf green, and lemon yellow paste food coloring

½   **teaspoon peppermint extract**

½   **teaspoon almond extract**

1   **teaspoon finely shredded lime peel**

1   **recipe Decorative Icing**

1. Beat butter and shortening for 30 seconds. Add sugar, sour cream, eggs, vanilla, baking powder, soda, and salt. Beat until combined. Beat in as much of the flour as you can. Stir in any remaining flour. Divide dough into six equal portions. Cover; chill dough 1 hour or until easy to handle.

2. Tint each of three portions a different color. (To make green color shown, combine leaf green and lemon yellow.) Knead each dough gently until evenly tinted. Leave three portions of dough untinted. Add peppermint to pink dough, almond to violet dough, and lime peel to green dough.

3. Break off pieces of a plain dough and a colored dough. Place pieces alternately on a floured pastry cloth to form an 11×7-inch rectangle, pressing pieces together. Roll into a 12-inch square that is ¼ inch thick, creating a marbled effect. Trim edges of the marbled square; cut into forty-eight 3×1-inch rectangles. Repeat with remaining dough portions. Place rectangles 1 inch apart on an ungreased cookie sheet.

4. Bake in a 375° oven for 7 to 8 minutes or until edges are very lightly browned. Transfer to a wire rack; let cool. Use Decorative Icing to pipe "Joy," "Noel," or "Peace" onto each cookie; let icing dry.

Decorative Icing: In a large bowl combine 4 cups sifted powdered sugar and 3 tablespoons milk; stir until smooth. Stir in additional milk, 1 teaspoon at a time, until piping consistency. Tint as desired with paste food coloring.

TO STORE: Place in layers separated by waxed paper in an airtight container; cover. Store at room temperature up to 3 days or freeze undecorated cookies up to 3 months. Thaw cookies; pipe on icing greetings.

Nutmeg *Softies*

Set aside some of these big, soft cookies for "one of those (bad) days." Served with a glass of milk, this comforting, old-fashioned treat will help get you back on your feet.

Makes: about 32 cookies

Oven: 350°F

½ **cup butter, softened**

½ **cup shortening**

1½ **cups granulated sugar**

1 **teaspoon baking soda**

1 **teaspoon ground nutmeg**

½ **teaspoon salt**

1 **cup dairy sour cream**

1 **egg**

1 **teaspoon vanilla**

4 **cups all-purpose flour**

   Colored decorating sugar

1. In a large mixing bowl beat butter and shortening with an electric mixer on medium to high speed for 30 seconds. Add granulated sugar, baking soda, nutmeg, and salt. Beat until combined, scraping sides of bowl occasionally. Beat in sour cream, egg, and vanilla until combined. Beat in as much of the flour as you can with the mixer. Stir in any remaining flour with a wooden spoon (dough will be sticky). Divide dough into three equal portions. Cover and chill dough about 2 hours or until easy to handle.

2. On a lightly floured surface, roll one portion of the dough at a time until ¼ inch thick. Using a floured 3-inch cookie cutter, cut into desired shapes. Place 1 inch apart on an ungreased cookie sheet. Sprinkle with decorating sugar.

3. Bake in a 350° oven about 10 minutes or until edges are firm and bottoms are golden. Transfer cookies to a wire rack and let cool.

TO STORE: Place in layers separated by waxed paper in an airtight container; cover. Store at room temperature up to 3 days or freeze up to 3 months.

The smart way to decorate with sugar

- Decorate cookies with granulated or colored sugar immediately after rolling and cutting. Once the surface dries a bit, the sugar won't stick well.
- Teach young helpers that more isn't better; only the sugar that touches the cookie dough will bake in place. The rest will burn on the pan or fall off.
- If you want to sprinkle sugar on iced cookies, work on just a few cookies at a time, and add the sugar while the icing is wet.

Shimmering Citrus Snowflakes

No two snowflakes are alike, and the same goes for these citrus-infused sweets. A simple drinking straw is all you'll need to give each cookie its one-of-a-kind pattern, making it easy for kids to help. *(photo, page 218)*

Makes: about 40 cookies

Oven: 375°F

½ cup butter, softened

⅓ cup shortening

1 cup granulated sugar

⅓ cup dairy sour cream

1 egg

1 teaspoon vanilla

2 teaspoons finely shredded
     lemon peel (optional)

½ teaspoon finely shredded
     lime peel (optional)

¾ teaspoon baking powder

¼ teaspoon baking soda

Dash salt

2½ cups all-purpose flour

Assorted colors edible glitter
     or decorating sugar

Sifted powdered sugar

1. In a large mixing bowl beat butter and shortening with an electric mixer on medium to high speed for 30 seconds. Add granulated sugar, sour cream, egg, vanilla, lemon and lime peels (if desired), baking powder, baking soda, and salt. Beat until combined, scraping sides of bowl occasionally. Beat in as much of the flour as you can with the mixer. Stir in any remaining flour with a wooden spoon. Divide dough in half. Cover and chill dough about 2 hours or until easy to handle.

2. On a lightly floured surface, roll half of the dough at a time until ⅛ to ¼ inch thick. Using floured 2½-inch cookie cutters, cut dough into circles, triangles, squares, and/or diamonds. Using straws or aspic or hors d'oeuvre cutters, cut random holes in the cutout shapes so they resemble snowflakes. Use a straw to cut half circles from the edges to flute them. Using a wide spatula, place 1 inch apart on an ungreased cookie sheet. Sprinkle with edible glitter.

3. Bake in 375° oven for 7 to 8 minutes or until edges are firm and bottoms are very lightly browned. Transfer cookies to a wire rack and let cool. Sprinkle with powdered sugar.

TO STORE: Place in layers separated by waxed paper in an airtight container; cover. Store at room temperature up to 3 days or freeze unsprinkled cookies up to 3 months. Thaw cookies; sprinkle with powdered sugar.

Swedish *Butter* Cookies

Swedish butter cookies don't always call for a dip in chocolate, but it's hard to resist,

knowing how good they taste together. If desired, purists can always skip that step.

Makes: about 36 cookies

Oven: 375°F

½ cup butter, softened

¼ cup sugar

¼ teaspoon vanilla

1 cup all-purpose flour

1½ teaspoons finely shredded
lemon peel

4 ounces semisweet chocolate,
chopped

2 teaspoons shortening

1. In a medium mixing bowl beat butter with an electric mixer on medium to high speed for 30 seconds. Add sugar and vanilla. Beat until combined, scraping sides of bowl occasionally. Beat in as much of the flour as you can with the mixer. Stir in any remaining flour and lemon peel with a wooden spoon. Cover and chill dough about 1 hour or until easy to handle.

2. On a lightly floured surface, roll dough until ⅛ to ¼ inch thick. Using floured 2-inch cookie cutters, cut into desired shapes. Place 1 inch apart on an ungreased cookie sheet.

3. Bake in a 375° oven for 5 to 7 minutes or until edges are lightly browned. Cool on cookie sheet for 1 minute. Transfer cookies to a wire rack and let cool.

4. In a small heavy saucepan melt chocolate and shortening over low heat, stirring constantly. Dip half of each cookie into melted chocolate; let stand until set.

TO STORE: Place in layers separated by waxed paper in an airtight container; cover. Store at room temperature up to 3 days or freeze undipped cookies up to 3 months. Thaw cookies; dip in chocolate.

Springtime Blossoms

Four heart-shape pieces of dough, positioned just right, blend during baking to create

a flower cookie. Consider it springtime's answer to the Christmas cutout!

Makes: about 60 cookies

Oven: 375°F

¹/₄ **cup butter, softened**

¹/₂ **cup sugar**

1 **egg**

1 **tablespoon milk**

¹/₂ **teaspoon vanilla**

1¹/₄ **cups self-rising flour**

1 **recipe Powdered Sugar Icing**

   Miniature candy-coated

   milk chocolate pieces

1. In a medium mixing bowl beat butter with an electric mixer on medium to high speed for 30 seconds. Add sugar; beat until combined, scraping sides of bowl occasionally. Beat in egg, milk, and vanilla until combined. Stir in flour with a wooden spoon. Divide dough in half. Cover and chill dough about 2 hours or until easy to handle.

2. Grease a large cookie sheet; set aside. On a lightly floured surface, roll half of the dough at a time until ¹/₈ inch thick. Using a floured 1-inch heart-shape cookie cutter, cut out dough. For each cookie, arrange 4 hearts on prepared cookie sheet, with points together and 1 or 2 of the sides overlapping slightly. Repeat with remaining dough.

3. Bake in a 375° oven for 6 to 7 minutes or until edges are lightly browned. Cool on cookie sheet for 1 minute. Transfer cookies to a wire rack.

4. Using a large pastry brush, brush warm cookies with Powdered Sugar Icing. Place a candy-coated chocolate piece in the center of each cookie; let icing dry.

Powdered Sugar Icing: In a small bowl stir together 1 cup sifted strawberry-flavored, lemon-flavored, or regular powdered sugar; 1 tablespoon milk; and ¹/₄ teaspoon vanilla. Stir in enough additional milk, 1 teaspoon at a time, to make drizzling consistency.

TO STORE: Place in layers separated by waxed paper in an airtight container; cover. Store at room temperature up to 3 days or freeze up to 3 months.

Watermelon **Cookies**

Not only are these cookies cute and delicious, you can eat the seeds! Celebrate summer's arrival with these melon look-alikes. Even before the first bite, their clever shape brings smiles.

Makes: about 48 cookies

Oven: 375°F

- ¹/₃ **cup butter, softened**
- ¹/₃ **cup shortening**
- ³/₄ **cup granulated sugar**
- 1¹/₂ **teaspoons baking powder**
- ¹/₂ **teaspoon salt**
- 1 **egg**
- 1 **tablespoon orange juice or milk**
- 1 **teaspoon vanilla**
- 2 **cups all-purpose flour**
  Red food coloring
- 1 **egg white**
- 1 **tablespoon water**
  Green decorating sugar
- ¹/₄ **cup miniature semisweet chocolate pieces**

1. In a large mixing bowl beat butter and shortening with an electric mixer on medium to high speed for 30 seconds. Add granulated sugar, baking powder, and salt. Beat until combined, scraping sides of bowl occasionally. Beat in egg, orange juice, and vanilla until combined. Beat in as much of the flour as you can with the mixer. Stir in any remaining flour with a wooden spoon. Transfer dough to waxed paper and knead in enough red food coloring for desired color. Divide dough in half. Cover and chill dough about 3 hours or until easy to handle.

2. Stir together egg white and water; set aside. On a lightly floured surface, roll half of the dough at a time until slightly less than ¼ inch thick. Using a floured 3-inch round cookie cutter, cut out dough. Cut cookies in half. Using a small brush, brush the egg white-water mixture on the rounded edges and a small portion of the sides of each cookie. Dip brushed edges in decorating sugar. Place 2 inches apart on an ungreased cookie sheet. Press a few chocolate pieces into each cookie for "seeds."

3. Bake in a 375° oven for 5 to 7 minutes or until bottoms just begin to brown (do not allow to brown on top). Transfer cookies to a wire rack and let cool.

TO STORE: Place in layers separated by waxed paper in an airtight container; cover. Store at room temperature up to 3 days or freeze up to 3 months.

Tropical *Pinwheels*

You'll love these pinwheels, inside and out. A mix of cream cheese, sugar, and coconut hides within the centers while nuts and sugar top the outside. *(photo, page 218)*

Makes: 32 cookies

Oven: 350°F

⅓ **cup butter, softened**

⅓ **cup shortening**

¾ **cup granulated sugar**

1½ **teaspoons baking powder**

¼ **teaspoon salt**

1 **egg**

4 **teaspoons milk**

1 **teaspoon vanilla**

2 **cups all-purpose flour**

1 **3-ounce package cream cheese, softened**

2 **tablespoons granulated sugar**

¼ **cup coconut**

¼ **cup finely chopped macadamia nuts or almonds**

   Colored decorating sugar (optional)

1 **recipe Tropical Icing (optional)**

1. In a large mixing bowl beat butter and shortening with an electric mixer on medium to high speed for 30 seconds. Add the ¾ cup granulated sugar, baking powder, and salt. Beat until combined, scraping sides of bowl occasionally. Beat in egg, milk, and vanilla until combined. Beat in as much of the flour as you can with the mixer. Stir in any remaining flour with a wooden spoon. Divide dough in half. Cover and chill dough about 3 hours or until easy to handle.

2. Meanwhile, for filling, in a small bowl stir together cream cheese and the 2 tablespoons granulated sugar; stir in coconut. Set filling aside.

3. On a lightly floured surface, roll half of the dough at a time into a 10-inch square. Using a fluted pastry wheel or a sharp knife, cut square into sixteen 2½-inch squares. Place 2 inches apart on an ungreased cookie sheet. Cut 1-inch slits from each corner toward the center of each square. Spoon a level teaspoon of the filling in each center. Fold every other tip to center to form a pinwheel, pressing lightly to seal the tips. Carefully sprinkle some of the chopped nuts onto the center of each pinwheel; press nuts lightly into the dough. If desired, sprinkle with decorating sugar.

4. Bake in a 350° oven for 8 to 10 minutes or until edges are lightly browned. Cool on cookie sheet for 1 minute. Transfer cookies to a wire rack and let cool. If desired, drizzle with Tropical Icing; let dry.

Tropical Icing: In a small bowl stir together ¾ cup sifted powdered sugar and enough pineapple juice (about 1 tablespoon) to make drizzling consistency.

TO STORE: Place in layers separated by waxed paper in an airtight container; cover. Store at room temperature up to 3 days or freeze undrizzled cookies up to 3 months. Thaw cookies; if desired, drizzle.

Buttered Rum Cutouts

With a little nutmeg and rum extract in the mix, these cookies exude the flavors of the tropics. Why not take the island theme a step further? Cut them into tropical shapes, such as coconut palm trees and bright shining suns, before decorating them with boldly colored icing. *(photo, page 219)*

Makes: about 55 cookies

Oven: 350°F

- 1 **cup butter, softened**
- ⅔ **cup packed brown sugar**
- 1 **teaspoon baking powder**
- 1 **teaspoon ground nutmeg**
- ¼ **teaspoon salt**
- 1 **egg**
- 1 **teaspoon rum extract
    or vanilla**
- 2⅔ **cups all-purpose flour**
- 1 **recipe Royal Icing Glaze**

1. In a large mixing bowl beat butter with an electric mixer on medium to high speed for 30 seconds. Add brown sugar, baking powder, nutmeg, and salt. Beat until combined, scraping sides of bowl occasionally. Beat in egg and rum extract until combined. Beat in as much of the flour as you can with the mixer. Stir in any remaining flour with a wooden spoon. Divide dough in half. If necessary, cover and chill dough about 1 hour or until easy to handle.

2. On a lightly floured surface, roll half of the dough at a time until ⅛ inch thick. Using floured cookie cutters, cut into desired shapes. Place 1 inch apart on an ungreased cookie sheet.

3. Bake in a 350° oven for 8 to 10 minutes or until edges are lightly browned. Transfer cookies to a wire rack and let cool. Frost with Royal Icing Glaze. If desired, add details with contrasting glaze; let glaze dry.

Royal Icing Glaze: In a small mixing bowl combine 2 cups sifted powdered sugar, ¼ cup warm water, 4 teaspoons meringue powder, and ¼ teaspoon cream of tartar. Beat with an electric mixer on low speed until combined. Beat on high speed for 7 to 10 minutes or until very stiff. Add 1 to 2 tablespoons additional warm water, 1 teaspoon at a time, until glazing consistency. If desired, divide glaze and tint each portion with a different paste food coloring. Use at once. Keep covered when not in use.

TO STORE: Place in layers separated by waxed paper in an airtight container; cover. Store at room temperature up to 3 days or freeze unfrosted cookies up to 3 months. Thaw cookies; frost.

holiday treat

Eggnog Cookies

This old-fashioned sugar cookie shines brighter than most. Golden butterscotch candies create stained-glass centers in light of the holiday season.

Makes: about 24 cookies

Oven: 375°F

2 cups all-purpose flour

1 cup granulated sugar

¾ teaspoon baking powder

¼ teaspoon ground nutmeg

¼ teaspoon salt

⅔ cup butter

1 slightly beaten egg

¼ cup dairy eggnog

½ cup finely crushed
    butterscotch- or rum-
    flavored hard candies
    (about twenty-five
    1-inch candies)

1 recipe Eggnog Glaze
  Yellow decorating sugar
    (optional)

1. In a large bowl stir together flour, granulated sugar, baking powder, nutmeg, and salt. Using a pastry blender, cut in butter until the pieces are the size of small peas. Make a well in center of flour mixture; set aside. In a small bowl combine egg and eggnog. Add all at once to flour mixture. Stir just until moistened. Cover and chill dough about 2 hours or until easy to handle.

2. Line a cookie sheet with foil; set aside. On a well floured surface, roll dough until ¼ inch thick. Using floured 2½-inch cookie cutters, cut into desired shapes. Place 1 inch apart on prepared cookie sheet. Cut small shapes out of cookie centers. Fill each center cutout with some of the crushed candy.

3. Bake in a 375° oven for 6 to 8 minutes or until edges are firm and lightly browned. Cool on cookie sheet for 5 minutes. Cool cookies on foil. Drizzle with Eggnog Glaze. If desired, immediately sprinkle with decorating sugar. Let glaze dry.

Eggnog Glaze: In a medium bowl stir together 3 cups sifted powdered sugar and ¼ teaspoon rum extract. Add enough dairy eggnog (2 to 3 tablespoons) to make drizzling consistency.

TO STORE: Place in layers separated by waxed paper in an airtight container; cover. Store at room temperature up to 3 days or freeze undrizzled cookies up to 3 months. Thaw cookies; drizzle.

Patchwork Mittens

These colorful patchwork cookies warm hearts as surely as real mittens warm fingers. To present these sweet mittens as a gift, tie a pastel-colored ribbon around the base of each cookie.

(photo, page 213)

Makes: about 18 cookies

Oven: 375°F

½ cup butter, softened

1 3-ounce package cream
   cheese, softened

1½ cups sifted powdered sugar

½ teaspoon baking powder

¼ teaspoon salt

1 egg

½ teaspoon vanilla

2¼ cups all-purpose flour

   Paste food coloring

   Clear edible glitter

1. In a large mixing bowl beat butter and cream cheese with an electric mixer on medium to high speed for 30 seconds. Add powdered sugar, baking powder, and salt. Beat until combined, scraping sides of bowl occasionally. Beat in egg and vanilla until combined. Beat in as much of the flour as you can with the mixer. Stir in any remaining flour with a wooden spoon. Cover and chill dough about 1 hour or until easy to handle.

2. Divide dough into five equal portions; place each portion in an individual bowl. Tint four of the dough portions a different color using paste food coloring. Knead each dough gently until it is evenly tinted. Wrap each portion in plastic wrap or waxed paper. Chill dough about 1 hour or until easy to handle.

3. On a lightly floured surface, roll one portion of the dough at a time until ⅛ inch thick. Cut into 1-inch-wide strips with a fluted pastry wheel; cut dough strips into squares, diamonds, and triangles. Overlap dough pieces in groups of about 10 on an ungreased cookie sheet until the group of pieces is slightly larger than a 3-inch mitten-shape cookie cutter. Using the floured mitten-shape cutter, cut out dough. (Reserve scraps; reroll to make marble cutouts.)

4. Bake in a 375° oven for 8 to 9 minutes or until edges are firm and bottoms are very lightly browned. Immediately sprinkle with edible glitter. Transfer cookies to a wire rack and let cool.

TO STORE: Place in layers separated by waxed paper in an airtight container; cover. Store at room temperature up to 3 days or freeze up to 3 months.

Patchwork Mittens, page 212

Honey and Poppy Seed Hearts, page 221

Honey and *Poppy Seed* Hearts

The addition of honey to these cinnamon-spiced cookies results in a dough that's soft and sweet. Their sentimental shapes and homespun appeal will no doubt pull a few heartstrings.

(photo, page 220)

Makes: about 36 cookies

Oven: 375°F

¾ cup butter, softened

⅔ cup sugar

3 tablespoons honey

2 teaspoons finely shredded
   lemon peel or orange peel

1 teaspoon baking powder

1 teaspoon ground cinnamon

¼ teaspoon baking soda

1 egg

2¼ cups all-purpose flour

1 egg white

1 tablespoon water

2 tablespoons poppy seeds

1. In a large mixing bowl beat butter with electric mixer on medium to high speed for 30 seconds. Add sugar, honey, lemon peel, baking powder, cinnamon, and baking soda. Beat until combined, scraping sides of bowl occasionally. Beat in the whole egg until combined. Beat in as much of the flour as you can with the mixer. Stir in any remaining flour with a wooden spoon. Divide dough in half. Cover and chill dough about 2 hours or until easy to handle.

2. Grease a large cookie sheet; set aside. On a lightly floured surface, roll half of the dough at a time until ¼ inch thick. Using a floured 2½- to 3-inch heart-shape cookie cutter, cut out dough. Place 2 inches apart on prepared cookie sheet. (If you plan to string a ribbon through the cookies, use a drinking straw to make a hole in the center of each cookie before baking.)

3. In a small bowl beat together egg white and water. Brush egg white-water mixture over tops of cookies; immediately sprinkle with poppy seeds.

4. Bake in a 375° oven for 8 to 10 minutes or until edges are golden brown. Transfer cookies to a wire rack and let cool.

TO STORE: Place in layers separated by waxed paper in an airtight container; cover. Store at room temperature up to 3 days or freeze up to 3 months.

Almond Galettes

In the vernacular of French cooking and baking, a galette is a round, rather flat cake. These little almond-infused "cakes" are the essence of simple sophistication. *(photo, page 218)*

Makes: about 36 cookies

Oven: 375°F

1 8-ounce can almond paste

1 cup butter, softened

½ cup sugar

2 teaspoons finely shredded
   lemon peel

½ teaspoon almond extract

2 cups all-purpose flour

2 egg yolks

4 teaspoons water

¼ teaspoon almond extract

   Sliced almonds

1. Grease a large cookie sheet; set aside. Crumble almond paste into a large mixing bowl. Beat with an electric mixer on medium to high speed for 30 seconds. Add butter; beat for 30 seconds more. Add sugar, lemon peel, and the ½ teaspoon almond extract. Beat about 2 minutes more or until combined, scraping sides of bowl occasionally. Beat in as much of the flour as you can with the mixer. Stir in any remaining flour with a wooden spoon. Divide dough in half.

2. On a lightly floured surface, roll half of the dough at a time until ¼ inch thick. Using a floured 2-inch square scalloped cookie cutter, cut out dough. Place 1 inch apart on prepared cookie sheet.

3. In a small bowl beat egg yolks, water, and the ¼ teaspoon almond extract until combined. Brush egg mixture over tops of cookies; immediately top each cookie with 2 almond slices.

4. Bake in a 375° oven for 7 to 9 minutes or until edges are firm and bottoms are very lightly browned. Cool on cookie sheet for 1 minute. Transfer cookies to a wire rack and let cool.

TO STORE: Place in layers separated by waxed paper in an airtight container; cover. Store at room temperature up to 3 days or freeze up to 3 months.

Syrup Snips

Though the name has been pared down and simplified, these Norwegian *sirupssippers* have lost none of their spicy goodness. Use a fluted pastry wheel to dress them up.

Makes: about 48 cookies

Oven: 375°F

½ **cup butter, softened**

½ **cup sugar**

¾ **teaspoon ground cardamom**

¼ **teaspoon baking soda**

⅛ **teaspoon salt**

1 **egg**

⅓ **cup dark-colored corn syrup**

2 **cups all-purpose flour**

 Whole blanched almonds

1. In a large mixing bowl beat butter with an electric mixer on medium speed for 30 seconds. Add sugar, cardamom, baking soda, and salt. Beat until combined, scraping sides of bowl occasionally. Beat in egg and corn syrup until combined. Beat in as much of the flour as you can with the mixer. Stir in any remaining flour with a wooden spoon. Divide dough into three equal portions. Cover and chill dough for several hours or overnight or until easy to handle.

2. Grease a large cookie sheet; set aside. On a lightly floured surface, roll one portion of the dough at a time until ⅛ inch thick. With a fluted pastry wheel, cut dough into 2×2-inch diamonds. Place 1 inch apart on prepared cookie sheet. Place an almond in the center of each diamond.

3. Bake in a 375° oven about 7 minutes or until edges are lightly browned. Transfer cookies to a wire rack and let cool.

TO STORE: Place in layers separated by waxed paper in an airtight container; cover. Store at room temperature up to 3 days or freeze up to 3 months.

The secret to tender rolled cookies

Too much flour and too much handling make sugar cookies tough or hard. For tender cookies, roll the dough on a pastry cloth with a stockinette-covered rolling pin, using only enough flour on the cloth to keep the dough from sticking. When rerolling scraps to make new cookies, handle the dough as little as possible.

Ruiskakut

In Finland, where rye grows better than wheat, rye flour more frequently appears in recipes. These flaky rye cutouts are a delicious case in point.

Makes: about 48 cookies

Oven: 350°F

1 cup butter, softened

⅔ cup granulated sugar

2 cups rye flour

1 cup all-purpose flour

3 tablespoons cold water

Green and white
decorating sugars

1. In a large mixing bowl beat butter with an electric mixer on medium to high speed for 30 seconds. Add granulated sugar; beat until combined, scraping sides of bowl occasionally. Beat in rye flour and all-purpose flour with the mixer on low speed until mixture resembles fine crumbs. Add water, tossing mixture with a fork until dough is moistened. Gently knead the dough until a ball forms.

2. On a lightly floured surface, roll dough until ⅛ inch thick. Using a floured 2½-inch oval cookie cutter, cut out dough. Place 1 inch apart on an ungreased cookie sheet. Prick each cookie all over with a fork; sprinkle with decorating sugars.

3. Bake in a 350° oven for 8 to 10 minutes or until firm and edges begin to brown. Transfer cookies to a wire rack and let cool.

TO STORE: Place in layers separated by waxed paper in an airtight container; cover. Store at room temperature up to 3 days or freeze up to 3 months.

Cookie cutting clues

- When rolling and cutting, work with half the dough at a time, keeping the other half refrigerated.
- Shapes can differ, but the size of cookies on the same sheet should be similar so they'll have similar baking times and brown evenly.
- Dip the cutter in flour between cuts to keep dough from sticking to it.
- Make cutouts as close together on the dough as possible so fewer rerolls will be needed.
- Place the cutouts 1 inch apart on the baking sheet so they don't run together during baking.

holiday treat

Biscochitos

Made at Christmastime throughout Mexico and the American Southwest, these anise-flavored biscuits are traditionally cut into birds, flowers, and other fanciful shapes. *(photo, page 217)*

Makes: about 36 cookies

Oven: 350°F

3 cups all-purpose flour

1½ teaspoons anise seeds,
    crushed

1 teaspoon baking powder

½ teaspoon salt

1¼ cups butter-flavored
    shortening

1 egg

½ cup sugar

3 tablespoons frozen
    orange juice concentrate,
    thawed, or brandy

1 teaspoon vanilla

Cinnamon-sugar (optional)

Crushed anise seeds (optional)

1. Grease a large cookie sheet; set aside. In a medium bowl stir together flour, the 1½ teaspoons anise seeds, baking powder, and salt; set flour mixture aside.

2. In a large mixing bowl beat shortening with an electric mixer on medium to high speed for 30 seconds. Add egg, sugar, orange juice concentrate, and vanilla. Beat until light, scraping sides of bowl occasionally. Beat in as much of the flour mixture as you can with the mixer. Stir in any remaining flour mixture with a wooden spoon (dough will be stiff). Divide dough in half.

3. On a lightly floured surface, roll half of the dough at a time until ¼ inch thick. Using floured 2½-inch cookie cutters, cut into desired shapes. Place 1 inch apart on prepared cookie sheet. If desired, sprinkle with cinnamon-sugar and additional crushed anise seeds.

4. Bake in a 350° oven about 9 minutes or until bottoms are golden brown. Transfer cookies to a wire rack and let cool.

TO STORE: Place in layers separated by waxed paper in an airtight container; cover. Store at room temperature up to 3 days or freeze up to 3 months.

Zaletti

In the Veneto region of Italy, and in Venice, its most visited city, these crunchy cookies are made with polenta—coarsely ground cornmeal—which could account for their name. In Venetian dialect, *zaletti* means "little yellow things." *(photo, page 218)*

Makes: about 54 cookies

Oven: 375°F

¾ **cup dried currants**

2 **tablespoons dark or light rum**

⅔ **cup butter, softened**

⅔ **cup sugar**

1 **teaspoon baking powder**

¼ **teaspoon salt**

1 **egg**

2 **teaspoons finely shredded orange peel**

½ **cup yellow cornmeal**

1½ **cups all-purpose flour**

Sugar

1. In a small bowl combine currants and rum; cover and let stand 30 minutes.

2. In a large mixing bowl beat butter with an electric mixer on medium to high speed for 30 seconds. Add the ⅔ cup sugar, baking powder, and salt. Beat until combined, scraping sides of bowl occasionally. Beat in egg and orange peel until combined. Beat in cornmeal and as much of the flour as you can with the mixer. Stir in any remaining flour with a wooden spoon. Stir in currant mixture. Divide dough in half. Cover and chill dough about 3 hours or until easy to handle.

3. On a lightly floured surface, roll half of the dough at a time into a 12×8-inch rectangle. Using a knife, cut dough rectangle diagonally into diamond shapes 3 inches long and 1¼ inches wide. Place 1 inch apart on an ungreased cookie sheet. Sprinkle with additional sugar.

4. Bake in a 375° oven for 6 to 8 minutes or until edges are lightly browned. Transfer cookies to a wire rack and let cool.

TO STORE: Place in layers separated by waxed paper in an airtight container; cover. Store at room temperature up to 3 days or freeze up to 3 months.

Is it done yet? Cutout cookies are done when the bottoms are very lightly browned and edges are firm. Remember to cool your cookies completely before storing them so they don't lose their shape.

Cornmeal Ribbons

Dress up these tender ribbons with Lemon Glaze and, if you wish, a sprinkling of sugar.

With their color so yellow, they make perfect treats to serve on sunny spring days.

Makes: about 32 cookies

Oven: 375°F

²/₃ **cup butter, softened**

²/₃ **cup granulated sugar**

1 **teaspoon baking powder**

¼ **teaspoon salt**

1 **egg**

1½ **teaspoons finely shredded**
     lemon peel

1 **teaspoon vanilla**

½ **cup yellow cornmeal**

1½ **cups all-purpose flour**

1 **recipe Lemon Glaze**
     Yellow decorating sugar
     (optional)

1. In a large mixing bowl beat butter with an electric mixer on medium to high speed for 30 seconds. Add granulated sugar, baking powder, and salt. Beat until combined, scraping sides of bowl occasionally. Beat in egg, lemon peel, and vanilla until combined. Beat in cornmeal and as much of the flour as you can with the mixer. Stir in any remaining flour with a wooden spoon. Divide dough in half. Cover and chill dough about 3 hours or until easy to handle.

2. On a lightly floured surface, roll half of the dough at a time into a 10×8-inch rectangle, smoothing edges. Cut rectangle in half lengthwise. Cut rectangle crosswise into 8 strips. Place 1 inch apart on an ungreased cookie sheet.

3. Bake in a 375° oven for 7 to 8 minutes or until edges are lightly browned. Transfer cookies to a wire rack and let cool. Frost with Lemon Glaze. If desired, immediately sprinkle with decorating sugar. Let glaze dry.

Lemon Glaze: In a small bowl stir together 1½ cups sifted powdered sugar and 2 teaspoons lemon juice. Add enough milk (1 to 2 tablespoons) to make spreading consistency.

TO STORE: Place in layers separated by waxed paper in an airtight container; cover. Store at room temperature up to 3 days or freeze unfrosted cookies up to 3 months. Thaw cookies; frost.

Coconut Washboards

The washboardlike ridges on these crisp cookies are made with the tines of a fork.

It's an easy step for little ones who want to join in the cookie-baking fun.

Makes: 40 cookies

Oven: 375°F

¾ **cup butter, softened**

1 **cup packed brown sugar**

¾ **teaspoon baking powder**

¼ **teaspoon ground cinnamon**

¼ **teaspoon ground nutmeg**

⅛ **teaspoon salt**

1 **egg**

1 **teaspoon vanilla**

½ **teaspoon almond extract**

2 **cups all-purpose flour**

1⅓ **cups coconut**

1. In a large mixing bowl beat butter with an electric mixer on medium to high speed for 30 seconds. Add brown sugar, baking powder, cinnamon, nutmeg, and salt. Beat until combined, scraping sides of bowl occasionally. Beat in egg, vanilla, and almond extract until combined. Beat in as much of the flour as you can with the mixer. Stir in any remaining flour with a wooden spoon. Stir in coconut. Divide dough in half. Cover and chill dough about 2 hours or until easy to handle.

2. On a lightly floured surface, roll half of the dough at a time into a 10×8-inch rectangle, smoothing edges. Cut rectangle in half lengthwise. Cut rectangle crosswise into 10 strips. Place 2 inches apart on an ungreased cookie sheet. Using a floured fork, gently press ridges into each dough strip.

3. Bake in a 375° oven about 8 minutes or until golden brown. Transfer cookies to a wire rack and let cool.

TO STORE: Place in layers separated by waxed paper in an airtight container; cover. Store at room temperature up to 3 days or freeze up to 3 months.

Coconut *Cutouts*

Piping the chocolate on top is a pretty, fancy touch, but if you're pressed for time, dip cookies into melted chocolate instead. Let the cookies stand on waxed paper until the chocolate is set.

Makes: about 48 cookies

Oven: 375°F

1¼ **cups coconut**

¾ **cup butter, softened**

¾ **cup sugar**

1½ **teaspoons baking powder**

2 **eggs**

1 **teaspoon vanilla**

2 **cups all-purpose flour**

6 **ounces semisweet chocolate, chopped**

1 **tablespoon shortening**

1. Place coconut in a food processor bowl. Cover and process until finely chopped. (Or finely chop coconut by hand.) Set coconut aside.

2. In a large mixing bowl beat butter with an electric mixer on medium to high speed for 30 seconds. Add sugar and baking powder. Beat until combined, scraping sides of bowl occasionally. Beat in eggs and vanilla until combined. Beat in as much of the flour as you can with the mixer. Stir in any remaining flour and the coconut with a wooden spoon. Divide dough in half. Cover and chill dough for 1 to 2 hours or until easy to handle.

3. On a lightly floured surface, roll half of the dough at a time until ⅛ inch thick. Using floured 2½-inch cookie cutters, cut into desired shapes. Place 1 inch apart on an ungreased cookie sheet.

4. Bake in a 375° oven about 8 minutes or until edges are lightly browned. Transfer cookies to a wire rack and let cool.

5. In a small heavy saucepan melt chocolate and shortening over low heat, stirring constantly. Spoon melted chocolate mixture into a small, heavy self-sealing plastic bag; seal bag. Snip a tiny piece off one corner of the bag. Pipe on cookies to decorate as desired; let stand until set.

TO STORE: Place in layers separated by waxed paper in an airtight container; cover. Store at room temperature up to 3 days or freeze undecorated cookies up to 3 months. Thaw cookies; decorate as desired.

Jam *Diamonds*

**Tender and not too sweet, these diamonds will remind you of European pastries. Rolling
and folding the rich dough is the secret to that luscious effect. *(photo, page 217)***

Makes: about 28 cookies

Oven: 400°F

  2 **cups all-purpose flour**

¼ **cup sugar**

  1 **cup butter, cut into**

      ½**-inch slices**

  1 **cup small-curd cottage cheese**

¼ **cup strawberry or cherry jam**

     Strawberry or cherry jam

  1 **recipe Powdered Sugar Icing**

1. In a medium bowl combine flour and sugar. Using a pastry blender, cut in butter and cottage cheese until mixture clings together (butter should remain in large pieces). Form into a ball. Turn dough out onto a floured pastry cloth. With floured hands, gently knead dough for eight strokes. Using a well-floured rolling pin, roll dough into a 12×10-inch rectangle. Fold dough crosswise into thirds to form a 4×10-inch rectangle. Give the dough a quarter turn and roll into a 12×10-inch rectangle. Fold, roll, and fold one more time. Wrap dough in plastic wrap; chill in the freezer for 20 to 30 minutes or until dough is firm but not stiff.

2. Grease a large cookie sheet; set aside. On a lightly floured surface, roll dough into a 15×11-inch rectangle. Using a pastry wheel or sharp knife, cut vertical parallel lines about 1½ inches apart. Then cut diagonal lines about 1½ inches apart, forming diamonds. Place 1 inch apart on prepared cookie sheet. Press an indentation into each diamond; spoon about ¼ teaspoon jam into each indentation.

3. Bake in a 400° oven about 10 minutes or until edges are golden. Transfer cookies to a wire rack and let cool. If desired, spoon in a little additional jam. Drizzle with Powdered Sugar Icing.

Powdered Sugar Icing: In a small bowl stir together 1 cup sifted powdered sugar and enough milk (1 to 2 tablespoons) to make drizzling consistency.

**TO STORE: Place in layers separated by waxed paper in an airtight container; cover.
Store at room temperature up to 3 days or freeze undrizzled cookies up to 3 months.
Thaw cookies; fill with additional jam, if desired, and drizzle.**

Mocha Cutouts

The sumptuous flavors of coffee and chocolate were made to meld! Here's a great take on the dynamite duo. Hint: If you prefer not to use alcohol, substitute strong brewed coffee for the coffee liqueur. *(photo, page 254)*

Makes: 18 to 24 cookies

Oven: 350°F

½ **cup butter, softened**

½ **cup packed brown sugar**

2 **teaspoons instant espresso coffee powder**

2 **teaspoons unsweetened cocoa powder**

Dash salt

1 **egg yolk**

1 **tablespoon coffee liqueur**

1½ **cups all-purpose flour**

¾ **cup semisweet chocolate pieces**

1 **tablespoon shortening**

1. In a medium mixing bowl beat butter with an electric mixer on medium to high speed for 30 seconds. Add brown sugar, coffee powder, cocoa powder, and salt. Beat until combined, scraping sides of bowl occasionally. Beat in egg yolk and coffee liqueur until combined. Beat in as much of the flour as you can with the mixer. Stir in any remaining flour with a wooden spoon. Divide dough in half. If necessary, cover and chill dough until easy to handle.

2. On a lightly floured surface, roll half of the dough at a time until ¼ inch thick. Using floured 2½- to 3-inch cookie cutters, cut dough into desired shapes. Place 1 inch apart on an ungreased cookie sheet.

3. Bake in a 350° oven about 12 minutes or until bottoms are lightly browned. Cool on cookie sheet for 1 minute. Transfer cookies to a wire rack and let cool.

4. In a small heavy saucepan melt chocolate pieces and shortening over low heat, stirring constantly. Dip a part of each cookie into melted chocolate; let stand until set.

TO STORE: Place in layers separated by waxed paper in an airtight container; cover. Store at room temperature up to 3 days or freeze undipped cookies up to 3 months. Thaw cookies; dip in chocolate.

holiday
treat

Gingerbread Cutouts

No book of all-time favorite cookies would be complete without a classic recipe for gingerbread cutouts, so here it is. Hint: If you want more than three or four dozen cookies, it's best to make extra batches separately rather than to double the recipe. *(photo, page 215)*

Makes: 36 to 48 cookies

Oven: 375°F

½ **cup shortening**

½ **cup sugar**

1 **teaspoon baking powder**

1 **teaspoon ground ginger**

½ **teaspoon baking soda**

½ **teaspoon ground cinnamon**

½ **teaspoon ground cloves**

½ **cup mild-flavored molasses**

1 **egg**

1 **tablespoon vinegar**

2½ **cups all-purpose flour**

1 **recipe Powdered Sugar Icing**
   (optional)

   Decorative candies (optional)

1. Beat shortening for 30 seconds. Beat in sugar, baking powder, ginger, soda, cinnamon, and cloves until combined. Beat in molasses, egg, and vinegar. Beat in as much of the flour as you can. Stir in any remaining flour. Divide dough in half. Cover and chill dough about 3 hours or until easy to handle.

2. Grease a large cookie sheet; set aside. On a lightly floured surface, roll half of the dough at a time until ⅛ inch thick. Using a floured 2½-inch cookie cutter, cut into shapes. Place 1 inch apart on prepared cookie sheet.

3. Bake in a 375° oven for 5 to 6 minutes or until edges are lightly browned. Cool on cookie sheet for 1 minute. Transfer to a wire rack; let cool. If desired, decorate cookies with Powdered Sugar Icing and candies; let dry.

Gingerbread People: Prepare as above, except use 5-inch gingerbread people cookie cutters. Bake as directed above. Decorate as desired. Makes about 25.

Powdered Sugar Icing: In a small bowl stir together 1 cup sifted powdered sugar, 1 tablespoon milk, and ¼ teaspoon vanilla. Stir in additional milk, 1 teaspoon at a time, to make drizzling consistency.

TO STORE: Place in layers separated by waxed paper in an airtight container; cover. Store at room temperature up to 3 days or freeze undecorated cookies up to 3 months. Thaw cookies; if desired, decorate.

Candyland trims **For a sweet and easy way to decorate a cookie, add a quick candy trim. Most candies melt if placed on cookies before baking, so it's best to arrange candy pieces on frosted cookies. Try sliced gumdrops and red cinnamon candy to make bells or holly and berries, or crushed peppermint for a cool and colorful finish.**

Gingerbread Cookies

Surprised to find coffee liqueur amongst the list of ingredients here? Adults love the way it deepens the flavors of this beloved cookie. Hint: You can find meringue powder for the icing in a store that sells cake-decorating supplies.

Makes: about 36 cookies

Oven: 350°F

⅓ **cup butter, softened**

⅓ **cup shortening**

1 **cup granulated sugar**

½ **cup packed brown sugar**

1 **teaspoon baking soda**

1 **teaspoon ground ginger**

½ **teaspoon ground cinnamon**

½ **teaspoon ground nutmeg**

1 **egg**

¼ **cup mild-flavored molasses**

2 **tablespoons coffee liqueur,**

strong coffee, or milk

2¼ **cups all-purpose flour**

1 **recipe Meringue Icing**

Colored decorating sugar or

edible glitter (optional)

1. In a large mixing bowl beat butter and shortening with an electric mixer on medium to high speed for 30 seconds. Add granulated sugar, brown sugar, baking soda, ginger, cinnamon, and nutmeg. Beat until combined, scraping sides of bowl occasionally. Beat in egg, molasses, and coffee liqueur until combined. Beat in as much of the flour as you can with the mixer. Stir in any remaining flour with a wooden spoon. Divide dough in half. Cover and chill dough about 3 hours or until easy to handle.

2. Grease a large cookie sheet; set aside. On a lightly floured surface, roll half of the dough at a time until ¼ inch thick. Using floured cookie cutters, cut into desired shapes. Place 1 inch apart on prepared cookie sheet.

3. Bake in a 350° oven for 6 to 8 minutes or until edges are lightly browned. Cool on cookie sheet for 1 minute. Transfer cookies to a wire rack and let cool.

4. Pipe Meringue Icing onto cookies to decorate as desired. If desired, immediately sprinkle with decorating sugar.

Meringue Icing: In a medium mixing bowl combine ⅓ cup warm water, 2 tablespoons meringue powder, and 1 tablespoon lemon juice. Beat lightly with a fork until combined. Add 3 to 3¼ cups sifted powdered sugar. Beat with an electric mixer on high speed until piping consistency. If desired, divide icing and tint each portion with a different paste food coloring.

TO STORE: Place in layers separated by waxed paper in an airtight container; cover. Store at room temperature up to 3 days or freeze undecorated cookies up to 3 months. Thaw cookies; decorate as desired.

Gossamer Spice Cookies

The word "gossamer" refers to something light and delicate, and perfectly describes these crisp, paper-thin cookies of northern European descent. *(photo, page 255)*

Makes: about 66 cookies

Oven: 375°F

1⅓ cups all-purpose flour

½ teaspoon ground ginger

½ teaspoon apple pie spice

¼ teaspoon ground cloves

¼ teaspoon ground cardamom

⅛ teaspoon ground red pepper

⅓ cup butter, softened

⅓ cup mild-flavored molasses

¼ cup packed dark brown sugar

1. In a medium bowl stir together flour, ginger, apple pie spice, cloves, cardamom, and red pepper; set flour mixture aside.
2. In a large mixing bowl beat butter with an electric mixer on medium to high speed for 30 seconds. Add molasses and brown sugar. Beat until combined, scraping sides of bowl occasionally. Beat in flour mixture until just combined. Divide dough in half. Cover and chill dough about 1 hour or until easy to handle.
3. On a lightly floured surface, roll half of the dough at a time until ¹⁄₁₆ inch thick. Using a floured 2-inch round scalloped cookie cutter, cut out dough. Place 1 inch apart on an ungreased cookie sheet.
4. Bake in a 375° oven for 5 to 6 minutes or until edges are lightly browned. Transfer cookies to a wire rack and let cool.

TO STORE: **Place in layers separated by waxed paper in an airtight container; cover. Store at room temperature up to 3 days or freeze up to 3 months.**

Sulfured vs. unsulfured molasses

If molasses is labeled "unsulfured," no sulfur was used in the processing. Unsulfured molasses usually is a bit lighter in color and has a cleaner sugarcane flavor. Either may be used in our recipes.

Joe *Froggers*

It's said that seafaring men from New England took these giant molasses cookies with them on long voyages. A lemony drizzle adds a touch of softness to an otherwise brawny batch.

Makes: about 24 cookies

Oven: 375°F

³/₄ **cup butter, softened**

1 **cup sugar**

1¹/₂ **teaspoons ground ginger**

1 **teaspoon baking soda**

¹/₂ **teaspoon ground cloves**

¹/₂ **teaspoon ground nutmeg**

¹/₄ **teaspoon ground allspice**

1 **cup mild-flavored molasses**

2 **tablespoons water**

2 **tablespoons rum or milk**

4 **cups all-purpose flour**

1 **recipe Lemon Frosting**
    (optional)

1. In a large mixing bowl beat butter with an electric mixer on medium to high speed for 30 seconds. Add sugar, ginger, baking soda, cloves, nutmeg, and allspice. Beat until combined, scraping sides of bowl occasionally. Beat in molasses, water, and rum until combined. Beat in as much of the flour as you can with the mixer. Stir in any remaining flour with a wooden spoon. Divide dough in half. Cover and chill dough at least 3 hours or until easy to handle.

2. Grease a large cookie sheet; set aside. On a lightly floured surface, roll half of the dough at a time until ¹/₄ inch thick. Using a floured 4-inch scalloped or plain cookie cutter, cut out dough. Place 1 inch apart on prepared cookie sheet.

3. Bake in a 375° oven for 9 to 11 minutes or until edges are firm and bottoms are just lightly browned. Cool on cookie sheet for 1 minute. Transfer cookies to a wire rack and let cool. If desired, drizzle with Lemon Frosting; let frosting dry.

Lemon Frosting: In a small bowl stir together 1 cup sifted powdered sugar, 1 tablespoon softened butter, and ¹/₂ teaspoon finely shredded lemon peel. Stir in 1 tablespoon lemon juice. Stir in enough milk (2 to 3 teaspoons) to make a frosting that is smooth and drizzling consistency.

TO STORE: Place in layers separated by waxed paper in an airtight container; cover. Store at room temperature up to 3 days or freeze undrizzled cookies up to 3 months. Thaw cookies; if desired, drizzle.

Spicy *Ginger Hearts*

Like Old World recipes, this one calls for a little ground pepper for extra spiciness.

Grated ginger—rather than powdered—provides a fresher and more intense ginger flavor.

(photo, page 216)

Makes: about 24 cookies

Oven: 350°F

¾ cup butter, softened

¾ cup packed brown sugar

2 tablespoons grated fresh

     ginger or 2 teaspoons

     ground ginger

1½ teaspoons finely ground

     black pepper

½ teaspoon baking soda

¼ teaspoon salt

¼ teaspoon ground cinnamon

¼ teaspoon ground nutmeg

1 egg

⅓ cup mild-flavored molasses

2¾ cups all-purpose flour

1 recipe Royal Icing or

     purchased decorator icing

     (optional)

    Red and white nonpareils

     or other small red candies

     (optional)

1. In a large mixing bowl beat butter with an electric mixer on medium to high speed for 30 seconds. Add brown sugar, ginger, pepper, baking soda, salt, cinnamon, and nutmeg. Beat until combined, scraping sides of bowl occasionally. Beat in egg and molasses until combined. Beat in as much of the flour as you can with the mixer. Stir in any remaining flour with a wooden spoon. Divide dough in half. Cover and chill dough for 4 to 24 hours or until easy to handle.

2. Grease a large cookie sheet or line with parchment paper; set aside. On a lightly floured surface, roll half of the dough at a time until ¼ inch thick. Using floured heart-shape cookie cutters of various sizes, cut out dough. Place 1 inch apart on prepared cookie sheet. (If you plan to hang the cookies, use a drinking straw to make a hole at the top of each cookie before baking.)

3. Bake in a 350° oven about 10 minutes or until tops appear dry. Cool on cookie sheet for 1 minute. Transfer cookies to a wire rack and let cool. If desired, decorate with Royal Icing and nonpareils; let icing dry.

Royal Icing: In a medium mixing bowl combine 2 cups sifted powdered sugar and 4 teaspoons meringue powder. Add 3 tablespoons warm water. Beat with an electric mixer on low speed until combined. Beat on medium to high speed for 5 to 8 minutes or until very stiff. (If mixture seems stiff while beating, add more water, ½ teaspoon at a time, until piping consistency.) If desired, divide glaze and tint one portion with red paste food coloring. Use at once. Keep covered when not in use.

TO STORE: Place in layers separated by waxed paper in an airtight container; cover. Store at room temperature up to 3 days or freeze undecorated cookies up to 3 months. Thaw cookies; if desired, decorate.

holiday treat

Pistachio Sugar Cookies

Cut these crisp cookies into simple shapes. Once they're baked, use your artistic flair to embellish them with melted chocolate and green candy coating. Look for colored candy-coating disks where cake decorating supplies are sold.

Makes: 54 to 72 cookies

Oven: 375°F

1 cup butter, softened

1 cup sugar

1½ teaspoons baking powder

Dash salt

1 egg

3 tablespoons half-and-half,
light cream, or milk

¼ teaspoon almond extract

3 cups all-purpose flour

½ cup ground pistachio nuts

Sugar

6 ounces semisweet chocolate,
chopped

2 teaspoons shortening

1 ounce green or pink
candy-coating disks, melted

1. In a large mixing bowl beat butter with an electric mixer on medium to high speed for 30 seconds. Add the 1 cup sugar, baking powder, and salt. Beat until combined, scraping sides of bowl occasionally. Beat in egg, half-and-half, and almond extract until combined. Beat in as much of the flour as you can with the mixer. Stir in any remaining flour and the ground pistachio nuts with a wooden spoon. Divide dough into three equal portions. Cover and chill dough about 3 hours or until easy to handle.

2. On a lightly floured surface, roll one portion of the dough at a time until ⅛ inch thick. Using floured 2½- to 3-inch cookie cutters, cut dough into desired shapes. Place 1 inch apart on an ungreased cookie sheet. Sprinkle with additional sugar.

3. Bake in a 375° oven for 7 to 8 minutes or until edges are firm and bottoms are very lightly browned. Transfer cookies to a wire rack and let cool.

4. In a small heavy saucepan melt chocolate and shortening over low heat, stirring constantly. Dip half of each cookie into melted chocolate; let stand until set. Spoon melted candy coating into a small, heavy self-sealing plastic bag; seal bag. Snip a tiny piece off a corner of the bag. Pipe in a loop design over chocolate-coated cookies; let stand until set.

TO STORE: Place in layers separated by waxed paper in an airtight container; cover. Store at room temperature up to 3 days or freeze undipped cookies up to 3 months. Thaw cookies; dip in chocolate and pipe on candy coating.

Cashew-Sugar Cookies

Here's a unique cookie that cashew lovers go nuts for! It's dainty, buttery, and nutty—the perfect treat to go with your afternoon tea or coffee.

Makes: about 42 cookies

Oven: 375°F

1¼ cups all-purpose flour

½ cup ground lightly salted
cashews or ground almonds

¼ cup granulated sugar

¼ cup packed brown sugar

½ cup butter

Granulated or coarse sugar

Whole cashews or blanched
whole almonds, toasted

1. In a medium bowl combine flour, ground nuts, the ¼ cup granulated sugar, and the brown sugar. Using a pastry blender, cut in butter until the pieces resemble fine crumbs. Form mixture into a ball and knead gently until smooth.

2. On a lightly floured surface, roll dough until ¼ inch thick. Using a floured 1½-inch cookie cutter, cut into desired shapes. Place 1 inch apart on an ungreased cookie sheet. Sprinkle with additional sugar. Lightly press a whole nut in the center of each cookie.

3. Bake in a 375° oven for 8 to 10 minutes or until lightly browned. Transfer cookies to a wire rack and let cool.

TO STORE: **Place in layers separated by waxed paper in an airtight container; cover. Store at room temperature up to 3 days or freeze up to 3 months.**

Tips for rerolling the scraps You'll most likely have dough scraps left over after you have cut out your cookies. To ensure that cookies cut from rerolled scraps are as tender as those you cut first, combine the scraps, handling the dough as little as possible. Reroll the dough on a very lightly floured surface. Using a pastry stocking and cloth will also help prevent the dough from sticking to the surface.

Zimtsterne

These unusual, nut-infused meringue-and-cinnamon cookies from Germany are a great way to use egg whites left over from another recipe. *(photo, page 219)*

Makes: about 32 cookies

Oven: 325°F

2 **egg whites**

1½ **cups almonds, toasted and ground**

¾ **cup hazelnuts (filberts), toasted and ground**

2 **tablespoons all-purpose flour**

1 **teaspoon ground cinnamon**

¼ **teaspoon ground nutmeg**

1 **cup granulated sugar**

   Sifted powdered sugar

1. In a large mixing bowl allow egg whites to stand at room temperature for 30 minutes. Meanwhile, grease a large cookie sheet; set aside.

2. In a medium bowl combine almonds, hazelnuts, flour, cinnamon, and nutmeg; set aside. Beat egg whites with an electric mixer on medium speed until soft peaks form (tips curl). Gradually add granulated sugar, 1 tablespoon at a time, beating on high speed until stiff peaks form (tips stand straight) and sugar is almost dissolved. Fold nut mixture into beaten egg whites. Cover and let stand for 30 minutes to let nuts absorb moisture.

3. Sprinkle some powdered sugar lightly over work surface. Roll dough on surface to ¼ inch thick. Using a floured 2- to 2½-inch star-shape cookie cutter, cut out dough. Place 1 inch apart on prepared cookie sheet.

4. Bake in a 325° oven about 10 minutes or until lightly browned and crisp. Transfer cookies to a wire rack and let cool. If desired, sprinkle lightly with additional powdered sugar.

TO STORE: Place in layers separated by waxed paper in an airtight container; cover. Store at room temperature up to 3 days or freeze up to 3 months.

Sesame-Pecan Wafers

When you think of Southern cooking, does only fried chicken come to mind? Two of that region's favorite ingredients are sesame seeds and pecans, joined here in one irresistibly nutty cookie.

Makes: about 56 cookies

Oven: 375°F

1 cup butter, softened

⅔ cup sugar

1 teaspoon vanilla

1¾ cups all-purpose flour

½ cup sesame seeds

½ cup ground pecans or almonds

4 ounces semisweet chocolate
   or white baking bars

1 teaspoon shortening
   Ground pecans or toasted
   sesame seeds

1. In a large mixing bowl beat butter with an electric mixer on medium to high speed for 30 seconds. Add sugar and vanilla. Beat until combined, scraping sides of bowl occasionally. Beat in as much of the flour as you can with the mixer. Stir in any remaining flour with a wooden spoon. Stir in the ½ cup sesame seeds and the ½ cup ground nuts. Divide dough in half. If necessary, cover and chill dough about 1 hour or until easy to handle.

2. On a lightly floured surface, roll half of the dough at a time until ⅛ inch thick. Using floured 2-inch cookie cutters, cut into desired shapes. Place 1 inch apart on an ungreased cookie sheet.

3. Bake in a 375° oven for 7 to 8 minutes or until edges are lightly browned. Transfer cookies to a wire rack and let cool.

4. In a small heavy saucepan melt semisweet chocolate and shortening over low heat, stirring constantly. Dip half of each cookie into melted chocolate; immediately sprinkle with additional ground pecans. Let stand until set.

TO STORE: Place in layers separated by waxed paper in an airtight container; cover. Store at room temperature up to 3 days or freeze undipped cookies up to 3 months. Thaw cookies; dip in chocolate and sprinkle with nuts.

Mantecados

These shortbreadlike cookies, infused with almond and lemon and topped with a shiny glaze, are a traditional Christmastime treat in both Spain and Mexico. *(photo, page 254)*

Makes: about 60 cookies

Oven: 350°F

1 cup butter, softened

1 cup sugar

2 cups all-purpose flour

½ cup blanched almonds, very finely ground

1 tablespoon finely shredded lemon peel

1 beaten egg

1 teaspoon water

1. In a large mixing bowl beat butter with an electric mixer on medium to high speed for 30 seconds. Add sugar; beat until combined, scraping sides of bowl occasionally. Beat in flour until combined. Stir in ground almonds and lemon peel with a wooden spoon. Divide dough into three equal portions. Cover and chill dough about 1 hour or until easy to handle.

2. On a lightly floured surface, roll one portion of the dough at a time until ⅛ to ¼ inch thick. Using floured 2-inch cookie cutters, cut into desired shapes. Place 1 inch apart on an ungreased cookie sheet. Combine egg and water; brush over tops of cookies.

3. Bake in a 350° oven for 8 to 10 minutes or until edges are lightly browned. Cool on cookie sheet for 2 minutes. Transfer cookies to a wire rack and let cool.

Chocolate-Dipped Mantecados: Prepare and bake as directed above. In a medium heavy saucepan melt 10 ounces chocolate-flavored candy coating over low heat, stirring occasionally. Meanwhile, in a small heavy saucepan melt 2 ounces vanilla-flavored candy coating over low heat, stirring occasionally. Dip half of each cookie into melted chocolate-flavored candy coating. Immediately swirl melted vanilla-flavored candy coating over chocolate. Place on waxed paper. Let stand until set.

TO STORE: Place in layers separated by waxed paper in an airtight container; cover. Store at room temperature up to 3 days or freeze undipped cookies up to 3 months. Thaw cookies; if desired, dip and swirl with candy coating.

Black *Walnut* Thins

Enjoy these rich, nut-studded butter cookies all year long. To make them extra-special at Christmastime, pipe their tops with white icing snowflakes. *(photo, page 255)*

Makes: about 36 cookies

Oven: 350°F

- 1 **cup butter, softened**
- 2¾ **cups sifted powdered sugar**
- ¾ **teaspoon vanilla**
- ¼ **teaspoon salt**
- 1 **egg**
- 2 **cups all-purpose flour**
- 1½ **cups black walnuts or hazelnuts (filberts), toasted and chopped**
- ½ **cup granulated sugar**
- ½ **cup black walnuts or hazelnuts (filberts), toasted and finely chopped**
- 1 **recipe Powdered Sugar Icing**

1. In a large mixing bowl beat butter with an electric mixer on medium to high speed for 30 seconds. Add powdered sugar, vanilla, and salt. Beat until combined, scraping sides of bowl occasionally. Beat in the egg until combined. Beat in as much of the flour as you can with the mixer. Stir in any remaining flour with a wooden spoon. Stir in the 1½ cups chopped nuts. Divide dough in half. Cover and chill dough about 2 hours or until easy to handle.

2. In a small bowl combine granulated sugar and the ½ cup finely chopped nuts; set sugar-nut mixture aside.

3. On a lightly floured surface, roll half of the dough at a time until ⅛ inch thick. Using a floured 2½-inch round cookie cutter, cut out dough. Place 1 inch apart on an ungreased cookie sheet. Sprinkle with the sugar-nut mixture.

4. Bake in a 350° oven for 8 to 10 minutes or until bottoms are just golden brown. Cool on cookie sheet for 1 minute. Transfer cookies to a wire rack and let cool. Pipe Powdered Sugar Icing on each cookie in a snowflake pattern. Let stand until dry.

Powdered Sugar Icing: In a small bowl stir together 1 cup sifted powdered sugar and ¼ teaspoon vanilla. Add enough milk (2 to 4 teaspoons) to make piping consistency.

TO STORE: Place in layers separated by waxed paper in an airtight container; cover. Store at room temperature up to 3 days or freeze undecorated cookies up to 3 months. Thaw cookies; pipe on icing.

Leckerle

These cookies hail from Switzerland, where honey serves as a popular sweetener for baked goods. Cookies made with honey tend to be chewier than those made with sugar. Hint: Mix the dough until it forms a ball. If you stop mixing too soon, the dough may be too crumbly.

Makes: about 60 cookies

Oven: 350°F

2½ **cups all-purpose flour**

1 **cup sugar**

1 **cup unblanched almonds, finely chopped**

¼ **cup candied orange peel, finely chopped**

¼ **cup candied lemon peel, finely chopped**

1 **teaspoon baking powder**

1 **teaspoon ground cinnamon**

½ **teaspoon ground nutmeg**

¼ **teaspoon ground cloves**

¾ **cup honey**

2 **tablespoons kirsch or brandy**

1 **beaten egg**

1 **recipe Citrus Glaze**

1. Grease a large cookie sheet; set aside. In a large bowl stir together flour, sugar, almonds, candied orange peel, candied lemon peel, baking powder, cinnamon, nutmeg, and cloves. Make a well in the center of the flour mixture. Add honey, kirsch, and beaten egg. Stir and knead dough, forming it into a ball. Divide dough in half.

2. On a lightly floured surface, roll half of the dough at a time until ¼ inch thick. Cut dough into 2½×1-inch strips. Place 1 inch apart on prepared cookie sheet.

3. Bake in a 350° oven about 10 minutes or until golden brown. Transfer cookies to a wire rack. Brush tops of warm cookies with Citrus Glaze; let glaze dry.

Citrus Glaze: In a small bowl stir together 1 cup powdered sugar, ½ teaspoon finely shredded lemon peel or orange peel, and 2 teaspoons lemon juice or orange juice. Add enough water (2 to 3 teaspoons) to make desired consistency.

TO STORE: Place in layers separated by waxed paper in an airtight container; cover. Store at room temperature up to 3 days or freeze up to 3 months.

Almond Crescents

These nutty shortbread cookies sport a sprightly twist. Lemon peel is responsible for the extra dimension.

Makes: about 62 cookies

Oven: 375°F

8 ounces unblanched
   whole almonds

1 cup butter, softened

1¼ cups granulated sugar

1⅔ cups all-purpose flour

2 teaspoons vanilla

¼ teaspoon salt

2 teaspoons finely shredded
   lemon peel

2 cups sifted powdered sugar

3 tablespoons milk

1. Place almonds in a food processor bowl. Cover and process until very finely ground but not a paste. Set aside.

2. In a large mixing bowl beat butter with an electric mixer on medium to high speed for 30 seconds. Add granulated sugar; beat until combined, scraping sides of bowl occasionally. Beat in ground almonds, flour, 1 teaspoon of the vanilla, and salt until combined. Stir in lemon peel with a wooden spoon. Knead dough until it clings together. Divide dough in half.

3. On a lightly floured surface, roll half of the dough at a time until ⅛ inch thick. Using a floured 3-inch crescent-shape cookie cutter, cut out dough. Place 2 inches apart on an ungreased cookie sheet.

4. Bake in a 375° oven about 10 minutes or until edges are lightly browned. Cool on cookie sheet for 2 minutes. Transfer cookies to a wire rack.

5. Meanwhile, for glaze, in a small bowl stir together powdered sugar, milk, and the remaining 1 teaspoon vanilla. Spread glaze over tops of warm cookies; let glaze dry.

TO STORE: Place in layers separated by waxed paper in an airtight container; cover. Store at room temperature up to 3 days or freeze up to 3 months.

Lime Zingers

Not just another pretty cookie, these cutouts wake up taste buds with the zippy taste of lime. The cream cheese frosting adds an extra zing, so decide if you want to slather it over the cookies or use it to pipe on a fanciful design.

Makes: about 72 cookies

Oven: 350°F

1 **cup butter, softened**

½ **cup granulated sugar**

2 **teaspoons finely shredded lime peel**

¼ **cup lime juice (about 2 limes)**

2 **teaspoons vanilla**

2¼ **cups all-purpose flour**

¾ **cup finely chopped Brazil nuts or hazelnuts (filberts)**

½ **of an 8-ounce package cream cheese, softened**

1 **cup sifted powdered sugar**

1 **tablespoon lemon juice or lime juice**

Green food coloring

1. In a large mixing bowl beat butter with an electric mixer on medium to high speed for 30 seconds. Add granulated sugar; beat until combined, scraping sides of bowl occasionally. Beat in lime peel, the ¼ cup lime juice, and 1 teaspoon of the vanilla until combined. Beat in as much of the flour as you can with the mixer. Stir in any remaining flour with a wooden spoon. Stir in nuts. Divide dough in half.

2. On a lightly floured surface, roll half of the dough at a time until ¼ inch thick. Using floured 1- or 2-inch cookie cutters, cut into desired shapes. Place 1 inch apart on an ungreased cookie sheet.

3. Bake in a 350° oven for 8 to 10 minutes or until edges are lightly browned. Transfer cookies to a wire rack and let cool.

4. For frosting, in a mixing bowl beat cream cheese, powdered sugar, the 1 tablespoon lemon juice, and the remaining 1 teaspoon vanilla with an electric mixer on medium speed until smooth. Tint as desired with green food coloring. Frost cookies or use frosting to pipe designs on cookies; let frosting dry.

TO STORE: **Place in layers separated by waxed paper in an airtight container; cover. Store at room temperature up to 3 days or freeze unfrosted cookies up to 3 months. Thaw cookies; frost.**

Freeze now, ice later **If you want to make iced cutouts ahead, we recommend that you freeze the cutouts before you ice them. When ready to serve, thaw the cookies, then ice. Frozen icing tends to discolor or dry out and fall off. Cookies frozen with icing also may be less crisp because they tend to absorb moisture from the icing.**

Shortbread

Name your pleasure: Bake this basic recipe for shortbread at its pure and simple best, or use it as the starting point for intriguing variations that integrate extras such as oatmeal and spices. *(photo, page 255)*

Makes: 16 wedges

Oven: 325°F

1¼ **cups all-purpose flour**

3 **tablespoons sugar**

½ **cup butter**

1. In a medium bowl combine flour and sugar. Using a pastry blender, cut in butter until mixture resembles fine crumbs and starts to cling. Form mixture into a ball and knead until smooth.

2. To make shortbread wedges, pat or roll the dough into an 8-inch circle on an ungreased cookie sheet. Crimp the edge of the dough circle. Use a long, sharp knife to cut circle into 16 wedges. Leave wedges in circle.

3. Bake in a 325° oven for 25 to 30 minutes or until bottom just starts to brown and center is set. Cut circle into wedges again while warm. Cool on cookie sheet for 5 minutes. Transfer wedges to a wire rack and let cool.

Cornmeal Shortbread: Prepare as above, except substitute ¼ cup cornmeal for ¼ cup of the flour. After cutting in butter, stir in ¼ cup snipped dried cranberries or dried tart cherries.

Lemon-Poppy Seed Shortbread: Prepare as above, except stir 1 tablespoon poppy seeds into flour mixture and add 1 teaspoon finely shredded lemon peel with the butter.

Oatmeal Shortbread: Prepare as above, except reduce flour to 1 cup. After cutting in butter, stir in ⅓ cup quick-cooking rolled oats.

Spiced Shortbread: Prepare as above, except substitute brown sugar for sugar and stir ½ teaspoon ground cinnamon, ¼ teaspoon ground ginger, and ⅛ teaspoon ground cloves into flour mixture.

TO STORE: Place in layers separated by waxed paper in an airtight container; cover. Store at room temperature up to 3 days or freeze up to 3 months.

 **holiday treat**

Holiday *Shortbread* Sticks

These festive shortbread cookies glisten with colorful candied fruits and peels. Dip one end of each cookie into white chocolate or semisweet chocolate, whichever you prefer.

Makes: 16 cookies

Oven: 325°F

1¼ cups all-purpose flour

3 tablespoons brown sugar

½ cup butter

¼ cup finely chopped mixed
candied fruits and peels
or candied red and/or
green cherries

½ teaspoon vanilla

3 ounces white chocolate
baking squares or
semisweet chocolate,
chopped

2 teaspoons shortening

¼ cup finely chopped pecans,
walnuts, or mixed nuts

1. In a medium bowl combine flour and brown sugar. Using a pastry blender, cut in butter until mixture resembles fine crumbs and starts to cling. Stir in candied fruits and peels. Sprinkle with the vanilla. Form mixture into a ball and knead until smooth.

2. On a lightly floured surface, roll dough into an 8×6-inch rectangle. Using a long, sharp knife, cut dough in half lengthwise; cut crosswise into 1-inch-wide strips. Place 1 inch apart on an ungreased cookie sheet.

3. Bake in a 325° oven for 20 to 25 minutes or until bottoms just start to brown. Transfer cookies to a wire rack and let cool.

4. In a small heavy saucepan melt white chocolate baking squares and shortening over low heat, stirring constantly. Dip one end of each cookie into melted chocolate. Immediately sprinkle with nuts; let stand until set.

TO STORE: Place in layers separated by waxed paper in an airtight container; cover. Store at room temperature up to 3 days or freeze undipped cookies up to 3 months. Thaw cookies; dip in chocolate and sprinkle with nuts.

Macadamia Nut Shortbread

The much-loved British goodie just got better—and richer—with a sprinkling of buttery macadamia nuts. Serve it alongside a little lemon curd for dipping, and the classic easily stands in as a luscious dessert! *(photo, page 255)*

Makes: 30 to 40 cookies
Oven: 325°F

1¼ cups all-purpose flour

  3 tablespoons brown sugar

½ cup butter

  2 tablespoons finely chopped
      macadamia nuts

      Sifted powdered sugar

      Purchased lemon curd
        (optional)

1. In a medium bowl stir together flour and brown sugar. Using a pastry blender, cut in butter until mixture resembles fine crumbs and starts to cling. Stir in macadamia nuts. Form mixture into a ball and knead until nearly smooth.

2. On a lightly floured surface, roll or pat dough into an 11¼×6-inch rectangle. Use a fluted pastry wheel to cut into 3×¾-inch or 2¼×¾-inch strips. Place 1 inch apart on an ungreased cookie sheet.

3. Bake in a 325° oven about 10 minutes or until bottoms just start to brown. Transfer cookies to a wire rack and let cool.

4. Just before serving, sprinkle powdered sugar lightly over cookies. If desired, serve cookies with lemon curd for dipping.

TO STORE: Place in layers separated by waxed paper in an airtight container; cover. Store at room temperature up to 3 days or freeze unsprinkled cookies up to 3 months. Thaw cookies; sprinkle with powdered sugar.

Elfin *Shortbread* Bites

Maybe elves do exist! It certainly is a wonder when a simple combination of flour, butter, and sugar is so easily transformed into home-baked magic like these sparkling bites.

(photo, page 254)

Makes: about 160 cookies

Oven: 325°F

1¼ **cups all-purpose flour**

3 **tablespoons sugar**

½ **cup butter**

2 **tablespoons colored sprinkles**

1. In a medium bowl stir together flour and sugar. Using a pastry blender, cut in butter until mixture resembles fine crumbs and starts to cling. Stir in colored sprinkles. Form mixture into a ball and knead until smooth.

2. Pat or roll the dough into an 8×5-inch rectangle on an ungreased cookie sheet; cut into ½-inch squares. Separate the squares on the cookie sheet.

3. Bake in a 325° oven for 12 to 14 minutes or until bottoms just start to brown. Transfer cookies to a wire rack covered with waxed paper and let cool.

TO STORE: Place in layers separated by waxed paper in an airtight container; cover. Store at room temperature up to 3 days or freeze up to 3 months.

Frosting tips With a little know-how and lots of colorful frosting, you can deftly transform your cutouts into miniature works of art.

- Cool cookies completely before frosting, allowing about 15 minutes.
- For easy cleanup, use disposable decorating bags.
- Arm yourself with a few basic decorating tips—a small writing tip, a star tip, and perhaps a small rose tip for special touches.
- Make the consistency of your frosting thick enough to hold the piping shape but thin enough to squeeze easily from the bag.
- For the brightest colors, use a frosting made with shortening instead of butter.
- Use either liquid or paste food coloring; paste gives more intense color without thinning the frosting.
- Squeeze frosting from the end of the decorating bag and use steady pressure to keep the frosting flowing evenly.
- Let frosted cookies stand on a rack until frosting is firm. Store in a single layer in cool, dry place.

Cherry Shortbread *Valentine* Hearts

Chopped maraschino cherries are responsible for the delicate pink hue of these shortbread hearts.

A dunk in melted chocolate properly prepares them for the job of sweetening up your valentine.

Makes: about 18 cookies

Oven: 325°F

½ **cup maraschino cherries**

1¼ **cups all-purpose flour**

3 **tablespoons sugar**

½ **cup butter**

1 **cup semisweet chocolate**

pieces

2 **teaspoons shortening**

1. Drain cherries well on paper towels; pat dry. Finely chop cherries; set aside. In a medium bowl stir together flour and sugar. Using a pastry blender, cut in butter until mixture resembles fine crumbs and starts to cling. Stir in cherries. Form mixture into a ball and knead until combined and nearly smooth.

2. On a lightly floured surface, roll dough until ½ inch thick. Using a floured 1½-inch heart-shape cookie cutter, cut out dough. Place 1 inch apart on an ungreased cookie sheet.

3. Bake in a 325° oven for 20 to 25 minutes or until bottoms just start to brown. Transfer cookies to a wire rack and let cool.

4. In a small heavy saucepan melt chocolate pieces and shortening over low heat, stirring constantly. Dip half of each cookie into melted chocolate; let stand until set.

TO STORE: Place in layers separated by waxed paper in an airtight container; cover. Store at room temperature up to 3 days or freeze undipped cookies up to 3 months. Thaw cookies; dip in chocolate.

Chocolate Shortbread

In the minds of true chocolate lovers, there's only one way to improve upon a classic such as this pure butter shortbread. Just add chocolate!

Makes: 12 wedges

Oven: 325°F

1½   **cups all-purpose flour**

  ⅓   **cup unsweetened cocoa**
        powder

  ¾   **cup butter, softened**

  ¾   **cup sifted powdered sugar**

  ½   **teaspoon vanilla**

  ½   **teaspoon almond extract**

  ⅛   **teaspoon salt**

 12   **almond slices**

1. Lightly grease a 9-inch fluted tart pan with a removable bottom or a cookie sheet; set aside. In a medium bowl combine flour and cocoa powder; set flour mixture aside.

2. In a large mixing bowl beat butter with an electric mixer on medium to high speed for 30 seconds. Add powdered sugar, vanilla, almond extract, and salt. Beat until combined, scraping sides of bowl occasionally. Add flour mixture and beat until mixture resembles fine crumbs and starts to cling. Form mixture into a ball and knead until smooth.

3. Pat dough evenly into prepared tart pan or pat into a 9-inch circle on the prepared cookie sheet. Use a long, sharp knife to cut dough into 12 wedges. Leave wedges in circle. Prick each wedge three times with a fork, making sure to go all the way through the dough. Press an almond slice into each wedge about ½ inch from the edge.

4. Bake in a 325° oven about 30 minutes or until top looks dry. Cut into wedges again while warm. Cool in pan or on cookie sheet for 5 minutes. Remove sides of tart pan, if using. Transfer wedges to a wire rack and let cool.

TO STORE: Place in layers separated by waxed paper in an airtight container; cover. Store at room temperature up to 3 days or freeze up to 3 months.

holiday treat

Chocolate *Reindeer*

Want to make friends with your child's classmates? Bake these adorable reindeer for a holiday-time homeroom treat, and you'll be the most popular parent at school. *(photo, page 253)*

Makes: 36 cookies

Oven: 375°F

    1 **cup butter, softened**

1½ **cups sugar**

    ⅓ **cup unsweetened cocoa powder**

    2 **teaspoons cream of tartar**

    1 **teaspoon baking soda**

    ½ **teaspoon salt**

    3 **eggs**

    1 **teaspoon vanilla**

3¼ **cups all-purpose flour**

  72 **small pretzel twists**

  72 **candy-coated milk chocolate pieces**

  36 **small red gumdrops**

1. In a large mixing bowl beat butter with an electric mixer on medium to high speed for 30 seconds. Add sugar, cocoa powder, cream of tartar, baking soda, and salt. Beat until combined, scraping sides of bowl occasionally. Beat in eggs and vanilla until combined. Beat in as much of the flour as you can with the mixer. Stir in any remaining flour with a wooden spoon. Divide dough into six equal portions. Cover and chill dough about 3 hours or until easy to handle.

2. On a lightly floured surface, roll one portion of the dough at a time into a 6-inch diameter circle. Using a sharp knife, cut each circle into 6 wedges. Place 2 inches apart on an ungreased cookie sheet.

3. For antlers, on each triangle lightly press a pretzel into the upper corners. Press in chocolate pieces for eyes. For a nose, press a red gumdrop into the dough triangle about ½ inch from the point.

4. Bake in a 375° oven for 7 to 9 minutes or until edges are firm (do not overbake). Cool on cookie sheet for 1 minute. Transfer cookies to a wire rack and let cool.

TO STORE: Place in layers separated by waxed paper in an airtight container; cover. Store at room temperature up to 3 days or freeze up to 3 months.

Chocolate Reindeer, page 252

Chocolate Buttons, page 257

Chocolate *Buttons*

In today's world of mega-size cookies, these old-fashioned, cute-as-a-button gems work their charm on the cookie tray. *(photo, page 256)*

Makes: about 144 cookies

Oven: 375°F

¼ cup butter, softened

½ cup packed dark brown sugar

¼ cup unsweetened cocoa
   powder

1 tablespoon milk

1 teaspoon vanilla

¼ teaspoon baking soda

⅔ cup all-purpose flour

4 ounces bittersweet chocolate,
   chopped

1½ teaspoons shortening

½ teaspoon mint extract

1. In a medium mixing bowl beat butter, brown sugar, cocoa powder, milk, and vanilla with an electric mixer on medium speed until combined, scraping sides of bowl occasionally. Beat in baking soda and as much of the flour as you can with the mixer. Stir in any remaining flour with a wooden spoon. Divide dough in half.

2. On a lightly floured surface, roll half of the dough at a time until $\frac{1}{16}$ inch thick. Using floured 1- to 1½-inch round cookie cutters, cut out dough. Place 1 inch apart on an ungreased cookie sheet.

3. Bake in a 375° oven for 4 to 5 minutes or until edges are firm. Cool on cookie sheet for 1 minute. Transfer cookies to a wire rack and let cool.

4. In a small heavy saucepan melt chocolate and shortening over low heat, stirring constantly. Remove from heat; stir in mint extract. Spoon melted chocolate mixture into a small, heavy self-sealing plastic bag; seal bag. Snip a tiny piece off a corner of the bag. Pipe on cookies to decorate as desired; let stand until set.

TO STORE: Place in layers separated by waxed paper in an airtight container; cover. Store at room temperature up to 3 days or freeze undecorated cookies up to 3 months. Thaw cookies; decorate as desired.

Spooky *Chocolate* Cutouts

Take frightfully good chocolate dough and cut it into a variety of shapes, such as bats,

cats, and witches, for a Halloween treat that's more whimsical than wicked.

Makes: about 20 cookies

Oven: 375°F

½ cup butter, softened

1 3-ounce package cream cheese

1½ cups sifted powdered sugar

¼ cup unsweetened cocoa
powder

½ teaspoon baking powder

¼ teaspoon ground cinnamon

1 egg

½ teaspoon vanilla

1½ cups all-purpose flour

1 recipe Powdered Sugar Icing

1. In a medium mixing bowl beat butter and cream cheese with an electric mixer on medium speed for 30 seconds. Add powdered sugar, cocoa powder, baking powder, and cinnamon. Beat until combined, scraping sides of bowl occasionally. Beat in egg and vanilla until combined. Beat in as much of the flour as you can with the mixer. Stir in any remaining flour with a wooden spoon. Divide dough in half. Cover and chill dough about 1 hour or until easy to handle.

2. On a lightly floured surface, roll half of the dough at a time until ⅛ inch thick. Using floured Halloween cookie cutters, cut out dough. Place 1 inch apart on an ungreased cookie sheet.

3. Bake in a 375° oven for 8 to 9 minutes or until edges are set. Cool on cookie sheet for 1 minute. Transfer cookies to a wire rack and let cool. Use Powdered Sugar Icing to pipe an outline on top of cookies.

Powdered Sugar Icing: In a medium bowl stir together 2 cups sifted powdered sugar and 2 tablespoons milk. Stir in additional milk, 1 teaspoon at a time, to make piping consistency.

TO STORE: Place in layers separated by waxed paper in an airtight container; cover. Store at room temperature up to 3 days or freeze undecorated cookies up to 3 months. Thaw cookies; outline with icing.

Fabulous Filled Cookies

Whoopie Pies

Appropriately named, these small pies have been known to conjure hoots and hollers from kids and adults alike. *(photo, page 291)*

Makes: 14 sandwich cookies
Oven: 350°F

½ cup shortening

1 cup granulated sugar

1 teaspoon baking soda

⅛ teaspoon salt

1¼ cups buttermilk or sour milk*

1 egg

2 teaspoons vanilla

2¼ cups all-purpose flour

⅔ cup unsweetened cocoa
   powder

¾ cup milk

¾ cup butter

2 cups sifted powdered sugar

1 recipe Chocolate Butter
   Frosting

1. Beat shortening with an electric mixer. Beat in granulated sugar, baking soda, and salt until combined. Beat in buttermilk, egg, and 1 teaspoon of the vanilla. Combine 2 cups of the flour and cocoa powder. Beat in as much of the flour mixture as you can. Stir in any remaining flour mixture.

2. Drop dough by rounded tablespoons 2 inches apart onto an ungreased cookie sheet. Bake in a 350° oven for 8 to 10 minutes or until the edges are firm. Transfer to a wire rack and let cool.

3. For filling, combine milk and the remaining ¼ cup flour. Cook and stir until thickened and bubbly. Cook and stir 2 minutes more. Remove from heat; cool. Beat butter for 30 seconds. Beat in powdered sugar and remaining 1 teaspoon vanilla until fluffy. Beat cooled milk mixture, 1 large spoonful at a time, into butter mixture. Beat on high speed about 1 minute or until fluffy.

4. Frost tops of half the cookies with Chocolate Butter Frosting. Spread bottoms of remaining cookies with filling. Top with frosted cookies.

*NOTE: For sour milk, place 1 tablespoon lemon juice or vinegar in a glass measuring cup. Add milk to make 1¼ cups total; stir. Let stand 5 minutes.

Chocolate Butter Frosting: Beat together ¼ cup unsweetened cocoa powder and 3 tablespoons butter. Gradually beat in 1 cup sifted powdered sugar. Beat in 2 tablespoons milk and ½ teaspoon vanilla. Gradually beat in 1 cup sifted powdered sugar. Beat in additional milk to make spreading consistency.

TO STORE: Place in layers separated by waxed paper in an airtight container; cover. Store in the refrigerator up to 3 days or freeze unfrosted and unfilled cookies up to 3 months. Thaw cookies; frost and fill.

Acorns

Round up the kids—they'll love molding the dough into replica acorns. For shaping, use a flatware teaspoon rather than a measuring spoon.

Makes: 16 sandwich cookies

Oven: 350°F

⅓ cup butter, softened

⅓ cup granulated sugar

½ teaspoon baking soda

1 egg yolk

1½ teaspoons vanilla

1 cup all-purpose flour

3 ounces semisweet chocolate, chopped

1 teaspoon shortening

Strawberry jam or hazelnut butter

Finely chopped hazelnuts (filberts) (about 2 tablespoons)

Pretzel twists, broken (optional)

1. Grease a cookie sheet; set aside. In a medium mixing bowl beat butter with an electric mixer on medium to high speed for 30 seconds. Add sugar and baking soda. Beat until combined, scraping sides of bowl occasionally. Beat in egg yolk and vanilla. Beat in as much of the flour as you can with the mixer. Stir in any remaining flour with a wooden spoon.

2. To shape, press a small amount of dough firmly and evenly into a teaspoon (not a measuring teaspoon). Gently tap the side of the spoon onto prepared cookie sheet to remove the shaped cookie. If necessary, use your finger to help remove dough from spoon. Reshape dough slightly on cookie sheet, if necessary. Place cookies 1 inch apart.

3. Bake in a 350° oven for 8 to 10 minutes or until lightly browned. Cool on cookie sheet on a wire rack.

4. In a small heavy saucepan melt chocolate and shortening over low heat, stirring constantly. Remove from heat; cool slightly.

5. Meanwhile, spread bottoms of half of the cookies with about 1 teaspoon strawberry jam. Top with remaining cookies, flat sides down. Dip wide end of each cookie sandwich into melted chocolate mixture. Place on a wire rack over waxed paper. Sprinkle with chopped nuts. If desired, insert a pretzel piece at the chocolate-dipped end of each cookie for stem. Let stand until set.

TO STORE: Place in a single layer in an airtight container; cover. Store in the refrigerator up to 1 week.

French *Pistachio* Buttercreams

Buttery and elegant. What else would you expect from a cookie with "French" and "buttercream" in its name?

Makes: 30 sandwich cookies

Oven: 350°F

  1 **cup unsalted butter, softened**

  1 **cup sifted powdered sugar**

 ½ **teaspoon salt**

  1 **egg**

1½ **cups all-purpose flour**

     Granulated sugar

  1 **teaspoon rum, cognac, or milk**

  6 **ounces semisweet chocolate**

       pieces or white baking

       pieces, melted

 ½ **cup shelled pistachio nuts,**

       chopped

1. In a medium mixing bowl beat ¾ cup of the butter with an electric mixer on medium to high speed for 30 seconds. Add ½ cup of the powdered sugar and the salt. Beat until combined, scraping sides of bowl occasionally. Beat in egg until combined. Beat in as much of the flour as you can with the mixer. Stir in any remaining flour with a wooden spoon. Cover and chill dough about 1 hour or until easy to handle.

2. Shape dough into ¾-inch balls. Place balls on an ungreased cookie sheet. Using the bottom of a glass dipped in granulated sugar, flatten each ball to a 1½-inch circle.*

3. Bake in a 350° oven about 8 minutes or until bottoms are lightly browned. Transfer cookies to a wire rack and let cool.

4. Meanwhile, for filling, in a small mixing bowl beat together the remaining ¼ cup butter, the remaining ½ cup powdered sugar, and rum with an electric mixer on medium to high speed until combined.

5. Spread the bottoms of half of the cookies with filling. Top with remaining cookies, flat sides down. Chill about 30 minutes or until filling is set. Spread each cookie with melted chocolate; sprinkle with nuts. Chill about 10 minutes or until chocolate is set.

*NOTE: So sugar will stick to the glass, first dip the bottom of the glass in the cookie dough. Next, dip it into sugar.

TO STORE: Place unfilled and undecorated cookies in layers separated by waxed paper in an airtight container; cover. Store at room temperature up to 3 days or freeze up to 3 months. Thaw frozen cookies; just before serving, fill and decorate cookies.

Chocolate-Hazelnut Sandwich Cookies

Chocolate-hazelnut spread is the key to the nutty and rich filling in these cookies. Check the baking aisles in large supermarkets.

Makes: 48 sandwich cookies

Oven: 375°F

½ cup shortening

⅓ cup granulated sugar

⅓ cup packed brown sugar

½ teaspoon baking powder

¼ teaspoon baking soda

⅛ teaspoon salt

1 egg

1 teaspoon vanilla

1½ cups all-purpose flour

¾ cup quick-cooking rolled oats

½ cup chocolate-hazelnut spread

1. In a medium mixing bowl beat shortening with an electric mixer on medium to high speed for 30 seconds. Add granulated sugar, brown sugar, baking powder, baking soda, and salt. Beat until combined, scraping sides of bowl occasionally. Beat in egg and vanilla until combined. Beat in as much of the flour as you can with the mixer. Stir in any remaining flour and the rolled oats with a wooden spoon.

2. Shape dough into ¾-inch balls. Place balls 1½ inches apart on an ungreased cookie sheet. Using the bottom of a glass, flatten dough into 1-inch circles.

3. Bake in a 375° oven for 5 to 7 minutes or until edges are firm and bottoms are lightly browned. Transfer cookies to a wire rack and let cool.

4. Spread bottoms of half the cookies with a scant ½ teaspoon chocolate-hazelnut spread. Top with remaining cookies, flat sides down.

Cashew-Filled Sandwich Cookies: Prepare as directed above, except fill cookies with Cashew-Butter Filling. For filling, in a small mixing bowl beat ⅓ cup cashew butter and 2 tablespoons softened butter with an electric mixer on medium to high speed until combined. Slowly beat in ½ cup sifted powdered sugar and 1 tablespoon milk. Beat in additional milk to make of spreading consistency. If desired, in a small heavy saucepan melt 1 cup semisweet chocolate pieces and 1 tablespoon shortening over low heat, stirring constantly. Drizzle over sandwich cookies; let stand until set.

TO STORE: Place in layers separated by waxed paper in an airtight container; cover. Store in the refrigerator up to 3 days or freeze unfilled cookies up to 3 months. Thaw cookies; fill.

Mini Madeleines with *Candied Orange*

Madeleines just got more dreamy. Here fancy minis are fitted together with a creamy, orange-flavored filling. Present them in paper or foil candy cups. *(photo, page 290)*

Makes: 60 sandwich cookies
Oven: 375°F

1²/₃ cups sifted powdered sugar

¹/₂ cup all-purpose flour

¹/₂ cup yellow cornmeal

4 eggs

¹/₂ cup butter, melted

1 tablespoon honey

¹/₄ cup candied orange peel,
      finely chopped

Nonstick cooking spray

1 recipe Orange-Butter Filling

Sifted powdered sugar

1. Combine the 1²/₃ cups powdered sugar, flour, and cornmeal; set aside. Beat eggs on high speed about 4 minutes or until eggs are thick and lemon-colored. Add sugar mixture; beat on low speed just until combined. Beat in butter and honey. Stir in orange peel. Cover and chill batter for 1 hour.

2. Coat 1¾-inch madeleine molds with cooking spray. Stir batter and spoon 1 teaspoon into each mold.

3. Bake in a 375° oven 7 to 8 minutes or until edges are golden. Immediately invert pan and gently tap on counter to unmold cookies. Using the tip of a knife, loosen cookies, if necessary. Transfer to a rack; let cool. Cool molds; wash, dry, and coat them with cooking spray for each remaining batch.

4. Pipe Orange-Butter Filling onto bottoms of half of the cookies. Top with remaining cookies, flat sides down. Sprinkle with powdered sugar.

*NOTE: If you do not have 1¾-inch madeleine molds, use 3-inch madeleine molds. Lightly coat large molds with cooking spray, or grease and lightly flour molds. Spoon 1 tablespoon chilled batter into each mold. Bake 8 to 9 minutes or until golden. Immediately invert pan and gently tap on counter to unmold cookies. Fill as directed. Makes about 20 sandwich cookies.

Orange-Butter Filling: Beat 3 tablespoons butter until fluffy. Gradually beat in 1 cup sifted powdered sugar. Slowly beat in 3 tablespoons orange juice and 1¾ cups sifted powdered sugar, scraping sides of bowl. Beat in additional orange juice, if needed, to make piping consistency.

TO STORE: Place in layers separated by waxed paper in an airtight container; cover. Store at room temperature up to 3 days or freeze unfilled cookies up to 3 months. Thaw cookies; fill and assemble sandwiches.

Pumpkin Patch Cookies

Why save pressed cookies for Christmas when they're equally good around Halloween?

Held together with chocolate icing and topped with a jelly bean stem, these make a

clever autumn party treat or after-school snack.

Makes: 60 sandwich cookies

Oven: 375°F

1½ cups butter, softened

 ¼ teaspoon orange paste

      food coloring

  1 cup sugar

  1 teaspoon baking powder

  1 egg

  1 teaspoon vanilla

3½ cups all-purpose flour

  1 cup purchased creamy

      chocolate frosting

 60 small green jelly beans

1. In a large mixing bowl beat butter and food coloring with an electric mixer on medium to high speed for 30 seconds. Add sugar and baking powder. Beat until combined, scraping sides of bowl occasionally. Beat in egg and vanilla until combined. Beat in as much of the flour as you can with the mixer. Stir in any remaining flour.

2. Pack dough into cookie press. Using a flower plate in the press, force dough through the press onto an ungreased cookie sheet.

3. Bake in a 375° oven for 6 to 8 minutes or until edges are lightly browned. Transfer cookies to a wire rack and let cool.

4. Spread the bottoms of half of the cookies with frosting. Top with remaining cookies, flat sides down, to form pumpkins. For stems, attach one jelly bean to the top of each cookie with frosting. Let stand for 1 to 2 hours or until frosting is slightly dry.

TO STORE: Place in layers separated by waxed paper in an airtight container; cover. Store at room temperature up to 3 days or freeze unfilled cookies up to 3 months. Thaw frozen cookies; fill.

Pumpkin-Cream Cheese Sandwiches

**Like coffee and chocolate, and peanut butter and jelly, pumpkin and cream cheese were
simply made for each other.**

Makes: 30 sandwich cookies

Oven: 400°F

- 1 **cup butter, softened**
- ½ **cup granulated sugar**
- ¾ **teaspoon baking powder**
- ¾ **teaspoon ground cinnamon**
- ½ **teaspoon ground nutmeg**
- ¼ **teaspoon ground ginger**
- ⅓ **cup canned pumpkin**
- 1 **egg**
- 1 **teaspoon vanilla**
- 2¾ **cups all-purpose flour**
  Ground nutmeg (optional)
  Sanding or coarse sugar
    (optional)
- 1 **recipe Cream Cheese Filling**

1. In a large mixing bowl beat butter with an electric mixer on medium to high speed for 30 seconds. Add granulated sugar, baking powder, cinnamon, nutmeg, and ginger. Beat until combined, scraping sides of bowl occasionally. Beat in pumpkin, egg, and vanilla until combined. Beat in as much of the flour as you can with the mixer. Stir in any remaining flour with a wooden spoon.

2. Pack dough into a cookie press. Using a flower plate in the press, force dough through the press onto an ungreased cookie sheet. If desired, sprinkle with nutmeg and/or sanding sugar.

3. Bake in a 400° oven for 6 to 8 minutes or until edges are firm but not brown. Transfer cookies to a wire rack and let cool.

4. Spread bottoms of half of the cookies with Cream Cheese Filling. Top with remaining cookies, flat sides down.

Cream Cheese Filling: In a small bowl stir together one 3-ounce package softened cream cheese, ½ cup sifted powdered sugar, 3 tablespoons whipping cream, 1 teaspoon vanilla, and ½ teaspoon finely shredded orange peel.

TO STORE: Place in layers separated by waxed paper in an airtight container; cover. Store in the refrigerator up to 3 days or freeze unfilled cookies up to 3 months. Thaw frozen cookies; fill.

Meringue Kiss *Sandwiches*

If you don't have a pastry bag with a star tip, spoon the meringue mixture onto the cookie sheet. Make the dollops as uniform in size as you can so they'll sandwich together nicely.

Makes: 30 sandwich cookies

Oven: 300°F

  2 **egg whites**

½ **teaspoon vanilla**

⅛ **teaspoon cream of tartar**

⅔ **cup sugar**

  Few drops red food coloring

2 **ounces semisweet**

  chocolate, melted

1. In a medium mixing bowl let egg whites stand, covered, at room temperature for 30 minutes. Lightly grease two cookie sheets; set aside.
2. Add vanilla and cream of tartar to egg whites. Beat with an electric mixer on medium speed until soft peaks form (tips curl). Add the sugar, 1 tablespoon at a time, and food coloring, beating on high speed until stiff peaks form (tips stand straight).
3. Using a decorating bag fitted with a ½-inch star tip, pipe mixture into 1½-teaspoon mounds 2 inches apart onto prepared cookie sheets.
4. Bake in a 300° oven about 15 minutes or until firm and bottoms are very lightly browned. Transfer cookies to a wire rack and let cool.
5. Spread bottoms of half of the meringues with about 1 teaspoon melted chocolate. Top with remaining meringues, flat sides down.

TO STORE: Place in layers separated by waxed paper in an airtight container; cover. Store at room temperature up to 3 days.

Baking in thin air Although more stable than cakes, cookie recipes may need to be adjusted a little if you live at high altitudes. Here are a few tricks to help ensure your cookies won't suffer too badly from that Rocky Mountain high.
- Increase the oven temperature by 25° and slightly decrease the baking time (try 1 to 2 minutes less).
- You may need to reduce the sugar slightly (try just a couple of tablespoons less to start).
- If a recipe calls for baking powder or soda, you may need to reduce the amount (try ⅛ teaspoon less).

Amaretti

The combination of ground nuts and amaretto doubles the almond flavor of these chewy,

Italian-style morsels.

Makes: 20 sandwich cookies

Oven: 300°F

2 egg whites

1 tablespoon amaretto or

   ¼ teaspoon almond extract

½ teaspoon vanilla

¼ teaspoon cream of tartar

½ cup sugar

2 tablespoons all-purpose flour

1½ cups ground almonds

½ cup semisweet chocolate

   pieces

1 teaspoon shortening

1. In a medium mixing bowl let egg whites stand, covered, at room temperature for 30 minutes. Line two cookie sheets with parchment paper, plain brown paper, or foil; set aside.

2. Add amaretto, vanilla, and cream of tartar to egg whites. Beat with an electric mixer on medium speed until soft peaks form (tips curl). Add sugar, 1 tablespoon at a time, beating on high speed about 7 minutes or until stiff peaks form (tips stand straight) and sugar is almost dissolved. Beat in flour just until combined. Gently stir in almonds.

3. Using a decorating bag fitted with a ½-inch round tip, pipe mixture into 1-inch mounds 1½ inches apart onto prepared cookie sheets. (Or place the mixture in a self-sealing plastic bag; seal. Snip a piece off one corner of the bag and pipe as above.)

4. Bake in a 300° oven for 10 minutes or until set. Turn off oven and let cookies dry in oven with door closed for 30 minutes. Peel cookies from paper; transfer to a wire rack and let cool.

5. In a small heavy saucepan melt chocolate pieces and shortening over low heat, stirring occasionally. Spread the bottoms of half of the cookies with ¼ teaspoon chocolate mixture. Top with remaining cookies, flat sides down. Let stand on a wire rack until chocolate is set.

TO STORE: Place in layers separated by waxed paper in an airtight container; cover. Store at room temperature up to 3 days. Do not freeze.

Stroopwafels

Dutch tradition calls for this oversize, caramel-filled cookie to be placed over the top of a cup of hot coffee or tea to warm its filling and make it scrumptiously gooey. There's more Caramel Filling than is needed, so make the extra into yummy candy squares. *(photo, page 290)*

Makes: 24 sandwich cookies

  2 **cups all-purpose flour**

  1 **tablespoon baking powder**

  2 **teaspoons ground cinnamon**

  3 **eggs**

  ¾ **cup sugar**

  ⅓ **cup butter, melted and cooled**

1½ **teaspoons vanilla**

  1 **recipe Caramel Filling**

1. Combine flour, baking powder, and cinnamon; set aside. In a medium mixing bowl beat eggs with an electric mixer on high speed 4 minutes or until thick and lemon-colored. Gradually beat in sugar. Beat in butter and vanilla. Add flour mixture; beat on low speed until combined.
2. Heat an electric mini pizzelle iron (for 3-inch-diameter cookies) according to manufacturer's directions. Place a slightly rounded teaspoon of batter in center of grid. Close lid. Bake according to manufacturer's directions. Transfer cookie to a paper towel; cool. Repeat, making about 48 cookies.
3. Prepare Caramel Filling. Immediately spoon 1 to 2 teaspoons filling onto half of the cookies, quickly covering filling with a second cookie.

Caramel Filling: Line a 9×5×3-inch loaf pan with foil. Lightly butter foil; set aside. In a heavy 3-quart saucepan melt ½ cup butter over low heat. Add 1 cup plus 2 tablespoons packed brown sugar, ⅔ cup sweetened condensed milk, and ½ cup light-colored corn syrup; mix well. Cook and stir over medium-high heat until mixture boils. Clip a candy thermometer to side of pan. Reduce heat to medium; continue boiling at a moderate, steady rate, stirring frequently, until thermometer registers 234°F, soft-ball stage (about 8 minutes). Remove from heat; remove thermometer. Stir in ½ teaspoon vanilla. Use about 1 cup of the filling for cookies. Pour remaining filling (about 1¼ cups) into the prepared loaf pan; cool. When firm, lift foil out of pan. Use a buttered knife to cut into squares. Wrap each caramel in plastic wrap. If caramels are slightly sticky, refrigerate them; store in the refrigerator.

TO STORE: Place in layers separated by waxed paper in an airtight container; cover. Store at room temperature up to 3 days or freeze unfilled cookies up to 3 months. Thaw cookies; fill.

Hickory Nut-Buttercream Sandwiches

The rich, pecanlike hickory nut lends its taste of the country to these double-decker cookies. Hickory nuts can be a bit tricky to find—seek them out at farmers' markets or use pecans or black walnuts instead.

Makes: 30 sandwich cookies

Oven: 325°F

1 cup butter, softened

¾ cup sugar

1½ teaspoons vanilla

1¾ cups all-purpose flour

¾ cup finely ground hickory nuts,
    pecans, or black walnuts

½ cup finely chopped
    hickory nuts, pecans,
    or black walnuts

3 ounces bittersweet
    chocolate, chopped

1 teaspoon shortening

1 recipe Buttercream

1. In a large mixing bowl beat butter with an electric mixer for 30 seconds. Add sugar and vanilla; beat until combined. Beat in as much of the flour as you can. Stir in any remaining flour and the ground nuts.

2. Divide dough in half. Shape each half into a 6-inch-long roll. Roll each dough roll in the finely chopped nuts. Wrap each roll in plastic wrap or waxed paper. Chill for 3 to 24 hours or until firm enough to slice.

3. Cut rolls into slightly less than ¼-inch slices. Place 1 inch apart on an ungreased cookie sheet. Bake in a 325° oven 12 to 15 minutes or until bottoms are very lightly browned. Transfer cookies to a rack; let cool.

4. Melt chocolate and shortening over low heat, stirring constantly. Using a small pastry brush, paint bottoms of half of the cookies with chocolate. Place cookies, chocolate sides up, on a wire rack; let stand until set.

5. Spread bottoms of the plain cookies with a rounded teaspoon of Buttercream. Top with chocolate-coated cookies, chocolate sides down.

Buttercream: Beat together 2 egg yolks; set aside. In a small heavy saucepan combine ⅓ cup sugar and 2 tablespoons water. Bring to boiling; remove from heat. Gradually stir about half of the sugar mixture into the egg yolks. Return entire egg yolk mixture to saucepan. Bring to a gentle boil; reduce heat. Cook and stir for 2 minutes more. Remove from heat. Stir in ½ teaspoon vanilla. Cool to room temperature. In a large mixing bowl beat ½ cup softened butter with an electric mixer on medium to high speed for 30 seconds. Add cooled sugar mixture; beat until combined. If necessary, chill until easy to spread.

TO STORE: Place in layers separated by waxed paper in an airtight container; cover. Store in refrigerator up to 1 week or freeze unfilled cookies up to 3 months. Thaw cookies; fill.

Lime *Sandwich* Cookies

If you like a little zing in your cookie, bake this recipe! The refreshing lime flavor brings a tantalizing tingle. Hint: To avoid flattening the dough, slip the logs into tall drinking glasses while they chill.

Makes: 40 sandwich cookies
Oven: 375°F

1 cup butter, softened

1 cup sugar

½ teaspoon baking powder

1 egg

1 teaspoon finely shredded
    lime peel (set aside)

2 tablespoons lime juice

3 cups all-purpose flour
    Several drops green
        food coloring

1 recipe Lime-Pistachio Filling

1. In a large mixing bowl beat butter with an electric mixer on medium to high speed for 30 seconds. Add sugar and baking powder. Beat until combined, scraping sides of bowl occasionally. Beat in egg and lime juice until combined. Beat in as much of the flour as you can with the mixer. Stir in any remaining flour and the lime peel with a wooden spoon. Knead in enough green food coloring for desired color.

2. Shape dough into two 8-inch-long rolls. Wrap in clear plastic wrap or waxed paper. Chill for 4 to 24 hours or until firm enough to slice.

3. Cut rolls into ⅛-inch slices. Place slices 1 inch apart on an ungreased cookie sheet. Bake in a 375° oven for 7 to 8 minutes or until bottoms are lightly browned. Transfer cookies to a wire rack and let cool. Spread bottoms of half of the cookies with about 1 tablespoon of Lime-Pistachio Filling. Top with remaining cookies, flat sides down.

Lime-Pistachio Filling: In a medium mixing bowl beat ¼ cup softened butter with an electric mixer on medium to high speed for 30 seconds. Gradually beat in 1⅓ cups sifted powdered sugar. Beat in 3 tablespoons lime juice until smooth. Gradually beat in enough sifted powdered sugar (1⅓ to 2 cups) to make of spreading consistency. Stir in ⅓ cup finely chopped pistachio nuts.

TO STORE: Place in layers separated by waxed paper in an airtight container; cover. Store at room temperature up to 3 days or freeze unfilled cookies up to 3 months. Thaw cookies; fill.

Mocha Squares

A sumptuous layer of creamy Coffee Liqueur Icing fills these delights. Hint: Use a small metal spatula to smooth and square off the sides of the dough log.

Makes: 20 sandwich cookies

Oven: 375°F

  1 tablespoon coffee liqueur
       or milk

  2 teaspoons instant espresso
       coffee powder or instant
       coffee crystals

  ½ cup butter, softened

  ¾ cup sugar

  ½ teaspoon baking powder

  1 egg

  1 ounce semisweet chocolate,
       melted and cooled

1¾ cups all-purpose flour

  1 recipe Coffee Liqueur Icing

1. In a small bowl or custard cup stir together coffee liqueur and espresso powder; set aside for a few minutes until powder dissolves.

2. In a large mixing bowl beat butter with an electric mixer on medium to high speed for 30 seconds. Add sugar and baking powder. Beat until combined, scraping sides of bowl occasionally. Beat in liqueur mixture, egg, and melted chocolate until combined. Beat in as much of the flour as you can with the mixer. Stir in any remaining flour with a wooden spoon. Cover and chill dough about 1 hour or until easy to handle.

3. Shape dough into a 1¾-inch-square log. Wrap in plastic wrap or waxed paper. Chill for 4 to 24 hours or until firm enough to slice.

4. Cut log into ¼-inch slices. Place slices 2 inches apart on an ungreased cookie sheet. Bake in a 375° oven for 9 to 11 minutes or until edges are firm. Cool on cookie sheet for 1 minute. Transfer cookies to a wire rack and let cool.

5. Up to 1 hour before serving, spread the bottoms of half of the cookies with 1 teaspoon Coffee Liqueur Icing. Top with remaining cookies, flat sides down. Store in refrigerator until serving time.

Coffee Liqueur Icing: In a small bowl stir together ¼ teaspoon instant coffee crystals and 2 tablespoons whipping cream until crystals dissolve. In a medium bowl stir together coffee mixture, 2 cups sifted powdered sugar, and 1 tablespoon coffee liqueur. Add enough whipping cream (1 to 2 tablespoons), 1 teaspoon at a time, to make spreading consistency.

TO STORE: Place unfilled cookies in layers separated by waxed paper in an airtight container; cover. Store at room temperature up to 1 week or freeze up to 3 months. Thaw frozen cookies; fill up to 1 hour before serving. Refrigerate until serving time.

Molasses *Slices*

If you're a made-from-scratch purist, substitute your favorite homemade frosting for the canned frosting used to make these homey snacks.

Makes: 36 sandwich cookies

Oven: 375°F

½ **cup butter, softened**

½ **cup shortening**

¾ **cup sugar**

1½ **teaspoons baking soda**

½ **teaspoon ground cinnamon**

¼ **teaspoon ground nutmeg**

¼ **teaspoon ground ginger**

¼ **teaspoon ground cloves**

1 **egg**

½ **cup molasses**

2¼ **cups all-purpose flour**

1¼ **cups canned vanilla frosting**

1. In a large mixing bowl beat butter and shortening with an electric mixer on medium to high speed for 30 seconds. Add sugar, baking soda, cinnamon, nutmeg, ginger, and cloves. Beat until combined, scraping sides of bowl occasionally. Beat in egg and molasses until combined. Beat in as much of the flour as you can with the mixer. Stir in any remaining flour with a wooden spoon. Cover and chill dough about 2 hours or until easy to handle.

2. Divide dough in half. Shape each half into a 9-inch-long roll. Wrap rolls in plastic wrap or waxed paper. Chill for 4 to 24 hours or until firm enough to slice.

3. Cut rolls into ¼-inch slices. Place slices about 2 inches apart on an ungreased cookie sheet. Bake in a 375° oven about 8 minutes or until edges are firm. Cool on cookie sheet for 2 minutes. Transfer cookies to a wire rack and let cool.

4. Just before serving, spread the bottoms of half of the cookies with frosting. Top with remaining cookies, flat sides down.

TO STORE: Place unfilled cookies in layers separated by waxed paper in an airtight container; cover. Store at room temperature up to 3 days or freeze up to 3 months. Thaw cookies; fill just before serving.

The sorghum substitute Sorghum is made by boiling down the juices from the grain plant sorghum. It can be substituted for molasses in baking.

Apricot-Sage Cookies

Herbs and cookies don't normally go hand in hand, but you'll love the melding of flavor that occurs when tart apricot meets soft sage.

Makes: 16 sandwich cookies

Oven: 375°F

1³/₄ cups all-purpose flour

¹/₃ cup sugar

¹/₄ cup yellow cornmeal

¹/₂ cup butter

2 tablespoons snipped fresh
    sage, lemon thyme,
    or rosemary, or
    2 teaspoons dried sage
    or rosemary, crushed

3 tablespoons milk

1 egg white

1 tablespoon water
    Fresh sage leaves (optional)
    Sugar

2 tablespoons apricot preserves

1. In a medium bowl stir together flour, sugar, and cornmeal. Using a pastry blender, cut in butter until mixture resembles fine crumbs and starts to cling. Stir in fresh herb. Add milk and stir with a fork to combine. Form mixture into a ball and knead until smooth. Divide dough in half.

2. On a lightly floured surface, roll half of the dough at a time until ¹/₈ inch thick. Using a floured 2¹/₂-inch round cookie cutter, cut out dough.

3. In a small bowl combine egg white and water. Brush half of the cutouts with the egg white-water mixture and, if desired, top with one or two small sage leaves. Brush leaves with egg white mixture. Sprinkle with sugar. Place cutouts 1 inch apart on an ungreased cookie sheet.

4. Bake in a 375° oven about 7 minutes or until edges are firm and bottoms are very lightly browned. Transfer cookies to a wire rack and let cool.

5. Snip any large pieces of fruit in apricot preserves. Spread preserves on the bottoms of cookies without sage leaves. Top with sage-topped cookies, flat sides down.

Sage Cookies: Prepare as directed above, except cut out with a 2¹/₂-inch oval or round cookie cutter. Brush cutouts as above. Top all cookies with fresh sage leaves. Brush and sprinkle with sugar as above. Omit apricot preserves. Makes 32 cookies.

TO STORE: Place in layers separated by waxed paper in an airtight container; cover. Store at room temperature up to 3 days or freeze unfilled cookies up to 3 months. Thaw cookies; fill.

Happy Faces

You won't be able to stop yourself from smiling back at these whimsical jam-filled sandwiches!

Crescent-shape aspic cutters are the secret to their jolly faces. *(photo, page 290)*

Makes: 36 sandwich cookies

Oven: 375°F

1½ **cups all-purpose flour**

1 **cup ground pecans**

½ **cup sugar**

⅔ **cup butter**

3 **tablespoons cold water**

½ **teaspoon vanilla**

Pink decorating sugar

(optional)

¾ **cup raspberry or**

strawberry jam

1. Combine flour, pecans, and sugar. Cut in butter until pieces are the size of coarse crumbs. Combine water and vanilla. Sprinkle over flour mixture a little at a time; mix with a fork until dough forms a ball. Wrap dough in plastic wrap. Chill for 1 to 2 hours or until easy to handle.
2. On a lightly floured surface, roll dough until ⅛ inch thick. Using a floured 2-inch fluted or plain round cookie cutter, cut out dough. Place cutouts 1 inch apart on an ungreased cookie sheet. Using a crescent-shape aspic cutter, cut out eyes and mouths from half the rounds. If desired, sprinkle "cheeks" with pink decorating sugar. Bake in a 375° oven for 7 to 10 minutes or until edges begin to brown. Transfer cookies to a wire rack and let cool.
3. Up to 1 hour before serving, spread bottoms of plain cookies with about 1 teaspoon raspberry jam. Top with cutout cookies, flat sides down.

TO STORE: Place unfilled cookies in layers separated by waxed paper in an airtight container; cover. Store at room temperature up to 3 days or freeze up to 3 months. Thaw cookies; fill up to 1 hour before serving.

A matter of degree If you've noticed that your cookies brown too fast or that they seem to take forever to bake and are pale, coarsely textured, and dry when they finally do come out of the oven, your oven might be a little bit off.

To check your oven temperature, set your oven at 350°F and let it heat for at least 10 minutes. Place an oven thermometer (available at hardware stores) in the oven and close the door for at least 5 minutes.

If the thermometer reads higher than 350°, reduce the oven setting specified in the recipe by the number of degrees between 350° and the thermometer reading. If it's lower, increase the temperature.

If it's off more than 50 degrees in either direction, have your thermostat adjusted.

Mascarpone Creams

Looking for a cookie that razzle-dazzles them? Extra-rich and creamy Italian cheese and a bittersweet chocolate spread team up for one super-sophisticated party cookie.

Makes: 64 sandwich cookies
Oven: 375°F

½ cup butter, softened

1 cup sugar

1 teaspoon baking powder

1 teaspoon freshly grated
    nutmeg or ground nutmeg

¼ teaspoon baking soda

    Dash salt

½ cup mascarpone cheese
    or dairy sour cream

1 egg

2½ cups all-purpose flour

1 recipe Powdered Sugar Icing

    White or pastel-color sprinkles

1 recipe Bittersweet Chocolate
    Spread

1. Beat butter for 30 seconds. Add sugar, baking powder, nutmeg, soda, and salt. Beat until combined. Beat in cheese and egg until combined. Beat in as much of the flour as you can. Stir in any remaining flour. Divide dough in half. Cover and chill dough for 1 to 2 hours or until easy to handle.

2. Lightly grease two cookie sheets; set aside. On a floured surface, roll half of the dough at a time until ⅛ inch thick. Using a floured 3-inch oval cookie cutter, cut out dough. Place 1 inch apart on prepared cookie sheets. Use an hors d'oeuvre cutter to cut out a smaller oval shape from centers of half of the cookies. (Bake whole cookies and cookies with cutouts on separate cookie sheets because they may bake at different rates.)

3. Bake in a 375° oven for 5 to 7 minutes or until edges begin to brown. Transfer to a wire rack and let cool. Glaze tops of cookies with cutouts with Powdered Sugar Icing. Sprinkle with white sprinkles; let icing dry.

4. Spread bottoms of whole cookies with about ½ teaspoon of Bittersweet Chocolate Spread. Top with cookies with cutouts, flat sides down.

Powdered Sugar Icing: Combine 1 cup sifted powdered sugar, ¼ teaspoon vanilla, and enough milk (2 to 4 teaspoons) to make spreading consistency.

Bittersweet Chocolate Spread: In a small heavy saucepan melt 6 ounces cut-up bittersweet chocolate and 2 tablespoons butter over low heat, stirring constantly. Cool slightly.

TO STORE: Place in layers separated by waxed paper in an airtight container; cover. Store at room temperature up to 3 days or freeze undecorated and unassembled cookies up to 3 months. Thaw cookies; decorate and fill.

Party Cookie *Tarts*

A fruit curd filling is sandwiched between a spice cookie and a butter cookie for a special-occasion treat. Hint: Look for ready-made strawberry, lemon, and other flavored curds in your supermarket. You'll find them alongside other baking fillings.

Makes: 20 sandwich cookies

Oven: 375°F

- 1 **cup butter, softened**
- 1 **cup sifted powdered sugar**
- 2 **egg yolks**
- 2 **teaspoons vanilla**
- ¼ **teaspoon ground cinnamon**
- ⅛ **teaspoon ground cloves**
- 2 **cups all-purpose flour**
- ⅛ **teaspoon salt**
- ½ **cup strawberry or lemon curd**
  Powdered sugar

1. For spice dough, in a small saucepan heat ½ cup of the butter over medium heat until butter is the color of light brown sugar. Remove from heat. Pour into a small mixing bowl; chill until butter is firm. Beat browned butter with an electric mixer on medium to high speed for 30 seconds. Add ½ cup of the powdered sugar, 1 of the egg yolks, 1 teaspoon of the vanilla, the cinnamon, and cloves. Beat until combined, scraping sides of bowl occasionally. Beat or stir in ¾ cup of the flour. Wrap dough in plastic wrap. Chill about 1 hour or until easy to handle.

2. For butter dough, in a medium mixing bowl beat the remaining ½ cup butter with an electric mixer for 30 seconds. Add the remaining ½ cup powdered sugar, 1 egg yolk, 1 teaspoon vanilla, and the salt. Beat until combined. Beat or stir in the remaining 1¼ cups flour. Wrap dough in plastic wrap. Chill about 1 hour or until easy to handle.

3. On a floured surface, roll each dough until ⅛ inch thick. Using a floured 2½- to 3-inch scalloped round cookie cutter, cut out dough. Using a 1-inch cutter, cut a shape from the center of each butter dough round. (Do not cut out shapes from spice dough rounds.) Place rounds 1 inch apart on an ungreased cookie sheet. Bake in a 375° oven for 7 to 8 minutes or until edges are very lightly browned. Transfer cookies to a wire rack; let cool.

4. Up to 1 hour before serving, spread bottoms of spice cookies with about 1 teaspoon strawberry curd. Top with butter cookies, flat sides down. Chill until serving time. Just before serving, sift powdered sugar over cookies.

TO STORE: Place unfilled cookies in layers separated by waxed paper in an airtight container; cover. Store at room temperature up to 1 week or freeze up to 3 months. Thaw frozen cookies; up to 1 hour before serving, fill and sprinkle with powdered sugar. Refrigerate until serving time.

Pastel *Cream* Wafers

So few ingredients, so much loveliness and sparkle! Hint: Sanding sugar—the secret to these shimmering gems—is a little coarser than granulated sugar. You'll find it where cake decorating supplies are sold and in mail-order catalogs.

Makes: 20 sandwiches cookies

Oven: 375°F

½ cup cold butter

1 cup all-purpose flour

3 to 4 tablespoons light cream
    or half-and-half

   Sanding sugar or
      granulated sugar

1 recipe Powdered Sugar
    Frosting

1. In a medium bowl use a pastry blender to cut butter into flour until pieces are the size of small peas. Sprinkle 1 tablespoon cream over part of mixture. Gently toss with a fork and push to side of bowl. Repeat until all flour mixture is moistened. Form into a ball.

2. On a lightly floured surface, roll dough until slightly less than ⅛ inch thick. Using a floured scalloped 1¾-inch round cookie cutter, cut out dough. Dip one side of each round in sugar. Place cutouts, sugared sides up, 1 inch apart on an ungreased cookie sheet. With a fork, prick four parallel rows in each cutout.

3. Bake in a 375° oven for 8 to 10 minutes or until edges just begin to brown. Transfer cookies to a wire rack and let cool.

4. Just before serving, spread the bottoms of half of the cookies with a scant 1 teaspoon Powdered Sugar Frosting. Top with remaining cookies, flat sides down.

Powdered Sugar Frosting: In a small bowl stir together 1 cup sifted powdered sugar, 1 tablespoon softened butter, ½ teaspoon vanilla, 1 drop food coloring, and enough light cream or half-and-half (about 1 tablespoon) to make of spreading consistency.

TO STORE: Place unfilled cookies in layers separated by waxed paper in an airtight container; cover. Store at room temperature up to 1 week or freeze up to 3 months. Thaw frozen cookies; fill just before serving.

Peanut Butter and Jelly *Sandwiches*

Adults and children alike never outgrow their fondness for peanut butter and jelly.

Here's a dressed-up way to enjoy that classic combination.

Makes: 45 sandwich cookies

Oven: 375°F

½ **cup shortening**

½ **cup peanut butter**

½ **cup granulated sugar**

½ **cup packed brown sugar**

¾ **teaspoon baking soda**

1 **egg**

2 **tablespoons milk**

1¾ **cups all-purpose flour**

Peanuts

Peanut butter

Grape jelly

1. In a large mixing bowl beat shortening and the ½ cup peanut butter with an electric mixer for 30 seconds. Add sugars and baking soda. Beat until combined. Beat in egg and milk until combined. Beat in as much of the flour as you can. Stir in any remaining flour. Divide dough in half. Cover and chill dough for 1 to 2 hours or until easy to handle.

2. On a lightly floured surface, roll half of the dough at a time until ⅛ inch thick. Using a 2-inch floured scalloped round cookie cutter, cut out dough. Place rounds 1 inch apart on an ungreased cookie sheet. Place a peanut half in the center of half the rounds.

3. Bake in a 375° oven about 8 minutes or until lightly browned. Transfer cookies to a wire rack and let cool.

4. Just before serving, spread the bottoms of the plain cookies with about 2 teaspoons peanut butter and 1 teaspoon jelly. Top with peanut-topped cookies, plain sides down.

TO STORE: Place unfilled cookies in layers separated by waxed paper in an airtight container; cover. Store at room temperature up to 3 days or freeze up to 3 months. Thaw frozen cookies; fill just before serving.

Cookie trivia (The first American cookies)

The first cookbook published in North America appeared in 1796 and included a recipe called "Another Christmas Cookey." It required "3 pounds of flour, a tea cup of fine powdered coriander seed, 1 pound of butter, and three 3 teaspoonfuls of pearl ash dissolved in a tea cup of milk." The author advised that the cookies would be "finer, softer, and better when 6 months old," after being stored in an earthen pot, dry cellar, or damp room. Note: Don't try this recipe at home; it doesn't have the Better Homes and Gardens Test Kitchen seal of approval!

Raspberry Gems

Filled with berries, dipped in chocolate, and sprinkled with almonds—this festive little cookie belongs on your list of favorite gems.

Makes: 36 sandwich cookies

Oven: 350°F

1½ **cups all-purpose flour**

1 **cup butter, softened**

½ **cup dairy sour cream**

3 **tablespoons raspberry spreadable fruit**

3 **tablespoons sugar**

1 **tablespoon water**

⅔ **cup semisweet chocolate pieces**

1 **tablespoon shortening**

½ **cup finely chopped almonds**

1. In a large bowl stir together flour, butter, and sour cream until thoroughly combined. Divide dough in half. Cover and chill dough about 3 hours or until easy to handle.

2. Lightly grease a cookie sheet; set aside. On a lightly floured surface, roll half of the dough at a time until ⅛ inch thick. Using a floured 1¾- to 2-inch floured round cookie cutter, cut out dough. Spread about ¼ teaspoon raspberry fruit on top of half of the cookies. Top with remaining cookies. Seal edges, pressing with your fingers.

3. Stir together sugar and water. Brush mixture over cookies. Place 1 inch apart on the prepared cookie sheet. Bake in a 350° oven for 15 to 20 minutes or until bottoms are lightly browned. Transfer cookies to a wire rack and let cool.

4. Meanwhile, in a small heavy saucepan melt chocolate pieces and shortening over low heat until melted, stirring constantly. Dip half of each cookie into melted chocolate. Place on a wire rack placed over waxed paper. Sprinkle with almonds. Let stand until set.

TO STORE: Place in layers separated by waxed paper in an airtight container; cover. Store at room temperature up to 3 days or freeze undipped cookies up to 1 month. Thaw cookies; dip in chocolate and sprinkle with nuts.

holiday treat

Sour Cream *Snowflakes*

The sour cream makes these raspberry-filled snowflakes extra tender. Hint: Use several jam flavors to produce a variety of cookies from just one recipe. *(photo, page 291)*

Makes: 48 cookies

Oven: 375°F

½ cup butter, softened

⅓ cup shortening

1 cup granulated sugar

¾ teaspoon baking powder

¼ teaspoon baking soda

⅓ cup dairy sour cream

1 egg

1 teaspoon vanilla

2½ cups all-purpose flour

⅓ cup raspberry jam

Sifted powdered sugar

1. In a large mixing bowl beat butter and shortening with an electric mixer on medium to high speed for 30 seconds. Add granulated sugar, baking powder, and baking soda. Beat until combined, scraping sides of bowl occasionally. Beat in sour cream, egg, and vanilla until combined. Beat in as much of the flour as you can with the mixer. Stir in any remaining flour with a wooden spoon. Divide dough in half. Cover and chill dough for 1 to 2 hours or until easy to handle.

2. On a lightly floured surface, roll half of the dough until ⅛ inch thick. Using a floured 2½-inch star-shape cookie cutter, cut out dough. Cut a small star shape from the center of half of the stars. Place cutouts 1 inch apart on an ungreased cookie sheet.

3. Bake in a 375° oven for 7 to 8 minutes or until edges are firm and bottoms are very lightly browned. Transfer cookies to a wire rack and let cool.

4. Spread the center of the plain star cookies with about ¼ teaspoon of jam. Top with cutout star cookies, flat sides down, offsetting the points of the top and bottom cookies. Sprinkle cookies with powdered sugar.

TO STORE: Place in layers separated by waxed paper in an airtight container; cover. Store at room temperature up to 3 days or freeze unfilled cookies up to 3 months. Thaw cookies; fill.

Cherry-Nut Rugalach

Starting with the same trio of ingredients—flour, butter, and sugar—cooks throughout the Old World came up with varied and wonderful treats. These fruit-filled pastries come from Eastern European Jewish communities.

Makes: 36 cookies

Oven: 350°F

1 cup dried cherries
  and/or dried apricots,
  finely snipped

¼ cup sugar

¼ cup water

2 teaspoons kirsch (optional)

½ cup finely chopped walnuts

1 cup butter, softened

1 3-ounce package cream
  cheese, softened

2 cups all-purpose flour

2 tablespoons sugar

  Milk

  Sugar (optional)

1. For filling, in a small saucepan combine dried cherries, the ¼ cup sugar, and water. Bring to boiling; reduce heat. Simmer, uncovered, about 5 minutes or until thickened, stirring occasionally. Remove from heat and, if desired, stir in kirsch; cool. Stir in walnuts.

2. Lightly grease a cookie sheet; set aside. For pastry, in a large mixing bowl beat butter and cream cheese with an electric mixer on medium to high speed for 30 seconds. Add flour and the 2 tablespoons sugar. Beat on low speed until crumbly. Knead until a dough forms. Divide dough into thirds.

3. On a lightly floured surface, roll one-third of the dough at a time into a 9-inch circle. Spread the dough with one-third of the cooled filling. Cut circle into 12 wedges. Beginning at wide end of each wedge, roll up dough. Place cookies, tip side down, about 2 inches apart on prepared cookie sheet. Brush each cookie with some milk and, if desired, sprinkle with sugar.

4. Bake in a 350° oven for 15 minutes or until golden brown. Transfer cookies to a wire rack and let cool.

TO STORE: **Place in layers separated by waxed paper in an airtight container; cover. Store at room temperature up to 3 days or freeze up to 3 months.**

Kipfel

These rich cookies feature two much loved hallmarks of Eastern European baking: the use of sour cream in the pastry and a plump, dumplinglike shape.

Makes: about 30 cookies

Oven: 375°F

½ cup butter

2 cups all-purpose flour

¾ cup granulated sugar

2 egg yolks

½ cup dairy sour cream

2 egg whites

1¼ cups ground nuts

1 tablespoon lemon juice

¾ teaspoon ground cinnamon

Sifted powdered sugar

Ground cinnamon

1. For pastry, in a medium bowl use a pastry blender to cut butter into flour until mixture resembles coarse crumbs. Stir in ¼ cup of the granulated sugar. Make a well in the center. In a small bowl combine egg yolks and sour cream. Add to flour mixture. Stir until mixture forms a ball.

2. Divide dough in half. Keeping half of the dough tightly covered, on a lightly floured surface, roll other half of dough until 1/16 inch thick. Using a floured 4-inch round cookie cutter, cut out dough.

3. For filling, in a medium bowl beat egg whites slightly. Stir in ground nuts, the remaining ½ cup granulated sugar, lemon juice, and cinnamon. Spread a rounded teaspoon of filling onto each round to within ¼ inch of edge. Roll up. With seam sides down, press ends with tines of a fork to seal. Place seam sides down on an ungreased cookie sheet.

4. Bake in a 375° oven for 10 to 12 minutes or until lightly browned. Transfer cookies to a wire rack and let cool. Sprinkle with a mixture of powdered sugar and cinnamon.

TO STORE: Place in layers separated by waxed paper in an airtight container; cover. Store in the refrigerator up to 3 days or freeze up to 3 months.

Italian Fig Cookies

Figs, citrus, and almonds often find their way into Sicilian treats at Christmastime. But there's no need to save these buttery filled slices for the holidays; they make terrific anytime treats during the fall and winter months. *(photo, page 291)*

Makes: about 36 cookies

Oven: 375°F

½ cup butter, softened

¼ cup granulated sugar

¼ cup packed brown sugar

¼ teaspoon baking soda

1 egg

1 teaspoon vanilla

1¾ cups all-purpose flour

1 recipe Fig Filling

1 recipe Lemon Glaze
   or powdered sugar

1. Beat butter for 30 seconds. Add sugars and soda. Beat until combined. Beat in egg and vanilla. Beat or stir in flour. Divide dough in half. Cover and chill 3 hours or until easy to handle. Meanwhile, prepare Fig Filling.

2. On a floured pastry cloth, roll a dough portion at a time into a 10×8-inch rectangle. Cut each rectangle lengthwise in half. Spread Fig Filling lengthwise down the middle of each strip. Using the cloth, lift up one long side of dough; fold it over filling. Lift up opposite side; fold it to enclose filling. Seal edges. Place seam sides down on an ungreased cookie sheet.

3. Bake in a 375° oven for 10 to 12 minutes or until lightly browned. Immediately slice strips diagonally into 1-inch pieces. Transfer pieces to a wire rack; let cool. Drizzle with Lemon Glaze or sift with powdered sugar.

Fig Filling: In a medium heavy saucepan combine 1 cup dried and chopped figs, stems removed; ⅔ cup raisins, finely chopped; ½ cup orange juice; ⅓ cup diced candied fruits and peels, finely chopped; 2 tablespoons granulated sugar; 1 teaspoon finely shredded lemon peel; and ¼ teaspoon ground cinnamon. Bring just to boiling; reduce heat. Simmer, covered, 5 to 8 minutes or until fruit is softened and mixture is thick, stirring occasionally. Stir in ⅓ cup blanched almonds, finely chopped. Cool to room temperature.

Lemon Glaze: In a small bowl combine ¾ cup sifted powdered sugar and enough lemon juice (2 to 3 teaspoons) to make of drizzling consistency.

TO STORE: Place in layers separated by waxed paper in an airtight container; cover. Store in the refrigerator up to 3 days or freeze unglazed cookies up to 3 months. Thaw cookies; glaze.

Chocolate-Mint Sticks

At first glance, these look like biscotti, but they're actually soft, not solid, with a creamy, mint-flavored white chocolate filling.

Makes: about 30 cookies

Oven: 350°F

½ cup butter, softened

¼ cup shortening

½ cup packed brown sugar

2 teaspoons milk

½ teaspoon vanilla

¼ teaspoon salt

1¾ cups all-purpose flour

½ cup miniature semisweet
    chocolate pieces

1¼ cups white baking pieces

¼ cup sweetened condensed milk

¼ teaspoon mint extract

2 or 3 drops red or green
    food coloring

2 teaspoons shortening

Few drops red or green
    food coloring (optional)

1. In a large mixing bowl beat butter and the ¼ cup shortening with an electric mixer on medium to high speed for 30 seconds. Add brown sugar, milk, vanilla, and salt. Beat until combined, scraping sides of bowl occasionally. Beat in as much of the flour as you can. Stir in any remaining flour and the semisweet chocolate pieces with a wooden spoon. If necessary, cover and chill dough about 30 minutes or until easy to handle.

2. Meanwhile, for filling, in a small saucepan combine ¾ cup of the white baking pieces and sweetened condensed milk. Cook and stir over low heat until baking pieces melt. Remove from heat; cool slightly. Stir in mint extract and 2 or 3 drops of red or green food coloring.

3. Lightly grease a cookie sheet; set aside. Divide dough in half. On a lightly floured surface, roll one portion of dough at a time into a 12×6-inch rectangle. Spread half of the filling lengthwise over half of each rectangle to within ½ inch of edges. Carefully fold dough rectangles in half to cover the filling; seal all edges. Transfer filled dough rectangles to the prepared cookie sheet.

4. Bake in a 350° oven for 15 to 20 minutes or until edges are lightly browned. Cool on cookie sheet on a wire rack. Transfer to a cutting board. Cut crosswise into ¾-inch strips.

5. In a small heavy saucepan melt the remaining ½ cup white baking pieces and the 2 teaspoons shortening over low heat, stirring occasionally. Remove from heat. If desired, stir in a few drops of red or green food coloring. Drizzle over cookie strips; let stand until set.

TO STORE: Place in layers separated by waxed paper in an airtight container; cover. Store at room temperature up to 3 days or freeze undrizzled cookies up to 3 months. Thaw cookies; drizzle.

Apple Butter *Crescents*

For an old-fashioned touch, use a fluted pastry wheel to cut the dough squares. The result is a dressed up, rickrack edge your grandmother would be proud of.

Makes: 32 cookies

Oven: 375°F

⅔ **cup butter, softened**

1 **cup sugar**

1 **teaspoon baking powder**

¼ **teaspoon salt**

2 **eggs**

1 **teaspoon vanilla**

3 **cups all-purpose flour**

⅔ **cup apple butter or seedless raspberry jam**

2 **tablespoons sugar**

½ **teaspoon ground cinnamon**

1. In a large mixing bowl beat butter with an electric mixer on medium to high speed for 30 seconds. Add the 1 cup sugar, baking powder, and salt. Beat until combined, scraping sides of bowl occasionally. Beat in eggs and vanilla until combined. Beat in as much of the flour as you can with the mixer. Stir in any remaining flour with a wooden spoon. Divide dough in half. Cover and chill dough about 3 hours or until easy to handle.

2. Line a cookie sheet with foil or parchment paper; set aside. On a lightly floured surface, roll half of the dough at a time into a 12-inch square. Cut into sixteen 3-inch squares.

3. Spread about 1 teaspoon apple butter down the middle of each square. Fold one edge of the dough over the filling; fold the other edge over. Place on prepared cookie sheet. On one long side of each cookie, make three cuts halfway through the width of cookie. Curve cookie slightly to separate cuts. Brush lightly with a little water.

4. In a small bowl combine the 2 tablespoons sugar and cinnamon. Sprinkle some of the sugar-cinnamon mixture over each cookie.

5. Bake in a 375° oven for 8 to 10 minutes or until golden brown. Transfer cookies to a wire rack and let cool.

TO STORE: **Place in layers separated by waxed paper in an airtight container; cover. Store at room temperature up to 3 days or freeze up to 3 months.**

Dutch Letters

The Dutch call these almond-filled cookies *Banketstaven*. At one time Dutch bakers made a whole alphabet of shapes, but today most of these treats are S-shaped.

Makes: 16 cookies

Oven: 375°F

4½ cups all-purpose flour

1 teaspoon salt

2 cups butter, cut into
    ½-inch slices

1 egg

1 cup water

1 8-ounce can almond paste

½ cup granulated sugar

½ cup packed brown sugar

2 egg whites

   Milk

   Granulated sugar

1. In a large bowl combine flour and salt. Stir butter slices into flour mixture, coating each butter piece to separate it. (Butter will be in large chunks.) In a small bowl combine egg and water. Add egg-water mixture all at once to flour mixture. Mix quickly. (Butter will still be in ½-inch pieces and flour will not be completely moistened.)

2. On a lightly floured surface, knead dough 10 times, pressing and pushing pieces together to form a rough-looking ball. Shape into a rectangle. (Dough still will have some dry-looking areas.) Flatten slightly.

3. On a well floured surface, roll dough into a 15×10-inch rectangle. Fold two short sides to meet in center; fold dough in half crosswise to form a 7½×5-inch rectangle. Repeat rolling and folding process. Cover; chill 20 minutes. Repeat rolling and folding two more times; chill 20 minutes.

4. Meanwhile, beat almond paste, ½ cup granulated sugar, brown sugar, and egg whites with an electric mixer until smooth. Cover; chill 20 minutes.

5. Cut chilled dough crosswise into four equal portions. (Keep unused dough chilled.) Roll one portion of dough at a time into a 12×10-inch rectangle. Cut into four 10×3-inch strips. Spread 1 slightly rounded tablespoon of almond mixture down center of each strip. Roll up each strip lengthwise around filling. Brush edge and ends with milk. Pinch to seal. Place seam side down on an ungreased cookie sheet, shaping each roll into an S shape or other letter shape. Brush with milk; sprinkle with granulated sugar.

6. Bake in a 375° oven for 25 to 30 minutes or until golden. Transfer cookies to a wire rack and let cool.

TO STORE: Place in layers separated by waxed paper in an airtight container; cover. Store at room temperature up to 3 days or freeze up to 3 months.

Quilt-Block Cookies

This cookie tastes wonderfully old-fashioned and it looks that way too. Pipe tiny lines of icing along the edges of the squares to resemble stitches on a quilt block. *(photo, page 289)*

Makes: 24 sandwich cookies

Oven: 375°F

¹/₂ cup butter, softened

¹/₂ cup packed brown sugar

¹/₂ teaspoon baking soda

¹/₂ teaspoon ground cardamom

    or 1 teaspoon ground

    cinnamon

 1 egg

¹/₃ cup honey

 1 teaspoon vanilla

 1 cup all-purpose flour

 1 cup whole wheat flour

 1 recipe Cherry Filling

 1 recipe Powdered Sugar Icing

1. In a medium mixing bowl beat butter for 30 seconds. Beat in brown sugar, soda, and cardamom. Beat in egg, honey, and vanilla. Beat in all-purpose flour. Stir in whole wheat flour. Divide dough in half. Cover and chill about 2 hours or until easy to handle. Meanwhile, prepare Cherry Filling.

2. On a lightly floured surface, roll half of the dough at a time into a 13×11-inch rectangle. Using a fluted pastry wheel, trim to a 12¹/₂×10-inch rectangle. Cut into twenty 2¹/₂-inch squares. Place half of the squares 1 inch apart on an ungreased cookie sheet. Spread 1 teaspoon of the Cherry Filling over center of each square. Using a 1-inch cutter, cut out and remove a shape from center of each of the remaining squares. Place a square with a cutout on top of each filled square; press edges to seal.

3. Bake in a 375° oven 6 to 8 minutes or until edges are lightly browned. Transfer to a wire rack; let cool. Pipe with Powdered Sugar Icing.

Cherry Filling: In a small heavy saucepan combine 1 cup dried cherries, ¹/₂ cup cherry-blend drink or apple juice, and 1 tablespoon lemon juice. Bring just to boiling; reduce heat. Simmer, uncovered, 10 minutes or until cherries are tender and most of the liquid is absorbed, stirring occasionally. Remove from heat; stir in 2 tablespoons sugar. Cool slightly. Transfer mixture to a food processor bowl. Cover and process until a paste forms. Cool completely.

Powdered Sugar Icing: Combine 1 cup sifted powdered sugar, ¹/₄ teaspoon vanilla, and enough milk (2 to 4 teaspoons) to make piping consistency.

TO STORE: Place in layers separated by waxed paper in an airtight container; cover. Store at room temperature up to 3 days or freeze unfrosted cookies up to 3 months. Thaw cookies; frost.

Quilt-Block Cookies, page 288

LEFT: Happy Faces, page 275 ABOVE: Stroopwafels, page 269
BELOW: Mini Madeleines with Candied Orange, page 264

ABOVE: Sour Cream Snowflakes, page 281; Whoopie Pies, page 260
BELOW: Italian Fig Cookies, page 284; Caramel-Chocolate Pockets, page 298

Pastry Pillows, page 293

Pastry Pillows

This recipe demonstrates how to use the food processor to make quick, easy work of pastry making. When using a food processor, be sure the butter and cream cheese are chilled first. If using a mixer, let the butter and cream cheese stand at room temperature 30 minutes to soften. *(photo, page 292)*

Makes: about 52 cookies

Oven: 375°F

  2 **cups all-purpose flour**

¼ **teaspoon salt**

  1 **cup butter, cut up**

  1 **8-ounce package cream
       cheese, cut up**

      **Apricot, peach, raspberry,
       strawberry, or cherry
       preserves**

      Almond paste

  1 **beaten egg**

  1 **tablespoon water**

      Coarse sugar or pearl sugar

1. In a food processor bowl combine flour and salt. Cover and process until mixed. Add butter and cream cheese. Cover and process until combined. (Or in a medium mixing bowl beat softened butter and softened cream cheese with an electric mixer for 30 seconds. Add flour and salt; beat on low speed just until combined.) Divide dough in half. Cover and chill dough at least 1 hour or until easy to handle.

2. On a lightly floured surface, roll half of the dough at a time until ⅛ inch thick. Cut dough into 2-inch squares. Place half of the squares on an ungreased cookie sheet. Place a scant ¼ teaspoon each of preserves and almond paste in the center of each square.

3. In a small bowl combine beaten egg and water. Brush edges of squares on cookie sheet with egg-water mixture. Top each layered square with a plain dough square. Lightly press together edges; seal with fork tines. Brush with egg-water mixture. Sprinkle lightly with coarse sugar.

4. Bake in a 375° oven for 10 to 12 minutes or until golden. Transfer cookies to a wire rack and let cool.

TO STORE: Place in layers separated by waxed paper in an airtight container; cover. Store in the refrigerator up to 3 days or freeze up to 3 months.

Orange-Cardamom Turnovers

An easy filling of marmalade plumps up these little pastries. The cardamom, a relative of ginger, adds a pleasing dose of spicy-sweet intrigue.

Makes: about 40 cookies

Oven: 375°F

2 cups all-purpose flour

⅓ cup granulated sugar

½ teaspoon ground cardamom

¾ cup butter

2 teaspoons finely shredded
    orange peel

¼ cup cold water

3 tablespoons orange juice

⅓ cup orange marmalade

Powdered sugar

1. Lightly grease a cookie sheet; set aside. In a large bowl stir together flour, granulated sugar, and cardamom. Using a pastry blender, cut in butter until mixture resembles coarse crumbs. In a small bowl combine orange peel, cold water, and orange juice. Sprinkle 1 tablespoon orange mixture over part of the flour mixture. Gently toss with a fork; push to side of bowl. Repeat with remaining orange mixture, 1 tablespoon at a time, until all flour mixture is moistened. Form into a ball.

2. Divide dough in half. On a lightly floured surface, roll half of the dough at a time until ⅛ inch thick. Using a floured 2½-inch scalloped or plain round cookie cutter, cut out dough. Using kitchen scissors, snip any large orange peel pieces in the marmalade. Place a rounded ¼ teaspoon of the marmalade on half of each round. Fold in half. Seal edges, pressing with your fingers. (Or, if using a plain cookie cutter, use a fork to seal edges.) Place 1 inch apart on the prepared cookie sheet.

3. Bake in a 375° oven for 10 to 12 minutes or until edges just begin to brown. Transfer cookies to a wire rack and let cool. Sift powdered sugar over tops of cookies.

TO STORE: Place in layers separated by waxed paper in an airtight container; cover. Store at room temperature up to 3 days or freeze unsugared cookies up to 3 months. Thaw cookies; sprinkle with powdered sugar.

Date and Orange *Pockets*

A drizzle of Golden Icing, made with browned butter, enhances the homespun flavor of these turnovers.

Makes: about 48 cookies

Oven: 375°F

½ cup butter, softened

⅔ cup packed brown sugar

1 teaspoon baking powder

½ teaspoon ground cinnamon

⅛ teaspoon salt

1 egg

½ teaspoon vanilla

1 cup all-purpose flour

⅔ cup whole wheat flour

1 8-ounce package sugar-coated
    chopped pitted dates

⅓ cup orange juice

¼ cup granulated sugar

¼ cup chopped walnuts
    or pecans

1 recipe Golden Icing

1. In a large mixing bowl beat butter with an electric mixer on medium to high speed for 30 seconds. Add brown sugar, baking powder, cinnamon, and salt. Beat until combined, scraping sides of bowl occasionally. Beat in egg and vanilla until combined. Beat in all-purpose flour with the mixer. Stir in whole wheat flour with a wooden spoon. Cover and chill dough about 1 hour or until easy to handle.

2. Meanwhile, for filling, in a food processor bowl or blender container combine dates, orange juice, granulated sugar, and nuts. Cover and process or blend until smooth, stopping as necessary to scrape sides.

3. On a lightly floured surface, roll dough until ⅛ inch thick. Using a floured 2½-inch round cookie cutter, cut out dough. Place cutouts ½ inch apart on an ungreased cookie sheet. Spoon 1 level teaspoon date filling onto center of each round. Fold in half. Seal edges, pressing with fork tines.

4. Bake in a 375° oven for 7 to 9 minutes or until edges are firm and bottoms are light brown. Transfer cookies to a wire rack and let cool. Drizzle with Golden Icing; let icing dry.

Golden Icing: In a small saucepan heat 2 tablespoons butter over medium-low heat for 10 to 12 minutes or until light brown. Remove from heat. Gradually stir in ¾ cup sifted powdered sugar and ¼ teaspoon vanilla (mixture will be crumbly). Gradually stir in enough milk (2 to 3 teaspoons) to make of drizzling consistency.

TO STORE: Place in layers separated by waxed paper in an airtight container; cover. Store at room temperature up to 3 days or freeze undrizzled cookies up to 3 months. Thaw cookies; drizzle.

Cranberry *Pockets*

A pleasing surprise awaits the recipients of these pockets. Inside, a sweet-tart cranberry filling is flavored with port wine. If you choose, substitute cranberry-apple drink for the port wine in the filling and the glaze.

Makes: about 42 cookies

Oven: 375°F

½ cup butter, softened

1 cup sugar

½ teaspoon baking powder

¼ teaspoon baking soda

¼ teaspoon ground nutmeg

Dash salt

½ cup dairy sour cream

1 egg

2 teaspoons finely shredded
orange peel

½ teaspoon vanilla

2⅔ cups all-purpose flour

1 recipe Cranberry-Port Filling

1 recipe Port Glaze

1 recipe Powdered Sugar Icing

1. Beat butter for 30 seconds. Beat in sugar, baking powder, soda, nutmeg, and salt. Beat in sour cream, egg, peel, and vanilla. Beat in as much of the flour as you can. Stir in any remaining flour. Divide dough in half. Cover; chill about 2 hours or until easy to handle. Meanwhile, prepare Cranberry-Port Filling.

2. On a floured surface, roll each dough half until ⅛ inch thick. Cut into 3-inch rounds. Place ½ inch apart on an ungreased cookie sheet. Spoon ½ teaspoon Cranberry-Port Filling onto center of each. Fold in half; seal.

3. Bake in a 375° oven for 7 to 8 minutes or until edges are firm and bottoms are very lightly browned. Transfer to a wire rack and let cool. Drizzle cooled cookies with Port Glaze and Powdered Sugar Icing.

Cranberry-Port Filling: Combine ¾ cup dried cranberries, ⅓ cup port wine, and 2 tablespoons orange juice. Bring just to boiling; reduce heat. Simmer, uncovered, 5 to 10 minutes or until most of liquid is absorbed, stirring occasionally. Stir in 3 tablespoons granulated sugar. Cool slightly. Transfer to a food processor. Process until cranberries are finely chopped. Cool completely.

Port Glaze: Combine 1 cup sifted powdered sugar and enough port wine (3 to 4 teaspoons) to make glaze of drizzling consistency. If desired, tint with a small amount of red food coloring.

Powdered Sugar Icing: Combine 1 cup sifted powdered sugar, ¼ teaspoon vanilla, and enough milk (3 to 4 teaspoons) to make of drizzling consistency.

TO STORE: Place in layers separated by waxed paper in an airtight container; cover. Store in the refrigerator up to 3 days or freeze undrizzled cookies up to 3 months. Thaw cookies; drizzle.

Double-Fudge Pockets

These doubly rich cookies have trufflelike centers between two layers of chocolate cookie. Those who crave even more chocolate are encouraged to top them with a drizzle of chocolate frosting or melted chocolate in place of powdered sugar.

Makes: about 30 cookies

Oven: 350°F

1 cup butter, softened

1 cup sugar

1 teaspoon baking powder

1 egg

1 egg yolk

1 teaspoon vanilla

½ cup unsweetened cocoa powder

2½ cups all-purpose flour

1 recipe Fudge Filling

Sifted powdered sugar

1. In a large mixing bowl beat butter with an electric mixer on medium to high speed for 30 seconds. Add sugar and baking powder. Beat until combined, scraping sides of bowl occasionally. Beat in whole egg, egg yolk, and vanilla until combined. Beat in cocoa powder and as much of the flour as you can with the mixer. Stir in any remaining flour with a wooden spoon. Divide dough in half. Cover and chill dough about 1 hour or until easy to handle. Meanwhile, prepare Fudge Filling.

2. On a lightly floured surface, roll half of the dough at a time until ⅛ inch thick. Using a floured scalloped round 2½-inch cookie cutter, cut out dough. Place half of the cutout rounds 1 inch apart on an ungreased cookie sheet. Spoon a rounded teaspoon of Fudge Filling into the center of each round. Place remaining rounds over of each of the filled rounds. Press edges together to seal.

3. Bake in a 350° oven for 10 to 12 minutes or until edges are firm. Cool on cookie sheet for 1 minute. Transfer cookies to a wire rack and let cool. Before serving, sprinkle with powdered sugar.

Fudge Filling: In a small heavy saucepan melt 4 ounces semisweet chocolate over low heat, stirring constantly. Remove from heat. Stir in ½ cup dairy sour cream and ¼ cup finely chopped walnuts. Mixture will stiffen as it cools.

TO STORE: Place in layers separated by waxed paper in an airtight container; cover. Store in the refrigerator up to 3 days or freeze unsugared cookies up to 3 months. Thaw cookies; sprinkle with powdered sugar.

Caramel-Chocolate Pockets

Chocolate-hazelnut spread, popular in Europe as a breakfast bread topper, is gaining fans on these shores. With new fans come new uses too. Here it lends its nutty flavor to caramel-filled cookies. *(photo, page 291)*

Makes: about 24 cookies
Oven: 375°F

¼ cup butter, softened

½ cup chocolate-hazelnut spread

1 cup sugar

½ teaspoon baking powder

1 egg

¼ cup milk

1 teaspoon vanilla

2½ cups all-purpose flour

32 vanilla or chocolate caramels, unwrapped (about 10 ounces)

2 tablespoons milk

¼ cup finely chopped toasted hazelnuts (filberts)

1. In a large mixing bowl beat butter and chocolate-hazelnut spread with an electric mixer on medium to high speed for 30 seconds. Add sugar and baking powder. Beat until combined, scraping sides of bowl occasionally. Beat in egg, the ¼ cup milk, and vanilla until combined. Beat in as much of the flour as you can with the mixer. Stir in any remaining flour with a wooden spoon.

2. Divide dough in half. Shape each half into a 6½-inch-long roll. Gently flatten each roll into a triangular shape. Wrap in plastic wrap or waxed paper. Chill for 4 to 24 hours or until firm enough to slice.

3. For filling, in a small saucepan melt 16 of the caramels and 1 tablespoon of the milk over low heat, stirring occasionally. Cool slightly. Stir in 2 tablespoons of the hazelnuts.

4. Reshape triangular logs, if necessary. Using a sharp knife, cut each log into ¼-inch slices. Place half of the slices 1 inch apart on an ungreased cookie sheet. Carefully spoon about ½ teaspoon filling over each. Top with remaining slices. Seal edges, pressing with fork tines.

5. Bake in a 375° oven for 9 to 11 minutes or until edges are firm. Cool on cookie sheet for 1 minute. Transfer cookies to a wire rack and let cool.

6. For drizzle, in a small saucepan melt remaining 16 caramels and 1 tablespoon milk over low heat, stirring occasionally. Drizzle over cooled cookies; sprinkle with remaining nuts. Let stand until caramel is set.

TO STORE: Place in layers separated by waxed paper in an airtight container; cover. Store at room temperature up to 3 days or freeze undrizzled cookies up to 3 months. Thaw cookies; drizzle.

Simple Shortcuts

Fry-Pan Cookies

Here's an oldie but goodie, one of the best recipes from the days when cooks first discovered the wonders of using packaged cereal as a baking ingredient. Hint: If the mixture is sticky, lightly coat the scoop with nonstick cooking spray or dip it in water between scoops. *(photo, page 327)*

Makes: about 48 cookies

1 tablespoon butter

½ cup sugar

2 beaten eggs

1½ cups chopped pitted dates

1 teaspoon vanilla

2½ cups crisp rice cereal

½ cup chopped nuts

3 cups coconut

1. Line a cookie sheet with waxed paper; set aside. In a large skillet melt butter over low heat. Stir together sugar and eggs. Add to skillet along with dates and vanilla. Cook and stir over low heat about 5 minutes or until thick. Remove from heat; stir in cereal and nuts.
2. Place coconut in a shallow dish. Drop mixture with a cookie scoop or small ice cream scoop (No. 100 size, about 1¼-inch diameter) into coconut; roll to coat. Place on prepared cookie sheet. Chill until firm.

TO STORE: Place in layers separated by waxed paper in an airtight container; cover. Refrigerate up to 1 week. Let chilled cookies stand 30 minutes at room temperature before serving.

Cherry-Coconut Drops

holiday treat

It's hard to believe just five ingredients add up to such delectable goodness. You can use red or green candied cherries, or both if you're celebrating the Christmas season.

Makes: about 24 cookies

Oven: 325°F

2⅔ cups coconut

2 tablespoons cornstarch

½ cup sweetened condensed milk

1 teaspoon vanilla

½ cup chopped candied cherries

1. Grease and flour a cookie sheet; set aside. In a medium bowl combine coconut and cornstarch. Stir in sweetened condensed milk and vanilla until combined. Stir in chopped cherries. Drop dough by small rounded teaspoonfuls about 1 inch apart onto prepared cookie sheet.
2. Bake in a 325° oven for 12 to 15 minutes or until bottoms are lightly browned. Cool on cookie sheet for 1 minute. Transfer cookies to a wire rack and let cool.

TO STORE: Place in layers separated by waxed paper in an airtight container; cover. Store at room temperature up to 3 days or freeze up to 1 month.

Chocolate-Oatmeal Cookies

Chocolate-hazelnut spread is the shortcut secret here. This one ingredient and its windfall of rich, nutty flavor make these cookies the favorites they are today. Look for it next to the peanut butter at your supermarket.

Makes: about 36 cookies

2 **cups sugar**

¼ **cup unsweetened cocoa**
   powder

½ **cup milk**

½ **cup butter**

1 **tablespoon light-colored**
   corn syrup

¼ **cup chocolate-hazelnut**
   spread or peanut butter

2 **cups quick-cooking rolled oats**

1. Line a cookie sheet with waxed paper; set aside. In a medium heavy saucepan combine sugar and cocoa powder; stir in milk. Add butter and corn syrup. Bring mixture to boiling, stirring occasionally. Boil mixture, uncovered, for 3 minutes. Stir in chocolate-hazelnut spread until smooth. Stir in rolled oats.

2. Return mixture to boiling. Remove saucepan from heat. Beat the mixture with a wooden spoon until slightly thickened. Let stand for 15 to 20 minutes or until the mixture mounds. Drop mixture from a teaspoon onto prepared cookie sheet. Let cool.

TO STORE: Place in layers separated by waxed paper in an airtight container; cover. Store at room temperature up to 3 days or freeze up to 3 months.

Cookies: special delivery Ensuring the safe arrival of cookies sent by mail takes some know-how on the part of the sender. Here are some tips *Better Homes and Gardens* editors have culled over the years.

- Choose sturdy cookies that will travel well. Most bar or soft, moist cookies are good choices. However, the filling or frosting in or on some cookies may soften, causing them to stick together or to the wrapping.
- Wrap cookies in pairs, back to back, or individually with plastic wrap.
- Choose a heavy box and line it with plastic wrap or foil. Place a generous layer of plastic bubble wrap; foam packing pieces; or crumpled tissue paper, paper towels, waxed paper, or brown paper bags on the bottom of the box.
- Layer the cookies and the filler. End with plenty of filler to prevent the contents from shifting during shipping.

Milk Chocolate and *Caramel* Clusters

Sticky, chewy, crunchy, nutty, and chocolaty—who could ask for more in a snack treat?

Certainly not your kids, who are sure to make these clusters disappear quickly.

Makes: about 28 cookies

12 vanilla caramels, unwrapped

½ cup milk chocolate pieces

2 tablespoons water

2 cups honey graham
   cereal, slightly crushed
   (about 1½ cups)

¾ cup peanuts

1. Line a cookie sheet with waxed paper; set aside. In a medium heavy saucepan combine caramels, chocolate pieces, and water. Heat and stir over low heat until caramels melt. Remove saucepan from heat. Stir in cereal and peanuts.

2. Working quickly, drop the mixture from a teaspoon onto prepared cookie sheet. Let stand until firm.

TO STORE: Place in layers separated by waxed paper in an airtight container; cover. Store at room temperature up to 3 days or freeze up to 3 months.

Host a cookie exchange Everyone is busy around the holidays and may not have time to make up multiple batches of cookies, but that doesn't mean you can't sample and enjoy a good variety. It's easy to stock up on an assortment of homemade cookies if you host a cookie exchange. Here's how it works:

- Ask guests to bring one kind of special homemade holiday cookie (no store-bought sweets allowed).
- Specify the number of cookies each person must bring, making sure there are enough to allow each guest to take home a good sampling (at least a dozen cookies).
- Suggest that everyone bring extra plastic bags or cartons so each type of cookie has its own container for the trip home. That way they're ready to pop into the freezer to enjoy later.
- To sample the cookies at the party, have guests bring a separate plate of cookies for a tasting buffet. Otherwise, there may not be enough cookies left to exchange. Depending on the time of day, you might also consider serving brunch, salad lunch, or potluck supper.

Peanut Butter Chocolate Cookies

Fast and easy, these drop cookies have what it takes to squash your peanut butter-chocolate craving in the most delightful way.

Makes: about 30 cookies

Oven: 375°F

1 package 1-layer-size devil's
   food cake mix

½ cup peanut butter

1 egg

2 tablespoons water

1 tablespoon cooking oil

½ cup miniature candy-coated
   semisweet chocolate pieces
   or miniature semisweet
   chocolate pieces

1. In a large mixing bowl combine cake mix, peanut butter, egg, water, and cooking oil. Beat with an electric mixer on medium speed until combined. Stir in chocolate pieces.

2. Drop dough by rounded teaspoons 2 inches apart onto an ungreased cookie sheet. Bake in a 375° oven for 9 to 11 minutes or until edges are firm. Transfer cookies to a wire rack and let cool.

TO STORE: Place in layers separated by waxed paper in an airtight container; cover. Store at room temperature up to 3 days or freeze up to 3 months.

Haystacks

Melt, stir, and drop. In just three steps these super-easy snacks are ready to eat.

Makes: 30 cookies

1 3-ounce can chow mein
   noodles (about 2 cups)

½ cup peanuts

⅔ cup sweetened condensed milk

½ cup semisweet chocolate pieces

½ cup butterscotch-flavored pieces

1. Line a cookie sheet with waxed paper; set aside. In a large bowl combine noodles and peanuts; set aside. In a medium saucepan combine condensed milk, chocolate pieces, and butterscotch pieces. Cook and stir over low heat about 5 minutes or until pieces melt. Pour chocolate mixture over noodles and peanuts. Stir until thoroughly coated.

2. Drop by rounded teaspoons onto prepared cookie sheet. Cool at room temperature or chill in the refrigerator until firm.

TO STORE: Place in layers separated by waxed paper in an airtight container; cover. Store in the refrigerator up to 1 week or freeze up to 3 months.

Tom *Thumbprints*

The thumbprints lose some of their depth when the cookies are baked. Re-press them after baking with the back of a round measuring spoon so they'll hold plenty of sweet preserves.

Makes: 48 cookies

Oven: 375°F

1 **18-ounce roll refrigerated sugar cookie dough**

2 **slightly beaten egg whites**

2 **tablespoons water**

1½ **cups finely chopped walnuts or pecans**

½ **cup cherry, strawberry, and/or apricot preserves or mint jelly**

1. Lightly grease a cookie sheet; set aside. Shape dough into ¾-inch balls. Combine egg whites and water. Roll balls in egg white mixture; roll in nuts. Place balls 1½ inches apart on prepared cookie sheet. Press your thumb into center of each ball.

2. Bake in a 375° oven about 10 minutes or until edges are firm and lightly browned. Immediately press indentations in center of cookies with the back of a round ½-teaspoon measuring spoon. Transfer to a wire rack and let cool.

3. Just before serving, snip any large pieces of fruit in preserves. Fill thumbprints with preserves, using about ½ teaspoon for each cookie.

TO STORE: Place unfilled cookies in layers separated by waxed paper in an airtight container; cover. Store at room temperature up to 3 days or freeze up to 3 months. Thaw cookies; fill just before serving.

Holiday Snowmen

Get your little kitchen helpers together. These cookies are so easy (and fun) to assemble, the kids won't be able to decide whether they like eating them or baking them better.

(photo, page 326)

Makes: 18 snowmen

Oven: 375°F

1   18-ounce roll refrigerated
    chocolate chip, sugar, or
    peanut butter cookie dough

1   cup sifted powdered sugar

¼   teaspoon vanilla

1   to 2 tablespoons milk
    Gumdrops
    Miniature semisweet
    chocolate pieces

1. Cut cookie dough into 18 equal pieces. Divide each dough piece into 3 balls: one large (about 1¼ inches in diameter), one medium (about 1 inch in diameter), and one small (about ¾ inch in diameter). Assemble each set of balls ¼ inch apart in a snowman shape on an ungreased cookie sheet, placing the largest balls 2 inches apart.

2. Bake in a 375° oven for 8 to 10 minutes or until edges are very lightly browned. Cool on cookie sheet for 3 minutes. Transfer cookies to a wire rack and let cool.

3. For glaze, in a small bowl stir together powdered sugar, vanilla, and 1 tablespoon of the milk. Stir in additional milk, 1 teaspoon at a time, to make drizzling consistency. Spread glaze over snowmen. Decorate as desired with gumdrops and/or chocolate pieces. Let glaze dry.

TO STORE: Place in a single layer in an airtight container; cover. Store at room temperature up to 3 days or freeze unglazed cookies up to 3 months. Thaw cookies; glaze and decorate.

Viennese *Coffee* Balls

No cooking, not even melting, is involved in making these incredibly easy but delicious little morsels. *(photo, page 326)*

Makes: about 30 cookies

2 cups crushed shortbread
   cookies

1¾ cups sifted powdered sugar

1 cup finely chopped nuts

2 tablespoons unsweetened
   cocoa powder

1½ teaspoons instant coffee
   crystals or instant
   espresso powder

¾ teaspoon ground cinnamon

4 to 5 tablespoons brewed
   espresso or strong
   coffee, or water

   Sifted powdered sugar
   (optional)

1. In a large bowl combine crushed cookies, 1¼ cups of the powdered sugar, nuts, cocoa powder, coffee crystals, and cinnamon. Stir in brewed espresso, adding just enough to moisten.

2. Shape mixture into 1¼-inch balls. Roll balls generously in the remaining ½ cup powdered sugar. Place balls on a sheet of waxed paper; let stand until dry (about 1 hour). If desired, roll balls again in powdered sugar before serving.

TO STORE: Place in layers separated by waxed paper in an airtight container; cover. Store at room temperature up to 3 days or freeze up to 3 months. Thaw cookies; roll balls again in powdered sugar.

More exchange ideas In addition to the basics
on how to host a cookie exchange (see tip, page 302), here are some more ideas you might try:

- Turn your cookie exchange into a fund-raiser for a favorite charity. Ask guests to bring a gift for a sponsored family, a local food pantry, or a holiday hat-and-mitten tree.
- Don't be too quick to mark men off your guest list. The women and men at a Midwest printing company have shared a combined potluck lunch and cookie exchange for years. It was the men who rallied to save it when it was in danger of being dropped.
- Combine holiday activities, such as tree-trimming or caroling, or winter sports, such as sledding, ice-skating, or cross-country skiing, with a family cookie exchange.
- Stick with a theme. Host an all-chocolate or nice-and-spicy exchange. Or assign each guest a country or region, requesting that they make a cookie from that part of the world.

Holiday Fruit Balls

Like sparkling gems, candied fruits make these cookies merry and bright. They're just right for Christmas gifts, either on their own or on a cookie tray.

Makes: about 60 cookies

⅔ cup crushed graham crackers

¾ cup chopped candied pineapple

¾ cup chopped candied cherries

¾ cup raisins

3 cups assorted chopped nuts

2 tablespoons butter

¼ cup evaporated milk

2½ cups tiny marshmallows

2 cups coconut

1. In a large bowl combine crushed crackers, candied fruits, raisins, and nuts. In a medium saucepan combine butter, evaporated milk, and marshmallows. Cook and stir until marshmallows melt. Stir marshmallow mixture into cracker mixture until combined.

2. With damp hands, shape mixture into 1-inch balls. Roll balls in coconut. Place balls in a single layer in a storage container; cover. Chill for 4 hours before serving.

TO STORE: Place in a single layer in an airtight container; cover. Store in the refrigerator up to 1 week or freeze up to 3 months.

No-Bake Orange Balls

These beautiful nut-studded gems are made with crumbled sugar cookies, giving new meaning to the phrase "that's the way the cookie crumbles." (photo, page 327)

Makes: about 40 cookies

2 cups finely crushed, crisp
  unfrosted sugar cookies

1 cup toasted hazelnuts or
  almonds, finely chopped

1 cup sifted powdered sugar

¼ cup light-colored corn syrup

2 tablespoons orange liqueur

2 tablespoons butter, melted

1. In a large bowl stir together cookie crumbs, nuts, powdered sugar, corn syrup, liqueur, and butter until well combined.

2. Shape mixture into 1-inch balls. Roll balls in additional powdered sugar. Place balls on a cookie sheet; cover. Let stand for 2 hours. Before serving, roll balls again in powdered sugar.

TO STORE: Place in layers separated by waxed paper in an airtight container; cover. Store at room temperature up to 3 days or freeze up to 3 months. Thaw cookies; roll balls again in powdered sugar.

Simple *Fudge* Tarts

How do you make luscious chocolate minitarts without having to whip up a pastry?

Use refrigerated cookie dough for a shortcut crust. *(photo, page 327)*

Makes: 24 tarts

Oven: 350°F

    Nonstick cooking spray

½ **of an 18-ounce roll**
    refrigerated peanut
    butter cookie dough

½ **cup semisweet chocolate**
    pieces

¼ **cup sweetened condensed milk**

1. Spray twenty-four 1¾-inch muffin cups with nonstick spray; set aside. Cut cookie dough into 6 equal pieces. Cut each piece into 4 equal slices. Press each slice of dough evenly into bottom and up sides of a prepared muffin cup.

2. Bake in a 350° oven about 9 minutes or until edges are lightly browned and dough is slightly firm but not set. Remove from oven. Gently press a shallow indentation in each tart shell with the back of a round ½-teaspoon measuring spoon.

3. Bake for 2 minutes more or until edges of tart shells are firm and light golden brown. Let tart shells cool in cups on a wire rack for 15 minutes. Carefully remove tart shells from cups. Cool completely on wire racks.

4. For filling, in a small saucepan combine chocolate pieces and sweetened condensed milk. Cook and stir over medium heat until chocolate melts. Spoon a generous teaspoon of filling into each cooled tart shell. Let stand until filling is set.

TO STORE: Place in a single layer in an airtight container; cover. Store at room temperature up to 3 days or freeze up to 3 months.

Peanut Butter and Chocolate *Pinwheels*

These pinwheels only look intricate and time-consuming. They're actually incredibly easy to put together, thanks to a head start with purchased cookie dough. If you're really in a hurry, cut the chilling step in half by placing the dough logs in the freezer about 30 minutes before slicing.

Makes: about 88 cookies

Oven: 375°F

1   18-ounce roll refrigerated
    peanut butter cookie dough

¼   cup all-purpose flour

1   18-ounce roll refrigerated
    sugar cookie dough

¼   cup unsweetened cocoa
    powder

½   cup finely chopped peanuts
    (optional)

1. In a large bowl stir together peanut butter cookie dough and flour with a wooden spoon. Divide dough in half. In another large bowl stir together sugar cookie dough and cocoa powder with a wooden spoon. Divide dough in half.

2. Between pieces of waxed paper, roll out half of the peanut butter dough and half of the sugar cookie dough into 12×6-inch rectangles. Remove the top pieces of waxed paper. Invert one rectangle on top of the other; press down gently to seal. Remove top piece of waxed paper. Roll up tightly, starting from a long side. Repeat with remaining dough portions.

3. If desired, sprinkle half of the peanuts onto waxed paper. Roll a roll of dough in peanuts. Wrap in waxed paper or plastic wrap. Repeat with remaining dough and peanuts, if desired. Chill dough rolls about 1 hour or until firm enough to slice.

4. Cut dough rolls into ¼-inch slices. Place slices 2 inches apart on an ungreased cookie sheet. Bake in a 375° oven for 8 to 10 minutes or until edges are firm. Transfer cookies to a wire rack and let cool.

TO STORE: Place in layers separated by waxed paper in an airtight container; cover. Store at room temperature up to 3 days or freeze up to 3 months.

Almond Twists

Easy-to-handle frozen puff pastry slashes hours of preparation time from these crisp, pastrylike cookies.

Makes: 28 cookies

Oven: 400°F

½ of a 17½-ounce package
     frozen puff pastry,
     thawed (1 sheet)

⅓ cup almond paste

1 egg yolk

3 tablespoons packed
     brown sugar

2 teaspoons water

1 recipe Icing
     Coarsely chopped
     sliced almonds

1. On a lightly floured surface, unfold pastry. Roll out into a 14-inch square. Using a fluted pastry wheel, cut square in half.

2. For filling, in a small mixing bowl crumble almond paste. Add egg yolk and brown sugar. Beat with an electric mixer on medium speed until smooth. Beat in water, 1 teaspoon at a time, until of spreading consistency.

3. Spread filling over one pastry half. Place remaining pastry half on top of filling. Using the pastry wheel, cut dough lengthwise into seven 14×1-inch strips. Cut each strip crosswise into quarters to make 28 pieces. Twist each piece twice. Place twists about 2 inches apart on an ungreased cookie sheet.

4. Bake in a 400° oven for 12 to 15 minutes or until golden. Transfer cookies to a wire rack and let cool. Drizzle Icing over cookies. Sprinkle with almonds. Let icing dry.

Icing: In a small bowl stir together 1 cup sifted powdered sugar, ¼ teaspoon vanilla, and enough milk (1 to 2 tablespoons) to make drizzling consistency.

TO STORE: Place in layers separated by waxed paper in an airtight container; cover. Store at room temperature up to 3 days.

Nut Wedges

If you're a fan of baklava, these pastry wedges are for you. Just like the classic Greek pastry, they're chock-full of nuts and flavored with honey. *(photo, page 326)*

Makes: 16 to 20 wedges

Oven: 375°F

1 **package piecrust mix**
   (for 2 crusts)

¼ **cup sugar**

3 **to 4 tablespoons water**

1 **cup finely chopped nuts**

⅓ **cup sugar**

2 **tablespoons honey**

1 **teaspoon ground cinnamon**

1 **teaspoon lemon juice**

   Milk

½ **cup semisweet chocolate**
   pieces

1 **teaspoon shortening**

1. In a medium bowl stir together piecrust mix and the ¼ cup sugar. Add enough of the water to form a ball. Divide dough in half. On a floured surface, roll each half of the dough into a 9-inch circle. Transfer 1 circle to an ungreased cookie sheet.

2. For filling, combine nuts, the ⅓ cup sugar, honey, cinnamon, and lemon juice. Spread over dough circle on cookie sheet. Top with remaining dough circle. Use a fork to seal edges and prick dough. Brush with milk.

3. Bake in a 375° oven for 15 to 20 minutes or until pastry starts to brown. Cool on cookie sheet on a wire rack for 10 minutes. While warm, cut into wedges. Cool completely.

4. In a small heavy saucepan melt chocolate pieces and shortening over low heat, stirring constantly. Drizzle chocolate over wedges; let stand until set.

TO STORE: Place in layers separated by waxed paper in an airtight container; cover. Store at room temperature up to 3 days or freeze undrizzled wedges up to 3 months. Thaw wedges; drizzle with chocolate.

Dazzle with a drizzle A drizzle of melted chocolate or candy coating may be just the thing to finish off your cookies in style. Here are some suggestions to ensure dazzling results:
- When melting chocolate for a drizzle, add 1 teaspoon shortening for each ½ cup (3 ounces) of chocolate to help the chocolate set.
- Place the cookies on a wire rack over waxed paper. Dip a fork into the melted chocolate or candy coating, letting the first clumpy bit land in the pan; pass the fork over the cookies, letting the chocolate drizzle off.
- For added color, melt tinted candy coating. Or tint melted white baking bar or candy coating with paste food coloring. Do not use liquid food coloring. The liquid coloring causes white baking bar to separate and curdle.

Chocolate *Sandwich* Cookies

Here flaky pastry envelops a luscious strawberry-cream cheese filling. They'll think you stayed in all day baking, but since this recipe calls for piecrust dough, it's surprisingly quick to make.

Makes: 15 sandwich cookies

Oven: 375°F

1 **package piecrust mix
   (for 2 crusts)**

½ **cup sugar**

¼ **cup unsweetened cocoa
   powder**

6 **tablespoons water**

1 **8-ounce tub cream cheese
   with strawberries**

1. In a medium bowl stir together piecrust mix, sugar, and cocoa powder. Sprinkle 1 tablespoon water over part of mixture; gently toss with a fork. Push moistened dough to the side of the bowl. Repeat moistening dough, using 1 tablespoon of water at a time, until all dough is moistened. Form dough into a ball. Divide dough into thirds.

2. On a floured surface, roll each portion of dough into a 6-inch circle. Cut each circle into 10 wedges. Prick dough with tines of a fork in a decorative design. Transfer wedges to an ungreased cookie sheet.

3. Bake in a 375° oven about 10 minutes or just until set. Transfer wedges to a wire rack and let cool.

4. To assemble, spread about 2 teaspoons cream cheese on bottoms of half of the pastry wedges. Top with remaining wedges, bottom sides down, pressing together lightly.

TO STORE: Place in layers separated by waxed paper in an airtight container; cover. Store in the refrigerator up to 1 week.

Chocolate-Peppermint *Sandwiches*

This idea isn't limited to the chocolate and peppermint combination. You can make these super-easy sandwich cookies with crushed cherry-, berry-, or orange-flavored hard candies instead of peppermints.

Makes: 22 sandwich cookies

½ cup canned vanilla or
   chocolate frosting

3 tablespoons finely
   crushed striped round
   peppermint candies

44 chocolate wafers

1. In a small bowl stir together frosting and crushed candies. Spread 1 level teaspoon frosting mixture on bottoms of half of the chocolate wafers. Top with remaining chocolate wafers, bottom sides down.

TO STORE: Place in layers separated by waxed paper in an airtight container; cover. Store at room temperature up to 3 days.

Chocolate-Mint Bars

Because the crumb crust is dark and the tops are light, it's best not to stack these chewy squares on the serving plate.

Makes: 48 bars
Oven: 350°F

1 tablespoon butter

1½ cups packaged chocolate
   cookie crumbs

1 cup chopped nuts

1 cup mint-flavored semisweet
   chocolate pieces

1 cup coconut

1 14-ounce can (1¼ cups)
   sweetened condensed milk

1. Generously grease the bottom of a 13×9×2-inch baking pan with the butter. Sprinkle crumbs evenly into the bottom of pan; sprinkle with nuts, chocolate pieces, and coconut. Drizzle sweetened condensed milk evenly over all.

2. Bake in a 350° oven for 20 to 25 minutes or until coconut is golden brown around edges. Cool completely in pan on a wire rack. Cut into bars.

TO STORE: Cover and store in the refrigerator up to 3 days.

Peanutty **Bars**

A drizzle of Peanut Butter Icing spruces up these bars for company, but they taste every bit as scrumptious without it.

Makes: 72 bars

Oven: 350°F

Nonstick cooking spray

1 18-ounce package refrigerated peanut butter cookie dough

1 12-ounce package semisweet chocolate pieces (2 cups)

1 14-ounce can (1¼ cups) sweetened condensed milk

1½ cups dry-roasted peanuts

1 10-ounce package peanut butter-flavored pieces

1 recipe Peanut Butter Icing (optional)

1. Lightly coat a 15×10×1-inch baking pan with nonstick spray. Using floured hands, press cookie dough evenly into bottom of prepared pan. Sprinkle chocolate pieces evenly over dough. Drizzle sweetened condensed milk evenly over chips. Top with peanuts and peanut butter pieces. Press down firmly.

2. Bake in a 350° oven about 25 minutes or until edges are firm. Cool completely in pan on a wire rack. Cut into bars. If desired, drizzle with Peanut Butter Icing; let icing dry.

Peanut Butter Icing: In a small mixing bowl beat ¼ cup peanut butter, 1 cup sifted powdered sugar, and 1 tablespoon milk with an electric mixer until combined. Beat in additional milk, 1 teaspoon at a time, to make drizzling consistency.

TO STORE: Cover and store in the refrigerator up to 3 days.

Sweetened condensed milk Many bar cookies get their sweet, rich flavor from sweetened condensed milk. When baking with this luscious ingredient, use a can opener to remove the entire end of the can. Stir the milk to thin the consistency for even drizzling.

Banana *Brownie Bars*

Banana chips and more crowd into these brownie bars, transforming an ordinary

package of brownie mix into something unique.

Makes: 24 bars

Oven: 325°F

    Nonstick cooking spray

1 **8- or 10-ounce package fudge**

    brownie mix

1 **cup quick-cooking rolled oats**

1 **egg**

2 **to 3 tablespoons water**

1 **cup broken banana chips**

1 **cup milk chocolate pieces**

1 **cup tiny marshmallows**

¾ **cup chopped walnuts**

1. Lightly coat a 13×9×2-inch pan with nonstick spray. In a medium bowl stir together brownie mix, oats, egg, and water. Using floured hands, spread mixture evenly into bottom of prepared pan. Bake in a 325° oven for 5 minutes.
2. Layer banana chips, chocolate pieces, marshmallows, and walnuts over partially baked crust. Press down gently. Bake for 15 minutes more. Cool completely in pan on a wire rack. Cut into bars.

TO STORE: **Cover and store at room temperature up to 3 days.**

> ***Perfect layered bars*** In some cases, the bar's ingredients are layered right in the pan. To help the layers hold together when cut, after adding the last layer, use the flat bottom of a spatula or pancake turner to pat down the surface.

Mocha-Chocolate Chip *Cheesecake* Bars

This bar cookie weds chocolate chip cookies and cheesecake. It's an irresistible marriage,

and it's irresistibly easy to make too!

Makes: 36 bars

Oven: 350°F

1 18-ounce package refrigerated
    chocolate chip cookie dough

1 8-ounce package cream cheese
    or reduced-fat cream cheese
    (Neufchâtel), softened

⅓ cup sugar

1 egg

1 tablespoon instant
    coffee crystals

1 teaspoon water

1 teaspoon vanilla

½ cup miniature semisweet
    chocolate pieces

1. For crust, in a 13×9×2-inch baking pan crumble cookie dough. Press evenly into bottom of pan; set aside.

2. In a medium bowl beat together cream cheese, sugar, and egg with a wooden spoon until smooth. In a small bowl or custard cup stir together coffee crystals, water, and vanilla until crystals dissolve. Stir coffee mixture into cream cheese mixture. Spread cream cheese mixture evenly over crust. Sprinkle with chocolate pieces.

3. Bake in a 350° oven about 20 minutes or until completely set. Cool completely in pan on a wire rack. Cut into bars.

TO STORE: Place in a single layer in an airtight container; cover. Store in the refrigerator up to 3 days or freeze up to 1 month.

Brownie Pizza

Like ordinary pizza, this sweet brownie version is a combination of crust and melted toppings.

Hint: If marshmallows are one of your topping choices and you prefer them less toasty, add them the last 4 minutes of baking instead of the last 8 minutes.

Makes: 16 servings

Oven: 350°F

½ cup finely chopped nuts

1 15-ounce package fudge brownie mix

1½ cups assorted toppings (semisweet chocolate pieces; candy-coated milk chocolate pieces; tiny marshmallows; candy bars, cut up; and/or small gumdrops, cut in half)

1. Grease a 12- or 13-inch pizza pan. Sprinkle with the finely chopped nuts; set aside. Prepare brownie mix according to package directions. Carefully spread batter into prepared pan.

2. Bake in a 350° oven about 15 minutes or until edges are set. Sprinkle partially baked brownie with desired toppings. Return to oven. Bake about 8 minutes more or until a wooden toothpick inserted near the center comes out clean. Cool completely on a wire rack. Cut into wedges.

TO STORE: Cover and store at room temperature up to 3 days.

Easy *Pecan* Bars

These yummy bars taste like pecan pie but, thanks to a cake mix, take only a fraction of the preparation time. Some of the cake mix goes into the crust; the rest goes into the filling.

Makes: 32 bars

Oven: 350°F

1 package 2-layer-size white
     or chocolate cake mix

¼ cup butter, softened

1 slightly beaten egg

3 eggs

¾ cup packed brown sugar

¾ cup dark-colored corn syrup

1 teaspoon vanilla

1¼ cups coarsely chopped pecans

1. Lightly grease a 13×9×2-inch baking pan; set aside. Set aside 1 cup cake mix for the filling. For crust, in a medium bowl combine remaining cake mix, butter, and the 1 slightly beaten egg. Stir with a fork until crumbly. With lightly floured hands, press mixture evenly into the bottom of prepared pan. Bake in a 350° oven for 12 minutes.

2. Meanwhile, for filling, in a medium bowl combine the 3 eggs, brown sugar, corn syrup, and vanilla. Add the 1 cup reserved cake mix. Stir with a fork just until blended. (Some tiny cake mix clumps will remain.) Spread filling evenly over partially baked crust. Sprinkle pecans on top.

3. Bake for 25 to 30 minutes more or until filling appears set when pan is gently shaken. Cool completely in the pan on a wire rack. Cut into bars.

TO STORE: Cover and store in the refrigerator up to 3 days.

Softening butter When the recipe calls for softened butter, be sure to allow enough time—about 30 minutes—for butter to reach room temperature. While you're waiting for butter to soften, you can measure and prepare other ingredients for your recipe.

Coconut-Cashew Bars

Pineapple and cashews lend these bars a taste of the tropics. Be sure to use dried pineapple,

not candied pineapple, for best results.

Makes: 72 bars

Oven: 350°F

 Nonstick cooking spray

1 **18-ounce package refrigerated**

 sugar cookie dough

1 **14-ounce can (1¼ cups)**

 sweetened condensed milk

1½ **cups chopped dried pineapple**

1 **cup semisweet chocolate pieces**

1⅓ **cups coconut**

1⅓ **cups cashew halves or coarsely**

 chopped macadamia nuts

1. Lightly coat a 15×10×1-inch baking pan with nonstick spray. With floured hands, press cookie dough into bottom of prepared pan. Drizzle with sweetened condensed milk, spreading evenly. Sprinkle with dried pineapple, chocolate pieces, coconut, and nuts. Press down firmly.

2. Bake in a 350° oven about 20 minutes or until lightly browned. Cool completely in pan on a wire rack. Cut into bars.

TO STORE: **Cover and store in the refrigerator up to 3 days.**

Quick *Panforte* Bars

These rich bars mimic traditional panforte—an Italian fruitcakelike pastry dense with nuts and candied fruit—in all ways except one: These are much easier to make! *(photo, page 328)*

Makes: 32 bars

Oven: 350°F

1 18-ounce roll refrigerated
   sugar cookie dough

1 10- to 12-ounce can
   unsalted mixed nuts,
   coarsely chopped

½ cup butterscotch-flavored
   pieces or semisweet
   chocolate pieces

½ cup mixed dried fruit bits,
   coarsely chopped dried
   apricots, or golden raisins

½ cup coconut

1. Lightly grease a 9×9×2-inch baking pan; set aside. In a large bowl stir sugar cookie dough with a wooden spoon until soft. Add nuts, butterscotch pieces, and dried fruit. Stir until well mixed. Pat dough evenly into the prepared pan. Sprinkle coconut over top; press in lightly.

2. Bake in a 350° oven about 30 minutes or until a wooden toothpick inserted near center comes out clean. Cool completely in pan on a wire rack. Cut into bars.

TO STORE: Place in layers separated by waxed paper in an airtight container; cover. Store at room temperature up to 3 days or freeze up to 3 months.

Salted *Peanut* Bars

Has it been a while since you've eaten a salted nut roll candy bar? One bite of these pleasingly sweet-and-salty bars will remind you of that classic treat. *(photo, page 326)*

Makes: 32 bars

Oven: 350°F

1 package 2-layer-size white
    or yellow cake mix

½ cup butter, melted

1 beaten egg

1 10-ounce package (2⅔ cups)
    peanut butter-flavored
    pieces

1 cup chopped salted peanuts

2 cups tiny marshmallows

1. In a large bowl stir together cake mix and melted butter. Stir in egg (dough will be stiff). Press dough into the bottom of an ungreased 13×9×2-inch baking pan. Sprinkle with peanut butter pieces and peanuts.

2. Bake in a 350° oven about 20 minutes or until edges are lightly browned. Remove from oven. Sprinkle with marshmallows. Return to oven and bake about 5 minutes more or until marshmallows are puffed and just starting to brown. Cool in pan on a wire rack for 1 hour. Cut into triangles or rectangles.

TO STORE: Place in layers separated by waxed paper in an airtight container; cover. Store at room temperature up to 3 days or freeze up to 3 months.

Peanut Butter *Crunch* Bars

One of the most kid-pleasing cookies in the *Better Homes and Gardens* archives, these bars

feature an unexpected crispy crunch.

Makes: 36 bars

5 cups crisp rice cereal

¾ cup coarsely chopped peanuts

1 cup light-colored corn syrup

½ cup sugar

1½ cups chunky peanut butter

½ cup semisweet chocolate

 pieces

1. Line a 13×9×2-inch baking pan with foil, extending foil over edges of pan. Set pan aside. In a large bowl combine cereal and peanuts; set aside.

2. In a small heavy saucepan cook and stir syrup and sugar over medium heat until mixture just boils. Remove saucepan from heat. Stir in peanut butter until combined.

3. Pour peanut butter mixture over cereal mixture; stir to mix well. Stir in chocolate pieces. Press mixture into prepared pan. Let stand for 1 hour. Lift foil from pan. Cut into bars.

TO STORE: Place in layers separated by waxed paper in an airtight container; cover. Store at room temperature up to 3 days or freeze up to 3 months.

Springtime Cookie Pizza

This extra-easy and super-colorful recipe is a great choice if you want to get kids involved in cooking.

Its beautiful pastel hues make it perfect for Easter, Mother's Day, Father's Day, or a springtime birthday.

Makes: 12 servings

Oven: 350°F

1 18-ounce roll refrigerated

 sugar cookie dough

1 16-ounce can vanilla frosting

 Yellow paste food coloring

¼ cup coconut

 Green food coloring

1½ cups jelly beans

1. Grease a 12- or 13-inch pizza pan. Cut dough into ¼-inch slices. Press cookie dough slices into pan. Bake in a 350° oven for 15 to 20 minutes or until golden. Cool completely in pan on a wire rack.

2. Tint frosting with yellow food coloring. Spread over cooled cookie. Tint coconut with green food coloring. Sprinkle tinted coconut and jelly beans over frosting before it sets.

TO STORE: Cover and store in the refrigerator up to 3 days.

Crispy Cereal Treats

Take one of your childhood favorites a step further and share it with the new generation. Fruit-flavored crisp rice cereal replaces the plain cereal and, if you desire, each treat gets dipped in yummy candy coating.

Makes: about 16 cookies

Nonstick cooking spray

3 tablespoons butter

1 10¹/₂-ounce package (about
   6 cups) tiny marshmallows

6 cups fruit-flavored crisp
   rice cereal

6 ounces chocolate-flavored
   or vanilla-flavored candy
   coating, chopped (optional)

1. Line a 13×9×2-inch baking pan with foil, extending the foil over edges of pan. Coat foil with cooking spray. Set pan aside.

2. In a large saucepan melt butter; add marshmallows. Cook and stir over low heat until marshmallows melt and mixture is smooth. Remove saucepan from heat. Stir in cereal. With the back of a buttered spoon, press cereal mixture into prepared pan. Let stand until cool.

3. Lift foil from pan. Using a 2¹/₂-inch cookie cutter, cut into desired shapes. (Or cut into serving-size pieces using a knife.)

4. If desired, in a small saucepan melt candy coating over low heat until melted, stirring constantly. Dip one-third of each cookie into the melted candy coating and place on waxed paper. Let stand until coating is set.

TO STORE: Place in layers separated by waxed paper in an airtight container; cover. Store at room temperature up to 3 days.

No-Bake *Butterscotch* Treats

Instead of cutting these treats into traditional bars, use cookie cutters to cut the chilled

mixture into an assortment of simple shapes. *(photo, page 325)*

Makes: 48 bars

  6 **tablespoons butter, melted**

  1 **cup creamy peanut butter**

1½ **cups sifted powdered sugar**

  1 **9-ounce package chocolate**

      wafers, crushed

  1 **12-ounce package (2 cups)**

      butterscotch-flavored pieces

¼ **cup whipping cream**

¾ **cup chopped peanuts**

1. In a large bowl stir together melted butter, peanut butter, and powdered sugar. Stir in crushed chocolate wafers. Press mixture into the bottom of an ungreased 13×9×2-inch baking pan.

2. In a medium heavy saucepan combine butterscotch pieces and whipping cream. Stir over low heat until pieces melt. Carefully spoon butterscotch mixture over crumb mixture, spreading evenly. Sprinkle peanuts over butterscotch mixture.

3. Cover and chill at least 2 hours. Cut into bars or use 2-inch cookie cutters to cut out shapes.

TO STORE: Place in layers separated by waxed paper in an airtight container; cover. Store in the refrigerator up to 1 week or freeze up to 3 months.

No-Bake Butterscotch Treats, page 324

ABOVE: Holiday Snowmen, page 305; Nut Wedges, page 311
BELOW: Viennese Coffee Balls, page 306; Salted Peanut Bars, page 321

ABOVE: No-Bake Orange Balls, page 307   RIGHT: Fry-Pan Cookies, page 300
BELOW: Simple Fudge Tarts, page 308

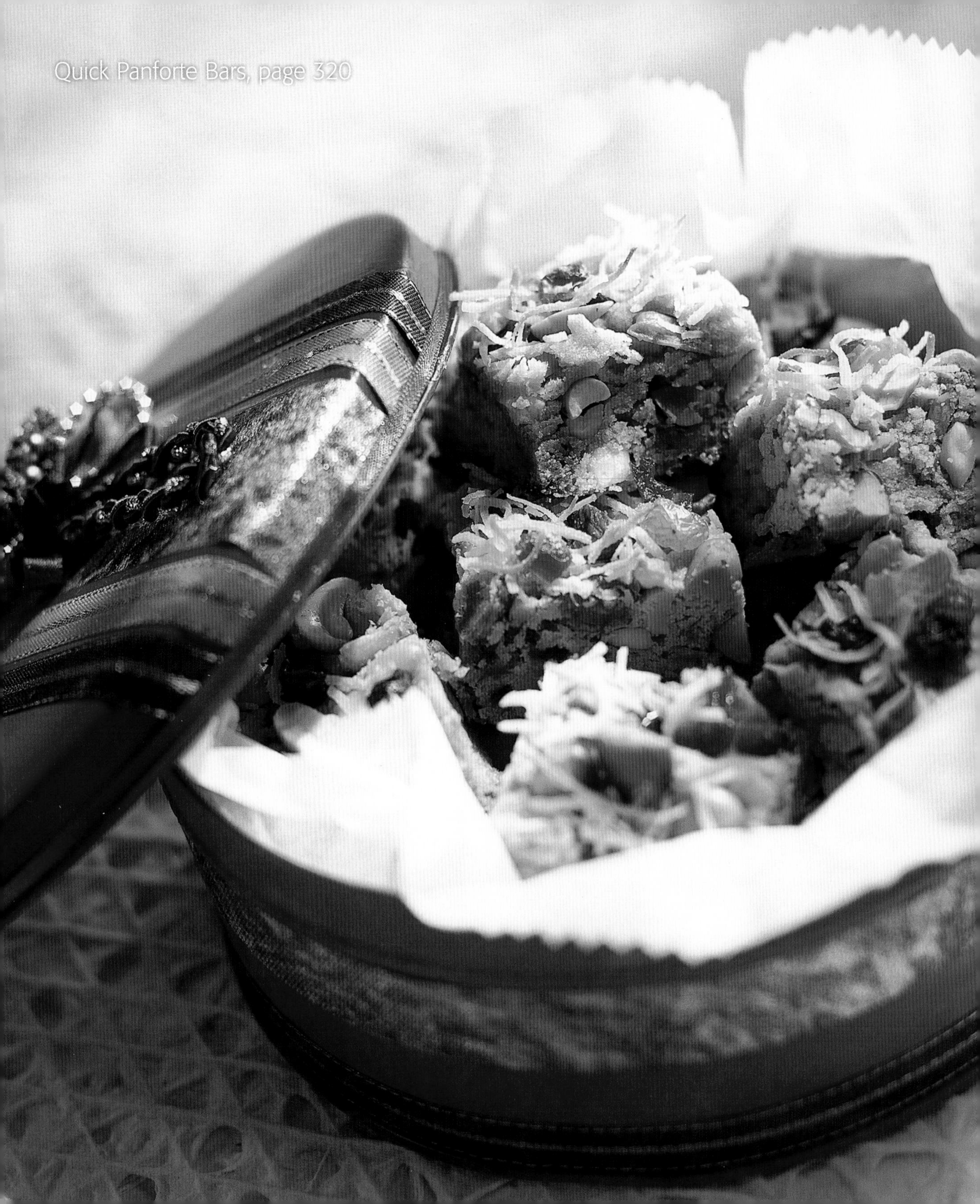

Quick Panforte Bars, page 320

Brown Sugar *Cookie* Mix

This handy mix is the key to three totally distinct cookies: Polka-Dot Cookie Bars (below),

Apricot Bars (page 330), and Cherry-Orange Drops (page 331).

Makes: about 8½ cups

3   cups all-purpose flour

1   cup whole wheat flour

2   cups packed brown sugar

2   teaspoons baking powder

½   teaspoon baking soda

1½   cups shortening

1. In a very large bowl stir together all-purpose flour, whole wheat flour, brown sugar, baking powder, and baking soda. Using a pastry blender, cut in shortening until mixture resembles fine crumbs.
2. Store mixture in a tightly covered container at room temperature up to 3 weeks. To measure, lightly spoon the mix into a measuring cup and level with a spatula.

Polka-Dot Cookie Bars

Dotted with colorful chocolate candies, these bars look as good as they taste. Plan on

10 minutes for mixing and 20 to 25 minutes for baking. How's that for fast?

Makes: 24 bars

Oven: 350°F

2   slightly beaten eggs

⅓   cup milk

2½   cups Brown Sugar Cookie Mix
    (recipe, above)

½   cup miniature candy-coated
    semisweet or milk
    chocolate pieces

1. Grease an 11×7×1½-inch baking pan; set aside. In a large bowl combine eggs and milk. Stir in Brown Sugar Cookie Mix until combined. Spread batter evenly into prepared pan.
2. Bake in a 350° oven for 10 minutes. Sprinkle chocolate pieces evenly over top of partially baked bars. Bake for 10 to 15 minutes more or until golden brown and firm around edges. Cool completely in pan on a wire rack. Cut into bars.

TO STORE: Place in layers separated by waxed paper in an airtight container; cover. Store at room temperature up to 3 days or freeze up to 3 months.

Apricot Bars

Of the delicious recipes you can make with Brown Sugar Cookie Mix, page 329, this one's the dressiest. To personalize, choose your favorite pie filling or preserves.

Makes: 24 bars

Oven: 350°

1 **slightly beaten egg**

1 **tablespoon water**

½ **teaspoon vanilla**

2½ **cups Brown Sugar Cookie Mix**
  (recipe, page 329)

1 **cup quick-cooking rolled oats**

1 **12-ounce can apricot or other**
  fruit cake and pastry filling
  or 1 cup apricot or other
  fruit preserves

¼ **teaspoon ground nutmeg**
  or ground cardamom

1 **recipe Lemon Icing (optional)**

1. Grease a 9×9×2-inch baking pan; set aside. For crust, in a large mixing bowl combine egg, water, and vanilla. Stir in 2 cups of the Brown Sugar Cookie Mix and ¾ cup of the rolled oats. Spread mixture into prepared pan.

2. Bake in a 350° oven for 10 minutes. Spread filling over top of partially baked crust. In a medium bowl combine the remaining ½ cup Brown Sugar Cookie Mix, the remaining ¼ cup rolled oats, and nutmeg. Sprinkle over filling. Bake about 15 minutes more or until top is golden brown. Cool completely in pan on a wire rack. If desired, drizzle with Lemon Icing; let icing dry. Cut into bars.

Lemon Icing: In a small bowl stir together ¾ cup sifted powdered sugar and enough lemon juice (3 to 4 teaspoons) to make drizzling consistency.

TO STORE: Place in layers separated by waxed paper in an airtight container; cover. Store at room temperature up to 3 days or freeze undrizzled bars up to 3 months. Thaw bars; if desired, drizzle.

Cherry-Orange *Drops*

Tangy-sweet dried cherries add chewy texture to these simple drops. If you like, experiment with the fruit and try dried cranberries, raisins, or mixed dried fruit bits in place of the cherries.

Makes: about 32 cookies

Oven: 350°F

1 **slightly beaten egg**

2 **tablespoons orange juice**

3 **cups Brown Sugar Cookie Mix**

   (recipe, page 329)

1 **cup dried cherries**

$\frac{1}{2}$ **cup slivered almonds**

$\frac{1}{2}$ **teaspoon ground cinnamon**

1 **recipe Orange Icing**

1. In a large bowl beat together egg and orange juice. Stir in Brown Sugar Cookie Mix, cherries, almonds, and cinnamon. Drop dough by rounded teaspoons 2 inches apart onto an ungreased cookie sheet.

2. Bake in a 350° oven for 12 to 14 minutes or until bottoms are lightly browned. Transfer cookies to a wire rack and let cool. Drizzle Orange Icing over tops of cooled cookies; let icing dry.

Orange Icing: In a small bowl stir together 1 cup sifted powdered sugar, $\frac{1}{2}$ teaspoon finely shredded orange peel, and enough orange juice (3 to 4 teaspoons) to make drizzling consistency.

TO STORE: Place in layers separated by waxed paper in an airtight container; cover. Store at room temperature up to 3 days or freeze undrizzled cookies up to 3 months. Thaw cookies; drizzle.

Basic *Peanut Butter* Dough

Add exponentially to your cookie stash by making this one basic cookie dough. Turtle Cookies (page 333), Quick Crisscrosses (below), and Peanut Butter Bells and Angels (page 333) all are based on this versatile dough.

1 **cup butter**

1 **cup creamy peanut butter**

1 **cup granulated sugar**

1 **cup packed brown sugar**

1 **teaspoon baking soda**

1 **teaspoon baking powder**

2 **eggs**

1 **teaspoon vanilla**

2½ **cups all-purpose flour**

1. In a large mixing bowl beat butter and peanut butter with an electric mixer on medium to high speed for 30 seconds. Add granulated sugar, brown sugar, baking soda, and baking powder. Beat until combined, scraping sides of bowl occasionally. Beat in eggs and vanilla until combined. Beat in as much of the flour as you can with the mixer. Stir in any remaining flour with a wooden spoon.

2. Divide dough into three equal portions. Wrap dough portions in plastic wrap or waxed paper. Chill for 1 to 2 hours or until easy to handle.

Quick Crisscrosses

Just like the traditional cookie, granulated sugar glistens on the outside. It's the sprinkling of colored sugar that dresses this favorite up for any holiday.

Makes: about 32 cookies

Oven: 375°F

1 **portion Basic Peanut Butter**
   Dough (recipe, above)

   Granulated sugar

   Colored Sugar

1. Shape Basic Peanut Butter Dough into 1-inch balls; roll in granulated sugar. Place balls 2 inches apart on an ungreased cookie sheet.

2. Flatten by crisscrossing with the tines of a fork. Sprinkle tops with colored sugar.

3. Bake in a 375° oven for 7 to 9 minutes or until bottoms are lightly browned. Transfer cookies to a wire rack and let cool.

TO STORE: Place in layers separated by waxed paper in an airtight container; cover. Store at room temperature up to 3 days or freeze up to 3 months.

Peanut Butter *Bells and Angels*

No cookie cutter needed! Here festive bell- and angel-shape cookies are only a few cuts and folds away.

Makes: about 24 cookies

Oven: 375°F

1 **portion Basic Peanut Butter**
   Dough (recipe, page 332)
   Colored sugar
   Large semisweet chocolate
   pieces

1 **cup powdered sugar**

1 **tablespoon milk**

1. Divide Basic Peanut Butter Dough in half. Shape each half into a 4-inch-long roll. For bells, roll in colored sugar. Wrap; chill overnight. Slice ¼-inch thick.

Bells: Place slices 2 inches apart on an ungreased cookie sheet. Fold over sides of a circle of dough, overlapping to make a triangle. Press a chocolate piece into dough near bottom of bell for clapper. Bake in a 375° oven for 7 to 9 minutes or until bottoms are lightly browned. Transfer to a wire rack and let cool.

Angels: Cut each slice into three pieces: one triangle and two curved pieces. On an ungreased cookie sheet, attach curved pieces (wings) to angel body (triangle) by overlapping slightly. Bake as directed for bells. In a small bowl stir together powdered sugar and milk. Use frosting to decorate cooled angels.

TO STORE: Place in layers separated by waxed paper in an airtight container; cover. Store at room temperature up to 3 days or freeze undecorated cookies up to 3 months. Thaw cookies; decorate angels.

Turtle Cookies

With chocolate inside as well as on top, and a turtle shape, these sweets delight kids of all ages.

Makes: 32 cookies

Oven: 375°F

1 **portion Basic Peanut Butter**
   Dough (recipe, page 332)

32 **½-inch squares milk chocolate**

96 **pecan halves**

¾ **cup semisweet chocolate pieces**

2 **teaspoons shortening**

1. Shape Basic Peanut Butter Dough into 1-inch balls. Wrap each ball around a candy square. Place balls 2 inches apart on an ungreased cookie sheet. Tuck three pecan halves under each ball.

2. Bake in a 375° oven for 9 to 10 minutes or until edges are lightly browned. Cool 1 minute; transfer cookies to a wire rack and let cool.

3. In a small heavy saucepan melt chocolate and shortening over low heat, stirring constantly. Spread chocolate over cookies; let stand until set.

TO STORE: Place in layers separated by waxed paper in an airtight container; cover. Store at room temperature up to 3 days or freeze unfrosted cookies up to 3 months. Thaw cookies; spread with chocolate.

Trio Cookie Dough

This butter cookie dough presents you with countless options. With simple stir-ins,

such as fruit pieces, chocolate nuggets, and nuts, you'll never get bored with this recipe.

¾ **cup butter, softened**

¾ **cup shortening**

1½ **cups sugar**

¼ **teaspoon baking soda**

1 **egg**

1 **egg yolk**

3 **tablespoons milk**

1½ **teaspoons vanilla**

4½ **cups all-purpose flour**

1. In a large mixing bowl beat butter and shortening with an electric mixer on medium to high speed for 30 seconds. Add sugar, baking soda, and ¼ teaspoon salt. Beat until combined, scraping sides of bowl occasionally. Beat in the whole egg, egg yolk, milk, and vanilla. Beat in as much of the flour as you can with the mixer. Stir in any remaining flour with a wooden spoon. Divide dough into three equal portions.

Cherry-Nut Slices

Keep a roll of this dough in the refrigerator so you can bake up cherry- and nut-studded

slices whenever you're in the mood for a rich and wonderful cookie.

Makes: about 36 cookies

Oven: 375°F

¾ **cup maraschino cherries,**
   drained and finely chopped

1 **portion Trio Cookie Dough**
   (recipe, above)

   Few drops red food coloring

½ **cup finely chopped pecans**
   or hazelnuts (filberts)

1. Pat cherries dry with paper towels. In a medium bowl combine cherries, cookie dough, and food coloring. With a wooden spoon, stir until thoroughly combined. Shape dough into a 10-inch-long roll. Roll dough in chopped nuts until covered. Wrap in plastic wrap or waxed paper. Chill at least 4 hours or until firm enough to slice.

2. Cut roll into ¼-inch slices. Place slices 2 inches apart on an ungreased cookie sheet. Bake in a 375° oven for 8 to 10 minutes or until edges are firm and bottoms are lightly browned. Transfer cookies to a wire rack and let cool.

TO STORE: Place in layers separated by waxed paper in an airtight container; cover. Store at room temperature up to 3 days or freeze up to 3 months.

Lemon-Almond Tea Cookies

With just a few added ingredients, the Trio Cookie Dough becomes a lovely lemon cookie that's well suited to tea party trays.

Makes: 28 cookies

Oven: 375°F

1 **portion Trio Cookie Dough**
  (recipe, page 334)

2 **teaspoons finely shredded**
  lemon peel

1 **teaspoon almond extract**

1 **recipe Lemon Frosting**

½ **cup sliced almonds, toasted**

1. In a medium bowl combine Trio Cookie Dough, lemon peel, and almond extract. With a wooden spoon, stir until thoroughly combined. Shape dough into an 8-inch-long roll. Wrap in plastic wrap or waxed paper. Chill for at least 4 hours or until firm enough to slice.

2. Cut roll into ¼-inch slices. Place slices 2 inches apart on an ungreased cookie sheet. Bake in a 375° oven for 8 to 10 minutes or until edges are firm and bottoms are lightly browned. Transfer cookies to a wire rack and let cool.

3. Spread about 1 teaspoon of the Lemon Frosting over each cookie. Sprinkle with sliced almonds. Let frosting dry.

Lemon Frosting: In a small mixing bowl beat ¼ cup softened butter with an electric mixer on medium to high speed for 30 seconds. Gradually add 1 cup sifted powdered sugar, beating until combined. Beat in 4 teaspoons milk, 1 teaspoon lemon juice, ¼ teaspoon vanilla, and a few drops almond extract. Gradually beat in 1 cup sifted powdered sugar until of spreading consistency.

TO STORE: Place in layers separated by waxed paper in an airtight container; cover. Store at room temperature up to 3 days or freeze unfrosted cookies up to 3 months. Thaw cookies; frost and sprinkle with almonds.

Chocolate-Mint Thumbprints

These peppermint and chocolate cookies bring to mind snowmen, ice-skating, and winter wonderlands.

Makes: about 36 cookies

Oven: 375°F

1 **portion Trio Cookie Dough**
 (recipe, page 334)

2 **ounces semisweet chocolate,**
 melted and cooled

2 **teaspoons milk**

1 **recipe Peppermint Filling**

¼ **cup chopped candy canes or**
 hard peppermint candies

1. In a medium bowl combine Trio Cookie Dough, chocolate, and milk. With a wooden spoon, stir until thoroughly combined. Shape dough into an 8-inch-long roll. Wrap in plastic wrap or waxed paper. Chill for at least 1 hour or until firm enough to slice.

2. Cut dough into ¾-inch slices. Cut each slice into quarters; roll each quarter into a ball. Place balls 2 inches apart on an ungreased cookie sheet. Press your thumb into the center of each ball.

3. Bake in a 375° oven for 8 to 10 minutes or until tops look dry. Transfer cookies to a wire rack and let cool. Spoon a scant teaspoon of Peppermint Filling into center of each cookie. Sprinkle with chopped candy.

Peppermint Filling: In a small mixing bowl beat ¼ cup softened butter with an electric mixer on medium speed for 30 seconds. Gradually beat in 1 cup sifted powdered sugar until combined. Beat in 2 tablespoons milk, ¼ teaspoon peppermint extract, and, if desired, a few drops of red or green food coloring. Gradually beat in 1 cup sifted powdered sugar until of spreading consistency.

TO STORE: Place in layers separated by waxed paper in an airtight container; cover. Store at room temperature up to 3 days or freeze unfilled cookies up to 3 months. Thaw cookies; fill and sprinkle with candy.

Microwaving chocolate If you use a microwave oven for melting chocolate, cook the chopped chocolate or chocolate pieces, uncovered, on 100% power (high) only until soft. Stir often to keep the heat evenly distributed through the chocolate. For 4 ounces of chocolate, allow 1 to 2 minutes. Stir after 1 minute and again after every 30 seconds.

Best Bars and Brownies

Oatmeal-Caramel Bars

Get the kids to help unwrap the caramels needed to make the topping. Just be sure most candies make it into the bowl rather than into their mouths.

Makes: 60 bars

Oven: 350°F

1 cup butter, softened

2 cups packed brown sugar

2 eggs

2 teaspoons vanilla

1 teaspoon baking soda

2½ cups all-purpose flour

3 cups quick-cooking rolled oats

1 cup semisweet chocolate
   pieces

½ cup chopped walnuts
   or pecans

30 vanilla caramels, unwrapped
   (8 ounces)

3 tablespoons milk

1. In a large mixing bowl beat butter with an electric mixer on medium to high speed for 30 seconds. Add brown sugar; beat until combined, scraping sides of bowl occasionally. Beat in eggs, vanilla, and baking soda. Beat or stir in the flour. Stir in the oats with a wooden spoon.

2. Press two-thirds (about 3⅓ cups) of the oat mixture into the bottom of an ungreased 15×10×1-inch baking pan. Sprinkle with chocolate pieces and nuts.

3. In a medium saucepan combine caramels and milk. Cook over low heat until caramels are melted, stirring occasionally. Drizzle caramel mixture over chocolate and nuts. Drop remaining one-third of the oat mixture by teaspoons over the top.

4. Bake in a 350° oven for 22 to 25 minutes or until top is light brown. Cool completely in pan on a wire rack. Cut into bars.

TO STORE: Place in layers separated by waxed paper in an airtight container; cover. Store at room temperature up to 3 days or freeze up to 3 months.

Fruit-Filled *Oatmeal* Bars

Choose your favorite filling—apricot, apple-cranberry, or raisin—for these treasured lunch-box treats. If you're pressed for time, use purchased pie filling.

Makes: 25 bars

Oven: 350°F

1 **cup all-purpose flour**

1 **cup quick-cooking rolled oats**

²/₃ **cup packed brown sugar**

¹/₄ **teaspoon baking soda**

¹/₂ **cup butter**

1 **recipe Apricot Filling,**
   Apple-Cranberry Filling,
   Easy Filling, or Raisin Filling

1. In a medium bowl combine flour, oats, brown sugar, and baking soda. Using a pastry blender, cut in butter until the mixture resembles coarse crumbs. Reserve ¹/₂ cup of the crumb mixture.

2. Press remaining crumb mixture into bottom of an ungreased 9×9×2-inch or 11×7×1¹/₂-inch baking pan. Spread with desired filling. Sprinkle with reserved crumb mixture. Bake in a 350° oven for 30 to 35 minutes or until the top is golden. Cool completely in pan on a wire rack. Cut into bars.

Apricot Filling: In a medium saucepan combine 1 cup snipped dried apricots and ³/₄ cup water. Bring to boiling; reduce heat. Simmer, covered, for 5 minutes. Meanwhile, combine ¹/₄ cup sugar and 1 tablespoon all-purpose flour; stir into apricot mixture. Cook and stir about 1 minute more or until thickened and bubbly.

Apple-Cranberry Filling: Combine 1 cup chunky applesauce, ²/₃ cup dried cranberries or blueberries, ¹/₂ teaspoon ground cinnamon, and dash ground cloves.

Easy Filling: Use 1¹/₂ cups canned mincemeat or one 21-ounce can cherry or peach pie filling.

Raisin Filling: In a medium saucepan combine ³/₄ cup water, 2 tablespoons sugar, and 2 teaspoons cornstarch. Add 1¹/₄ cups golden raisins. Cook and stir until thickened and bubbly.

TO STORE: Place in layers separated by waxed paper in an airtight container; cover. Store at room temperature up to 3 days or freeze up to 3 months.

Blueberry Bars

When you yearn for crumb-topped blueberry pie but don't want to fuss with rolling out a pie pastry, mix up these easy bars. They feature the same tasty oats and blueberry filling and require less effort.

Makes: 25 bars

Oven: 350°F

1½ cups quick-cooking rolled oats

1 cup all-purpose flour

¾ cup packed brown sugar

¾ cup butter

1 cup frozen blueberries

½ cup blueberry, raspberry, or strawberry preserves

1 teaspoon finely shredded lemon peel

1. Line an 8×8×2-inch baking pan with foil, extending foil over edges of pan. Set pan aside. In a medium bowl combine oats, flour, and brown sugar. Using a pastry blender, cut in butter until pieces are the size of small peas. Reserve 1 cup of the mixture.

2. Press remaining oat mixture into the bottom of the prepared baking pan. Bake in a 350° oven for 25 minutes.

3. Meanwhile, for filling, in a small bowl combine frozen blueberries, preserves, and lemon peel. Carefully spread over baked crust. Sprinkle with reserved oat mixture; press lightly into blueberry mixture.

4. Bake about 30 minutes more or until top is golden. Cool completely in pan on a wire rack. Cut into bars.

TO STORE: Place in layers separated by waxed paper in an airtight container; cover. Store at room temperature up to 2 days or freeze up to 3 months.

Double-Cherry Streusel Bars

The season for fresh cherries is brief, but you can enjoy this very cherry bar any time of the year because it is made with dried tart cherries and cherry preserves. *(photo, page 363)*

Makes: 48 bars

Oven: 350°F

2 **cups water**

1 **cup dried tart cherries or**
   dried cranberries, snipped

2 **cups quick-cooking rolled oats**

1½ **cups all-purpose flour**

1½ **cups packed brown sugar**

1 **teaspoon baking powder**

½ **teaspoon baking soda**

1 **cup butter**

½ **cup coarsely chopped**
   slivered almonds

2 **12-ounce jars cherry preserves**

1 **teaspoon finely shredded**
   lemon peel

½ **cup semisweet chocolate**
   pieces

1 **teaspoon shortening**

1. In a small saucepan bring water to boiling; remove from heat. Add dried cherries and let stand about 10 minutes or until softened. Drain and set aside.

2. For crust, in a large bowl combine oats, flour, brown sugar, baking powder, and baking soda. Using a pastry blender, cut in the butter until mixture resembles coarse crumbs. Reserve 1 cup of the crumb mixture. Stir the almonds into the reserved crumb mixture; set aside.

3. Press remaining crumb mixture into the bottom of an ungreased 15×10×1-inch baking pan. Bake in a 350° oven for 12 minutes.

4. Meanwhile, for filling, stir together the drained cherries, cherry preserves, and lemon peel. Spread filling evenly over partially baked crust. Sprinkle with reserved crumb mixture. Bake for 20 to 25 minutes more or until top is golden brown. Cool completely in pan on a wire rack.

5. In a small heavy saucepan melt chocolate pieces and shortening over low heat, stirring constantly. Drizzle chocolate mixture over top of bars. Let stand until chocolate is set. Cut into bars.

TO STORE: Place in layers separated by waxed paper in an airtight container; cover. Store at room temperature up to 3 days. To freeze, wrap undrizzled, uncut bars in heavy foil. Freeze up to 3 months. Thaw; drizzle and cut into bars.

Apricot-Nut Diamonds

To cut diamonds, first cut straight lines down the length of the pan. Then cut diagonal lines across the pan. Trim the end pieces into triangles, rectangles, or squares.

Makes: about 30 diamonds

Oven: 375°F

1 cup all-purpose flour

    Dash salt

¼ cup butter

½ cup snipped dried apricots

¾ cup packed brown sugar

2 eggs

1 cup chopped walnuts

½ cup coconut

1 teaspoon vanilla

2 tablespoons all-purpose flour

1 recipe Powdered Sugar Icing

1. Grease an 11×7×1½-inch baking pan; set aside. For crust, in a medium bowl combine the 1 cup flour and salt. Using a pastry blender, cut in butter until mixture is crumbly. Press into the bottom of the prepared baking pan. Bake in a 375° oven for 12 minutes.

2. Meanwhile, in a small saucepan place apricots in enough water to cover. Bring to boiling; reduce heat. Simmer, covered, for 10 minutes; drain.

3. For topping, in a medium bowl stir together brown sugar and eggs. Stir in drained apricots, walnuts, coconut, and vanilla. Add the 2 tablespoons flour; stir until combined.

4. Spread topping evenly over partially baked crust. Bake for 15 minutes more. Cool completely in pan on a wire rack. Drizzle with Powdered Sugar Icing. Let icing dry. Cut into diamonds or bars.

Powdered Sugar Icing: In a small bowl stir together 1 cup sifted powdered sugar, ¼ teaspoon vanilla, and 1 tablespoon milk. Stir in additional milk, if necessary, 1 teaspoon at a time, until icing is smooth and of drizzling consistency.

TO STORE: Cover and store in the refrigerator up to 3 days. To freeze, wrap undrizzled, uncut bars in heavy foil. Freeze up to 3 months. Thaw; drizzle and cut into bars.

holiday
treat

Brandied *Cranberry-Apricot* Bars

These bars will remind you of a tart, but they're so much easier to make! For a grand finale,

serve large slices on your prettiest dessert plates.

Makes: 16 bars

Oven: 350°F

¹/₃ **cup golden raisins**

¹/₃ **cup dark raisins**

¹/₃ **cup dried cranberries**

¹/₃ **cup snipped dried apricots**

¹/₂ **cup brandy or water**

1¹/₂ **cups all-purpose flour**

1¹/₃ **cups packed brown sugar**

¹/₂ **cup butter**

2 **eggs**

1 **teaspoon vanilla**

¹/₃ **cup chopped pecans**

Sifted powdered sugar

1. In a small saucepan stir together golden raisins, dark raisins, cranberries, apricots, and brandy. Bring to boiling; remove from heat. Let stand for 20 minutes; drain.

2. For crust, in a medium bowl combine 1 cup of the flour and ¹/₃ cup of the brown sugar. Using a pastry blender, cut in butter until mixture resembles coarse crumbs. Press mixture into bottom of an ungreased 8×8×2-inch baking pan. Bake in a 350° oven about 20 minutes or until golden.

3. For topping, in a medium mixing bowl beat eggs with an electric mixer on low speed for 4 minutes. Stir in the remaining 1 cup brown sugar, the remaining ¹/₂ cup flour, and the vanilla just until combined. Stir in pecans and drained fruit.

4. Pour topping over baked crust, spreading evenly. Bake about 40 minutes more or until a wooden toothpick inserted in center comes out clean (if necessary, cover loosely with foil the last 10 minutes of baking to prevent overbrowning). Cool completely in pan on a wire rack. Sprinkle with sifted powdered sugar. Cut into bars.

TO STORE: Place in layers separated by waxed paper in an airtight container; cover. Store in the refrigerator up to 3 days or freeze up to 3 months. Thaw; sprinkle with additional powdered sugar.

Cranberry-Macadamia Bars

If you're looking for an easy bar cookie that's festive enough for the holidays, try this one.

Ruby red cranberries, like shiny holly berries, bring to mind merry Christmases.

Makes: 24 bars

Oven: 350°F

1¼ cups all-purpose flour

2 cups sugar

½ cup butter

1 cup finely chopped

macadamia nuts, hazelnuts

(filberts), or pecans

2 slightly beaten eggs

2 tablespoons milk

1 teaspoon finely shredded

orange peel

1 teaspoon vanilla

1 cup finely chopped cranberries

½ cup coconut

1. For crust, in a medium bowl stir together flour and ¾ cup of the sugar. Using a pastry blender, cut in butter until mixture resembles coarse crumbs. Stir in ½ cup of the nuts. Press mixture into the bottom of an ungreased 13×9×2-inch baking pan. Bake in a 350° oven for 10 to 15 minutes or until the crust is light brown around the edges.

2. Meanwhile, for topping, in a medium bowl beat together the remaining 1¼ cups sugar, the eggs, milk, orange peel, and vanilla. Pour topping over baked crust. Sprinkle with the remaining ½ cup nuts, cranberries, and coconut. Bake about 30 minutes more or until golden. Cool slightly in pan on a wire rack. Cut into bars while warm. Cool completely.

TO STORE: Place in layers separated by waxed paper in an airtight container; cover. Store in the refrigerator up to 3 days or freeze up to 3 months.

> ## *A new look for bar cookies* Think outside the square (or rectangle!). To give brownies and bars a new look, cut them into triangles and diamonds.
> • To make triangles, cut bars into 2- or 2½-inch squares. Cut each square in half diagonally. Or cut bars into rectangles and cut each diagonally into triangles.
> • To make diamonds, first cut parallel lines 1 or 1½ inches apart down the length of the pan. Then cut diagonal lines the same distance apart across the pan, forming diamond shapes.

Lemon Bars *Deluxe*

When assembling a platter of assorted cookies, include these lemony favorites. Their tangy sweet flavor offers a pleasing contrast to other, less sprightly, cookies.

Makes: 30 bars

Oven: 350°F

2¼ cups all-purpose flour

½ cup sifted powdered sugar

1 cup butter

4 slightly beaten eggs

1½ cups granulated sugar

1 to 2 teaspoons finely shredded lemon peel (set aside)

⅓ cup lemon juice

½ teaspoon baking powder

Powdered sugar

1. For crust, in a medium bowl combine 2 cups of the flour and the ½ cup powdered sugar. Using a pastry blender, cut in butter until mixture clings together. Press dough into the bottom of an ungreased 13×9×2-inch baking pan. Bake in a 350° oven for 20 to 25 minutes or until light brown.

2. Meanwhile, for filling, in a medium bowl stir together eggs, granulated sugar, and lemon juice. In another bowl combine the remaining ¼ cup flour and the baking powder. Stir flour mixture into egg mixture along with the lemon peel.

3. Pour filling over baked crust. Bake for 25 minutes more. Cool completely in pan on a wire rack. Sift powdered sugar over top. Cut into bars.

TO STORE: Place in layers separated by waxed paper in an airtight container; cover. Store in the refrigerator up to 3 days.

Orange-Coconut Bars

No time to sit down for breakfast? Eat one of these zingy bars on the go. Hint: Use fresh-squeezed orange juice for the sprightliest flavor. *(photo, page 363)*

Makes: 16 bars

Oven: 350°F

½ cup all-purpose flour

1 cup granulated sugar

¼ cup butter

½ cup finely chopped pecans

2 slightly beaten eggs

2 tablespoons all-purpose flour

1½ teaspoons finely shredded
    orange peel

3 tablespoons orange juice

¼ teaspoon baking powder

1 cup coconut

1. For crust, in a medium bowl combine the ½ cup flour and ¼ cup of the sugar. Using a pastry blender, cut in butter until mixture resembles coarse crumbs. Stir in pecans. Press mixture into the bottom of an ungreased 8×8×2-inch baking pan. Bake in a 350° oven for 18 to 20 minutes or until golden.

2. Meanwhile, for topping, in a medium mixing bowl combine the remaining ¾ cup sugar, the eggs, the 2 tablespoons flour, orange peel, orange juice, and baking powder. Beat with an electric mixer on low speed about 2 minutes or until combined. Stir in coconut.

3. Pour topping over baked crust. Bake about 20 minutes more or until edges are light brown and center is set. Cool completely in pan on a wire rack. Cut into bars.

TO STORE: Place in layers separated by waxed paper in an airtight container; cover. Store in the refrigerator up to 3 days.

Merry Christmas Bars

Red and green cherries bring to mind sparkling ornaments on a Christmas tree.

For Valentine's Day, decorate the bars only with red cherries.

Makes: 24 bars

Oven: 350°F

1 cup all-purpose flour

½ cup packed brown sugar

⅓ cup butter, softened

½ cup finely chopped pecans

1 8-ounce package cream
   cheese, softened

1 egg

¼ cup granulated sugar

2 tablespoons milk

2 tablespoons lemon juice

½ teaspoon vanilla

¼ teaspoon almond extract

½ cup red and/or green
   maraschino cherries, finely
   chopped and well drained

   Red and green maraschino
   cherries (optional)

1. In a medium mixing bowl combine flour, brown sugar, and butter. Beat with an electric mixer on low speed until mixture resembles coarse crumbs. Stir in pecans. Reserve 1 cup of the mixture for topping.

2. Press remaining nut mixture into the bottom of an ungreased 8×8×2-inch baking pan. Bake in a 350° oven for 8 to 10 minutes or until light brown.

3. Meanwhile, for filling, in another medium mixing bowl combine cream cheese, egg, granulated sugar, milk, lemon juice, vanilla, and almond extract. Beat with an electric mixer on medium speed until smooth. Stir in chopped red and green cherries. Pour filling over the partially baked crust. Sprinkle with reserved nut mixture.

4. Bake for 25 to 30 minutes more or until light brown and set. Cool completely in pan on a wire rack. Cut into bars. If desired, decorate each piece with red and green maraschino cherries.

TO STORE: **Cover and store in the refrigerator up to 3 days.**

holiday treat

Italian Cheese Bars

The light texture and classic flavor of a traditional Italian cheesecake is replicated here, with the help of cherries, almonds, golden raisins, and ricotta cheese. *(photo, page 398)*

Makes: 20 bars

Oven: 350°F

- ½ cup butter
- 1¼ cups finely crushed graham crackers (about 18)
- 1 15-ounce container fat-free ricotta cheese
- 1 egg
- ¼ cup sugar
- 2 tablespoons all-purpose flour
- 2 teaspoons finely shredded orange peel
- 1 teaspoon almond extract
- ½ cup sliced almonds or chopped hazelnuts (filberts)
- ⅓ cup chopped candied cherries
- ⅓ cup golden raisins

1. Place butter in a 9×9×2-inch baking pan. Place the pan in a 350° oven about 6 minutes or until butter is melted. Remove from oven. Stir crushed crackers into melted butter. With a wooden spoon, press the crumb mixture firmly and evenly into the bottom of the pan. Set aside.

2. In a blender container or food processor bowl combine the ricotta cheese, egg, sugar, flour, orange peel, and almond extract. Cover and blend or process until smooth. Carefully spread cheese mixture over crumb mixture. Combine the almonds, cherries, and raisins; sprinkle over cheese layer.

3. Bake for 25 to 30 minutes or until edges are puffed and golden. Cool in pan on a wire rack for 1 hour. Cover and chill for 2 hours. Cut into bars.

TO STORE: **Cover and store in the refrigerator up to 3 days.**

> ***The right pan*** To achieve bar cookie success, you must select the right pan for the job. Use a metal baking pan for the fastest, most even baking, and always use the pan size called for in the recipe. Too large a pan yields bars that are too thin to be appetizing. Too small a pan leaves you with bars too thick to bake evenly in the designated cooking time.

Golden Fig *Diamonds*

Dried fruits have long been the centerpiece of wintertime baking and a boon to creative holiday cooks. These Italian-style cookies celebrate tradition with a citrus twist. *(photo, page 362)*

Makes: about 18 diamonds

Oven: 350°F

8 ounces dried Calimyrna
(golden) figs, chopped
(1½ cups)

1 teaspoon finely shredded
orange peel

¾ cup orange juice

¼ cup packed brown sugar

Dash ground cinnamon

1 teaspoon vanilla

½ cup butter, softened

½ cup granulated sugar

⅛ teaspoon salt

1⅓ cups all-purpose flour

1 tablespoon granulated sugar

Orange peel twists (optional)

1. Lightly grease an 8×8×2-inch baking pan; set aside. For filling, in a medium saucepan combine figs, ½ teaspoon of the orange peel, orange juice, brown sugar, and cinnamon. Bring to boiling; reduce heat. Simmer, uncovered, over medium-low heat about 5 minutes or until figs are soft and mixture begins to thicken, stirring frequently (mixture will thicken more while cooling). Remove from heat. Stir in ½ teaspoon of the vanilla. Cool completely.

2. For crust, in a large mixing bowl beat butter with an electric mixer on medium to high speed for 30 seconds. Add the ½ cup granulated sugar, the remaining ½ teaspoon of the vanilla, and salt. Beat until combined, scraping sides of bowl occasionally. Beat in as much of the flour as you can with the mixer. Stir in any remaining flour with a wooden spoon (mixture will be crumbly). Set aside ¾ cup of the mixture for topping.

3. Press remaining mixture evenly into bottom of the prepared baking pan. Bake in a 350° oven about 20 minutes or until edges are golden brown.

4. Spread cooled fig mixture on top of hot crust. Sprinkle reserved crust mixture over filling. In a small bowl combine the 1 tablespoon sugar and the remaining ½ teaspoon orange peel; sprinkle on top. Bake about 30 minutes more or until crust is golden brown. Cool completely in pan on a wire rack. Cut into diamonds. If desired, top diamonds with orange peel twists.

TO STORE: Place in layers separated by waxed paper in an airtight container; cover. Store at room temperature up to 3 days or freeze up to 3 months. Thaw; if desired, top with orange peel twists.

holiday treat

Pear-Mince Streusel Bars

Christmas wouldn't be Christmas without mincemeat pie, but who has time for pie when there's so much cookie-baking to do? These easy bars are a faster, no-hassle alternative.

Makes: 32 bars

Oven: 375°F

1 recipe Fresh Pear-Mince Filling

1 cup butter, softened

⅓ cup granulated sugar

⅓ cup packed brown sugar

½ teaspoon baking soda

2½ cups all-purpose flour

½ cup chopped walnuts

1. Prepare Fresh Pear-Mince Filling. Set aside to cool slightly.
2. Meanwhile, for crust, in a large mixing bowl beat butter with an electric mixer on medium to high speed for 30 seconds. Add the granulated sugar, brown sugar, and baking soda. Beat until combined, scraping sides of bowl occasionally. Beat in as much of the flour as you can with the mixer. Sir in any remaining flour with a wooden spoon (mixture will be crumbly). Reserve 1 cup of the mixture for topping.
3. Press remaining crust mixture into the bottom of an ungreased 13×9×2-inch baking pan. Bake in a 375° oven about 12 minutes or until golden.
4. Carefully spread Fresh Pear-Mince Filling over hot crust. In a small bowl combine the 1 cup reserved crumb mixture and walnuts. Sprinkle over filling. Bake for 20 to 25 minutes more or until golden. Cool completely in pan on a wire rack. Cut into bars.

Fresh Pear-Mince Filling: In a medium saucepan combine 3 medium pears (1 pound), peeled, cored, and coarsely chopped; ⅓ cup dried currants or snipped raisins; ¼ cup packed brown sugar; 2 tablespoons brandy or orange juice; ½ teaspoon ground nutmeg. Bring to boiling, stirring constantly; reduce heat. Simmer, uncovered, about 5 minutes or until pear pieces are tender, stirring occasionally. Remove from heat.

TO STORE: Place in layers separated by waxed paper in a airtight container; cover. Store at room temperature up to 3 days or freeze up to 3 months.

Cherry-Berry Bars

Bursting with red cherries and black raspberries, these yummy bars steal the show at neighborhood block parties, family reunions, and summertime gatherings.

Makes: 32 bars

Oven: 375°F

4 cups fresh or one 16-ounce
    package frozen pitted
    red tart cherries

4 cups fresh or one 16-ounce
    package frozen black
    raspberries or blackberries

3½ cups all-purpose flour

1 teaspoon salt

1 cup shortening

1 egg yolk

    Milk

2 cups cornflakes

1 cup sugar

1 teaspoon ground cinnamon

1 slightly beaten egg white

    Sugar

1. If using frozen fruits, partially thaw; do not drain. In a large bowl stir together 3¼ cups of the flour and the salt. Using a pastry blender, cut in shortening until crumbs are the size of small peas. Place egg yolk in a 1-cup glass measuring cup; lightly beat with a fork. Add enough milk to egg yolk to make ½ cup. Beat until combined. Add milk mixture to flour mixture 1 tablespoon at a time, tossing lightly with a fork until all is moistened. Divide dough in half. Shape each half into a ball.

2. On a lightly floured surface, roll half of the dough into a 17×12-inch rectangle. Wrap the pastry around rolling pin. Unroll onto an ungreased 15×10×1-inch baking pan. Gently ease pastry into pan. Trim pastry even with sides of pan. Sprinkle cornflakes over pastry.

3. In a very large mixing bowl stir together the 1 cup sugar, the remaining ¼ cup flour, and the cinnamon. Add fruit; toss to coat. Sprinkle fruit mixture over cornflakes.

4. Roll remaining dough into a 17×12-inch rectangle. Arrange over fruit. Trim pastry to ½ inch beyond sides of pan. Seal top pastry to bottom pastry; crimp edges. Cut slits in top pastry.

5. Brush egg white over top of pastry; sprinkle with sugar. Bake in a 375° oven about 45 minutes or until golden brown. Cool in pan on a wire rack. Cut into bars.

TO STORE: Cover and store at room temperature up to 2 days.

Danish *Pastry Apple Bars*

If your family loves apple pie (and whose doesn't?), these bars will be a sure winner at dessert time. The perfect pastry—so tender and so flaky—tops off the spiced apple filling. (photo, page 399)

Makes: 32 bars

Oven: 375°F

2½ cups all-purpose flour

1 teaspoon salt

1 cup shortening

1 egg yolk

  Milk

1 cup cornflakes

8 to 10 tart baking apples,
    such as Cortland, Rome,
    or Granny Smith; peeled
    and sliced (8 cups)

½ cup granulated sugar

1 teaspoon ground cinnamon

1 egg white

1 tablespoon water

  Sifted powdered sugar or
    whipped cream (optional)

1. For pastry, in a large bowl stir together the flour and salt. Using a pastry blender, cut in shortening until mixture resembles coarse crumbs. Place egg yolk in a 1-cup glass measuring cup; lightly beat with a fork. Add enough milk to egg yolk to make ⅔ cup; mix well. Add egg yolk mixture to flour mixture; mix well. Divide dough in half.

2. On a lightly floured surface, roll half of the dough into an 18×12-inch rectangle. Fit dough rectangle into and up the sides of an ungreased 15×10×1-inch baking pan. Sprinkle with cornflakes; top with apples. Combine granulated sugar and cinnamon; sprinkle over apples.

3. Roll remaining dough into a 16×12-inch rectangle. Arrange over apples. Seal top pastry to bottom pastry. Cut slits in top pastry.

4. Beat together egg white and water. Brush mixture over pastry. Bake in a 375° oven about 50 minutes or until golden. Cool in pan on a wire rack. Serve warm or cool. If desired, top with powdered sugar or whipped cream.

TO STORE: Cover and store at room temperature up to 2 days.

Linzer Bars

Travelers to Austria often fall in love with Linzer torte, a distinctive dessert with a nutty base, raspberry jam filling, and lattice-crust topping. This concept is parlayed into an equally fancy bar cookie.

Makes: 32 bars

Oven: 350°F

²/₃ **cup butter, softened**

²/₃ **cup granulated sugar**

½ **teaspoon ground cinnamon**

¼ **teaspoon ground cloves**

1 **egg**

1 **tablespoon cherry liqueur,**

   cherry brandy, or water

1½ **cups all-purpose flour**

1 **cup ground hazelnuts**

   (filberts) or almonds

1 **teaspoon finely shredded**

   lemon peel

2 **tablespoons all-purpose flour**

1 **cup seedless red raspberry jam**

   Powdered sugar (optional)

1. In a large mixing bowl beat butter with an electric mixer on medium to high speed for 30 seconds. Beat in granulated sugar, cinnamon, and cloves. Beat in egg and liqueur. Stir in the 1½ cups flour, nuts, and lemon peel. Divide dough in half. Stir the 2 tablespoons flour into half of the dough. Wrap doughs in plastic wrap (label the dough containing the additional flour); chill for 1 hour.

2. Roll the dough that has the additional flour between two pieces of waxed paper into a 15×10-inch rectangle. Remove top piece of waxed paper. Cut rectangle into 10×½-inch strips. Using waxed paper with dough strips, slide dough onto a large baking sheet. Chill dough strips about 15 minutes or until firm and easy to handle.

3. Meanwhile, line a 13×9×2-inch baking pan with foil, extending foil 1 inch beyond edges of pan. Grease foil. Pat the dough without additional flour into bottom of the prepared pan. Spread jam evenly over dough in pan. Using a long narrow-blade metal spatula, peel chilled dough strips from waxed paper. Carefully place half of strips across jam about ½ inch apart; trim ends. Piece together dough strips as necessary by overlapping slightly. Place remaining strips diagonally across pan, forming diamonds.

4. Bake in the 350° oven about 30 minutes or until crust is golden. Cool completely in pan on wire rack. Using foil, lift out baked mixture. Cut into bars. Carefully remove foil. Just before serving, sift powdered sugar over bars.

TO STORE: Place in layers separated by waxed paper in an airtight container; cover. Store in the refrigerator up to 3 days or freeze up to 3 months.

Almond-Toffee Bars

A cookie recipe that requires no bowl and no stirring? Believe it! For these rich bars,

you simply layer the ingredients right in the baking pan.

Makes: 48 bars

Oven: 325°F

$\frac{1}{2}$ cup butter

$1\frac{1}{2}$ cups quick-cooking rolled oats

$\frac{1}{2}$ cup graham cracker crumbs

1 cup semisweet chocolate
pieces

1 cup almond brickle pieces

1 cup sliced or chopped almonds

1 14-ounce can ($1\frac{1}{4}$ cups)
sweetened condensed milk

1. Place butter in a 13×9×2-inch baking pan. Place pan in a 325° oven about 6 minutes or until butter is melted. Remove pan from oven. Sprinkle oats and graham cracker crumbs evenly over melted butter. Press lightly into bottom of pan with the back of a large metal spoon. Sprinkle chocolate pieces, brickle pieces, and almonds evenly over crumb mixture. Drizzle with sweetened condensed milk.

2. Bake in a 325° oven for 25 to 30 minutes or until edges are bubbly and center is just lightly browned. Remove from oven and immediately run a narrow metal spatula or table knife around edges of pan to loosen the cookie. Cool completely in pan on a wire rack. Cut into bars.

Toffee-Fruit Bars: Prepare as above, except substitute $\frac{1}{2}$ cup snipped dried apricots for $\frac{1}{2}$ cup of the chocolate pieces.

TO STORE: Cover and store in the refrigerator up to 3 days.

Apple *Butter* Bars

With the spiciness and subtle fruit flavor of apple butter, these moist cakelike bars capture the feel of a crisp fall morning. Add them to a brown bag lunch for a special treat.

Makes: 36 bars

Oven: 350°F

1 6-ounce package (1½ cups)
   mixed dried fruit bits

½ cup butter, softened

¾ cup packed brown sugar

½ teaspoon baking soda

½ teaspoon ground cinnamon

¼ teaspoon salt

2 eggs

½ cup apple butter

1½ cups all-purpose flour
   Sifted powdered sugar

1. Grease a 13×9×2-inch baking pan; set aside. Place fruit bits in a small bowl. Pour enough boiling water over fruit to cover. Let stand for 5 minutes; drain.

2. Meanwhile, in a large mixing bowl beat butter with an electric mixer on medium to high speed for 30 seconds. Add brown sugar, baking soda, cinnamon, and salt. Beat until combined, scraping sides of bowl occasionally. Beat in eggs and apple butter until combined. Beat in as much flour as you can with the mixer. Stir in remaining flour and drained fruit with a wooden spoon.

3. Pour batter into the prepared baking pan, spreading evenly. Bake in a 350° oven for 25 to 30 minutes or until a wooden toothpick inserted near center comes out clean. Cool completely in pan on a wire rack. Sprinkle with sifted powdered sugar. Cut into bars.

TO STORE: Place in layers separated by waxed paper in an airtight container; cover. Store at room temperature up to 3 days or freeze up to 3 months. Thaw; sprinkle with additional powdered sugar.

Spiced *Apricot* Bars

Looking for a low-fat treat? These bars substitute applesauce for most of the oil, making them a good choice.

Makes: 24 bars

Oven: 350°F

  1 **cup all-purpose flour**

 ½ **teaspoon baking powder**

 ¼ **teaspoon baking soda**

 ¼ **teaspoon ground cardamom or**

      ⅛ **teaspoon ground nutmeg**

  1 **slightly beaten egg**

 ½ **cup packed brown sugar**

 ½ **cup apricot nectar**

      or orange juice

 ¼ **cup unsweetened applesauce**

  2 **tablespoons cooking oil**

 ½ **cup finely snipped**

      dried apricots

  1 **recipe Apricot Icing**

1. In a medium bowl combine flour, baking powder, baking soda, and cardamom; set aside. In another bowl stir together the egg, brown sugar, apricot nectar, applesauce, and oil until combined. Add egg mixture to flour mixture, stirring just until combined. Stir in the apricots.

2. Pour batter into an ungreased 11×7×1½-inch baking pan, spreading evenly. Bake in a 350° oven for 20 to 25 minutes or until a wooden toothpick inserted near center comes out clean. Cool completely in pan on a wire rack. Drizzle with Apricot Icing; let icing dry. Cut into bars.

Apricot Icing: In a small bowl stir together ½ cup sifted powdered sugar and enough apricot nectar or orange juice (2 to 3 teaspoons) to make icing of drizzling consistency.

TO STORE: Cover and store at room temperature up to 3 days. To freeze, wrap undrizzled, uncut bars in heavy foil. Freeze up to 3 months. Thaw; drizzle with icing and cut into bars.

> *Beautiful bars* Besides their great taste, much of the beauty of bar cookies is the ease in making them: just stir, bake, and eat. If you'd like to dress them up a bit, try one of the following simple garnishes:
> • For unfrosted bars, lay waxed-paper strips across the top in a pattern. Sprinkle with a mixture of powdered sugar and a spice that's called for in the recipe.
> • For frosted bars, sprinkle with grated chocolate or chocolate curls, miniature chocolate chips, chopped nuts, or dried or candied fruit.

Carrot and *Zucchini* Bars

This is one way to get your family to eat some extra veggies! A citrusy cream cheese frosting is the crowning glory on these moist bars.

Makes: 36 bars

Oven: 350°F

1 1/2 cups all-purpose flour

3/4 cup packed brown sugar

1 teaspoon baking powder

1/2 teaspoon ground ginger

1/4 teaspoon baking soda

2 slightly beaten eggs

1 1/2 cups shredded carrots

1 medium zucchini, shredded
      (1 cup)

1/2 cup raisins

1/2 cup chopped walnuts

1/2 cup cooking oil

1/4 cup honey

1 teaspoon vanilla

1 recipe Citrus-Cream
      Cheese Frosting

1. In a large bowl combine flour, brown sugar, baking powder, ginger, and baking soda. In another large bowl stir together eggs, carrots, zucchini, raisins, walnuts, oil, honey, and vanilla. Add carrot mixture to flour mixture, stirring just until combined.

2. Pour batter into an ungreased 13×9×2-inch baking pan, spreading evenly. Bake in a 350° oven about 25 minutes or until a wooden toothpick inserted near the center comes out clean. Cool completely in pan on a wire rack. Frost with Citrus-Cream Cheese Frosting. Let frosting dry. Cut into bars.

Citrus-Cream Cheese Frosting: In a medium mixing bowl beat one 8-ounce package softened cream cheese and 1 cup sifted powdered sugar with an electric mixer on medium speed until fluffy. Stir in 1 teaspoon finely shredded lemon peel or orange peel.

TO STORE: Cover and store in the refrigerator up to 3 days. To freeze, wrap unfrosted, uncut bars in heavy foil. Freeze up to 3 months. Thaw; frost and cut into bars.

Banana Bars

A splash of brandy in the buttery frosting lends sophistication to these toffee-flecked bars. If you're baking them with kids in mind, use the milk instead of the brandy for a family-friendly treat.

Makes: 48 bars

Oven: 350°F

½ cup butter, softened

1⅓ cups sugar

1½ teaspoons baking powder

½ teaspoon baking soda

¼ teaspoon salt

1 egg

1 cup mashed bananas
   (about 3 medium)

½ cup dairy sour cream

1 teaspoon vanilla

2 cups all-purpose flour

¾ cup chocolate-covered
   toffee pieces or almond
   brickle pieces

¾ cup toasted chopped almonds
   (optional)

1 recipe Brandied Brown
   Butter Frosting

1. Lightly grease a 15×10×1-inch baking pan; set aside. In a large mixing bowl beat butter with an electric mixer on medium to high speed for 30 seconds. Add sugar, baking powder, baking soda, and salt. Beat until combined, scraping sides of bowl occasionally. Beat in the egg, mashed bananas, sour cream, and vanilla until combined. Beat or stir in the flour. Stir in toffee pieces and, if desired, almonds.

2. Pour batter into the prepared baking pan, spreading evenly. Bake in a 350° oven about 25 minutes or until a wooden toothpick inserted near center comes out clean. Cool completely in pan on a wire rack. Spread with Brandied Brown Butter Frosting; let frosting dry. Cut into bars.

Brandied Browned Butter Frosting: In a small saucepan heat ⅓ cup butter over low heat until melted. Continue heating until the butter turns light brown; remove from heat. Pour butter into a medium mixing bowl. Add 2½ cups sifted powdered sugar, 1 tablespoon brandy or milk, and 1 teaspoon vanilla. Beat with an electric mixer on low speed until combined. Beat on medium to high speed, adding enough milk to make frosting of spreading consistency. Use immediately.

TO STORE: Cover and store at room temperature up to 3 days. To freeze, wrap unfrosted, uncut bars in heavy foil. Freeze up to 3 months. Thaw; frost and cut into bars.

Pumpkin Bars

Celebrate fall's pumpkin harvest by making these frosted bars anytime from Halloween through New Year's Day. The rest of the year, you can make them with applesauce.

Makes: 48 bars

Oven: 350°F

  2 **cups all-purpose flour**

1½ **cups sugar**

  2 **teaspoons baking powder**

  2 **teaspoons ground cinnamon**

  1 **teaspoon baking soda**

  ¼ **teaspoon salt**

  ¼ **teaspoon ground cloves**

  4 **beaten eggs**

  1 **15-ounce can pumpkin**

  1 **cup cooking oil**

  1 **recipe Cream Cheese Frosting**

1. In a large bowl stir together the flour, sugar, baking powder, cinnamon, baking soda, salt, and cloves. Stir in the eggs, pumpkin, and oil until combined. Pour batter into an ungreased 15×10×1-inch baking pan, spreading evenly.

2. Bake in a 350° oven for 25 to 30 minutes or until a wooden toothpick inserted near center comes out clean. Cool completely in pan on a wire rack. Spread with Cream Cheese Frosting; let frosting dry. Cut into bars.

Cream Cheese Frosting: In a medium mixing bowl beat half of an 8-ounce package cream cheese, softened; ¼ cup softened butter; and 1 teaspoon vanilla with an electric mixer on medium to high speed until light and fluffy. Gradually add 1 cup sifted powdered sugar, beating well. Gradually beat in additional sifted powdered sugar (1¾ to 2¼ cups) until frosting is of spreading consistency.

Applesauce Bars: Prepare as above, except substitute one 15-ounce jar applesauce for the pumpkin.

TO STORE: Cover and store in the refrigerator up to 3 days. To freeze, wrap unfrosted, uncut bars in heavy foil. Freeze up to 3 months. Thaw; frost and cut into bars.

Malted Mocha Bars

Malted milk makes everything better, and these bars get a double dose—in both batter and icing.

(photo, page 361)

Makes: 36 bars

Oven: 350°F

²/₃ **cup butter, softened**

²/₃ **cup packed brown sugar**

1½ **cups all-purpose flour**

3 **slightly beaten eggs**

¹/₃ **cup granulated sugar**

2 **teaspoons vanilla**

1½ **cups coconut**

¾ **cup chocolate-flavored instant malted milk powder**

1½ **teaspoons instant espresso powder or instant coffee crystals**

¼ **teaspoon baking powder**

¼ **teaspoon salt**

1 **recipe Mocha Icing**

1. Grease a 13×9×2-inch baking pan; set aside. For crust, in a large mixing bowl combine butter and brown sugar. Beat with an electric mixer on medium to high speed until combined. Beat or stir in 1¼ cups of the flour. If necessary, gently knead to mix. Pat crust mixture evenly into the bottom of the prepared baking pan. Bake in a 350° oven about 15 minutes or until set.

2. Meanwhile, in a medium bowl stir together eggs, granulated sugar, and vanilla. Stir in coconut, malted milk powder, the remaining ¼ cup flour, espresso powder, baking powder, and salt. Carefully spread mixture over partially baked crust. Bake for 20 to 25 minutes more or until set. Cool completely in pan on a wire rack. Spread Mocha Icing over cooled bars; let frosting dry. Cut into bars.

Mocha Icing: In a medium mixing bowl beat 2½ cups sifted powdered sugar, ¼ cup malted milk powder, ½ teaspoon instant espresso powder or instant coffee crystals, 2 teaspoons vanilla, and 4 teaspoons boiling water with an electric mixer on medium to high speed until combined. If necessary, beat in a little additional boiling water until icing is of spreading consistency.

TO STORE: Cover and store at room temperature up to 3 days. To freeze, wrap unfrosted, uncut bars in heavy foil. Freeze up to 3 months. Thaw; frost and cut into bars.

Malted Mocha Bars, page 360

Pumpkin Cheesecake Bars, page 365

holiday treat

Pumpkin *Cheesecake* Bars

A spicy gingersnap crust is the perfect foil for the rich, creamy pumpkin cheesecake filling.

Hint: The crispiest gingersnaps produce the best crust. *(photo, page 364)*

Makes: 24 bars

Oven: 325°F

2 **cups finely crushed gingersnaps (about 30 cookies)**
¼ **cup butter, melted**
⅓ **cup canned pumpkin**
1 **tablespoon all-purpose flour**
1 **teaspoon pumpkin pie spice**
3 **8-ounce packages cream cheese, softened**
1 **cup sugar**
1½ **teaspoons vanilla**
3 **eggs**

1. Lightly grease a 13×9×2-inch baking pan; set aside. For crust, in a small bowl combine gingersnaps and melted butter. Press mixture evenly into bottom of the prepared pan. Bake in a 325° oven about 10 minutes or until crust is firm; cool.

2. Meanwhile, for pumpkin batter, in a medium bowl stir together pumpkin, flour, and pumpkin pie spice; set aside.

3. For cream cheese batter, in a large mixing bowl beat cream cheese with an electric mixer on medium to high speed until smooth. Add sugar and vanilla, beating until combined. Add eggs, 1 at a time, beating after each addition on low speed just until combined. Stir one-third of the cream cheese batter (about 1½ cups) into the pumpkin batter until smooth. Pour remaining cream cheese batter over crust, spreading evenly. Place large spoonfuls of pumpkin batter randomly over cream cheese batter. Using the tip of a table knife or a thin metal spatula, gently swirl the two batters together.

4. Bake for 25 to 30 minutes more or until center is just set. Cool completely in pan on a wire rack. Cover and chill for 4 to 24 hours before cutting into squares or bars.

TO STORE: Cover and store in the refrigerator up to 3 days.

Honey-Nut Bars

A drizzle of icing and a sprinkle of chopped walnuts make eye-catching—not to mention, palate-pleasing—toppings for these honey-sweetened bars. *(photo, page 363)*

Makes: 24 bars

Oven: 350°F

½ cup butter, softened

¼ cup shortening

1 cup honey

1 teaspoon baking powder

¼ teaspoon salt

3 eggs

1 teaspoon vanilla

1½ cups all-purpose flour

1 cup coconut

1 cup chopped walnuts

1 recipe Powdered Sugar Icing

Chopped walnuts

1. Grease a 13×9×2-inch baking pan; set aside. In a large mixing bowl beat butter and shortening with an electric mixer on medium to high speed for 30 seconds. Add honey, baking powder, and salt. Beat until combined, scraping sides of bowl occasionally. Beat in eggs and vanilla until combined. Beat in as much of the flour as you can with the mixer. Stir in any remaining flour. Stir in coconut and the 1 cup walnuts.

2. Pour batter into the prepared pan, spreading evenly. Bake in a 350° oven for 25 to 30 minutes or until a wooden toothpick inserted near center comes out clean. Cool completely in pan on a wire rack. Drizzle with Powdered Sugar Icing; sprinkle with nuts. Let icing dry. Cut into bars.

Powdered Sugar Icing: In a small bowl stir together 1 cup sifted powdered sugar, ¼ teaspoon vanilla, and 1 tablespoon milk. Stir in additional milk, 1 teaspoon at a time, until icing is of drizzling consistency.

TO STORE: **Cover and store at room temperature up to 3 days. To freeze, wrap undrizzled, uncut bars in heavy foil. Freeze up to 3 months. Thaw; drizzle and sprinkle with nuts. Cut into bars.**

Honey of a sweetener The flavor and color of honey depend on the flowers from which it is made. Most honey is made from clover, which gives it a mild flavor and pale color.

Store honey in a dry place up to 1 year. If honey crystallizes during storage, you can still use it. Place the jar of honey in a container of warm water, and occasionally stir the honey until the crystals dissolve. Change the warm water as necessary.

To use honey in baking, you'll get the best results when you follow a specially formulated recipe. Substituting honey for part of the sugar requires adjusting the amount of liquid, the leavening, and the baking temperature.

Pecan *Pie* Bars

These easy-to-make bars boast a scrumptious pecan pie filling baked over a buttery shortbread crust.

Makes: 24 bars

Oven: 375°F

1¼ cups all-purpose flour

  3 tablespoons brown sugar

 ½ cup butter

  2 slightly beaten eggs

 ½ cup packed brown sugar

 ¾ cup chopped pecans

 ½ cup light-colored corn syrup

  2 tablespoons butter, melted

  1 teaspoon vanilla

1. For crust, in a medium bowl combine flour and the 3 tablespoons brown sugar. Using a pastry blender, cut in the ½ cup butter until mixture resembles coarse crumbs. Pat crumb mixture into an ungreased 11×7×1½-inch baking pan. Bake in a 375° oven for 20 minutes.

2. Meanwhile, for filling, in a medium bowl stir together eggs, the ½ cup brown sugar, pecans, corn syrup, the 2 tablespoons melted butter, and vanilla. Pour filling over baked crust, spreading evenly.

3. Bake for 20 to 25 minutes more or until filling is set. Cool completely in pan on a wire rack. Cut into bars.

TO STORE: Place in layers separated by waxed paper in an airtight container; cover. Store in the refrigerator up to 3 days or freeze up to 3 months.

Mixed Nut Bars

This bar is at its nutty best. The buttermilk provides a distinctive, and perhaps unexpected,

tang. Hint: For nice, even edges, chill the bars for an hour or two before cutting. *(photo, page 399)*

Makes: 32 bars

Oven: 350°F

  2 **cups all-purpose flour**

 ³/₄ **cup butter, softened**

 ¹/₃ **cup packed brown sugar**

1²/₃ **cups granulated sugar**

  1 **cup buttermilk or sour milk***

  3 **eggs**

 ¹/₄ **cup butter, melted**

1¹/₂ **teaspoons vanilla**

  2 **cups coarsely chopped mixed**
        nuts (no peanuts)

     Sifted powdered sugar
        (optional)

1. For crust, in a large mixing bowl combine 1¾ cups of the flour, the ¾ cup butter, and brown sugar. Beat with an electric mixer on medium to high speed until combined (mixture will be crumbly). Pat mixture into the bottom and ½ inch up the sides of an ungreased 13×9×2-inch baking pan. Bake in a 350° oven for 10 minutes.

2. Meanwhile, in a medium mixing bowl beat together granulated sugar, the buttermilk, eggs, the remaining ¼ cup flour, the ¼ cup melted butter, and vanilla with an electric mixer on low speed until combined. Stir in nuts. Pour into partially baked crust.

3. Bake about 25 minutes more or until golden and center is set. Cool in pan on a wire rack. Cover and chill for 1 to 2 hours before cutting into bars. If desired, sprinkle with sifted powdered sugar.

*****NOTE:** To make sour milk, place 1 tablespoon lemon juice or vinegar in a glass measuring cup. Add enough milk to make 1 cup total; stir. Let mixture stand for 5 minutes before using.

TO STORE: Place in layers separated by waxed paper in an airtight container; cover. Store in the refrigerator up to 3 days or freeze up to 3 months.

Toffee *Squares*

These irresistible layered delights are similar to those sold in espresso bars across North America. Bring the treat home with this easy recipe.

Makes: about 36 triangles

Oven: 350°F

¾ cup butter, softened

¾ cup packed brown sugar

1 egg yolk

1½ cups all-purpose flour

¼ teaspoon salt

1 14-ounce can (1¼ cups)
        sweetened condensed milk

2 tablespoons butter

2 teaspoons vanilla

1 12-ounce package semisweet
        chocolate pieces (2 cups)

1 cup almond brickle pieces or
        toasted chopped pecans

1. Grease a 13×9×2-inch baking pan; set aside. For crust, in a large mixing bowl beat the ¾ cup butter and brown sugar with an electric mixer on medium speed until combined. Beat in the egg yolk. Stir in the flour and salt with a wooden spoon until well mixed. Using floured hands, press dough into the bottom of the prepared baking pan. Bake in a 350° oven about 20 minutes or until light brown. Cool on a wire rack.

2. For filling, in a small heavy saucepan heat and stir the sweetened condensed milk and the 2 tablespoons butter over medium heat until bubbly. Cook and stir for 5 minutes more. (Mixture will thicken and become smooth.) Stir in the vanilla. Spread filling over baked crust. Bake for 12 to 15 minutes more or until top layer is golden brown.

3. Sprinkle chocolate pieces evenly over top of baked layers. Bake for 1 to 2 minutes more or until chocolate pieces melt. Remove from oven; set on a wire rack. Using a flexible spatula, immediately spread chocolate evenly over baked layers. Sprinkle with almond brickle pieces. Cool completely on a wire rack. Cover and chill until chocolate is set. Cut into squares or triangles.

TO STORE: Place in layers separated by waxed paper in an airtight container; cover. Store in the refrigerator up to 3 days.

Terrific *Toffee* Bars

These yummy morsels are named for the candy they resemble. A layer of melted chocolate tops a layer of brown sugar cookie; chopped nuts and toffee candy finish the bars in style.

Makes: 36 bars

Oven: 350°F

½ cup butter, softened

¾ cup packed brown sugar

1 egg

½ teaspoon vanilla

1 cup all-purpose flour

⅛ teaspoon salt

¾ cup semisweet chocolate
   pieces

⅓ cup chopped walnuts
   or pecans

⅓ cup chocolate-covered
   toffee pieces

1. In a large mixing bowl beat butter with an electric mixer on medium to high speed for 30 seconds. Add brown sugar, egg, and vanilla. Beat until combined, scraping the sides of the bowl occasionally. Beat in the flour and the salt until combined.

2. Pour batter into an ungreased 13×9×2-inch baking pan, spreading evenly. Bake in a 350° oven about 15 minutes or until edges begin to brown and surface is dry. Remove from oven and immediately sprinkle with chocolate pieces. Let stand about 2 minutes or until chocolate is softened. Using a flexible spatula, spread chocolate evenly over baked layer. Sprinkle with nuts and toffee pieces. Immediately cut into bars. Cool on a wire rack.

TO STORE: Place in layers separated by waxed paper in an airtight container; cover. Store in the refrigerator up to 3 days.

Lining the pan For easier serving, neater bars, and fuss-free cleanup, *Better Homes and Gardens* food stylists like to line the baking pan with heavy foil, extending it over the sides of the pan. After baking and cooling, they use the foil to lift the cookie out of the pan, transferring it to a cutting board. Next they peel away the foil and cut the cookie into bars with a large knife, such as a chef's knife.

Peanut *Brittle* Bars

Earmark this page! Fifteen minutes of preparation time, a super-easy crust, and an even easier topping guarantee you'll be back again and again. *(photo, page 398)*

Makes: 36 bars

Oven: 350°F

2   **cups all-purpose flour**

½   **cup packed brown sugar**

⅔   **cup butter**

2   **cups cocktail peanuts**

1   **cup milk chocolate pieces**

1   **12½-ounce jar caramel**
      ice cream topping

3   **tablespoons all-purpose flour**

1. Line a 15×10×1-inch baking pan with foil, extending foil over edges of pan. Grease foil; set pan aside. For crust, in a medium bowl combine the 2 cups flour and the brown sugar. Using a pastry blender, cut in butter until mixture is crumbly. Press mixture into bottom of prepared pan. Bake in a 350° oven about 12 minutes or until golden brown.

2. Sprinkle peanuts and milk chocolate pieces over crust. For topping, in a small bowl stir together caramel topping and the 3 tablespoons flour. Drizzle topping over nuts and chocolate. Bake for 12 to 15 minutes more or until topping is bubbly. Cool completely in pan on a wire rack. Using foil, lift bars out of pan. Carefully peel foil from sides of bars. Cut into bars.

TO STORE: Place in layers separated by waxed paper in an airtight container; cover. Store at room temperature up to 3 days or freeze up to 3 months.

Ultimate Bar Cookies

Read the ingredients list and you'll see why these bars are "the ultimate." With walnuts, macadamia nuts, milk chocolate, and white chocolate, they couldn't be anything but.

Makes: 36 bars

Oven: 350°F

2 cups all-purpose flour

1 cup packed brown sugar

½ cup butter, softened

1 cup coarsely chopped walnuts

1 3½-ounce jar macadamia nuts, coarsely chopped (1 cup)

1 6-ounce package white baking bars, coarsely chopped

1 cup milk chocolate pieces

¾ cup butter

1. For crust, in a medium mixing bowl beat flour, ½ cup of the brown sugar, and the ½ cup softened butter with an electric mixer on medium speed until mixture forms fine crumbs.

2. Press mixture firmly into the bottom of an ungreased 13×9×2-inch baking pan. Bake in a 350° oven about 15 minutes or until light brown. Place pan on a wire rack. Sprinkle walnuts, macadamia nuts, white baking bars, and milk chocolate pieces over hot crust.

3. In a medium saucepan cook and stir the ¾ cup butter and the remaining ½ cup brown sugar over medium heat until bubbly. Cook and stir for 1 minute more. Pour evenly over layers in baking pan. Bake about 15 minutes more or until just bubbly around edges. Cool completely in pan on a wire rack. Cut into bars.

TO STORE: **Place in layers separated by waxed paper in an airtight container; cover. Store at room temperature up to 3 days or freeze up to 3 months.**

Blondies

A Southern cook's preference for brown sugar over granulated sugar resulted in these butterscotch bars many years ago. They've been a favorite ever since.

Makes: 36 bars

Oven: 350°F

2 **cups packed brown sugar**

²⁄₃ **cup butter**

2 **eggs**

2 **teaspoons vanilla**

2 **cups all-purpose flour**

1 **teaspoon baking powder**

¼ **teaspoon baking soda**

1 **cup semisweet chocolate pieces**

1 **cup chopped nuts**

1. Grease a 13×9×2-inch baking pan; set aside. In a medium saucepan heat brown sugar and butter over medium heat until butter melts and mixture is smooth, stirring constantly. Cool slightly. Add eggs, 1 at a time, beating with a wooden spoon after each addition just until combined. Stir in vanilla. Stir in flour, baking powder, and baking soda.

2. Pour batter into prepared baking pan, spreading evenly. Sprinkle with chocolate pieces and nuts. Bake in a 350° oven for 25 to 30 minutes or until a wooden toothpick inserted near center comes out clean (avoid chocolate pieces). Cool slightly in pan on a wire rack. Cut into bars while warm.

TO STORE: Place in layers separated by waxed paper in an airtight container; cover. Store at room temperature up to 3 days or freeze up to 3 months.

Chocolate sense **When a recipe calls for chocolate, the higher the quality of the chocolate you use, the better the results. Chocolate is a combination of cocoa butter, chocolate "liquor" (the pressed liquid from roasted cocoa beans), and sugar. Makers of imitation chocolate may substitute vegetable fat for the cocoa butter.**

Some recipes call for white chocolate. Although not truly chocolate, since it contains none of the chocolate liquor from the cocoa bean, high-quality white chocolate does contain cocoa butter. Use only a high-quality white chocolate when baking.

Browned Butter and Cashew *Shortbread*

Loved for its rich, nutty taste, browned butter is a favored ingredient of cookie chefs.

Hint: When browning the butter, watch carefully. The butter quickly transgresses from

a little too pale to much too dark.

Makes: 24 bars

Oven: 325°F

 ²/₃ **cup butter**

 ½ **teaspoon vanilla**

1¼ **cups all-purpose flour**

 3 **tablespoons brown sugar**

 ½ **cup sifted powdered sugar**

 2 to 3 **teaspoons milk**

 2 **tablespoons finely chopped**

   toasted cashews

1. Line an 8×8×2-inch baking pan with foil, extending foil over edges of pan. Set pan aside. In a medium saucepan heat butter over medium heat until butter turns the color of light brown sugar, stirring frequently. Remove from heat; cool slightly. Set aside 2 tablespoons of the butter at room temperature for the icing. Stir vanilla into remaining browned butter. Chill browned butter mixture about 1 hour or until firm.

2. In a medium bowl combine flour and brown sugar. Using a pastry blender, cut the chilled browned butter mixture into flour mixture until it resembles fine crumbs and the mixture starts to cling together.

3. Press dough firmly into the bottom of the prepared baking pan. Bake in a 325° oven about 25 minutes or until firm but not brown. Immediately use foil to lift shortbread out of pan. Cut shortbread into bars. Again use foil to transfer bars to a wire rack; cool completely on foil.

4. For icing, stir together reserved browned butter, the powdered sugar, and enough of the milk to make an icing of drizzling consistency. Drizzle icing over cooled shortbread. Sprinkle with cashews. Let icing dry.

TO STORE: Place in layers separated by waxed paper in an airtight container; cover. Store at room temperature up to 3 days or freeze undrizzled bars up to 3 months. Thaw bars; drizzle with icing and sprinkle with cashews.

Butterscotch Shortbread Bars

If you're looking for something wonderfully sweet and old-fashioned, you can hardly do better than this classic concoction of butterscotch and nuts over a shortbread cookie crust.
(photo, page 362)

Makes: 24 bars

Oven: 350°F

1¼   cups all-purpose flour

3   tablespoons brown sugar

¼   teaspoon baking powder

¾   cup butter

⅓   cup granulated sugar

⅓   cup packed brown sugar

⅓   cup light-colored corn syrup

1   tablespoon water

¼   teaspoon salt

½   cup coarsely chopped cashews

¼   cup whipping cream

1   teaspoon vanilla

1. Line a 9×9×2-inch baking pan with foil, extending foil over edges of pan. Butter foil; set pan aside. For crust, in a medium bowl combine flour, the 3 tablespoons brown sugar, and the baking powder. Using a pastry blender, cut in ½ cup of the butter until mixture resembles coarse crumbs. Press mixture into the bottom of the prepared baking pan. Bake in a 350° oven about 25 minutes or until golden brown.

2. Meanwhile, for butterscotch sauce, in a medium heavy saucepan melt the remaining ¼ cup butter. Stir in granulated sugar, the ⅓ cup brown sugar, corn syrup, water, and salt. Stir in cashews. Bring mixture to boiling over medium-high heat, stirring constantly. Boil, uncovered, for 5 minutes, stirring often. Remove saucepan from heat. Stir in whipping cream and vanilla.

3. Spread butterscotch mixture evenly over baked crust. Bake for 12 to 15 minutes more or until most of the surface is bubbly. Cool completely in pan on a wire rack. Using the foil, lift bars out of the pan. Carefully peel foil from sides of bars. Cut into bars.

TO STORE: Place in layers separated by waxed paper in an airtight container; cover. Store at room temperature up to 3 days or freeze up to 3 months.

holiday
treat

Peanut Butter and *Chocolate Chip* Bars

Turn these everyday hits into holiday favorites: Use colored frosting and small candies to decorate them to look like presents, Christmas trees, or other symbols of the season.

Makes: about 16 bars

Oven: 350°F

¾ **cup peanut butter**

¼ **cup cooking oil**

 1 **cup packed brown sugar**

 2 **eggs**

½ **teaspoon baking powder**

¼ **teaspoon baking soda**

 1 **cup all-purpose flour**

¾ **cup milk**

¾ **cup rolled oats**

½ **cup miniature semisweet**
    chocolate pieces

⅓ **cup chopped peanuts**

   Purchased frosting

   Assorted small candies

1. Grease a 13×9×2-inch baking pan; set aside. In a large mixing bowl beat peanut butter and oil with an electric mixer on low to medium speed for 30 seconds. Add brown sugar, eggs, baking powder, and baking soda. Beat until combined, scraping sides of bowl occasionally. Beat in flour; beat in the milk. Stir in rolled oats, chocolate pieces, and peanuts with a wooden spoon.

2. Spread batter in the prepared baking pan. Bake in a 350° oven for 25 to 30 minutes or until a wooden toothpick inserted near center comes out clean. Cool completely in pan on a wire rack. Cut into triangles, circles, and squares that are about 2½ inches across. Decorate with purchased frosting and candies. Let frosting dry.

TO STORE: Place in layers separated by waxed paper in an airtight container; cover. Store at room temperature up to 3 days or freeze undecorated bars up to 3 months. Thaw bars; decorate.

Peanut Butter Bars

These homespun peanut butter and oatmeal bars make a wholesome after-school snack.

They taste even better with a glass of cold milk.

Makes: 20 bars

Oven: 375°F

¼ **cup peanut butter**

¼ **cup shortening**

½ **cup packed brown sugar**

¼ **teaspoon baking soda**

1 **egg**

1 **tablespoon milk**

½ **teaspoon vanilla**

⅔ **cup all-purpose flour**

¼ **cup quick-cooking rolled oats**

1 **recipe Peanut Butter Frosting**

1 **ounce semisweet chocolate,**

   melted (optional)

1. In a medium mixing bowl beat peanut butter and shortening with an electric mixer on medium to high speed for 30 seconds. Add brown sugar and baking soda. Beat until combined, scraping sides of bowl occasionally. Beat in egg, milk, and vanilla. Beat in flour. Stir in rolled oats with a wooden spoon.

2. Spread batter in an ungreased 8×8×2-inch baking pan. Bake in a 375° oven about 15 minutes or until a wooden toothpick inserted near center comes out clean. Cool completely in pan on a wire rack. Frost with Peanut Butter Frosting. If desired, drizzle with melted chocolate. Let stand until chocolate is set. Cut into bars.

Peanut Butter Frosting: In a small mixing bowl beat 3 tablespoons creamy peanut butter and 1 cup sifted powdered sugar with an electric mixer on medium speed until combined. Slowly beat in 3 tablespoons milk and 1 teaspoon vanilla. Beat in 1¼ cups sifted powdered sugar. Beat in additional milk, if necessary, to make frosting of spreading consistency.

TO STORE: Cover and store at room temperature up to 3 days. To freeze, wrap unfrosted, uncut bars in heavy foil. Freeze up to 3 months. Thaw; frost and cut into bars.

holiday
treat

Peanut Butter *Pizza*

If pizza were a dessert, this is how it would look. It's hard to improve on pizza's perfection, but turning it into a cookie and adding peanut butter might just push pizza's popularity off the chart.

Makes: 12 wedges

Oven: 350°F

½ **cup butter, softened**

½ **cup peanut butter**

½ **cup packed brown sugar**

⅓ **cup granulated sugar**

1 **egg**

1 **teaspoon vanilla**

1 **cup all-purpose flour**

½ **cup semisweet chocolate
    pieces**

½ **cup peanut butter pieces**

¾ **cup tiny marshmallows**

⅔ **cup peanuts**

½ **cup miniature candy-coated
    semisweet chocolate pieces**

1. In a large mixing bowl beat butter and peanut butter with an electric mixer on medium to high speed for 30 seconds. Add brown sugar, granulated sugar, egg, and vanilla. Beat until combined, scraping sides of bowl occasionally. Beat in the flour on low speed.

2. Spread dough evenly in an ungreased 12- or 13-inch pizza pan. Bake in a 350° oven for 15 to 18 minutes or until golden. Remove from oven. Sprinkle with chocolate and peanut butter pieces. Let stand about 2 minutes or until chocolate pieces are softened. Spread melted pieces over crust. Top with marshmallows, peanuts, and miniature candy pieces.

3. Bake about 5 minutes more or until the marshmallows are golden. Cool completely in pan on wire rack. Cut into wedges.

TO STORE: Cover and store at room temperature for up to 2 days.

Triple Peanut Bars

Fans of old-fashioned peanut butter cookies will love these bars. Melted chocolate and a peanut butter icing top a peanutty cookie crust. *(photo, page 362)*

Makes: 48 bars

Oven: 350°F

¾ cup peanut butter

¼ cup cooking oil

½ cup granulated sugar

½ cup packed brown sugar

½ teaspoon baking powder

¼ teaspoon baking soda

 2 eggs

¾ cup milk

 1 teaspoon vanilla

1½ cups all-purpose flour

⅔ cup chopped peanuts

1½ cups semisweet chocolate
       pieces

 1 recipe Peanut Butter Icing
       Coarsely chopped peanuts
       (optional)

1. Grease a 15×10×1-inch baking pan; set aside. In a large mixing bowl beat peanut butter and oil with an electric mixer on low to medium speed for 30 seconds. Add granulated sugar, brown sugar, baking powder, and baking soda. Beat until combined, scraping sides of bowl occasionally. Beat in eggs, milk, and vanilla. Beat in flour. Stir in the ⅔ cup peanuts with a wooden spoon.

2. Spread dough evenly in the prepared baking pan. Bake in a 350° oven about 20 minutes or until a wooden toothpick inserted near center comes out clean. Remove from oven. Sprinkle with chocolate pieces. Let stand about 5 minutes or until chocolate pieces are melted. Spread melted pieces over surface. Let cool completely. Drizzle with Peanut Butter Icing. If desired, sprinkle with additional peanuts. Let icing dry. Cut into bars.

Peanut Butter Icing: In a small mixing bowl beat together ¾ cup sifted powdered sugar, ¼ cup creamy peanut butter, and enough milk (2 to 3 tablespoons) with an electric mixer on medium to high speed to make icing of drizzling consistency.

TO STORE: Cover and store at room temperature for up to 3 days.

Chocolate and Peanut Butter Bars

With a creamy peanut butter filling, a chocolate chip-crumb topping, and a chewy oat crust made with whole wheat flour, these delectable bars meld the sweet and the healthful.

Makes: 48 bars

Oven: 350°F

  2 **cups quick-cooking rolled oats**

1³⁄₄ **cups packed brown sugar**

  1 **cup all-purpose flour**

 ¹⁄₂ **cup whole wheat flour**

  1 **teaspoon baking powder**

 ¹⁄₂ **teaspoon baking soda**

  1 **cup butter**

 ¹⁄₂ **cup chopped peanuts**

  1 **12-ounce package (2 cups)**
      semisweet chocolate pieces

  1 **slightly beaten egg**

  1 **14-ounce can (1¹⁄₄ cups)**
      sweetened condensed milk

 ¹⁄₃ **cup creamy peanut butter**

1. For crumb mixture, in a large bowl combine oats, brown sugar, all-purpose flour, whole wheat flour, baking powder, and baking soda. Using a pastry blender, cut in the butter until mixture resembles fine crumbs. Stir in peanuts.

2. For topping, in a medium bowl combine 1³⁄₄ cups of the crumb mixture and the chocolate pieces; set aside.

3. For crust, stir the egg into the crumb mixture without the chocolate pieces. Press into the bottom of an ungreased 15×10×1-inch baking pan. Bake in a 350° oven for 15 minutes.

4. For filling, stir together sweetened condensed milk and peanut butter until smooth. Pour filling evenly over partially baked crust, spreading as necessary. Sprinkle topping evenly over filling.

5. Bake for 12 to 15 minutes more or until light brown around the edges. Cool completely in pan on a wire rack. Cut into bars.

TO STORE: Place in layers separated by waxed paper in an airtight container; cover. Store in the refrigerator up to 3 days or freeze up to 3 months.

The milk that made life sweeter Sweetened condensed milk has been around for almost a century and a half, but it wasn't invented with cookies in mind. In the days before refrigeration, it served as a reliable source of milk that wouldn't spoil. Everyone from babies to Civil War troops drank it. Industrious cooks quickly discovered that the product added something very special to baking. In 1931, one manufacturer offered home cooks $25 for original recipes using condensed milk, and more than 80,000 recipes rolled in!

Chocolate *Revel* Bars

The *Better Homes and Gardens*ᵣ Test Kitchen developed these bars in the late 1960s, and they've been an all-time favorite recipe ever since. Hint: Because they're so rich, cut them into small rectangles.

Makes: 60 bars

Oven: 350°F

1   **cup butter, softened**

2   **cups packed brown sugar**

1   **teaspoon baking soda**

2   **eggs**

4   **teaspoons vanilla**

2½ **cups all-purpose flour**

3   **cups quick-cooking rolled oats**

1½ **cups semisweet chocolate**
    pieces

1   **14-ounce can (1¼ cups)**
    sweetened condensed milk

½   **cup chopped walnuts**
    or pecans

1. Set aside 2 tablespoons of the butter. In a large mixing bowl beat remaining butter with an electric mixer on medium to high speed for 30 seconds. Add brown sugar and baking soda. Beat until combined, scraping sides of bowl occasionally. Beat in eggs and 2 teaspoons of the vanilla. Beat in as much of the flour as you can with the mixer. Stir in remaining flour and rolled oats with a wooden spoon.

2. For filling, in a medium saucepan combine reserved 2 tablespoons butter, chocolate pieces, and condensed milk. Cook and stir over low heat until chocolate melts and mixture is smooth. Remove from heat. Stir in nuts and the remaining 2 teaspoons vanilla.

3. Press two-thirds (about 3⅓ cups) of the oat mixture into the bottom of an ungreased 15×10×1-inch baking pan. Pour filling evenly over oat mixture, spreading as necessary. Dot remaining oat mixture on top of filling.

4. Bake in a 350° oven about 25 minutes or until top is light brown (chocolate filling will still look moist). Cool completely in pan on a wire rack. Cut into bars.

TO STORE: Place in layers separated by waxed paper in an airtight container; cover. Store in the refrigerator up to 3 days or freeze up to 3 months.

Chocolate and *Sherry Cream* Bars

Not a fan of sherry? Customize your gourmet bars with kirsch, clear crème de cacao, orange liqueur, or another flavored clear liqueur. No matter what flavor you choose, the results will be dreamy. *(photo, page 363)*

Makes: 60 bars

Oven: 350°F

1 cup butter

4 ounces unsweetened chocolate

4 slightly beaten eggs

2 cups granulated sugar

1 teaspoon vanilla

1 cup all-purpose flour

4 cups sifted powdered sugar

½ cup butter, softened

¼ cup half-and-half

    or light cream

¼ cup sherry

1 cup chopped walnuts

½ cup semisweet chocolate

    pieces

2 tablespoons butter

4 teaspoons sherry or water

1. Grease a 15×10×1-inch baking pan; set aside. For crust, in a large saucepan melt the 1 cup butter and the unsweetened chocolate over low heat, stirring occasionally. Remove from heat. Stir in eggs, granulated sugar, and vanilla. Lightly beat with a wooden spoon just until combined. Stir in flour. Spread mixture in prepared baking pan. Bake in a 350° oven for 25 minutes. Cool in pan on a wire rack. (Crust will be moist.)

2. For filling, in a large mixing bowl combine powdered sugar and the ½ cup softened butter. Beat with an electric mixer on low speed until combined. Gradually add half-and-half and the ¼ cup sherry; beat well. Stir in walnuts. Spread filling over crust. Chill until firm.

3. For topping, in a small saucepan melt chocolate pieces and 2 tablespoons butter over low heat, stirring constantly. Remove from heat. Stir in the sherry until smooth. Drizzle topping over chilled filling. Chill slightly until mixture is set but not firm. With a knife, score top to outline bars; chill until firm. Cut into bars.

TO STORE: Place in layers separated by waxed paper in an airtight container; cover. Store in the refrigerator up to 3 days.

Chocolate-Caramel Bars

Four different goodies—pecans, coconut, caramels, and milk chocolate—pile onto a buttery shortbread crust and melt together in the oven. Delectable!

Makes: 48 bars

Oven: 350°F

  1 **cup all-purpose flour**

  ½ **cup packed brown sugar**

  ½ **cup butter**

  2 **cups coarsely chopped pecans**

  1 **cup coconut**

  1 **14-ounce can (1¼ cups)**

      sweetened condensed milk

  2 **teaspoons vanilla**

20 **vanilla caramels, unwrapped**

  2 **tablespoons milk**

  6 **ounces semisweet baking**

      chocolate, coarsely chopped

1. For crust, in a medium bowl stir together flour and brown sugar. Using a pastry blender, cut in butter until mixture resembles coarse crumbs. Press crumb mixture into the bottom of an ungreased 13×9×2-inch baking pan. Bake in a 350° oven for 15 minutes.

2. Sprinkle pecans and coconut over partially baked crust. Combine sweetened condensed milk and vanilla. Pour milk mixture over crust, spreading evenly. Bake for 25 to 30 minutes more or until the filling is set. Cool in pan on a wire rack for 10 minutes.

3. In a small saucepan combine caramels and milk. Cook and stir over medium-low heat just until caramels are melted. Drizzle caramel mixture over baked filling. Sprinkle top with chocolate. Cool completely. Cut into bars.

TO STORE: Place in layers separated by waxed paper in an airtight container; cover. Store in the refrigerator up to 3 days or freeze up to 3 months.

Cutting bars Take a tip from *Better Homes and Gardens* food stylists who have found the secret to creating sharp, clean edges when cutting bar cookies: Cool the cookie completely or chill it in the pan in the refrigerator before cutting.

Super-Easy Chocolate Bars

To ensure nice, even squares, cool the baked bars thoroughly before you cut them. That way, the ultracreamy chocolate filling has time to set up.

Makes: about 25 bars

Oven: 350°F

1 cup butter, softened

½ cup sugar

⅛ teaspoon salt

2 cups all-purpose flour

1 14-ounce can (1¼ cups) sweetened condensed milk

1 cup semisweet chocolate pieces

½ cup chopped walnuts or pecans

½ teaspoon vanilla

1. For crust, in a large mixing bowl beat butter with an electric mixer on medium to high speed for 30 seconds. Add sugar and salt. Beat until combined, scraping sides of bowl occasionally. Beat in the flour until combined. Press two-thirds of the crust mixture into the bottom of an ungreased 13×9×2-inch baking pan.

2. For filling, in a medium saucepan combine sweetened condensed milk and chocolate pieces. Cook and stir over low heat until chocolate melts and mixture is smooth. Remove from heat. Stir in nuts and vanilla. Spread hot mixture over the crust. Sprinkle remaining crust mixture over chocolate mixture.

3. Bake in a 350° oven about 35 minutes or until golden. Cool completely in pan on a wire rack. Cut into squares.

TO STORE: **Place in layers separated by waxed paper in an airtight container; cover. Store in the refrigerator up to 3 days.**

Chocolate *Malt* Bars

The old-fashioned lure of the malted milk shake finds a home in these bars. Don't be afraid to use the fudge frosting to top other bar cookies and snack cakes too.

Makes: 16 bars

Oven: 350°F

¹/₃ cup butter, softened

¹/₂ cup sugar

  1 egg

¹/₂ cup chocolate-flavored instant
      malted milk powder

¹/₄ cup milk

  1 teaspoon baking powder

  1 teaspoon vanilla

1¹/₄ cups all-purpose flour

  1 cup malted milk balls,
      coarsely chopped

  1 recipe Quick Fudge Frosting

1. Lightly grease a 9×9×2-inch baking pan; set aside. In a large mixing bowl beat butter and sugar with an electric mixer on medium speed until combined. Add egg, malted milk powder, milk, baking powder, and vanilla. Beat about 2 minutes more or until combined. Gradually add flour, beating just until combined. Fold in the chopped malted milk balls. Pour batter into the prepared baking pan, spreading evenly.

2. Bake in a 350° oven about 25 minutes or until a wooden toothpick inserted near center comes out clean. Cool completely in pan on a wire rack. Frost with Quick Fudge Frosting; let dry. Cut into bars.

Quick Fudge Frosting: In a medium mixing bowl combine 2¹/₂ cups sifted powdered sugar, ¹/₄ cup unsweetened cocoa powder, and 2 tablespoons chocolate-flavored instant malted milk powder. Add ¹/₄ cup softened butter, 3 tablespoons boiling water, and ¹/₂ teaspoon vanilla. Beat with an electric mixer on low speed until combined. Beat for 1 minute on medium speed. Cool for 20 to 30 minutes or until of spreading consistency.

TO STORE: Cover and store at room temperature up to 3 days. To freeze, wrap unfrosted, uncut bars in heavy foil. Freeze up to 3 months. Thaw; frost and cut into bars.

Buttermilk Brownies

When you consider this recipe's rich chocolate flavor and its almost foolproof method,

you can see why the cakelike brownie ranks as a favorite time and time again. *(photo, page 398)*

Makes: 24 brownies

Oven: 350°F

2 cups all-purpose flour

2 cups sugar

1 teaspoon baking soda

¼ teaspoon salt

1 cup water

1 cup butter

⅓ cup unsweetened cocoa
   powder

2 eggs

½ cup buttermilk or sour milk*

1½ teaspoons vanilla

1 recipe Chocolate-Buttermilk
   Frosting

1. Grease a 15×10×1-inch baking pan; set aside. In a large mixing bowl combine flour, sugar, baking soda, and salt; set aside.
2. In a medium saucepan combine water, butter, and cocoa powder. Bring mixture just to boiling, stirring constantly. Remove from heat. Add the chocolate mixture to the flour mixture. Beat with an electric mixer on medium speed until combined. Add eggs, buttermilk, and vanilla. Beat for 1 minute (batter will be thin). Pour batter into prepared baking pan, spreading evenly.
3. Bake in a 350° oven about 25 minutes or until a wooden toothpick inserted in center comes out clean. Pour warm Chocolate-Buttermilk Frosting over the warm brownies, spreading evenly. Cool completely in pan on a wire rack. Cut into bars.

*NOTE: To make sour milk, place 1½ teaspoons lemon juice or vinegar in a glass measuring cup. Add enough milk to make ½ cup total; stir. Let mixture stand for 5 minutes before using.

Chocolate-Buttermilk Frosting: In a medium saucepan combine ¼ cup butter, 3 tablespoons unsweetened cocoa powder, and 3 tablespoons buttermilk or sour milk.* Bring mixture to boiling. Remove from heat. Add 2¼ cups sifted powdered sugar and ½ teaspoon vanilla. Beat with an electric mixer on medium to high speed until smooth. If desired, stir in ¾ cup coarsely chopped pecans.

TO STORE: Cover and store in the refrigerator up to 3 days.

Cake *Brownies*

Put away your mixer! All you need is a big bowl and a wooden spoon to mix up

these no-sweat brownies.

Makes: 48 brownies

Oven: 350°F

³/₄ **cup butter**

1¼ **cups sugar**

½ **cup unsweetened cocoa**

   powder

2 **eggs**

1 **teaspoon vanilla**

1½ **cups all-purpose flour**

1 **teaspoon baking powder**

¼ **teaspoon baking soda**

1 **cup milk**

1 **cup chopped walnuts**

   or pecans

1 **recipe No-Cook Fudge Frosting**

1. Grease a 15×10×1-inch baking pan; set aside. In a medium saucepan melt butter over medium heat; remove saucepan from heat. Stir in sugar and cocoa powder until combined. Add eggs and vanilla. Beat lightly with a wooden spoon just until combined.

2. In a small bowl combine flour, baking powder, and baking soda. Add flour mixture and milk alternately to cocoa mixture, beating with a wooden spoon after each addition. Stir in nuts.

3. Spread batter in the prepared baking pan. Bake in a 350° oven for 15 to 18 minutes or until a wooden toothpick inserted near center comes out clean. Cool completely in pan on a wire rack. Frost with No-Cook Fudge Frosting. Let frosting dry. Cut into bars.

No-Cook Fudge Frosting: In a large mixing bowl combine 4½ cups sifted powdered sugar (about 1 pound) and ½ cup unsweetened cocoa powder. Add ½ cup softened butter, ⅓ cup boiling water, and 1 teaspoon vanilla. Beat with an electric mixer on low speed until combined. Beat for 1 minute on medium speed. If necessary, cool for 20 minutes or until frosting is of spreading consistency.

TO STORE: Cover and store at room temperature up to 3 days. To freeze, wrap unfrosted, uncut brownies in heavy foil. Freeze up to 3 months. Thaw brownies; frost and cut into bars.

Fudgy Brownies

If you like rich, dense, and moist brownies, these bars are for you. Feel particularly indulgent?

Skip the frosting and serve the brownies with vanilla ice cream and hot fudge sauce. Of course,

no one will complain if you add whipped cream and a cherry too!

Makes: 16 brownies

Oven: 350°F

½ **cup butter**

3 **ounces unsweetened**

    chocolate, coarsely chopped

1 **cup sugar**

2 **eggs**

1 **teaspoon vanilla**

⅔ **cup all-purpose flour**

¼ **teaspoon baking soda**

½ **cup chopped nuts (optional)**

1 **recipe Chocolate-Cream Cheese**

    Frosting (optional)

1. Grease an 8×8×2-inch or 9×9×2-inch baking pan; set aside. In a medium saucepan melt butter and unsweetened chocolate over low heat, stirring constantly. Remove from heat; let cool.
2. Stir sugar into cooled chocolate mixture in saucepan. Add the eggs, 1 at a time, beating with a wooden spoon after each addition just until combined. Stir in the vanilla.
3. In a small bowl stir together the flour and baking soda. Add flour mixture to chocolate mixture; stir just until combined. If desired, stir in nuts. Spread batter in the prepared baking pan.
4. Bake in a 350° oven for 30 minutes for 8-inch pan or 25 minutes for 9-inch pan. Cool completely in pan on a wire rack. If desired, frost with Chocolate-Cream Cheese Frosting. Let frosting dry. Cut into bars.

Chocolate-Cream Cheese Frosting: In a small heavy saucepan melt 1 cup semisweet chocolate pieces over low heat, stirring constantly. Remove from heat; cool. In a small bowl stir together two 3-ounce packages softened cream cheese and ½ cup sifted powdered sugar. Stir in melted chocolate until smooth.

TO STORE: Cover and store frosted brownies in the refrigerator up to 3 days. (Store unfrosted brownies at room temperature.) To freeze, wrap unfrosted, uncut brownies in heavy foil. Freeze up to 3 months. Thaw brownies; frost, if desired, and cut into bars.

Triple-Decker *Brownies*

Three sweet layers—a chewy oatmeal crust, a fudgy brownie, and a creamy frosting—stack up to one delectable treat.

Makes: 32 brownies

Oven: 350°F

1 cup quick-cooking rolled oats

½ cup all-purpose flour

½ cup packed brown sugar

¼ teaspoon baking soda

½ cup butter, melted

1 egg

¾ cup granulated sugar

⅔ cup all-purpose flour

¼ cup milk

¼ cup butter, melted

1 ounce unsweetened chocolate, melted and cooled

1½ teaspoons vanilla

¼ teaspoon baking powder

½ cup chopped walnuts

1 ounce unsweetened chocolate

2 tablespoons butter

1½ cups sifted powdered sugar

Walnut halves (optional)

1. For bottom layer, in a medium bowl stir together oats, the ½ cup flour, the brown sugar, and baking soda. Stir in the ½ cup melted butter. Press mixture into the bottom of an ungreased 11×7×1½-inch baking pan. Bake in a 350° oven for 10 minutes.

2. Meanwhile, for middle layer, in another bowl stir together egg, granulated sugar, the ⅔ cup flour, milk, the ¼ cup melted butter, the 1 ounce melted chocolate, 1 teaspoon of the vanilla, and baking powder until smooth. Fold in chopped walnuts. Spread batter evenly over baked layer in pan. Bake in the 350° oven about 25 minutes more or until a wooden toothpick inserted in center comes out clean. Place on a wire rack while preparing top layer.

3. For top layer, in a medium saucepan melt the 1 ounce chocolate and the 2 tablespoons butter over low heat, stirring constantly. Stir in the powdered sugar and the remaining ½ teaspoon vanilla. Stir in enough hot water (1 to 2 tablespoons) to make a mixture that is almost pourable. Spread over brownies. If desired, garnish with walnut halves. Cool completely in pan on wire rack. Cut into bars.

TO STORE: Cover and store at room temperature up to 3 days.

Creamy, *Fudgy*, Nutty Brownies

The creamy topping on these brownies is essentially a chocolate cheesecake mixture,

making it necessary to store baked bars in the refrigerator.

Makes: 12 brownies

Oven: 350°F

4 ounces unsweetened
   chocolate, chopped

½ cup butter

1 cup all-purpose flour

½ cup chopped walnuts
   or pecans, toasted

¼ teaspoon baking powder

1¾ cups sugar

4 eggs

1½ teaspoons vanilla

3 ounces semisweet
   chocolate, chopped

2 3-ounce packages cream
   cheese, softened

1 tablespoon milk

1. Grease and lightly flour an 8×8×2-inch baking pan; set aside. In a small heavy saucepan melt unsweetened chocolate and butter over low heat, stirring constantly. Remove from heat; set aside to cool slightly. In a medium bowl stir together flour, nuts, and baking powder; set aside.

2. In a large bowl stir together the melted chocolate mixture and 1½ cups of the sugar. Add 3 of the eggs and 1 teaspoon of the vanilla. Lightly beat mixture with a wooden spoon just until combined (don't overbeat or brownies will rise too high, then fall). Stir in flour mixture. Spread batter in the prepared baking pan. Bake in a 350° oven for 40 minutes.

3. Meanwhile, for topping, in a small heavy saucepan melt semisweet chocolate over low heat. Remove from heat; cool slightly. In a medium mixing bowl combine the cream cheese, melted semisweet chocolate, the remaining egg, the remaining ¼ cup sugar, the 1 tablespoon milk, and the remaining ½ teaspoon vanilla. Beat with an electric mixer on medium to high speed until combined.

4. Carefully spread topping evenly over hot brownies. Bake about 10 minutes more or until topping appears set. Cool completely in pan on a wire rack. Cover and chill at least 2 hours before serving. Cut into bars.

TO STORE: Cover and store in the refrigerator up to 3 days.

Mint Brownies

Not only is the light green and deep brown color combo aesthetically pleasing, it signifies a sweet chocolate and cool mint delicacy. The chocolate indulges, while the mint refreshes. Hint: To make two-tone chocolate-mint curls, use a vegetable peeler to shave curls from the side of a layered mint candy.

Makes: about 50 brownies

Oven: 350°F

1 cup all-purpose flour

1 cup sugar

1 16-ounce can (1½ cups) chocolate-flavored syrup

4 eggs

½ cup butter, softened

1 recipe Mint Cream

1 recipe Chocolate Topping

Chocolate-mint candy curls (optional)

1. Grease a 13×9×2-inch baking pan; set aside. In a large mixing bowl combine flour, sugar, chocolate-flavored syrup, eggs, and butter. Beat with an electric mixer on low speed until combined. Beat on medium speed for 1 minute.

2. Pour batter into the prepared baking pan, spreading evenly. Bake in a 350° oven for 30 to 35 minutes or until top springs back when lightly touched. (Top may still appear wet.) Cool completely in pan on a wire rack.

3. Meanwhile, prepare Mint Cream and Chocolate Topping (allow Chocolate Topping to cool 10 to 15 minutes before spreading on cooled brownies).

4. Spread Mint Cream over cooled brownies. Pour slightly cooled Chocolate Topping over mint layer. Cover and chill at least 1 hour. Cut into bars. If desired, top with chocolate-mint candy curls.

Mint Cream: In a medium mixing bowl combine 2 cups sifted powdered sugar, ½ cup softened butter, 1 tablespoon water, ½ teaspoon mint extract, and, if desired, 3 drops green food coloring. Beat until smooth.

Chocolate Topping: In a small heavy saucepan melt 1 cup semisweet mint-flavored chocolate pieces or semisweet chocolate pieces and 6 tablespoons butter over low heat, stirring frequently.

TO STORE: **Cover and store in the refrigerator up to 3 days.**

Orange-Glazed Brownies

Irresistibly orange and wonderfully chocolaty, these oversize brownies make an indulgent dessert for any style of dinner—from country casual to black-tie elegant.

Makes: 9 brownies

Oven: 350°F

4 ounces unsweetened chocolate, chopped

½ cup butter

1 cup sugar

2 eggs

2 teaspoons finely shredded orange peel

1 teaspoon vanilla

¾ cup all-purpose flour

½ cup coarsely chopped walnuts or pecans

1 recipe Chocolate-Orange Glaze

1. In a medium saucepan melt chocolate and butter over low heat, stirring constantly. Remove from heat. Stir in sugar, eggs, orange peel, and vanilla. Lightly beat mixture with a wooden spoon just until combined. Stir in flour and nuts.

2. Spread batter in an ungreased 8×8×2-inch baking pan. Bake in a 350° oven for 30 minutes. Cool completely in pan on a wire rack. Pour Chocolate-Orange Glaze over the cooled brownies, spreading to glaze the top evenly. Let stand until glaze is set. Cut into squares.

Chocolate-Orange Glaze: In a small heavy saucepan bring ⅓ cup whipping cream to a gentle boil over medium-low heat, stirring constantly. Remove from heat. Add 3 ounces finely chopped semisweet chocolate and 1 teaspoon finely shredded orange peel. Let stand for 1 minute. Stir mixture with a wooden spoon until chocolate is melted. Cool glaze for 5 minutes before using.

TO STORE: Cover and store in the refrigerator up to 3 days. To freeze, wrap unglazed, uncut brownies in heavy foil and freeze up to 3 months. Thaw brownies; glaze and cut into bars.

Freezing bar cookies Did you know that most bar cookies freeze well? To freeze, before spreading the batter in the pan, line it with foil (see tip, page 370). Follow the recipe for baking and cooling. Lift the bars out of the pan using the foil edges. Wrap the uncut and unfrosted bars in heavy foil or place in freezer bags or airtight containers. Seal, label, date, and freeze. For best quality, use within 3 months. Thaw the bars at room temperature about 15 minutes. Once they're thawed, you can frost and cut the bars.

Top-of-the-World Brownies

Special occasions call for special brownies. Reward good work done at school or celebrate good times with friends with these special treats. Hint: A billowy dollop of chocolate meringue bakes right on each bar, so plan the placement of the dollops carefully. *(photo, page 398)*

Makes: 16 brownies

Oven: 350°F

¾ cup butter

3 ounces unsweetened chocolate, chopped

2 cups sugar

2 teaspoons vanilla

3 eggs

1 cup all-purpose flour

3 tablespoons unsweetened cocoa powder

½ cup coarsely chopped hazelnuts (filberts) or pecans

2 egg whites

1. Line an 8×8×2-inch baking pan with foil, extending foil over edges of pan. Grease foil and set aside. In a medium heavy saucepan melt butter and chocolate over low heat, stirring constantly. Remove from heat. Stir in 1⅓ cups of the sugar and vanilla. Cool about 5 minutes.

2. Add eggs, 1 at a time, beating with a wooden spoon after each addition just until combined. Stir in flour and 2 tablespoons of the cocoa powder just until combined. Spread batter evenly in the prepared baking pan. Sprinkle with nuts; set aside.

3. For meringue, in a small mixing bowl beat egg whites with an electric mixer on medium to high speed about 1 minute or until soft peaks form (tips curl). Gradually add the remaining ⅔ cup sugar, beating on high speed until stiff peaks form (tips stand straight) and sugar is almost dissolved. Reduce speed to low; beat in the remaining 1 tablespoon cocoa powder.

4. Using a tablespoon, carefully spoon the meringue in 16 even mounds on top of the brownie batter, keeping about ½ inch of space between them. (Or pipe the meringue mixture on top of the batter.)

5. Bake in a 350° oven about 1 hour or until a wooden toothpick inserted near center of brownie portion comes out clean. Cool brownies in pan on a wire rack at least 1 hour. Using foil, lift brownies from pan. Cut into squares.

TO STORE: Place in a single layer in an airtight container; cover. Store in the refrigerator up to 3 days.

Brownie *Ice Cream* Cones

Kids and adults alike will be pleasantly surprised when they bite into these whimsical cones and find their favorite brownies camouflaged within. Serve ice cream on the side, if you like.

Makes: 12 brownies

Oven: 350°F

½ cup butter

2 ounces unsweetened
   chocolate, chopped

1 cup sugar

2 eggs

1 teaspoon vanilla

¾ teaspoon baking powder

¾ cup all-purpose flour

½ cup chopped pecans or
   walnuts (optional)

12 flat-bottom wafer
   ice cream cones

1 cup semisweet chocolate
   pieces

2 teaspoons shortening
   Red and green nonpareils
   or candy sprinkles

1. In a medium saucepan melt butter and unsweetened chocolate over low heat, stirring constantly. Remove from heat. Stir in sugar, eggs, vanilla, and baking powder with a wooden spoon just until combined. Stir in flour and, if desired, nuts.

2. Place cones inside 2½-inch muffin cups. Divide batter among cones. Bake in a 350° oven for 30 to 35 minutes or until a wooden toothpick inserted in center comes out clean. Cool completely in muffin cups on a wire rack.

3. In a small heavy saucepan melt semisweet chocolate pieces and shortening over low heat, stirring constantly. Remove from heat. Dip tops of cones into chocolate, covering all of brownie. Stand upright. Sprinkle with nonpareils. Let stand until chocolate is set.

TO STORE: **Place in an airtight container and store at room temperature up to 2 days.**

Chocolate *Cappuccino* Brownies

Here a coffee-with-cream filling cozies up to two super-rich chocolate layers. Tempt all coffee lovers by decorating each square with a coffee bean. *(photo, page 399)*

Makes: 16 brownies

Oven: 350°F

½ **cup butter**

3 **ounces unsweetened chocolate, chopped**

1 **cup granulated sugar**

2 **eggs**

1 **teaspoon vanilla**

⅔ **cup all-purpose flour**

¼ **teaspoon baking soda**

1 **teaspoon instant coffee crystals**

1 **tablespoon whipping cream**

1 **cup sifted powdered sugar**

2 **tablespoons butter, softened**

1 **recipe Chocolate Frosting**

16 **coffee beans (optional)**

1. Grease an 8×8×2-inch baking pan; set aside. In a medium saucepan melt the ½ cup butter and the unsweetened chocolate over low heat, stirring constantly. Remove from heat; cool slightly. Stir in granulated sugar. Add eggs, 1 at a time, beating with a wooden spoon after each addition just until combined. Stir in vanilla.

2. In a small bowl stir together flour and baking soda. Add flour mixture to chocolate mixture; stir just until combined. Spread batter in the prepared baking pan. Bake in a 350° oven for 30 minutes.

3. Meanwhile, for topping, dissolve coffee crystals in whipping cream. In a small mixing bowl beat together powdered sugar and the 2 tablespoons butter with an electric mixer on medium speed. Add whipping cream mixture and beat until creamy. If necessary, add a little additional whipping cream until mixture is of spreading consistency. Spread over the warm brownies. Chill about 1 hour or until topping is set. Carefully spread Chocolate Frosting over brownies. Chill until frosting is set. Cut into bars. If desired, top each brownie with a coffee bean.

Chocolate Frosting: In a small saucepan combine 1 cup semisweet chocolate pieces and ⅓ cup whipping cream. Cook and stir over low heat until chocolate is melted and mixture begins to thicken.

TO STORE: Cover and store in the refrigerator up to 3 days.

Candy Bar Brownies

As candy makers and kids discovered long ago, getting chocolate in your peanut butter (or peanut butter in your chocolate) is a mix-up of the most delicious kind! *(photo, page 397)*

Makes: 50 to 70 small brownies

Oven: 350°F

1¼ cups finely crushed graham crackers (about 18 crackers)

1¼ cup sugar

¼ cup finely chopped dry-roasted peanuts

½ cup butter, melted

½ cup butter

2 ounces unsweetened chocolate, chopped

2 eggs

1 teaspoon vanilla

⅔ cup all-purpose flour

½ cup chopped peanuts

1 recipe Peanut Butter Frosting

¼ cup honey-roasted peanuts or regular peanuts

1. For crust, in a medium bowl combine graham crackers, ¼ cup of the sugar, and the ¼ cup finely chopped peanuts. Stir in the ½ cup melted butter. Press mixture evenly into bottom of an ungreased 11×7×1½-inch baking pan. Bake in a 350° oven for 5 minutes; cool.

2. For filling, in a large heavy saucepan melt ½ cup butter and the chocolate over low heat, stirring occasionally. Remove from heat. Stir in the remaining 1 cup sugar, the eggs, and vanilla. Stir just until combined. Stir in flour and the ½ cup chopped peanuts. Spread evenly over crust.

3. Bake for 20 minutes more. Cool completely in pan on a wire rack. Spread with Peanut Butter Frosting. Cut into small squares. (Or cut into 24 larger bars.) Place a few honey-roasted or regular peanuts on each square. If desired, place each brownie in a small candy cup.

Peanut Butter Frosting: In a small mixing bowl beat ¼ cup softened butter and 2 tablespoons peanut butter with an electric mixer on low speed for 30 seconds. Gradually add 1 cup sifted powdered sugar, beating well. Beat in 1 tablespoon milk and ½ teaspoon vanilla. Gradually beat in 1 cup additional sifted powdered sugar and enough milk to make a frosting of spreading consistency.

TO STORE: **Cover and store at room temperature up to 3 days. To freeze, wrap unfrosted, uncut bars in heavy foil. Freeze up to 3 months. Thaw; frost and cut into bars.**

Candy Bar Brownies, page 396

ABOVE: Top-of-the-World Brownies, page 393; Italian Cheese Bars, page 348
BELOW: Buttermilk Brownies, page 386; Peanut Brittle Bars, page 371

ABOVE: Danish Pastry Apple Bars, page 352   RIGHT: Mixed Nut Bars, page 368
BELOW: Chocolate Cappuccino Brownies, page 395

Raspberry and White Chocolate Brownies, page 401

Raspberry and *White Chocolate* Brownies

Always a class act, raspberry and white chocolate make an elegant duo even when they appear in a simple bar cookie. Hint: You'll need fresh raspberries for these brownies. Frozen raspberries release too much moisture during baking, causing wet areas. *(photo, page 400)*

Makes: about 20 brownies

Oven: 350°F

½ cup butter

2 ounces white baking bar
    or squares, chopped

2 eggs

⅔ cup sugar

1 teaspoon vanilla

1 cup all-purpose flour

½ cup chopped almonds, toasted

½ teaspoon baking powder

Dash salt

1 cup fresh raspberries

2 ounces white baking bar
    or squares, melted

1. Line an 8×8×2-inch baking pan with foil, extending foil over edges of pan. Grease foil; set pan aside.

2. In a medium heavy saucepan melt butter and the chopped white baking bar over low heat, stirring constantly. Remove from heat. Stir in eggs, sugar, and vanilla with a wooden spoon. Lightly beat just until combined. Stir in flour, almonds, baking powder, and salt.

3. Spread batter in the prepared baking pan. Sprinkle with raspberries. Bake in a 350° oven for 30 to 35 minutes or until golden. Cool completely in pan on a wire rack. Using foil, lift brownies from pan. Cut with a 2-inch round cutter or cut into bars. Drizzle cutouts or bars with melted white baking bar; let stand until set.

TO STORE: Place in a single layer in an airtight container; cover. Store at room temperature up to 3 days or freeze undrizzled brownies up to 3 months. Thaw brownies; drizzle.

Melt chocolate the easy way To melt chocolate over direct heat, put the chopped chocolate or chocolate pieces in a small heavy saucepan over low heat. (If using chocolate squares, coarsely chop the chocolate before melting. This makes it melt more quickly and with less danger of scorching.) Stir constantly with a wooden spoon until the chocolate just begins to melt. Remove the saucepan from the heat and continue stirring until smooth. If necessary, return the pan to the heat for a few seconds.

While it's all right to melt chocolate in a double boiler, it's not necessary. In fact, using a double boiler increases the chance of getting a drop or two of water in the chocolate, which will cause it to seize, or stiffen.

Cream Cheese Brownies

You'll want to stash a few of these elegant, chocolate-glazed, marbled beauties in a secret corner of the fridge to enjoy after everyone goes home.

Makes: 32 brownies

Oven: 350°F

8 ounces semisweet chocolate, chopped

3 tablespoons butter

4 eggs

1¼ cups sugar

⅓ cup water

2 teaspoons vanilla

1 cup all-purpose flour

¾ cup chopped macadamia nuts, toasted

1 teaspoon baking powder

¼ teaspoon salt

1 8-ounce package cream cheese, softened

⅔ cup sugar

2 tablespoons all-purpose flour

1 tablespoon lemon juice

1 recipe Chocolate Glaze

1. Line a 13×9×2-inch baking pan with foil, extending foil over edges of pan. Grease foil; set pan aside. In a large heavy saucepan melt the chocolate and butter over low heat, stirring constantly. Remove from heat; cool.

2. In a large mixing bowl beat 2 of the eggs with an electric mixer on medium speed until foamy. Add the 1¼ cups sugar, the water, and 1 teaspoon of the vanilla. Beat about 5 minutes or until mixture is thick and lemon-colored. Beat in cooled chocolate mixture. Stir in the 1 cup flour, macadamia nuts, baking powder, and salt. Spread half of the batter in prepared baking pan. Set remaining batter and pan aside.

3. In a medium mixing bowl beat the remaining 2 eggs, the remaining 1 teaspoon vanilla, the cream cheese, the ⅔ cup sugar, the 2 tablespoons flour, and the lemon juice with an electric mixer on medium speed until smooth. Spread evenly over batter in pan. Spoon remaining batter evenly over cream cheese mixture. Swirl batter with a knife to marble. Bake in a 350° oven for 45 minutes. Cool completely in pan on a wire rack. Frost with Chocolate Glaze. Chill about 1 hour or until glaze is set. Using foil, lift brownies from pan. Cut into bars.

Chocolate Glaze: In a small heavy saucepan cook and stir ⅓ cup whipping cream and 6 ounces finely chopped semisweet chocolate over low heat until chocolate melts.

TO STORE: Place in a single layer in an airtight container; cover. Store in the refrigerator up to 3 days. To freeze, wrap unglazed, uncut brownies in heavy foil and freeze up to 3 months. Thaw brownies; glaze and cut into bars.

Index

Holiday Treats

Metric Information

The charts on this page provide a guide for converting measurements from the U.S. customary system, which is used throughout this book, to the metric system.

Product Differences

Most of the ingredients called for in the recipes in this book are available in most countries. However, some are known by different names. Here are some common American ingredients and their possible counterparts:

- Sugar (white) is granulated, fine granulated, or castor sugar.
- Powdered sugar is icing sugar.
- All-purpose flour is enriched, bleached or unbleached white household flour. When self-rising flour is used in place of all-purpose flour in a recipe that calls for leavening, omit the leavening agent (baking soda or baking powder) and salt.
- Light-colored corn syrup is golden syrup.
- Cornstarch is cornflour.
- Baking soda is bicarbonate of soda.
- Vanilla or vanilla extract is vanilla essence.
- Golden raisins are sultanas.

Volume and Weight

The United States traditionally uses cup measures for liquid and solid ingredients. The chart below shows the approximate imperial and metric equivalents. If you are accustomed to weighing solid ingredients, the following approximate equivalents will be helpful.

- 1 cup butter, castor sugar, or rice = 8 ounces = ½ pound = 250 grams
- 1 cup flour = 4 ounces = ¼ pound = 125 grams
- 1 cup icing sugar = 5 ounces = 150 grams

Canadian and U.S. volume for a cup measure is 8 fluid ounces (237 ml), but the standard metric equivalent is 250 ml.

1 British imperial cup is 10 fluid ounces.

In Australia, 1 tablespoon equals 20 ml, and there are 4 teaspoons in the Australian tablespoon.

Spoon measures are used for smaller amounts of ingredients. Although the size of the tablespoon varies slightly in different countries, for practical purposes and for recipes in this book, a straight substitution is all that's necessary. Measurements made using cups or spoons always should be level unless stated otherwise.

Common Weight Range Replacements

Imperial / U.S.	Metric
½ ounce	15 g
1 ounce	25 g or 30 g
4 ounces (¼ pound)	115 g or 125 g
8 ounces (½ pound)	225 g or 250 g
16 ounces (1 pound)	450 g or 500 g
1¼ pounds	625 g
1½ pounds	750 g
2 pounds or 2¼ pounds	1,000 g or 1 Kg

Oven Temperature Equivalents

Fahrenheit Setting	Celsius Setting*	Gas Setting
300°F	150°C	Gas Mark 2 (very low)
325°F	160°C	Gas Mark 3 (low)
350°F	180°C	Gas Mark 4 (moderate)
375°F	190°C	Gas Mark 5 (moderate)
400°F	200°C	Gas Mark 6 (hot)
425°F	220°C	Gas Mark 7 (hot)
450°F	230°C	Gas Mark 8 (very hot)
475°F	240°C	Gas Mark 9 (very hot)
500°F	260°C	Gas Mark 10 (extremely hot)
Broil	Broil	Grill

*Electric and gas ovens may be calibrated using celsius. However, for an electric oven, increase celsius setting 10 to 20 degrees when cooking above 160°C. For convection or forced air ovens (gas or electric) lower the temperature setting 25°F/10°C when cooking at all heat levels.

Baking Pan Sizes

Imperial / U.S.	Metric
9×1½-inch round cake pan	22- or 23×4-cm (1.5 L)
9×1½-inch pie plate	22- or 23×4-cm (1 L)
8×8×2-inch square cake pan	20×5-cm (2 L)
9×9×2-inch square cake pan	22- or 23×4.5-cm (2.5 L)
11×7×1½-inch baking pan	28×17×4-cm (2 L)
2-quart rectangular baking pan	30×19×4.5-cm (3 L)
13×9×2-inch baking pan	34×22×4.5-cm (3.5 L)
15×10×1-inch jelly roll pan	40×25×2-cm
9×5×3-inch loaf pan	23×13×8-cm (2 L)
2-quart casserole	2 L

U.S. / Standard Metric Equivalents

⅛ teaspoon = 0.5 ml	
¼ teaspoon = 1 ml	
½ teaspoon = 2 ml	
1 teaspoon = 5 ml	
1 tablespoon = 15 ml	
2 tablespoons = 25 ml	
¼ cup = 2 fluid ounces = 50 ml	
⅓ cup = 3 fluid ounces = 75 ml	
½ cup = 4 fluid ounces = 125 ml	
⅔ cup = 5 fluid ounces = 150 ml	
¾ cup = 6 fluid ounces = 175 ml	
1 cup = 8 fluid ounces = 250 ml	
2 cups = 1 pint = 500 ml	
1 quart = 1 litre	